Principles and Agents

THE DAVID BRION DAVIS SERIES

SINCE ITS FOUNDING IN 1998, the Gilder Lehrman Center for the Study of Slavery, Resistance, and Abolition, which is part of the Mac-Millan Center for International and Area Studies, has sponsored an annual international conference on major aspects of slavery, its ultimate destruction, and its legacies in America and around the world. The Center's mission is to increase knowledge of this story across time and all boundaries, and to reach out to the broader public—in schools, museums, and historic sites, and through filmmakers and general readers—where there is a growing desire to understand race, slavery, abolition, and the extended meanings of this history over time.

In the name of David Brion Davis, the founder of the Center, Sterling Professor Emeritus at Yale, and the world's leading scholar of slavery in international perspective, we have established an occasional lecture series. A single distinguished scholar, or a group of noted writers on a subject, is invited to speak on a theme out of which we then produce an original book such as this one.

Because the research, discoveries, and narratives presented at our conferences do so much to enrich our knowledge of one of humanity's most dehumanizing institutions and its place in the founding of the modern world, as well as of the first historical movements for human rights, we are immensely grateful to Yale University Press for engaging in this joint publication venture. The Gilder Lehrman Center is supported by Richard Gilder and Lewis Lehrman, generous Yale alumni and devoted patrons of American history. The Center aspires, with Yale University Press, to offer to the broadest possible audience the best modern scholarship on a story of global and lasting significance.

DAVID W. BLIGHT
Class of 1954 Professor of History at Yale University, and Director,
Gilder Lehrman Center for the Study of Slavery, Resistance, and Abolition

Principles and Agents

The British Slave Trade and Its Abolition

David Richardson

Yale
UNIVERSITY PRESS
New Haven & London

Published with assistance from the Annie Burr Lewis Fund.

Published with assistance from the foundation established in memory of
Amasa Stone Mather of the Class of 1907, Yale College.

Yale University Press books may be purchased in quantity for educational,
business, or promotional use. For information, please e-mail sales.press@yale.edu
(US office) or sales@yaleup.co.uk (UK office).

Set in Monotype Bulmer by Westchester Publishing Services.
Printed in the United States of America.

Library of Congress Control Number: 2021932825
ISBN 978-0-300-25043-5 (hardcover : alk. paper)

A catalogue record for this book is available from the British Library.

This paper meets the requirements of ANSI/NISO Z39.48-1992 (Permanence of Paper).

10 9 8 7 6 5 4 3 2 1

Contents

Acknowledgments

SOME OF THE ideas underlying this book were first raised in the David Brion Davis Lectures I delivered at Yale University in March 2007 under the same title as that of this book. Their delivery coincided with the bicentennial of the abolition of the British slave trade in March 1807. The lectures were intended to throw light on a question that had fascinated historians across the intervening two centuries: why Parliament chose in 1807 to outlaw an economic activity in which Britain had proved preeminently successful in the preceding 150 years. In this book, I elaborate on the reflections in 2007. Sadly, David Brion Davis, who attended the lectures, died before I completed the book. It has nonetheless benefited from suggestions David offered at the time the lectures were delivered. Like so many others, I remain in admiration of the standard of scholarship on slavery that his work embodied and grateful for the encouragement he gave to those who have tried to walk in his steps. In working on this book, I have realized the scale of that task.

Readers of this book will soon understand how much I owe to others with whom I have collaborated in publishing some of the studies cited herein. They include Steve Behrendt, David Eltis, the late Frank Lewis, Paul Lovejoy, Robin Pearson, and Joel Quirk. I have benefited, too, from conversations and discussions with Seymour Drescher, Stan Engerman, John Oldfield, and Judith Spicksley about several issues. In the case of the last two, the conversations took place as colleagues at the Wilberforce Institute at Hull, as did work on the papers I have published since 2004 with Robin Pearson and Joel Quirk. All four have influenced my thinking more than they imagine, and I thank them for their continuing collegiality and interest in my work. None bear any responsibility for errors of fact or interpretation contained in this book. I am grateful also to Nick Evans, another Hull colleague, and to Suzanne Schwarz for allowing me to use unpublished material from their joint research to inform my arguments in chapter 6.

I conceived the idea of writing on British abolitionism in 2004 when I was a visiting scholar at Yale's Gilder Lehrman Center for Slavery, Abolition, and Resistance and had opportunities to discuss issues relating to it with David Brion Davis. David Blight, Davis's successor as the center's director, helped me to begin to crystallize my thoughts by inviting me to deliver the 2007 David Brion Davis Lectures. He then encouraged me to write up the lectures for several years after they were delivered. That process has been made easier by unfailing support from editor Adina Berk of Yale University Press. Adina commissioned valuable and constructive reports on an initial manuscript submitted almost three years ago. Since then she has displayed exemplary patience and offered important insights into the structuring of the manuscript's argument that allowed me to transform that initial text into a publishable one. I am extremely grateful to David and to Adina and others on the Yale team, notably Laura Jones Dooley, Ash Lago, and Susan Laity, for their sustained support and encouragement in bringing this book to fruition.

Last, but most important, I express huge, heartfelt thanks to Susan, my wife and companion in life for over a half a century. Throughout my academic career she has offered constant moral support and encouragement to all my research endeavors. None has been more important than in the past few years as I have worked to complete this book. She is not a historian, but without her love, her sacrifice of time together, and her patient acceptance of my mental distractions, this book, like so many others of my scholarly projects, could not have been completed. I dedicate this book to her and our son, John, in pride at their own achievements.

Introduction

Interpreting British Slave Trade Abolition

Personalities, not principles, move the age.

—Oscar Wilde, *The Picture of Dorian Gray,* 1891

THE DECISION OF Parliament in 1807 to outlaw Britain's trafficking of enslaved Africans has widely been considered a seminal moment in modern history. One nineteenth-century historian, W. E. H. Lecky, deemed Britain's crusade against slavery, which the act of 1807 effectively launched, "among the three or four perfectly virtuous acts recorded in the history of nations," a view that historian David Brion Davis considers still to have much merit.[1] The act has also been seen as initiating a process that, together with the Haitian Revolution of 1791–1804 and the American Civil War of 1861–65, would precipitate the formal outlawing of slavery throughout the Americas by 1889 and a century later throughout the rest of the world.[2] For others the act helped to define modernity and to propel issues of human rights and social justice to the top of global or at least Western political agendas, thereby reminding us that debates around such issues were not confined to Britain.[3] In each case, however, the long-term significance of Parliament's decision in 1807 was underscored by widespread public support, which legitimized intervention, and by Britain's hegemony and emergence as a global superpower by 1815. That power, in turn, was reflected in victories over Napoleonic France at Trafalgar and Waterloo in 1805 and 1815, respectively, and in Britain's rise as the first industrial nation. Without the resources that its military, diplomatic, industrial, and financial power afforded the nation, it is unlikely that Parliament's action in 1807 and

1

its subsequent support for the nation's antislavery crusade could have ever achieved the global reach that it did. If the British were not wholly exceptional in initially formulating ideas opposed to slavery, they were remarkable in the scale and persistence with which they sought to translate antislavery principles into political praxis from the late eighteenth century onward.[4]

Yet therein lies a puzzle with which historians have wrestled almost from the very moment that Parliament proscribed British slave carrying in 1807. Contemporary opponents of that measure claimed that slave carrying and the production of British colonial goods that depended on the traffic in enslaved Africans had itself elevated Britain from 1640 onward into the front rank of European nations. Later historians raised such arguments to an even higher plane, claiming that profits and wealth from Caribbean slavery and the slave trade from Africa fertilized British industrial capitalism.[5] And even should one regard such propositions as exaggerated and, in the case of contemporary assertions, largely self-serving, it still remains evident that in 1807 Britain's slave trade was at or close to its historic peak, that Britons were Europe's largest and most successful traffickers by some margin, and that parliamentary outlawing of their activities occurred at the height of a titanic struggle with Napoleon for European and therefore global dominance. It was the sheer scale of Britain's ongoing commitment to and perceived national dependence on colonial slavery as a source of wealth and power that made its supporters so incredulous of abolitionists' moves to outlaw it, especially when the nation's security was under threat. Equally, however, it was the extent of Britain's entanglement with and apparent dependency on slavery that outraged British abolitionists, motivating them to oppose it on grounds of humanitarianism, morality, and, ultimately, sound policy and national interest. Yet even as abolitionist sentiment grew, so, too, did British investment in slave trafficking: more enslaved Africans reached the Americas in the nation's ships in 1783–1807 than in any other quarter century in British history.[6]

All of which begs two key questions: First, why were the British such efficient and successful slave traffickers? And second, how and why did abolitionists succeed in convincing Parliament, guardian of the country's

national interest and security, to outlaw British participation in such trafficking in its prime, denying traffickers continuing opportunities to add to
the nation's coffers in time of war? This book seeks to provide answers to
those questions while shedding new light on an issue that has helped to define the modern world.

In his *History of the Rise, Progress, and Accomplishment of the Abolition of the Slave Trade*, published in London in 1808, abolitionist Thomas
Clarkson described how a London committee organized in May 1787 to
pursue abolition of the British slave trade had labored "under Providence"
to close down "in the space of twenty years" a business "which measuring
its magnitude by its crimes and sufferings, was the greatest practical evil
that ever afflicted the human race."[7] Britain's share of that "evil" was by
any reckoning large. In the very year that the committee was established,
British ships are estimated to have taken some 29,322 enslaved Africans
from their home continent, of whom 26,337 are estimated to have reached
the Americas alive. Moreover, despite the introduction of restrictions on
the carrying capacity of British slave ships from 1788 and reinforced in 1799,
with a view to lessening the suffering of Africans in transit, British slaving
activities reached new heights after 1787. In 1793, British ships took over
46,200 Africans as slaves from their homeland. In 1799, that figure reached
almost 49,900 captives. Before 1807, only the French exceeded in any single year—1790—the level of embarkation of enslaved Africans that British
carriers achieved in 1799.[8] Britain's addiction to slave trading, which had
its roots in the mid-seventeenth century, thus showed no sign of abating
until Parliament intervened decisively in 1807. In that respect Clarkson's
intuition was right: it was the perceived evil or immorality of the slave trade,
not its unprofitability as a form of business transaction, that brought it to a
close. Parliament's action, in short, ended the legal sanction under which
human trafficking by Britons had developed and prospered since the 1640s.
Without that intervention, there seems little doubt that Britons would have
continued to be among the principal carriers of enslaved Africans across
the Atlantic beyond 1807. Understanding British prowess in slaving activities, even in the face of regulation from 1787 onward, provides therefore an
important backcloth to measuring the achievement of those who opposed

it. In attacking the British slave trade abolitionists were not tilting at wind-mills or at some decaying edifice but confronting what before 1787 was widely accepted as, and even after 1787 remained, a vibrant species of com-merce in Africans, the legal ending of which was described in 1807 as "the most glorious measure, that had ever been adopted by any legislative body in the world."[9] That was perhaps an overstatement, but to see it otherwise is surely to do a severe disservice to those who fought against British traf-fickers of slaves.

This study seeks first to explain Britons' success in human traffick-ing through a focus on the growing demand for enslaved Africans in Brit-ish America as well as on the factors that allowed British traders efficiently to meet that demand. Demand for captives drove the growth of British slav-ing both before and after the abolitionist campaign began. Hence, exam-ining the shifting parameters of market demand for slaves in British America is necessary for understanding how the British slave trade came to be as large as it was. Market demand is, however, insufficient on its own to ac-count for the long-term success of Britons in trafficking. That hinged, too, on their comparative advantage in the activity, which enabled them to eclipse rival carriers and to continue to grow their business through 1807. Uncovering Britons' advantages in slave carrying is thus critical to explain-ing their success. Those advantages centered, among other things, on in-novations in commercial and financial organization and practices that occurred within a changing home-based economic landscape in which the hub of British slaving activity shifted decisively from southeast to north-west England. That process mirrored and anticipated larger transforma-tions in Britain's economy that we commonly identify with the Industrial Revolution. Slave trafficking, however, was also a high-investment, long-distance trade that typically required its financiers to delegate in-voyage decision-making to designated agents operating abroad. Investors in slav-ing voyages thus faced agency dilemmas or principal-agent issues charac-teristic of many other long-distance voyages at that time.[10] But we will see how practices adopted in the slave trade to address agency dilemma evolved in ways that reinforced incentive mechanisms for agents to maximize slave deliveries and revenues from slave sales in the Americas. Reinforcing such developments was the growth of trade axes or networks with specific ports in Atlantic Africa that ultimately proved most efficient in supplying large numbers of enslaved people at competitive prices. These may be seen, among other things, as transcending what may be described as microhistorical approaches to studies of slavery and Atlantic history, which emphasize the cumulative effects of individual behaviors and revolve around interactions between enslaving parties and the enslaved in various localities, including the slave ship.[11] There were likely elements of contingency, even serendipity, in some of these interactions, notably in Africa and in the infamous middle passage from Africa to the Americas. It is, nonetheless, difficult to uncouple critical sources of efficiency gain in British slaving from innovations and changes in other areas of domestic socioeconomic life that had growth-related repercussions for the nation's economy as a whole and its share of global long-distance trades. That broad line of argument is, ironically, not dissimilar to that now commonly adopted to explain the rise of British abolitionism, though the roots of abolitionism were evidently different from those shaping the growth of British slave-trading capabilities.

From the moment that Parliament outlawed British slave trading scholars have debated the relative importance of people and principles in determining its decision. That has generated a huge literature around the issue of slave trade abolition, one given added interest by the bicentennial of the 1807 act. But, unlike the belief of the fictional Dorian Gray, to whom Oscar Wilde attributed the words quoted in this chapter's epigraph, historians have rarely, if ever, thought that principles were inferior to persons, especially "persons with no principles," in deciding Parliament's decision.[12] Humanitarian, philosophical, religious, and economic ideas continue to inform debates about why Parliament elected to outlaw British slave trading in 1807 as much as the contributions made by particular individuals or groups to their translation into public policy. Even though detaching principles from those who espoused them may be problematic, even impossible, we can detect differences among historians in the weight they attach to specific ideas or to particular actors or agents in shaping debates over abolition or even in determining the timing of the passing of the Abolition Act in 1807. Some emphasize humanitarianism, based on changing philosophical or other ideas, in driving abolitionism; others prefer to emphasize economic principles. Some attribute leadership in the anti–slave trade movement to its parliamentary champion, William Wilberforce; others place greater weight on such extraparliamentary advocates as Thomas Clarkson or, especially in the years leading up to the passing of the act, on parliamentarians other than Wilberforce. This is to be expected; one finds similar sources of debate in studies of other social movements and change, among them the origins of human rights, an issue that appears to have had parallels and connections with antislavery.[13] Among the issues explored in this book are the balance between ideas and human agency as well as which ideas were paramount and whose agency mattered most when it came to delivering abolition of the British slave trade in 1807.

Though he recognized the motivating power of religion in shifting values, Thomas Clarkson, the writer of the first history of slave trade abolition, published in 1808, placed considerable weight on agency, personal and collective, in moving abolition forward politically. Offering evidence of his own extraparliamentary activities, notably in the late 1780s, in support of the anti–slave trade cause, Clarkson's story line was thereafter largely one of parliamentary debates and processes, interwoven with excerpts from parliamentary speeches. In some respects his treatment reflected the shifting arenas in which the discourse about the slave trade would evolve between the late 1780s and 1807. Insofar as it also emphasized leadership, whether outside or within Parliament, it may also be considered as consistent with views attributed to the cultural anthropologist Margaret Mead. In her words, "All social movements are founded by, guided by, motivated and seen through by the passion of individuals." She also proposed that "a small group of thoughtful, committed, citizens can change the world"; indeed, she asserted, it "is the only thing that ever has."[14] It is not certain that Mead ever expressed such thoughts verbally or in print, but assuming she did, Clarkson may, as he reflected on the anti–slave trade movement, have seen much merit in them. After writing a prize-winning essay at Cambridge University on the unlawfulness of slavery, he dedicated his life to the antislavery cause. His Cambridge paper was published in 1786.[15] During the following sixty years until his death in 1848 he would work tirelessly for the antislavery cause. His commitment to traveling the length and breadth of Britain after 1787 collecting and preparing evidence in support of outlawing the slave trade assumed legendary status. Few would match the energy and service he brought to the cause, but Clarkson acknowledged the passion and commitment of others, too. He listed in his *History* the names of the initial London committee formed in 1787 to pursue politically slave trade abolition, known as the Society for Effecting the Abolition of the Slave Trade. All but two of its earliest twelve members were Quakers. An Anglican, Clarkson was one of the non-Quakers. The other was Granville Sharp, who became the society's first chair and was said to be the "father of the cause in England," thereby recognizing his work before 1787 to liberate enslaved Africans residing in England. Clarkson went on to describe the evangelical William Wilberforce, MP for Hull and then for Yorkshire, as the campaign's "Parliamentary head," a role he assumed from 1789 through 1807.[16] One result of underlining those individuals' roles in pursuing abolition, and in his, Sharp's, and Wilberforce's cases seeing the campaign through to success in 1807, was to create a vision of British antislavery that was in some respects Meadlike in nature; one that, essentially male and white, was heroic and underpinned by a moral fervor and a commitment rooted primarily in religious belief.

Clarkson's approach to slave trade abolition, with its emphasis on religiously inspired humanitarianism and on parliamentary maneuverings, framed the historical discourse on the issue for more than a century. It was reflected in W. E. H. Lecky's remarks on Anglo-Saxon nations' "sense of duty, the power of pursuing a course which they believe to be right." Such attributes, Lecky argued, produced "men careless indeed for glory but very careful of honour," men who made "moral rectitude the guiding principle of their lives," refusing to "deviate one hair's breadth from the course they believed to be their duty" and thereby ensuring England's "unweary, unostentatious, and inglorious crusade" against slavery.[17] Lecky's was a description that a later scholar, Sir Reginald Coupland, was content to endorse. The author of a study of the British antislavery movement, Coupland identified the key actors in the anti–slave trade campaign, among them Clarkson, Wilberforce, "and their little band of propagandists," while

elevating the movement into a more global moral force.[18] At the same time
he and subsequent historians followed Clarkson in highlighting the contributions of individuals or groups identified with the promotion and delivery of slave trade abolition and of other moral reforms in the early
nineteenth century. Their writings included several biographies of Wilberforce, commonly seen as the leading champion of the cause.[19] But attention was given to others, including those who came to compose what would
later be labeled the Clapham Sect, after the place south of London where
some of its members lived and others regularly gathered to meet. Historians have questioned the accuracy of the term "sect" to describe the group's
members and activities, but, emerging during the 1790s, its membership
and, it is argued, its influence over the anti–slave trade campaign grew in
time. It comprised, among others, churchmen as well as a number of MPs
who would be closely associated with the final push in Parliament for slave
trade abolition in the following decade. Wilberforce was one of its members. Uncharitably labeled the "saints" by some contemporaries on account
of their evangelical zeal for reform, the group continues to attract, as Wilberforce does, historians' interest and has gained a place in the online *Oxford Dictionary of National Biography*. Collectively, modern studies portray
the Clapham Saints as a tightly knit community or network, forged by shared
moral and Christian spiritual values, by social activism, and by mutual affection and marriage. Two centuries on from Clarkson's history of British
slave trade abolition, his approach to the issue, with its emphasis on morality and its focus on a Meadlike body of architects, still finds echoes in
historical research.[20]

The Clarkson tradition remains alive, but it no longer wholly commands the field where interpretation of the cause and significance of British slave trade abolition is concerned. One important break with the
Clarkson-inspired narrative occurred in 1938 when the West Indian–born
scholar C. L. R. James published his *Black Jacobins*.[21] It has since been
republished numerous times. A study of the slave uprising in 1791 in
France's premier sugar colony, Saint-Domingue, that resulted in the founding of Haiti as a free Black republic in 1804, James's book reminded historians that the enslaved were not bystanders in debates over slavery but with

commitment, leadership, and organization could, in revolutionary times in Europe, become agents of their own emancipation and thereby a factor in the politics of slavery in France, in Britain, and beyond. The Saint-Domingue uprising (or Haitian Revolution) and its causes, course, and effects continue to fascinate historians eighty years after James published his seminal work.[22] I shall return to certain aspects of James's writings later, but I note here that his book was instrumental in initiating lines of research that not only focus on the specifics of African resistance to enslavement wherever it occurred but, equally importantly, examine how by their behavior enslaved as well as liberated Africans intruded themselves into the day-to-day workings of transatlantic slavery, into the processes that eventuated in its decline and downfall, and even into the construction of post-slavery societies. That research continues. It prompts analysis of the relative significance and effectiveness of rebellion, fugitive activity, and other forms of behavior as forms of slave resistance.[23] It prompts discussions of the meaning of slave or Black agency in terms of the politics of slavery and antislavery.[24] And in the specific context of this study, it prompts reflection on how evidence of Africans' resistance to enslavement before and after Saint-Domingue informed and shaped British debates about the nation's participation in the Atlantic slave trade. The Saint-Domingue uprising and Haiti's emergence as an independent Black republic would haunt lawmakers and invite political comment around the Atlantic basin throughout the nineteenth century.[25] What also bears reflection, however, is how the behavior of Africans under British jurisdiction was instrumental in redefining the nation's perception of their humanity before the uprising occurred on the French sugar colony in 1791. An issue almost totally overlooked by Clarkson, it is one that I explore in chapter 7.

A second and more direct challenge to the Clarkson-inspired narrative on British abolitionism came in the decade after James published his seminal work when the Trinidad-born, Oxford-trained scholar Eric Williams published in 1944 a revised version of his doctoral thesis under the title of *Capitalism and Slavery*.[26] Central to Williams's book was a rejection of arguments placing humanitarianism at the heart of explanations of abolition of the British slave trade and ultimately British Caribbean slavery itself. Williams, instead, identified abolitionism with the rise of British industrial capitalism and with resulting shifts in perceptions of Britain's economic self-interest. But implicit in Williams's study was a dialectical framework whereby he associated the growth of British industrial prowess with profits and wealth from British transatlantic slavery and abolitionism's emergence from the 1780s with the beginnings of a decline in the relative importance of slavery to Britain's overall economic well-being. In transforming the nation's global economic standing, industrialization, he believed, encouraged the abandonment of mercantilist or protectionist ideologies involving slavery in favor of free trade and free labor.

The causal relation between slavery and British industrialization that Williams postulated was and remains contentious. Some continue to advocate it.[27] Others tend to see Caribbean plantation slavery itself as an offshoot or extension of European capitalism, rather than vice versa, thereby reducing its economic significance to the rise of late eighteenth-century industrial capitalism.[28] Be that as it may, it is important to note that Williams, like his predecessors, still saw British abolitionism as primarily homegrown as well as white and male dominated, but unlike earlier historians, he essentially tied it to economic calculation rather than considerations of humanity. In identifying Parliament's outlawing of the British slave trade with the Industrial Revolution, Williams's dialectical materialist approach radically recast the conceptual framework of British abolitionism. In the process he elevated the role of class interest and downgraded the influence of personality in shaping abolitionism. In the Western intellectual and political environment that emerged after the Second World War and in the context of European decolonization and the US civil rights movements from the late 1950s onward, Williams's approach would take on increasing academic and other significance, redefining the parameters within which abolitionism not just in Britain but more widely in the Atlantic world has been debated since its publication. The relation among social values, economic interest, and change transcends British abolitionism. It now lies at the heart of discourses around historic and indeed contemporary slavery.[29]

Important elements of Williams's explanation of Parliament's moves to outlaw British slaving in 1806–7 have attracted criticism. Among the more contentious were assumptions about the economic health of British West Indian slavery and about the changing contribution of slave-grown products to British overseas commerce and wealth accumulation before the slave trade was formally outlawed. On both counts, Williams was pessimistic, prompting him to paint a gloomy picture of Caribbean slavery in crisis and decline in the quarter century before 1807 and of its diminishing significance economically to Britain as the nation industrialized. That argument, often referred to as the "decline thesis," drew inspiration from Lowell Ragatz's classic study of the fall of the British Caribbean planter class but was reinforced by Williams's own portrayal of the American Revolution as "the first stage in the decline of the sugar colonies" and of the underlying inefficiency of slavery itself as a labor institution, the survival of which he saw as depending on "ever fresh conquests" of new lands to sustain it.[30] Such arguments were consistent with some contemporary views on slavery, and they continue to draw support among historians who, like Williams, see a sustainability crisis in the British Caribbean as pivotal to Parliament's decision to outlaw the slave trade.[31] Other historians, however, have challenged and even contradicted such claims, noting the continuing importance through 1807 of, among other things, sugar and other slave-based trades to Britain's international commerce and of the resilient productivity and profit performance of the British Caribbean slave economy, attributes reflected in the continuing attractiveness of the slave trade to British investors even as the abolition campaign gathered pace.[32] That does not mean that economic factors were irrelevant to abolitionism. It does suggest, however, that decline in British Caribbean slavery, when it occurred, was more a consequence than a cause of the 1807 legislation.

The decline thesis no longer carries the weight in explaining abolition of the British slave trade that is sometimes assumed, but two other elements in the confluence of contingent forces that, Williams argued, inspired and shaped the course and outcome of British abolitionism have attracted more positive responses, though not necessarily in precisely the way that Williams himself imagined. The first was the American Revolution, which, in addition to precipitating an alleged crisis in British West Indian slave economies, Williams saw as provoking that "growing feeling of disgust with the colonial system which Adam Smith was voicing and which rose to a veritable crescendo of denunciation at the height of the free trade era."[33] Smith's own analysis of mercantilist regulations as impediments to the operation of market forces is endorsed by modern assessments of rent-seeking behavior under mercantilism, whereby British West Indian slave-owners profited at the expense not only of slaves but also of British consumers.[34] More recently, historian Christopher Brown has identified a more specific connection between Britain's loss of its thirteen colonies and the launch of the campaign against the slave trade, arguing that defeat provoked a crisis of national and imperial identity and a reevaluation of British colonial policy, thereby transforming what was a rising British unease in some quarters about slavery into an open political campaign in 1787 against British human trafficking.[35] It is also the case that war with Britain and the resulting independence of the thirteen colonies was associated with moves to end slavery and slave trading in some former colonies. Such moves anticipated the commitment during the ratification process in 1787–89 of the new federal constitution to outlaw slave trafficking by sea by US nationals within twenty years.[36] Seen in an international perspective, it is now evident that the American Revolution politicized antislavery, with implications for British abolitionism. Revolutions in 1789 in France and 1791 in France's prize sugar colony, Saint-Domingue, both in the name of liberty and equality, reinforced that process, though not always to British abolitionists' immediate advantage.

The other radical force identified by Williams in shaping British abolitionism was a revolution closer to home—the Industrial Revolution. More than anything else it was, for Williams, the rise of industrial capitalism, and its identification with forms of labor other than slavery, that drove British antislavery and to which his eagerness to cite Smith's analysis of the virtues of free labor offered testimony.[37] Where Clarkson had discerned noble intent, Williams saw self-serving cynical motives. Elevating economic theory and economic determinism above humanitarianism, he transformed antislavery into a vehicle of free market ideology identifiable with the onset of British industrialization. In this scenario, abolitionist champions such as Clarkson and Wilberforce, though not irrelevant to Williams, were nonetheless innocent or unwitting agents of deeper capitalist forces rapidly turning Britain into the first industrial nation and politically remodeling the British state and its policies to suit their interests. With its Marxist undertones, Williams's argument fitted with historiographical traditions linking social change in Britain to class-based or capitalist ideology but associated for the first time, in Williams's case, with the rise of antislavery. As Marxist interpretations of British history and specifically the Industrial Revolution gained momentum after 1945, it is perhaps not surprising that Williams-type views of the financing and development of British industrialization as well as of abolitionist impulses gained traction in the historical literature.[38] Echoes of Williams's influence still persist.[39]

Historian Joseph Miller has urged scholars to historicize slaving (and by implication its abolition) to locate them within the specific intellectual and social contexts in which they occurred globally.[40] After Williams, that has certainly been the case with scholars of antislavery, for whom it is now impossible to conceive of antislavery movements in general and British antislavery in particular without reference to the wider transformations in society one associates with industrialization. That is true even for those who take issue with Williams on specific aspects of his work. Stanley Engerman, who, with David Eltis, has questioned Williams's arguments regarding slavery resourcing British industrialization, nonetheless acknowledges that "while the specific links remain difficult to establish, the coincidence in timing between the political and economic modernization of Western Europe and the ending of slavery throughout the world seems striking."[41] In a similar vein, Seymour Drescher, whose book *Econocide,* published in 1977 and reissued in 2010, offers one of the most sustained attacks on Williams's decline thesis, had earlier noted that it was not accidental that "abolition coincided with Britain's industrial revolution" but, anticipating Engerman, observed that "what the nature of that connection was has proven more elusive than Williams imagined it to be."[42]

One historian other than Williams who sought to imagine what the connection might be was David Brion Davis. Nearly fifty years ago he proposed one based on the social functions of ideology. To do so, Davis adopted the theoretician Antonio Gramsci's notion of hegemony, whereby a dominant group is said through its social and intellectual prestige and supposedly superior function in the world of production to gain spontaneously the loyalty of others to its ideas.[43] For Davis the critical issue was to explain how antislavery came to reinforce and legitimize such hegemony in the context of Britain's transition to industrial capitalism. More specifically, he sought to show how the "antislavery movement, like Smith's political economy, reflected the needs and values of the emerging capitalist order" and how, also like Smith's economic theory, antislavery was committed to demonstrating, in an age of political reaction, the belief "that all classes and segments of society share a natural identity of interest," even in the pursuit of humanitarianism. Davis uncovered support for this argument in the compatibility of antislavery with emergent economic theory, not only at the theoretical level but also in the support for the movement among leading advocates politically of Smith's economics. Davis noted, too, the growing "significance of antislavery as a channel for political action" and the emergence of antislavery literature, including poetry, as "a medium for resolving conflicts inherent in the emerging system of liberal values." He found support for that argument in William Cowper's poem *Charity,* published in 1782, which he cited at length. For Davis, therefore, as abolitionists looked to gain support from those holding power and from middle-class opinion, they discovered, "though not without travail, the common denominators that gave both zeal and limits to an emerging consensus." In doing so, they transformed "a sincere humanitarianism" into "an integral part of class ideology, and thus of British culture." In short, abolitionism embodied more than simply collective motivation: rather, it involved a paradigmatic shift in patterns of thought and values, helping to define "new conceptions of social reality" as well as policy and political action.

At first glance Davis's Gramscian-inspired argument may be seen as a more sophisticated and nuanced elaboration of Williams's thesis linking industrial capitalism to British antislavery. His class-based approach to antislavery was consistent with Williams's, as was his insistence in identifying antislavery with the ideological purposes of the British establishment and of an emergent industrial bourgeoisie.[44] On closer inspection, however, Davis's argument was qualitatively and conceptually very different from

Williams's. He assumed a much wider lens to explore linkages between capitalism and antislavery and reached a conclusion that belied the narrow-minded cynicism that underpinned Williams's analysis. Where Williams posed a binary divide between economic interest and morality, Davis transcended it, embedding antislavery ideas within a "sincere humanitarianism" as part of a paradigmatic shift in values that would ultimately advance politically a reform agenda that extended beyond antislavery. That proposition built on his earlier work on the history of slavery in Western culture.[45] By reincorporating religion and moral values into the story of British abolitionism, it anticipated, too, his own future study of slavery and human progress while perhaps inspiring others not only to investigate the tensions between British ideas of personal liberty and the building of a slave-based empire abroad but also to identify antislavery with wider reform impulses within British society from the 1780s as part of what has more recently been called a "humanitarian revolution" that extended beyond Britain.[46] In embracing Cowper's poetry as a means of exploring the humanitarian impulse that he believed underlay British antislavery, Davis went beyond the economic treatises and other philosophical works that underpinned Williams's analysis, thereby exposing the intellectual and cultural breadth of the shift in values he proposed and encouraging research on imaginative literature and other art forms as sources of antislavery thinking that continues through the present day.[47] Such research sheds light on the psychology and motivations of abolitionist supporters, especially in what has been described, in the context of the rise of the novel, as an "explosion in reading" in later eighteenth-century Britain, while also reminding us that Britain was not alone in embracing new humanitarian ideas, including antislavery ones, in that period.[48] The weight one elects to attach to any specific ideas and their sources in shaping British antislavery from the 1780s is, of course, open to debate, as the historiography demonstrates. But out of the welter of research surrounding literature, art, and eighteenth-century British society that emerged after Davis offered his Gramsci-led interpretation of British antislavery, one conclusion now seems evident. There may be a growing acceptance that the politicization of British antislavery from the 1780s was linked to the rise of industrial capitalism, but

in the so-called Age of Enlightenment in which both occurred, the intellectual and social currents that helped to shape that linkage were far more
diverse in origin, content, and form and in the breadth of their articulation or public expression than Williams assumed. One aim of this book is
to shed light on the relative importance of those various currents of change.

Even as one identifies British antislavery sentiment within broader
middle-class reform agendas that emerged in tandem with industrial capitalism, the anti–slave trade campaign still retained exceptional or distinctive characteristics. Among the struggles for reform that historians have
noted, the intended beneficiaries of those who campaigned to end British
slaving were outsiders to British society. They were enslaved Africans
whose cultural characteristics and pagan traditions, as much as their race,
not only separated them culturally from the vast majority of Britons but also
were among the very factors that helped historically to legitimize their enslavement in the minds of most Britons and western Europeans for several
centuries. Implicit in the rise of antislavery, therefore, was a shift in British attitudes toward the humanity of Africans that requires explanation
separate from being simply part of a broad humanitarian revolution. Equally
striking was how quickly the anti–slave trade campaign, launched formally
in 1787, acquired a nationwide following, giving it a political legitimacy,
which, because of the orthodoxy of the campaigning processes it adopted,
would be retained through 1807. Though largely neglected by Williams and
by Davis in his early work, both of whose interests chiefly lay in the ideological shifts underlying antislavery, the mass mobilization of support transformed the campaign into a social movement of exceptional reach, energy,
commitment, and durability. The movement's attributes were built on the
support of agents and agencies more numerous and varied in nature than
Williams and most of his predecessors acknowledged. They were manifest
in the unprecedented mass petitioning of Parliament in favor of slave trade
abolition that erupted in 1787–92. It was the start of an antislavery movement unparalleled in history and that would become the largest and most
persistent of all the campaigns for social justice and human rights in Britain before 1834 in what historical sociologist Charles Tilly has described
as the age of mass politics.[49] Though historians have studied the mass

mobilization of 1787–92 associated with the anti–slave trade campaign, why so many in Britain were prepared to protest publicly against the nation's continuing participation in the trafficking of Africans from 1787 onward has yet to be fully explained. Nor do we wholly understand the impact that public outrage had on the course of the parliamentary campaign that effectively began in 1788 and culminated in the Abolition Act of 1807.

My search for answers to these issues invites reflection on where the respective influences of agency, contingency, and ideology began and ended in determining Parliament's decision in 1807 to outlaw a trade from which the nation was profiting. Because achieving abolition involved a political process, resolving that conundrum also requires us to investigate whose agency mattered most at specific moments in time and why. I believe that clues to answers to those questions are to be found in the pathbreaking work of C. L. R. James. In exploring interactions between Europe and the Caribbean in shaping antislavery, James anticipated in form, if not substance, some of Williams's arguments in *Capitalism and Slavery*.[50] He also showed how appeals to liberty and equality in France in 1789 helped to promote antislavery; provided a valuable corrective to white, Anglocentric approaches to that process; and encouraged generations of Caribbean and other scholars to investigate African resistance and leadership in confronting slavery and other forms of social injustice.[51] Of more immediate significance here is that in reflecting on the writing of history, James proposed a methodology that navigated between traditional narrative approaches, whose authors, he suggested, "wrote so well because they saw so little," and those who, while continuing to personify historical processes, tended to see human beings as "merely or nearly instruments in the hands of economic destiny." "As so often," he continued, "the truth does not lie in between." "Great men," James posited, "make history, but only such history as it is possible for them to make." Elaborating on the latter, with its Nietzschean undertones, he wrote that "freedom of achievement [of such men] is limited by the necessities of their environment. To portray the limits of those necessities and the realization, complete or partial, of all possibilities, that is the true business of the historian."[52]

In seeking to apply these historical principles to his study of Saint-Domingue's transformation into an independent Haiti, James wrote as follows:

> In a revolution, when the ceaseless slow accumulation of centuries bursts into volcanic eruption, the meteoric flares and flights above are a meaningless chaos and lend themselves to infinite caprice and romanticism unless the observer sees them always as projections of the sub-soil from which they came. The writer [James] has sought not only to analyse, but demonstrate in their movement, the economic forces of the age; their moulding of society and politics, of men in the mass and individual men; the powerful reaction of these on their environment at one of those rare moments when society is at boiling point and therefore fluid.[53]

Underpinning his analysis of the Haitian Revolution, with its references to economic context, mass action and politics, leadership, social values, and the fluidity surrounding possibilities of change in times of social turbulence, James's statement, with its rich metaphorical content, has considerable relevance to the historical understanding of the British slave trade and its abolition. It reminds us of the importance of identifying the slave trade as an economic enterprise, the long-standing pursuit of which came increasingly to be questioned in the face of accumulating doubts about its morality and even its efficacy as part of sustainable socioeconomic order. It reminds us of how those questions assumed political traction, according to some historians, courtesy of the American Revolution and the Industrial Revolution, which disturbed the subsoil of the social order, not least through their impact on the growth of mass politics in late eighteenth-century Britain. And it reminds us of how two other revolutions—the French and the Haitian, which James saw as intertwined—created obstacles to, but ultimately could not prevent, the statutory ending of the British slave trade in 1807 at a time of fluidity and deepening crisis in the nation's international relations. Above all else, however, James's philosophy, with its emphasis on how leadership can be constrained by wider sociopolitical forces or the "necessities" of the environment when setting and achieving its objectives, is a reminder of the need to understand the changing balance and interplay of ideas, human agency, and events in determining historical change and political outcomes. James's words inform my discussion of the politics of slave trade abolition in 1791–1807. More generally, however, his approach provides a rationale for the principle-agent terminology that underlies most of this book's analysis.

Principal-agent theory, also known as agency dilemma, is one commonly used by economists and political scientists to examine how, in delegating decision-making, one party (the principal) ensures that the party to whom such responsibility is given (the agent) acts in the principal's interest. The theory has been significant in studying long-distance trade and in investigating the efficacy (or otherwise) of measures introduced to deliver positive commercial outcomes.[54] For this book, principal-agent theory is particularly relevant to consideration of how investors in transatlantic slaving voyages managed the risks associated with their pursuit, thereby improving their prospects of financial success and thus growth in their number. But it is also pertinent to analysis of abolitionist politics through at least 1807; among other things, it offers insights into how rebellious slaves or authors of so-called slave narratives became representatives or agents of the larger African population victimized by British traffickers, of which they were an integral part. Such usages of conventional principal-agent theory, however, are not to be confused with the more generic ideas pertaining to principles and agents adopted in this book. These are concerned, respectively, with the values and beliefs that underlie behavior in general and with the authority and power of those who sought to make those principles operational in terms of social practice or change.[55] At the heart of this book is the issue of why an activity generally thought by many if not all Britons as a wholly unexceptional, even banal, species of commerce for more than a century came to be viewed by 1807 with such public distaste or abhorrence that Parliament ultimately decided, after a twenty-year political campaign outside and inside the legislature, to abolish it as contrary to Britain's national interest. Resolving that conundrum requires us to move

beyond the more circumscribed concerns of standard principal-agent theory. It behooves us instead to follow James's advice and to look at how,
despite seemingly insuperable domestic obstacles and a daunting and uncertain international environment, a political campaign launched in 1787
by a small group of people to reverse what was an accepted, even natural,
right of Britons to traffic enslaved Africans achieved its goal twenty years
later. It was a peaceful victory—a "will to power" in Friedrich Nietzsche's
language—for humanity over a perceived evil rarely equaled before 1807 in
recorded history.[56]

PART ONE

Trade

ONE

A *"Diabolical Traffic"*

British Slave Trading, 1640–1807

AMONG THE VARIOUS reasons the Abolition Act of 1807 has attracted so much attention from historians is that in the quarter century before its passing Britons were by some margin Europe's leading carriers of enslaved Africans across the Atlantic. It had not always been so. In the first century and a half after Columbus landed in the Americas in 1492, merchants from Iberia dominated the transatlantic slave trade, shipping enslaved Africans to Brazil and Spanish America, where they were employed in producing sugar and mining precious metals for export to Europe. In that period, the English briefly entered the trade in 1562–68, seeking to profit from breaking Spain's efforts to restrict trade with its American possessions to its own nationals or authorized merchants.[1] But without demand for enslaved workers in the nation's own American colonies before 1640, British merchants looked to Africa in that period as a source of commodities other than people, with one adventurer, Richard Jobson, famously declaring, when offered enslaved African women in the Gambia in the early 1620s, that "we were a people, who did not deale in any such commodities, neither did wee buy or sell one another, or any that had our owne shapes."[2] To the contrary, at the time that Jobson wrote, the English were likely more fearful of being enslaved themselves by Barbary corsairs than contemplating enslaving Africans, some of whom had long been resident as free people in England.[3]

Jobson, of course, overlooked Sir John Hawkins, who had commanded England's slaving activities half a century earlier, but the somewhat pious attitude toward enslaving Africans he expressed changed

decisively in the 1640s, if not earlier.[4] A decade marked in English history
for Parliament's violent confrontation with Charles I in defense of English
liberties, the 1640s witnessed also a "sugar revolution" in the English West
Indian colony of Barbados.[5] Transforming the commercial outlook of an
island colonized by England from 1627, and giving rise to a production regime there that would subsequently revolutionize economic life throughout the Caribbean basin, events in Barbados were instrumental in turning
Britons from possible indifference or even skepticism to enthusiastic support for trading in enslaved Africans. Despite the distractions of civil war at
home, in the 1640s alone British and British colonial merchants invested in
no fewer than 50 slaving voyages to Africa. And in the following 157 years
through 1807, they would outfit some 12,855 more as they endeavored to
satisfy the burgeoning demand for enslaved labor created in British and
other parts of the Americas by the commercial exploitation of land for sugar
and other crops to sell in Europe.[6] Demographic catastrophes among
American Indigenous peoples allied to a disinclination to enslave fellow
Christians in Europe helped to ensure that Africans were the slaves of
choice among white planters in the Americas.[7] In total, ships outfitted in
British and British colonial ports took an estimated 3.4 million Africans
from their home continent as slaves in 1640–1808. Some 2.8 million survived the infamous Atlantic crossing (or middle passage) from Africa to the
Americas, the vast majority to be sold to labor-hungry planters in Britain's
expanding sugar colonies.[8] Unfortunately, the 600,000 who perished before reaching America were only a fraction of those who would be consumed
through what the poet William Cowper described in 1788 as a "diabolical
traffic," having publicly denounced it six years earlier in his poem *Charity*.[9]
The trade's ultimate purpose was to sustain Britons' seemingly insatiable
craving for sugar and such other slave-produced goods as tobacco.

Cowper's poem appeared at a time when the nation's slave trade
had already reached unprecedented levels in the decade before 1776 and
when Britain was on the cusp of losing political control of its mainland
North American slave-owning and other colonies. Cowper was far from
being alone in the 1780s in denouncing the trade, but his and others' condemnation of it could not stem their compatriots' enthusiasm for the slaving business.

Table 1.1. Estimated slave embarkations in Africa,
British-flagged ships, 1651–1808

Period	British embarked	Annual average (British)	Share of all carriers (%)
1651–75	122,400	4,900	25.1
1676–1700	272,200	10,900	37.9
1701–25	410,600	16,400	37.7
1726–50	554,000	22,200	37.6
1751–75	832,000	33,300	43.2
1776–1808	1,032,600	32,300	38.0
1783–1807	907,600	37,800	39.7

Note: Numbers have been rounded to the nearest hundred.

Source: Voyages/transatlantic/estimates/flag = Great Britain/embarkations/25- and 1-year
(1776–1808 and 1783–1807) plus flag = USA (pre-1776).

The estimated annual numbers of enslaved Africans boarding British-flagged vessels rose from just under 5,000 to over 33,000 between the third quarters of the seventeenth and the eighteenth centuries (table 1.1). From accounting for 25 percent of American-bound slave embarkations in Africa in 1651–75, Britons increased their share of the trade to over 43 percent a century later, making them the largest national carrier of slaves across the Atlantic by that date. In the process they eclipsed the Portuguese, their closest rivals, who operated principally from Brazil. They largely overshadowed, too, the French, who, like the British, had entered the slave trade relatively late.[10]

Britain's involvement in slaving through 1807 remained near or somewhat above the levels reached in 1751–75, thereby maintaining its general leadership in the trade and ensuring that, as far as outfitting slaving voyages from Europe was concerned, it even increased. In the quarter century after the American Revolution, shipments of African captives on British vessels averaged almost 38,000 individuals a year. In some years after 1782, moreover, total British shipments surpassed the previous annual peaks reached in 1774–75, reaching, according to current estimates, over 48,000 enslaved persons a year in 1799 and 1800. French carriers, encouraged by recent nationally enhanced state subsidies, exceeded that annual total in 1790, but no other national carrier matched the sustained level of slave carrying that the British did across the quarter of a century before Parliament outlawed the business in 1807.[11] That included their nearest long-term rivals, the Portuguese, whose level of slave carrying exceeded that achieved by the British in 1783–1807 only after Britons had been forced by law to quit it. Remarkably, Britain's preeminence in those years occurred despite Parliamentary restrictions from 1788 onward on British ships' slave-carrying capacities, which raised their operating costs.[12] It occurred, too, despite more or less continuous war with revolutionary and Napoleonic France from 1793 onward, when participation in slave trafficking by ships from continental European ports collapsed. While Portuguese traders based in Brazil operated through 1807 and beyond, Britons were almost total masters of the European-based slave trade in 1793–1807. That position seemed almost unimaginable a century and a half earlier. The questions that need to be answered are how and why the British trade became so big and so sustainable, even in times of war, thus making Parliament's decision to outlaw it so significant historically.

To explain the long-term growth trajectory of British slaving we need to examine components of the demand for slaves as well as changes in the business's structure and organization. I focus first on two of the three geographical apexes of the British transatlantic slave-trading triangle, Britain and America, before looking at Africa. Because the growth of slaving was primarily demand driven—evinced by rising long-term real slave prices in tandem with increasing slave shipments—it is appropriate to begin by looking at American markets for British slave traders before turning to ports of provenance of ships, notably in Britain, where the bulk of slave ships were outfitted, and finally to the "ports" in Africa, which, though far from being European models "of neatness" where physical infrastructure was concerned, nonetheless performed vital functions in terms of slave supply.[13] Ultimately, what dictated the efficiency and profitability with which Britons conducted their slaving operations was the integration of these three elements in the transatlantic triangle and the costs of moving slaves and of managing flows of goods and credit relating to such market integration. In the final analysis, slaving was a commercial activity driven by greed or profit motives. Without a reasonable return on their voyage investments, British merchants would not have sustained their enthusiasm for slave carrying through 1807. It is imperative therefore to appreciate the trade's financial as well as commercial structure.

Major shifts in American markets for enslaved Africans underpinned the growth of British and British colonial slaving activity between 1640 and 1807 (table 1.2). The remarkable growth of British slave deliveries resulted not only from mercantilist doctrines but from their breaching, including Spain's relaxation of them in 1788, which facilitated a substantial widening of market opportunities for British traders.[14] In 1641–65 almost two-thirds of all the slaves that British traders landed in the Americas were reported as disembarking first in Barbados, then undergoing its sugar revolution. Some two in five of the rest disembarked in Jamaica, but even in 1641–65 British slave traders showed a preparedness to engage with other markets in British America and beyond. Slaves were delivered to such emergent British sugar islands as Nevis and St. Kitts as well as to tobacco-growing Chesapeake planters, and modest numbers of enslaved Africans were delivered to Spanish American colonies, to Dutch Guiana, and even, exceptionally it seems, to Bahia in Brazil.[15] Despite these early signs of British traders' enterprise in breaching contemporary national mercantilist policy, the colony of Barbados would continue for at least another half century to be among their prime markets for slaves and from 1641 through 1807 would receive nearly half a million (or about 18 percent) of all the enslaved Africans British ships disembarked in the Americas.

In that same half century after 1640, however, Jamaica, seized from Spain in 1655, expanded its share of the British slave trade, and by 1720 the island became the principal first destination of slaves carried by British-flagged ships. It retained that position through 1807. In 1783–1807, Jamaica accounted for no fewer than 299,000 (or nearly two in five) of the 784,500 enslaved Africans recorded as being disembarked by British ships in the Americas (table 1.2, panel B). And over the whole period from 1640 through abolition in 1807, the island probably accounted for

Table 1.2. Slave arrivals in British-flagged ships in the Americas by place of first disembarkation, 1641–65 and 1783–1807

Panel A. 1641–65

Barbados	14,757
Jamaica	3,186
St. Kitts	397
Nevis	170
Other British Caribbean	425
Maryland	158
Virginia	128
Bahia	356
Dutch Guiana	373
Hispaniola	380
Other Caribbean	647
Rio de la Plata	155
Spanish Americas	259
Americas, unspecified	1,118
Total	22,500

Panel B. 1783–1807

Jamaica	299,379
British Guiana	66,582
Grenada	64,288
Dominica	55,990
St. Vincent	42,900
Cuba	34,974
Barbados	28,395
Trinidad	24,323
Dutch Guiana	23,078
Martinique	20,864
Danish West Indies	20,318
South Carolina	19,564
Others (25 markets)	83,852
Total	784,507

Notes: The total for 1641–65 includes slaves landed in vessels outfitted in British America but excludes 128 slaves reported as landed in Spain. Panel A includes all reported places of disembarkation in that period; Panel B includes selected places of disembarkation based on a minimum 2% share of the overall British total in that period. The dates cover years of arrival of slaves in the Americas.

Source: Voyages/estimates/transatlantic/specified period/flag = Great Britain plus USA (panel A)/specific disembarkation regions.

over 1 million (or some 37 percent) of the 2.7 million or so enslaved Africans British traders are estimated to have delivered to the New World. Jointly accounting for over half of British slave disembarkations, the two sugar islands of Barbados and Jamaica were foundational to Britain's emergence as Europe's leading slave power by 1750.

Jamaica was not alone, however, in supplanting Barbados as a prime market destination for British slave traders as the eighteenth century unfolded. By 1783–1807, five other venues—British Guiana, Cuba, Dominica, Grenada, and St. Vincent—were each more important destinations than Barbados to British traders (table 1.2, panel B). Moreover, five other territories—the Danish West Indies, Martinique, South Carolina, Surinam (Dutch Guiana), and Trinidad—were by that stage not far behind Barbados in overall importance and in some years were more important. As in 1641–65, some of the markets in 1783–1807 were foreign. They included Cuba, Dutch Guiana, Martinique, the Danish West Indies, and South Carolina, reminders of the continuing willingness of Britons to traffic slaves across imperial or mercantilist boundaries. Nevertheless, the largest markets for slaves carried in British ships in 1783–1807, as in earlier years, were in British America, and, despite a not insignificant trade in slaves to British mainland North America in the half century before 1775, were always located primarily in British territories in the Caribbean basin. From there some slaves were commonly reexported to other markets, notably mainland Spanish America. Though focused on the Caribbean, the market opportunities available to British slave traders were nonetheless wide and growing through 1783–1807, stretching from South Carolina and the Bahamas in the north to Rio de la Plata in the south. Such opportunities gave British merchants confidence to invest in slaving voyages, secure in the knowledge that demand for slaves remained buoyant in British America and beyond.

Various phenomena lay behind the proliferation of market opportunities available to British slave traders. One was international conflict between Britain and the leading Catholic powers of Spain and France from the mid-1650s through 1807. In such conflicts, Britain's blue-water policy and increasing naval supremacy allowed it to make both permanent as well as temporary territorial gains, particularly in the Caribbean basin, at the expense of its rivals. To Barbados and the Leeward Islands, colonized before 1640, the British would permanently add Jamaica, the Ceded Islands (Grenada, Dominica, St. Vincent), British Guiana, and Trinidad and Tobago, among other colonies, to its Caribbean maritime empire between 1655 and 1802. Other foreign colonies, including Cuba (Havana), Martinique, Guadeloupe, and Dutch Guiana, would come temporarily under British control in wartime, too. Some have suggested that in the age of mercantilism Britain went to war for trade.[16] Such claims may be exaggerated, but there is little doubt that in terms of Caribbean possessions Britain made substantial net gains before 1807, the most important in the long term from the slave traders' perspective being Jamaica, seized from Spain in 1655, and the Ceded Islands taken from France in 1763. National success in war also gave British merchants legitimate access in 1713–39 to the Spanish American market for slaves. This was three-quarters of a century before Spain officially relaxed its restrictions on trade with its American empire in 1788, allowing British traders legal access to the burgeoning Cuban market for slaves in 1789–1808.[17] War also brought Britain losses, of course, not least through American independence in 1776–83. By raising shipping and other costs, war tended to dampen levels of trade in general and slave trading in particular as long as conflict continued. Insofar as long-run growth of British slaving was concerned, however, the nation's maritime power ensured that, on balance, international conflict would prove, as the data for 1783–1808 reveal, more an ally than an enemy in expanding market opportunities for the nation's slave merchants. No other European-based group of merchants could make such a claim.

Britain's success as a slave-trading nation may have reflected its growing maritime prowess, but it also reflected other phenomena that translated the commercial possibilities created by such power into widening and deepening demand for slaves in markets served by British traders. As chattels, newly imported enslaved Africans were put to work in a variety of tasks in their new homes, but the great majority found themselves producing goods for export, primarily to Europe, the earnings from which would ultimately be used, among other things, to pay for the slaves themselves. Some newly arrived Africans would be employed in mining precious metals, notably in Spanish America; others would produce tobacco, rice, and indigo, particularly in areas of British mainland North America that came to form part of the United States; yet others would grow cocoa, cotton, and pimento on Caribbean plantations or cut logwood in coastal Central America. All these activities influenced, directly or indirectly, the distributions through time and space of newly imported African slaves in British ships into the Americas. But it was the production of sugar and its derivatives such as rum that generated the principal demand for slaves delivered by British ships and that dictated the rhythms of growth and geographical patterns of slave arrivals in such ships in the Caribbean basin. Modern estimates suggest that up to four-fifths of all slaves taken to the Americas in 1500–1867 would be employed in one way or another in sugar production, refining, and marketing.[18] There seems no reason to assume that the ratio was lower among the 2.8 million slaves entering the Americas in 1640–1808 on British-flagged ships.[19] The widening of slave sales from British ships across Caribbean markets reflected the island hopping of the sugar revolution from Barbados to other colonies and its spread to the nearby mainland in the century and a half after 1640. It reflected, too, the remarkable rise of sugar consumption in the British Isles, which encouraged continuing growth and geographical expansion of Caribbean sugar output, as well as long-term increases in labor productivity in sugar cultivation.[20] The last was linked to the breaking in of new land, thereby allowing new entrants into sugar production to compete with established participants for supplies of newly imported slaves.[21] The outcome of such a combination of factors was what one late seventeenth-century writer, Nicholas Barbon, with great prescience, described as an expanding Atlantic-wide British maritime and commercial empire based on naval power.[22] A later writer, Malachy Postlethwayt, saw it in 1745 as "a magnificent superstructure of American commerce and naval power on an African foundation."[23] By 1807, the Caribbean component of that empire, which ultimately dictated the magnitude of the British slave trade, was formally and informally appreciably larger in scale, in productive capacity, and in the use of enslaved African labor than that in which the sugar revolution had been born a century and a half earlier or even that which Postlethwayt described in 1745.

Though expanding output and labor efficiency in sugar production to satisfy Britain's sweet tooth undergirded demand for slaves in British and other colonies through 1807, they are insufficient to explain why so many enslaved Africans entered the Caribbean in British ships through 1807. The opening up and breaking of new land into sugar production, often in previously underexploited territories or islands, clearly remained an important factor in slave labor recruitment from Africa through 1807. But reinforcing that was a chronic consumption of Africans that afflicted Caribbean slave societies and created a persistent and likely growing replacement demand for fresh recruits from Africa. The human cost of slavery to Africans was identified by contemporaries, nowhere more so than in the writings of abolitionist Thomas Clarkson. He wrote in 1788 that "out of every annual supply [of captives] that is shipped from the coast of Africa, forty-five thousand lives are regularly expended, including the number that perish on the voyage, and in the seasoning [in the Americas], even before it can be said, that there is really any additional stock for the colonies."[24] Other abolitionists would later echo Clarkson's remarks.[25] But modern historians have extended such arguments by reminding us of the demographic tragedy that continued to befall enslaved Africans once forcibly resettled in the Americas. That tragedy was at its most acute in the Caribbean, including British territories in the region, and existed from the dawn of large-scale slave arrivals there. Despite playwright Thomas Southerne's observation in 1696 on the value of men and women slaves intermingling "for Procreation-sake, and the good of the Plantation," historian Richard Dunn described the British West Indies before 1713 as a "demographic disaster area."[26] Another historian, Barry Higman, has observed how the "crisis" of slave reproduction affected slavery throughout most of the British Caribbean between 1750 and 1834.[27] And more recent quantitative assessments have allowed us to put figures on the crisis's scale, with estimates showing that although some places, including Barbados, may have achieved natural growth of slave populations by the end of the eighteenth century, most places in the British Caribbean still faced chronic annual "deficits" in slave reproduction of up to 2.5 percent or so.[28] If accurate, such a figure would imply a replacement demand in the British Caribbean alone equivalent to up to 45 percent of all newly imported slaves entering the colonies at the time that Clarkson published his study of the human costs of slavery. And if extrapolated to the whole era of British slave trading, it would suggest that as many as 1 million (or about a third) of the 3.4 million slaves taken from Africa in British ships were required not to increase but simply to sustain existing levels of British Caribbean slave populations.[29] Ironically, contemporary Europeans attributed to enslaved Africans boarding ship for the Americas a mistaken belief that their captors intended to cannibalize them.[30] This was a false assumption on the part of the victims, but their "consumption" under Caribbean slavery gave it profound metaphorical significance. Without it, the ongoing demand for newly imported Africans and thus the scale of Britain's slave trade would both have been significantly smaller than they actually were.

Historians differ in the emphasis they place on the causes of Caribbean slavery's lamentable demographic history.[31] Some stress the disease environment and nutritional status of the enslaved, which affected their vital rates, especially among the very young.[32] Others see connections between poor vital rates and levels of Caribbean slave family formation or between cultural habits and rates of female pregnancy and patterns of infant care, all of which were reflected in low ratios of children to women, thus perhaps anticipating twentieth-century poet Philip Larkin's advice against handing on misery through reproduction.[33] The life of all slaves, male and female, was one of unremitting toil, so others have not surprisingly attributed trends in slave demography to the crop-related work regimes that enslaved Africans were forced to endure. In particular, attention has focused on the demands made on slaves in the land clearing, holing, and fertilizing associated with cultivating sugar cane even before they became embroiled in what was typically a prolonged, strenuous, and round-the-clock harvest season. One of the most distinguished historians of Caribbean slavery, Barry Higman, has argued that the "natural decrease" of slaves in Jamaica "was related directly to the labour requirements of sugar," reinforcing his argument with suggestions that only hired jobbing

gangs, often charged with the heaviest work, began to approach "the extremely high rate of natural decrease on the sugar estates," which, it is
claimed, employed nearly half of all the slaves in Jamaica in 1807–34.[34]
Others have added weight to such arguments by comparing the Caribbean
with slave-owning societies in the former British mainland North America colonies, where slaves were employed in tobacco, rice, and later cotton
cultivation and where slave numbers actually increased naturally even before the American Revolution.[35] In continuing to do so, they sustained
growth and geographical expansion of US southern plantation agriculture
through 1861. On the basis of comparative research, historian Michael Tadman, echoing Higman's argument, suggested that the combination of
"sugar and the Atlantic slave trade represented the worst of all worlds" for
enslaved Africans, producing "lethal" demographic outcomes.[36] If we assume that Higman and Tadman are right, the adage proclaimed by economist Alfred Marshall one hundred years ago, when reflecting on the
"Mercantilist slave trade," that "silver and sugar rarely came to Europe
without a stain of blood" seems more than justified, at least as far as sugar
was concerned. Marshall chose to note its "demoralising influence" on "the
population of the great western ports of England." But the associated waste
of life also heaped more misery on Africa, increasing the demand for slaves
carried on British ships.[37]

Sugar production may have drained the life and reproductive will out
of the enslaved, allowing abolitionists at times to paint their drivers—
the British Caribbean planter class and its local agents, the plantation
overseers—as inhuman. It did not prevent that class, however, from profiting from the crop as long as slavery continued to exist.[38] Buoyant and protected markets in Britain for sugar provided one prop for such profits.
Another, as noted, was the upward trend in labor productivity in the sugar
islands, which was often linked to the continuing availability of previously
uncultivated land. Yet another source of profit, however, may have been the
availability of fresh slaves from Africa at prices lower than the cost of gen-
erating them through natural reproduction within the islands. There was
in all slave-owning parts of the Americas, including those that concentrated
on sugar cultivation, a growing population of Creole or native-born

slaves. They generally assumed the status of their birth mother. Among eighteenth-century observers, some thought that locally born slaves who survived to early adolescence were ultimately likely to prove more durable, competent, and less unruly workers than those imported from Africa.[39] That was to have profound significance in debates over slave trade abolition by 1804–7. Despite those contemporary opinions, it remains the view of some historians that West Indian planters believed that, as long as fresh supplies of young adult slaves from Africa were available, it was cheaper and less risky from a business perspective to rely on them than to invest in nurturing and supporting Creole sources.[40] Such arguments were anticipated by early British abolitionists such as James Currie, who claimed in 1788 that planters "can now buy a full-grown African cheaper than they can rear a child from birth to the age of labour." On that premise, Currie went on to suggest that planters "are thus, in the treatment of their slaves, freed from those restraints which interest imposes on the most merciless."[41] Such suggestions are consistent with assumptions that, provided imports were possible, planters were prepared literally to work slaves to death.[42] Yet, even if that judgment seems overly harsh, Currie's remarks on the competitiveness of slave imports remind us that in seeking explanations of why the British became such prominent human traffickers, we need to look not just at the demand conditions they encountered but also at their ability to supply enslaved Africans at prices that West Indian planters, among others, could afford and were willing to pay. That requires us, in turn, to examine the competencies and incentive mechanisms that British merchants brought to bear in financing and conducting transatlantic slaving voyages in response to changing market demands for slaves, thereby determining their profitability as business ventures.

Between 1640 and 1807 merchants in Britain dispatched some 11,219 slaving voyages to Africa.[43] Other British slaving voyages were also outfitted in colonial ports, including almost 700 in British mainland North America before 1776.[44] Our focus here is on British ports, particularly London, Bristol, and Liverpool, which collectively accounted for some 90 percent (or 3.05 million) of the 3.4 million slaves estimated to have been carried

from Africa in British-flagged ships in 1640–1808.[45] All British slaving voyages from 1640 onward were funded by private capital and, with the exception of a few hundred dispatched by trading companies mainly in the
late seventeenth century, by trading firms or partnerships of varying size
which were commonly known by their "ship's husband," "agent," or "managing owner."[46] The three principal ports in question were not only Britain's leading slave ports but also Europe's in 1640–1807. Their closest
continental rival was Nantes, which like Bristol and Liverpool became a
regular slave port only after 1700. Liverpool ships, which ultimately dominated the British trade, carried more Africans into American slavery than
all French slave ships combined.[47]

    Of the British three, London was easily the principal slave port before
1700. Its entry into the trade from the 1640s was critical in establishing Britain's leadership in the late seventeenth-century European-based slave
trade.[48] London's dominance reflected its standing as Britain's trading emporium, which gave its merchants access to a ready supply of merchant
vessels, to the capital to finance voyages, and to national and international
suppliers of the manufactures needed to buy African slaves.[49] It was also
tied to the city's position as the headquarters of the chartered trading companies that governed the nation's trade with Atlantic Africa from the Restoration through 1698.[50] Thereafter, for political as much as economic
reasons, some of them connected with the Glorious Revolution of 1689,
steps were taken to liberalize entry into the trade, a task finally completed
in 1712.[51] In the succeeding era of "free trade," London merchants would
find it difficult to retain their earlier dominance of British slaving, and in
the century before 1807 it would be merchants in the country's provincial
ports, notably Bristol and Liverpool, who would lead the way in growing
British interest in slaving. That would result in a national geographical re-
configuration in the center of gravity of British slaving matched only
by the shift southward of the epicenter of slaving in Brazil from Recife to
Bahia and finally to Rio de Janeiro between 1600 and 1800. In Brazil's
case, the shift reflected patterns of slave-based agricultural production; in
Britain's, it reflected shifts in the competitive standing of ports in terms of
participation in slaving per se.

It was the merchants of Britain's second port, Bristol, jealous of London's leading position in British Atlantic trade, who first overhauled the capital's merchants as slave traders, taking on the mantle previously held by Londoners around 1730.[52] Though later described as "a dark den of slave traders," Bristol merchants' level of control of British slave carrying never matched that of their predecessors, and by the late 1740s they lost primacy in British slaving to Liverpool merchants; the latter, in the striking phrase of one nineteenth-century historian, "filched that commerce" from their southern rivals and then continued steadily to strengthen their grip on it as time wore on, becoming the trade's "great emporium."[53] Between 1750 and 1807, Liverpool would dispatch almost 4,400 slaving voyages to Africa and deliver over one million slaves to the Americas. On both scores, this was more than twice as many as Bristol and London combined.[54] This commerce also entailed an investment in money terms by Liverpool merchants, minor players in British overseas trade before 1720, of some £1 million or more a year in slaving voyages by 1790.[55] That was four times the equivalent of Bristol's investment in slaving voyages around 1790.[56] Even more strikingly, however, it was four to five times greater than that for all British slave traders around 1715, when London and Bristol were in control.[57] If, in the century after 1640, it was the ambitions of merchants at the last two ports that fired Britain's response to growing American demand for slaves, from the 1740s it was Liverpool merchants who took that response to unprecedented levels. Understanding that outcome requires us to explain the remarkable rise and exceptional performance of Liverpool as Europe's and indeed the Atlantic world's principal slave port in 1740–1807.[58]

In seeking to do that, we do well to remember that in a competitive environment marginal advantages can generate sweeping changes in patterns of economic activity. Some have located those advantages in social capital, specifically the larger size of Liverpool groupings' investment in slave voyages relative to Bristol, which, it is argued, gave greater access to knowledge, skills, and resources.[59] But as others have noted and I shall show, personal connections can be instruments to deceive.[60] And it is also useful to recall that such human traits as "sharpness, greed, acquisitiveness, meanness, egotism and self-interest" are ones that society commonly detests but are often "the traits of success" where economic performance is concerned.[61] That helps to put into context claims by James Wallace, a late eighteenth-century writer, who attributed Liverpool's initial entry into slaving before 1730 to its merchants' frugality in remuneration of ship officers, crew, and American slave factors and to their willingness to engage in contraband trafficking of slaves to Spanish America, notably Cuba. The low payments, he alleged, allowed Liverpool traders to undersell by £4 to £5 Bristol and London rivals in supplying slaves and still earn profits while trade with Cuba provided access to ready money in the form of Spanish bullion, enabling merchants to offer credit to British Caribbean planters who sought it in their own slave purchases.[62]

Wallace's portrayal of how Liverpool's pioneering slave traders secured a foothold in the business in the face of competition from Bristol and London is difficult to verify in the absence of Liverpool ship muster rolls and slave voyage accounts before 1730. There is, however, some circumstantial, if not conclusive, evidence to support his assessment. For example, wage rates in some economic sectors in northern England were probably lower than in London and southwest England before 1750.[63] Further, large numbers of slaves were trafficked from the British Caribbean islands to Spanish America up to the 1730s, with Jamaica playing a central role in those transactions; Cuba was one destination for such slaves.[64] There is specific evidence, too, that Liverpool merchants were keen from the very start of their involvement in slaving to sell slaves in Spanish America, thereby accessing ready money or silver coinage in return.[65] The known overall scale of such intra-American transactions, however, exceeded Liverpool's total estimated slave deliveries to the Americas in 1700–1730, indicating that the port's merchants were far from being alone in their pursuit; Bristol and London traders were participants also through the early 1730s, prizing the bullion they yielded.[66] Nonetheless, insofar as Liverpool traders were involved, Wallace's argument about the significance to them of the pre-1730 traffic to Spanish America, like the one about their economizing on running costs, may still have contained grains of plausibility, thereby contributing to the port's emergence as a significant player in the business.

Even if true, Wallace's may not have been Liverpool merchants' only advantages in seeking to expand their trading regime from the early eighteenth century. In his tour of Britain, published in 1724–27, Daniel Defoe described Bristol as "the greatest, the richest, and the best port of trade in Great Britain, London only excepted," but he also highlighted Liverpool's emerging challenge to Bristol's position. To Defoe, this reflected in part Bristol's "greatest inconveniences"; they included the city's "situation" or location and its obstinacy in refusing to allow "any, who are not subjects of their city sovereignty, (that is to say, freemen), to trade within the chain of their own liberties."[67] By contrast, Defoe saw Liverpool as "one of the wonders of Britain," which, he noted, "still visibly encreases [*sic*] in both wealth, people, business and buildings," and where growth of trade with Virginia "and the English island colonies in America" was "in a fair way" threatening "to exceed and eclipse" Bristol's. Among the factors to which Defoe attributed Liverpool's success was its investment in a wet dock, completed in 1715, where "ships lye, as in a mill-pond, with the utmost safety and convenience." Such evidence prompted him to urge other "trading places in Britain who want such a convenience," such as Bristol, to build such a facility, or "for want of it, lose their trade."[68] Though Defoe noted that the trade of Liverpool is "not my particular province" and failed to mention the port's slave trade, which in any case remained modest when he made his last visit to the city, his remarks on the value of wet dock facilities may well have struck a chord locally, for four further docks were subsequently added to the city's complement in 1754–96, strengthening its advantages over Bristol and, if Defoe's analysis was correct, advancing Liverpool's overall commercial success as well as, more particularly, its position in the slave trade.[69] Investments in water and road transport eastward and southward from Liverpool at the same time reflected and reinforced such success.[70]

If infrastructural investment and an open door to strangers are measures of personal and civic ambition and self-confidence, then Liverpool and its merchants were evidently not lacking in such qualities relative to their closest rivals in the eighteenth century. Such "traits of success" were, moreover, reinforced by other local or regional factors that improved the city's comparative advantages as a slave port over time.[71] One was the city's location, which until 1765 gave its merchants easy access through the Isle of Man to contraband goods for trade with Africa and across the wider period from 1739 to 1815 afforded it some protection against wartime depredations by the nation's enemies in European waters. This protected location allowed Liverpool merchants to sustain to their long-term benefit higher levels of wartime trade to Africa than all its British and continental European competitors. Another factor was a steady inward migration of new merchants and capital from Ireland, Lancashire, Yorkshire, and other places, including London, attracted by Liverpool's increasingly rich and specialist knowledge of markets for slaves in Africa and the Americas and by the profits from investing in the slave trade that such knowledge helped to create. And yet another was the revolutionary change in textile production in Liverpool's hinterland that we commonly identify with the Industrial Revolution. Sometimes—and probably mistakenly—seen as a principal cause of Liverpool's emergence as Britain's leading slave port, the growth of factory-produced cotton-linen checks and other so-called Manchester textiles extended significantly and perhaps increasingly displaced the imported linens from Ireland and other places that had helped Liverpool to gain a foothold in the slave trade in the first place. By the last quarter of the eighteenth century, at least, Manchester textiles constituted noticeably higher proportions of Liverpool's exports to Africa than its domestic rivals.[72] In so doing, they created opportunities for Liverpool merchants both to compete more effectively for slaves in some traditional coastal markets of Atlantic Africa and to open up new ones. In what was to prove a revolutionary age economically within Britain, new blood, new capital, new knowledge, and new products all combined to enlarge Liverpool's position and to improve its long-term performance as a slave trading port.

For each Liverpool investor in slaving voyages, as for others elsewhere, the principal objective was to achieve a return on the investment commensurate with the risks involved. Some of that investment was based on credit, described by British abolitionist, banker, and political economist Henry

Thornton in 1802 as "that confidence which subsists among commercial men in respect to their mercantile affairs."[73] The evidence suggests that credit was always part of the financial equation of British slave voyages. Its mismanagement could sometimes ruin slave merchants, as several British cases attest, but, when efficiently managed, allowed them to grow their business.[74] The accounts of one major Liverpool slave merchant, William Davenport, suggest that in the third quarter of the eighteenth century credit covered about half of the outset costs (that is, trade goods plus ship and its outfitting) of over seventy of his voyages, with credit for trade goods, notably wares supplied from Birmingham, London, and Manchester, being particularly important.[75] Davenport's reliance on credit was not unusual but may have been more modest than that of some of his contemporaries. Evidence for some fifty-five other Liverpool slave voyages in 1759–98 involving a number of merchants reveals an overall ratio of credit to cash in payment of voyage outset costs of over 60 percent, with ratios closer to 70 percent in some cases (table 1.3). Underlying the general picture, however, some other features of credit provision in the Liverpool trade are apparent. One is that reliance on credit was typically significantly and consistently much higher in procuring trade goods than in equipping ships for sea; many of the trade goods came from outside the city, whereas the outfitting of ships depended more on local tradesmen and merchants.[76] Another was that, though the surviving evidence is uneven through time, use of credit to fund voyages seems to have been higher among some merchants than others before the national financial crisis of 1772 than in the years after.[77] On that evidence, Liverpool's consolidation of its dominance in British slaving may have occurred in tandem with what for some merchants at least was an extended credit bubble through 1772, and one that also coincided with what historian Richard Pares once described as the "silver age of sugar" in the British Caribbean.[78] By contrast, the city's post-1783 hegemony in British slaving rested more, if far from completely, on its accumulated wealth from slave-based and other activities.[79] Either way, the ability to draw on credit permitted investors to prepare more slaving voyages at any one time than the limits of their own financial resources dictated, thereby increasing the sum total of their activity.[80]

Table 1.3. Ratios of disbursements (cash) to credit (notes)
in outfitting costs of Liverpool slave ships, 1759–98

Merchant records (Voyages)	Cash outlays	Credit notes	Total outlays	Credit share
Tomlinson-Knight 1759–73 (20)	£25,506	£55,126	£80,632	68.4%
Hasell 1764–72 (8)	£13,586*	£29,805	£43,391	68.7%
Tuohy 1766–86 (21)	£60,443	£94,109	£154,552	60.9%
Leyland 1783–98 (6)	£29,761	£31,531	£61,292	51.4%
Overall 1759–98 (55)	£129,296	£210,571	£339,867	62.0%

Note: * Excludes £3,326 of ship values.

Sources: Tomlinson-Knight = John Tomlinson accounts current with John Knight, Account Book, 1757–1777, 380 MD 127, LRO; Hasell = accounts of Christopher Hasell, Hasell Family Papers, Private Collection; Tuohy = Ship papers, 380 TUO 4/1–10, Tuohy Papers, LRO; Leyland = 387 MD 40–44, LRO, and Dumbell Papers, University Library, Liverpool.

Credit, however, was not cost-free. It inflated outset charges, as indicated by the willingness of some suppliers of trade goods sometimes to give substantial discounts for ready or immediate payment for the goods they supplied. Just as important, credit also had to be repaid, and preferably within the time limits specified in contracts, if the confidence that Thornton regarded as fundamental to the system was to be sustained. And that, in turn, created pressures on slave voyage schedules and on the recovery of other trade-related debts incurred in Africa and the Americas, yet more elements of the larger credit-based financial edifice on which slave trading generally depended.

Although it was beneficial to the expansion of slaving and vital to Liverpool's success as a slave port, credit provision in preparing voyages to Africa added to the commercial risks and uncertainties that contemporary writers such as James Wallace thought were naturally inherent in the business. In 1795, Wallace wrote that "in every other species of traffic, some general prescription is discovered to guide opinion, but the African commerce holds forward one constant train of uncertainty, the timing of slaving is precarious, the length of the middle passage uncertain, a vessel may be in part, or wholly cut off, mortalities may be great, and various other incidents may arise impossible to be foreseen; an attempt therefore to determine the gains of an African cargo can only be supported by probable calculation."[81]

Wallace's listing of the hazards of slave voyages was incomplete, but historians have followed his advice and often calculated slave voyage profitability. Based it seems on a comparison of slave prices in Africa and the West Indies, Alfred Marshall suggested that the "profits of the slave trade would have been enormous if any large part of the victims had survived the voyage."[82] In varying degrees others have since echoed that proposition.[83] Closer inspection of actual voyage accounts, however, whether partial or complete, has revealed a different story. The financial returns per voyage varied widely and even, if one believes some participants' remarks, from one year to another.[84] Variations in profit margins are what one would anticipate given the hazards that Wallace and others adumbrated. But overall *annual* net profits from the trade in slaves were more modest than some historians have proposed, probably reaching not much more than 8–10 percent during the period of Liverpool's ascendancy in British slaving through 1807.[85] With investment in African voyages running at around £1 million a year by 1790, that rate could still have yielded returns of some £85,000–£100,000 annually to the city's merchants. That, moreover, was not the only way in which Liverpool merchants profited from slaving.[86]

Annual returns around 8 percent from voyages were seemingly enough by themselves to attract continuing investment into slaving, often from sources some distance from Liverpool. They certainly accorded with

Liverpool merchants' own publicly stated general expectations.[87] They also likely exceeded what merchants could earn on most other investments at home and were evidently higher overall than the cost of borrowing to invest in voyages. The last went some way toward explaining the willingness of slave-trading merchants to resort to credit to finance these voyages.[88] There are indications, too, that profits in the Liverpool trade were at least comparable to and in some cases noticeably higher than those achieved by other merchant groups in ports at home and abroad.[89] Such findings all help to explain continuing investment in and therefore growth of Liverpool's slave trade. But, equally, they beg fundamental questions about how Liverpool merchants were able to make the slave trade pay so well or, to put it another way, how they successfully managed for the most part the risks that Wallace and others associated with its pursuit. Part of the answer doubtless lies with economic matters discussed here, such as ship operating costs, access to African trade good assortments, and reduced exposure to enemy privateers in wartime. Additional insights into their success, however, are also to be gained from reviewing other aspects of the trade, notably the patterns of Liverpool trade in Africa, the geographical apex of the slave voyage triangle so far overlooked, as well as the city's merchants' handling of agency and financial risks inherent in slaving as a long-distance trade founded on credit.

Managing the "Train of Uncertainty"

Liverpool and the Bight of Biafra

AS EUROPE'S LEADING slave trading community from 1750 through 1807, Liverpool merchants were beneficiaries of a geographically expanding British West Indian sugar economy, with major additions to that economy occurring as Liverpool consolidated its hold over British slaving. The merchants also benefited from developments closer to home, including locally sponsored port improvements that can be easily overlooked when explaining Liverpool's rise. But as the late eighteenth-century writer James Wallace observed, investors in what he called "the African commerce" faced a "constant train of uncertainty," factors over which by definition they had only limited direct control but which they looked to manage in order to maximize opportunities for personal gain in the business.[1] A closer look at the uncertainties that Wallace identified reveals that, almost without exception, they related to African elements of the trade. He specified problems or uncertainties of timing voyages; over the length of the middle passage (or Atlantic crossing); of ships being attacked or "cut off" at the African coast; of shipboard slave mortality; and, as he noted, of various other incidents that were "impossible" to foresee. Though lengthy, his list was still incomplete, for, among other things, European slave traders depended for slave supplies in Africa on inland and coastal dealers with whom, directly or indirectly, they had to negotiate and, equally importantly, to whom they often had to advance credit to procure slave supplies. The processes involved could be long or short depending on local market conditions or the level of competition for slaves from rival carriers, but they commonly took months rather than days or even weeks. In a business,

however, in which "dispatch" was a refrain that investors constantly urged
on commanders of their ships, how quickly ships could procure slaves at
the African coast was almost universally seen as fundamental to survival
rates of slaves in transit and to the financial outcomes of voyages. Delays in
loading ships with their human cargo cost lives and money within what
historian Joseph Miller graphically described as a "way of death."[2] Seen
in that context, the ability of carriers to minimize or manage the risks or
"train of uncertainties" relating to the logistics of slaving in Africa was pivotal to sustaining success in the business.

   The risks just outlined were, of course, ones shared by all shippers
of enslaved Africans, regardless of nationality. Liverpool merchants were
not immune to them. But there are indications that they managed them
more successfully than most. That was not just implicit in the long-term
growth of the city's and therefore Britain's slaving business during the
course of the eighteenth century. It was also reflected in trends in such vari-
ables as loading rates of slaves per ship at the coast and the survival rate of
slaves in the Atlantic crossing that contributed to sustaining that growth.
Loadings tended to rise as the century wore on, diminishing only where
mean loadings per ship were concerned by measures introduced by Parliament from 1788 on to limit them, while losses of slaves in transit tended
to fall and did so for some time before Parliament looked to regulate the
trade in 1788.[3] Such trends were not unique to ships outfitted by Liverpool
merchants, but there are signs that advance on both counts more than
matched most of their rivals.[4] Factors other than trading conditions in Africa contributed to the general decline in shipboard slave mortality. They
included innovations in maritime health and ship technology unconnected
with slaving but that Liverpool merchants introduced into trade practices
from midcentury on.[5] An analysis of trading patterns at the African coast
also reveals, however, ways in which Liverpool merchants in particular
profited from specific developments in slave supply systems in the Bight of
Biafra that proved especially beneficial to their success from the 1740s on.

Advances in data collection and analysis, inspired by Philip Curtin's census of the Atlantic slave trade published over half a century ago, now

make it possible to explore in remarkable detail changes in the pattern of slave trading in Atlantic Africa on the basis of national or local carriers, regions of slave embarkation, and even port of loading.[6] Our focus here is the patterns of Liverpool's slave purchases at African ports and—in our quest to explain the city's growing and exceptional standing in the trade— how such patterns affected Liverpool's own performance as a slave port. Liverpool ships sought slaves at some sixty-six African ports or trading venues, many of which were identified by a map printed in 1744 by an advocate for maintaining British forts in Atlantic Africa and subsequently presented to Parliament as part of a petition in early 1745 (see map, below). Most venues were visited infrequently, however, and Liverpool merchants concentrated their activities at a small proportion of them.[7] Insights into how the city's merchants managed the trade in Africa can be gained by examining the ten leading African ports at which Liverpool ships bought slaves in 1726–1808. For some voyages there are documented loadings of slaves at an identified principal port of embarkation (table 2.1, panel A), and for others estimated embarkations at such ports are available, yielding higher totals (table 2.1, panel B). The estimated embarkations involve, among other things, redistributing slave embarkations to specific ports in regions where, for example, only the region of trade was documented.

The distribution of Liverpool slave purchases across these leading ports for 1726–1808 disguise variations within that period. For example, at Bonny in the Niger Delta, which lay within the broader coastal region

---

(Overleaf) The Coast of Africa from Cape Blanco to the Coast of Angola, showing Forts and Settlements, with a large insert map of the Gold Coast, probably designed by Charles Hayes and engraved by Richard Seale, and printed for the Royal African Company (1744), 19 ¼ in. × 26 in. The map contains manuscript additions in brown ink and hand coloring (color not reproduced here), likely added by Hayes to help to explain to members of Parliament the need for government financial support for maintaining the forts and settlements. Bonny is not referenced on the map, perhaps because Hayes was on the African coast around 1730, before the port rose to prominence in British slaving. Reproduced courtesy of Beecher House Center for Equal Rights—Documenting Venture Smith Project; image courtesy of Daniel Crouch Rare Books, CrouchRareBooks.com.

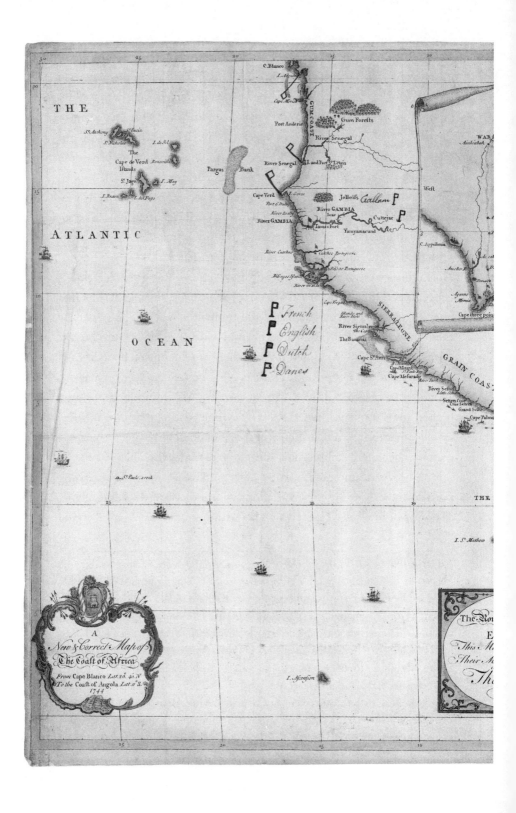

THE

ATLANTIC

OCEAN

C. Blanco
I. Arguin
Cape Mirik
GUM COAST
Gum Forests
Port Anderie
River Senegal
River Senegal I. and Fort S.t Lewis
WAR
Anchobah

St Anthony S.t Lucia
S.t Nicholas I. de S.l
The
Cape de Verd I.
Islands Bonavista
St Jago I. May
I. Bravo I. del Fugo

Pargas Bank

West

Cape Verd I. Gorse
Port o' Dally
River Sedly Jolloiss Gallam
River GAMBIA River GAMBIA P
near P
James Fort Cultejar P
Yamyamacund
C. Appollonia

River Cacheo Anicher R.
Cacheo Portugueze
Bissao Portugueze
Aquina
Menia
Bissagos Islands Cape three poin
River Grande Cape Verga

Islands and River Islet

French River Sierraleona
English the Cape SIERRA LEONE
Dutch The Banginas
Danes
Cape S.t Ann
Cape Mount GRAIN COAST
St Paulo River Mesurado
Cape Mesurado
River Sestro
Little Sestro
Setteri Crevia
Cue Setters
Grand Sestro
Cape Palmas

St Paulo, a rock

THE

I. S.t Matheo

A
New & Correct Map of
The Coast of Africa

From Cape Blanco Lat.20.40.N
To the Coast of Angola Lat.11 S.
1744

I. Ascension

The Ro
E
This M
Their M
Th

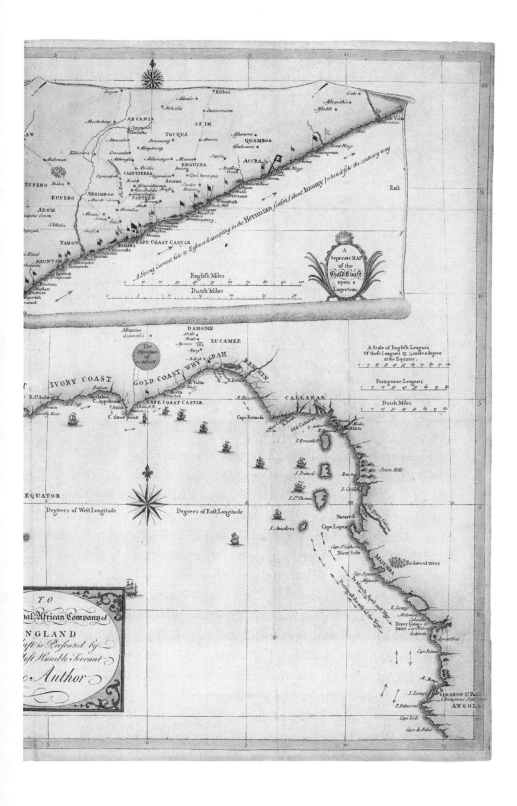

Table 2.1. Slave embarkations on Liverpool ships by
African port, 1726–1808

Panel A: Documented

Port	Number	Share (%)
Bonny	259,814	68.8 (1)
Calabar	101,660	57.3 (1)
Anomabu	51,462	38.4 (1)
New Calabar*	41,223	63.0 (1)
Sierra Leone**	39,423	84.4 (1)
Gambia	32,749	37.1 (1)
Congo River	31,504	66.1 (1)
Cape Mount	31,024	80.1 (1)
Cameroons	29,826	95.0 (1)
Whydah	24,865	14.1 (3)

Total 10 ports 626,783
Total shipped 850,342
Named ports (%) 73.7

that historians label the Bight of Biafra, purchases were largely continuous from at least the late 1720s, whereas purchases were concentrated in 1750–75 at Sierra Leone estuary and at Cape Mount on what was called the Windward Coast and in the period after 1782 at the Congo River in the region known as Angola. Disparities in African ports' contribution to Liverpool slave shipments may also have been less in some subperiods than the totals for 1726–1808 suggest. That said, the evidence suggests that across this longer period Liverpool traders were the leading buyers of slaves at most of the ten ports identified and major buyers at most of the others.[8] The two main exceptions were Malembo (on the Loango Coast to the south of the Bight of Biafra) and Whydah (in the Bight of Benin to the west), where in most of the years from 1726 to 1808 traders from other nations, including France and the Netherlands, tended to congregate.

Some differences in the general composition and individual rankings of ports by documented and estimated numbers of enslaved Africans loaded

Table 2.1. *Continued*

Panel B: Estimated

Port	Number	Share (%)
Bonny	389,200	70.0 (1)
Calabar	155,050	44.3 (1)
Anomabu	147,256	31.6 (1)
Gambia	81,270	31.5 (2)
Whydah	70,422	12.1 (3)
New Calabar*	67,308	47.4 (1)
Sierra Leone**	58,904	39.8 (1)
Cape Coast	51,516	16.2 (2)
Malembo	49,610	11.0 (5)
Congo River	48,576	17.4(1)
Total 10 ports 1,119,046		
Total shipped 1,338,000		
Named ports (%) 83.6		

Notes: * Also known as Elem Kalabari; ** river estuary, not region. "Share" refers to the proportion of slaves taken in Liverpool ships from the place specified. Figures in parentheses under Share (%) refer to Liverpool's ranking among carriers of slaves from the port indicated. All totals refer to shipments in Liverpool ships. "Total shipped" under Panel A excludes reported or imputed embarkations at unspecified places such as Africa or "regional" designations such as Windward Coast or Gold Coast. The estimates of numbers of slaves embarked in Panel B are based on data that typically cover periods longer than 1726–1808 but are allocated here according to the percentage of all captives leaving the port specified by the home port of the ships carrying them reported in the source cited. Though not strictly comparable to those in Panel A, therefore, they provide some indication of the documented *and undocumented* totals of slaves taken by Liverpool ships from the specific places identified in 1726–1808. The longer time periods underlying the sources of data in Panel B largely explain differences between the panels in percentage shares and rankings of Liverpool ships in carrying slaves from the same ports.

Sources: Panel A: Voyages/database/transatlantic/1726–1808/itinerary/departure port = Liverpool/ tables/African ports of embarkation and same/itinerary/principal place of purchase/tables/port of departure (search date 20 August 2020); Panel B: David Eltis and David Richardson, *Atlas of the Transatlantic Slave Trade* (New Haven: Yale University Press, 2010).

are evident. Overall, however, their similarities rather than their differences are most striking. They reveal a very clear pattern of Liverpool's trade with Africa for slaves. First, the ten ports accounted for close to or over four in five of all the slaves taken from Africa in Liverpool ships through 1808. Second, eight ports are common to both the documented and the estimated lists, and the same three ports head both categories. In ascending order, those three are Anomabu, on what was known as the Gold Coast; Calabar, on the Cross River in the eastern part of the Bight of Biafra; and Bonny in the Niger Delta, also in the Bight of Biafra. At Anomabu, trade was conducted at a British fort there. At the two Biafran ports traders dealt directly with local African merchants.[9] Roughly two-thirds of the slaves received by Liverpool ships at the leading ten ports boarded at these three ports, accounting for over half of all slaves taken by such ships from Africa in 1726–1808. Anomabu and Calabar combined accounted for about 300,000, or between a fifth and a quarter of the total, depending on the list selected. But, overlooked by the mapmaker of 1744, who omitted to identify it (see map, above), Bonny overshadowed both, accounting alone for perhaps around 400,000 enslaved Africans, or almost 30 percent of those entering Liverpool ships in the same period. The Merseyside port's ascendancy in British slave trafficking therefore was built in Africa on limited, specific commercial axes, with ports in the Bight of Biafra in the Gulf of Guinea being central to that strategy. In response to Wallace's "train of uncertainty," Liverpool's merchants seemingly looked to mitigate African-centered risks in slaving by building regular contacts with a few trading venues. As a strategy, it was not dissimilar to that pursued by other transatlantic slave carriers.[10] In Liverpool's case it was based heavily on ports in the Bight of Biafra but extended to some venues in other African coastal regions.

Liverpool merchants were prepared to invest in building trading alliances with a number of ports across the various coastal African regions that historians have identified. They included Gambia, Sierra Leone estuary, and Cape Mount in the north through Malembo on the Loango Coast and Congo River estuary in the south (see map, above). The contribution of commercial alliances forged by such efforts to Liverpool merchants' capacity to grow their slave trade in 1740–1807 should not be understated, particularly in the context of temporal variations in the incidence of Liverpool's trade with certain ports across that period. Trade at Cape Mount, for example, grew particularly rapidly in 1763–75, while that at the Congo estuary did so thirty years later. But such surges in Liverpool trade at particular places and times should not disguise the central importance consistently of Bonny on the Benue River of the Niger Delta to Liverpool's African commerce. Put simply, Bonny was the cornerstone of Liverpool's trade in enslaved Africans. By the same token, for the merchants of Bonny ties with Liverpool were fundamental to their export business through 1808. Equally importantly, the leading position of Liverpool carriers as shippers of slaves from other ports in the Bight of Biafra, such as Calabar, Bonny's neighbor New Calabar (or Elem Kalabari), and the Cameroons east of Calabar, also ensured that it was that coastal region more than any other upon which Liverpool's own success as a slave carrying port depended in the longer term. Moreover, just as Liverpool relied heavily on commercial relations with Biafran ports, so those same ports depended on Liverpool carriers of slaves to generate most of their exports earnings. Overall, Liverpool ships accounted for over 60 percent of the Bight of Biafra's slave exports between the 1720s and 1808.[11] Such patterns of interdependence between specific African communities of slave dealers and overseas carriers of slaves were not confined to Liverpool's trade with Biafran ports. Nonetheless, in seeking to understand Liverpool's contribution to the continuing growth of British slaving, the intensity and durability of its connections with those ports raises important questions. How did Liverpool merchants come to dominate slave exports from Biafran ports? What attracted them in such numbers to trade there? And what advantages, if any, accrued to Liverpool traders in dealing for slaves in the region, thereby mitigating the trade's risks and fostering Liverpool's emergence as Britain's and Europe's leading slave port? In sum, were slave suppliers in the Bight of Biafra active, if unconscious, partners in Liverpool and British slave trading success?

Liverpool did not initiate European slave trading at the Bight of Biafra. Nor was it the first European port to seek slaves at Bonny, the region's

principal slave port in 1750–1807. Liverpool's dominance was instead
built on a record of successful exploitation of trading opportunities there
over the previous century in which London and then Bristol merchants
had played prominent parts. As a result, by the early eighteenth century
Pidgin English had become a commercial lingua franca in the region, facilitating investment in social capital and networking that would shape
ongoing cross-cultural business. That investment began at the dawn of
the nation's regular participation in trafficking Africans during the 1640s
sugar revolution in Barbados. In the sixty years from 1641, the Bight of
Biafra was the source of some 140,000 slaves. That was equivalent to a third
of the 428,000 slaves estimated to have boarded British-flagged ships in
Africa in those years. Those ships, in turn, accounted for over three-
quarters of the 181,000 slaves calculated to have been carried away from
the Bight of Biafra at that time.[12] London merchants dominated that burgeoning connection, largely by trading before 1700 at New Calabar and
Calabar. Responsible for the great majority of the region's slave exports at
that time, Londoners founded a commercial axis with Biafra upon which
other British merchants could successfully build.[13]

Without ending, the intensity of British slaving in the Bight of Biafra
initially declined with the opening up of the trade to merchants outside the
Royal African Company, which formally lost its monopoly of English trade
to Africa from 1698. New entrants into the trade before 1720 focused their
energy on other regions, notably the Gold Coast, but in the following decade annual levels of British slave shipments from Biafra approximated
those before 1700. That marked a revival in British slaving in the region
that would continue to grow over the years through abolition in 1807. From
the 1760s, the British regularly shipped 10,000 or more enslaved Africans
each year from the Bight of Biafra. Such numbers easily outstripped those
they took from any other single region in Atlantic Africa, reflecting their
continuing and deepening commercial ties with the region.[14] The resurgence of shipments that began in the 1720s was associated primarily with
Bristol traders but with Liverpool ones in attendance. Together they sup-
planted London traders in the region. Bristol's ascendancy in controlling
slave exports from the region, which coincided with its emergence as

Britain's leading slave port in the 1730s, persisted through 1740. It was largely based on trade with Calabar on the Cross River east of the Niger Delta but was also identified with developing ties with Bonny in the delta from the late 1720s. The return from around 1720 of British slave trading in the Bight of Biafra to levels similar to those before 1700 was associated therefore with structural changes on both the British and Biafran sides. Such changes would accelerate from the 1740s, prompting a new configuration of trade relations by the 1750s in which an emergent Bonny-Liverpool axis increasingly overshadowed the preceding Calabar-Bristol one.[15] Thereafter Liverpool's influence in the region continued to grow, dominating Bonny, eclipsing Bristol at Calabar, and opening up trade with the Cameroons.

The principal catalyst of change from the British side was events in Europe. More specifically it was the outbreak of war between Britain and France in 1743. Continuing through 1748, the Anglo-French conflict dampened enthusiasm for outfitting slaving voyages among all British merchants, but its impact on Liverpool was less than on Bristol and London, where relative to Liverpool there was a collapse in outfitting ships for Africa in 1744–47.[16] In the absence of rivals, Liverpool merchants, who maintained a substantial rate of outfitting ships for Africa in the same period, seized opportunities to consolidate the commercial links with the Bight of Biafra, and Bonny in particular, that they had begun to establish before 1743. The continuity in trade relations that Liverpool merchants maintained with Bonny and Calabar in wartime stood them in good stead when peace between Britain and France was restored in 1748, enabling them to hold on to the leadership in trade with the region that the war had aided. Further consolidation of their commercial status in the region occurred from the mid-1750s with moves to open up slave supplies from the Cameroons east of Calabar. It was a move that paid financial dividends to the Liverpool merchants involved.[17] Emboldened perhaps by such returns and by the acquisition of potential new sugar colonies in the West Indies following the nation's victory over France in the Seven Years' (or French and Indian) War in 1756–63, Liverpool merchants were foremost in expanding slave shipments before 1776 from previously largely neglected potential sources of enslaved Africans at Sierra Leone and the Windward Coast as well as increasing those from Biafran ports and Anomabu on the Gold Coast. It was a pattern they repeated later in the century, notably at the Congo River estuary. Reflecting a mixture of single-minded opportunism and enterprise, the behavior of Liverpool merchants shifted decisively the historical geography of British slaving activity at home and in some cases in Africa, with their seizure of leadership of trade in the Bight of Biafra in general and Bonny in particular symbolizing their city's emergence out of London's and Bristol's shadows to become the nation's and Europe's new slaving capital. They were qualities that would sustain Liverpool's continuing growth as a slave port through 1807, allowing its merchants to exploit the commercial benefits that its market power in the Bight of Biafra afforded it.

When James Wallace discussed the complexities in 1795 of African commerce, he was probably aware that the assortments of trade goods exchanged for slaves differed widely among African trading places, with goods in demand at some places failing to find a market at others.[18] Depending on the comparative advantages of investors in slaving voyages in accessing assortments, such variations in African tastes doubtless influenced where they directed their ships to trade and in time cemented the concentrations of trading activities among different carriers at individual African ports, of which Liverpool's dealings with ports in the Bight of Biafra are a prime example. What Wallace did not acknowledge in his text, however, was that within the list of uncertainties or risks that he suggested outfitters of slaving voyages faced, their incidence was not random across places of trade in Africa. There were, in fact, some significant, even profound, differences among places of trade in Africa. It is now known, for example, that risks of ships being cut off at the coast or experiencing shipboard slave revolts were not evenly distributed across trading venues in Africa. To the contrary, they were very heavily skewed toward such places as Senegal, Gambia, and the Windward Coast and much lower at, for instance, the Bight of Biafra.[19] Similarly, there is firm evidence from both contemporary observations and voyage records that risks of shipboard slave mortality varied according to where the captives boarded in Africa. The same evidence points to similar variations in coastal turnaround times of ships waiting to load slaves. In judging where to send their ships in Africa, therefore, all investors in slaving voyages had to measure and balance security concerns against commercial opportunities. It was a fine line, subject, as Wallace noted, to careful calculation. But it appears, too, from closer inspection of the historical evidence that in the circumstances that Wallace described Liverpool merchants' concentration of so much of their resources in seeking slaves in the Bight of Biafra, and even more at Bonny, was a sound judgment, optimizing a balancing of economic opportunity and risk mitigation in pursuit of commercial rewards. As such, the Bight of Biafra became a critical pillar in sustaining the growth of Liverpool and thus British slaving.

Those not directly involved in trading to the Bight of Biafra sometimes depicted it in very negative terms. Some criticized the qualities of the enslaved people shipped from the region. American planters typically prized young adult male slaves, but slaves boarding ship in the Bight of Biafra commonly included higher proportions of females and children than those taken from elsewhere.[20] Others focused on their alleged character flaws. Igbo people, who comprised the majority of the enslaved shipped from the region to British America, were often viewed less favorably as potential workers than other ethnic groups, being characterized by some as lethargic, melancholic, and even suicidal.[21] Compounding such negativity toward slaves from the Bight of Biafra was the fact that their survival rate in transit to the Americas was generally lower than that among those shipped from anywhere else in Atlantic Africa. In the later eighteenth century, almost 18 percent (or nearly one in five) of the enslaved Africans entering British ships leaving the region died before reaching an American port, whereas mean losses on British ships leaving from elsewhere were typically 7–10 percent.[22] Even allowing for substantial variability of losses in the middle passage and for the fact that some ships leaving Biafran ports lost comparatively few slaves in transit, there was nonetheless a strong perception that slave trafficking in the region carried exceptional risks where slave quality and health were concerned. By the 1780s that view, for some, applied most particularly to slaves taken from Calabar, but that still did not deter Liverpool merchants from looking to that port as well as Bonny for many of their slaves at that time.[23]

The scale and persistence of Liverpool's investment in voyages to the Bight of Biafra in 1750–1807 may prompt us to assume that in its merchants' minds there were compensating advantages to trading in the region sufficient to mitigate its known risks. To uncover them we must look outside Wallace's list of uncertainties in the African trade and focus instead on other aspects of the Biafran trade that encouraged Liverpool merchants to invest so heavily and regularly in it. It is possible to identify and even measure some of the factors involved. Britain's lengthy history of commercial engagement with the region before Liverpool's rise to prominence almost certainly provided cultural and institutional foundations capable of enabling further export growth in the era of Liverpool's dominance. Other factors likely to attract Liverpool investment were relatively low export prices for slaves in the region, for which there is some evidence, as well as a low incidence of shore-based attacks on ships or of shipboard slave rebellions on vessels leaving all the major Biafran ports.[24] These specific attributes were not all peculiar to the Bight of Biafra, but in tandem they may have reassured Liverpool merchants aware of the trade's risks and looking for a comparatively safe and secure commercial environment in which to purchase slaves. In effect, the social capital that earlier generations of British traders had built up in the Bight of Biafra laid a platform for later Liverpool success.

There was, however, one set of positive reasons for Liverpool merchants to commit so consistently to voyages to the Bight of Biafra, and particularly to Bonny. It concerned turnaround times and loading rates of ships. For any owner of ships, to have one's vessel sitting idly in port was uneconomic, but in the slave trade, where British investors usually owned the ships they employed and where monthly wage bills were inflated by the hire of crew to oversee the human cargo in transit, turnaround times of ships in Africa were always of great concern. The erosion of ship hulls in tropical waters through attacks from the naval shipworm (*Teredo navalis*) added to such concerns, even prompting innovations in copper sheathing on British slave ships from the late 1760s. Such concerns were manifest also in investors' urgings to shipmasters to make haste in their trade at the coast or, as one set of owners exhorted in 1798, not to "procrastinate your purchase."[25] Competition among carriers for slaves was often a barrier to meeting such demands. It likely contributed at times to driving up turnaround times of ships moored off African ports and thus extending the overall length of triangular slave voyages. By the time that Liverpool merchants began to assume ascendancy in slaving in the early 1750s, mean loading times of slave ships in Africa generally hovered around six months; that was almost double what it had been a quarter century earlier. It remained high through 1776 but then, for reasons that are not wholly clear, fell back between 1783 and Britain's abolition of its trade in 1807.[26] Other things being equal, lengthening turnaround times in Africa raised voyage running costs and lowered capital turnover in the trade.[27] In such circumstances any advantage that slave merchants could gain in turning around their ships in Africa was likely therefore to enhance growth in their trade relative to others. The indications are that trading in the Bight of Biafra gave Liverpool merchants just such an advantage in 1750–1807.

Several commentators in the 1780s on the British trade remarked on Bonny's efficiency in supplying slaves fast.[28] Even Calabar merchants, concerned at Bonny's competitiveness, recognized it around 1780.[29] Given Bonny's reputation, we would expect to find Bonny attracting a disproportionate share of the ships seen as capable of carrying the largest conceivable numbers of slaves. The evidence supports that expectation. In 1741–1808, for example, the mean number of slaves boarding British ships trading at Bonny was 363 (sample = 988 voyages). That figure was some 50 more on average than that for British ships trading at all ports in the Bight of Biafra (2,321 voyages) and some 84 more than that for all British ships involved in slaving voyages (6,982 voyages).[30] Bonny seemed, in effect, to have attracted disproportionate numbers of ships owned by what were called by the 1780s Liverpool's leading capital houses in the slave trade.

Even more compelling evidence of Bonny's exceptional capacity to load ships fast lies in comparative data relating to loading rates per day for Liverpool ships across a spectrum of African trading venues (table 2.2). Daily loading rates in 1750–1805 improved across most places, a finding that is consistent with other studies of productivity change in slaving voyages and implying that in the closing years of British slave trading Liverpool

Table 2.2. Loading rates of slaves per day:
Liverpool ships in Africa, 1750–1805

Place	1750–75	1791–97	1800–1805
Gambia	1.0 (23)		
Windward Coast	1.0 (135)	1.5 (36)	
Gold Coast	1.3 (61)	2.2 (14)	3.0 (36)
Bight of Biafra			
Bonny	3.1 (60)	5.0 (38)	5.7 (59)
Calabar	1.5 (52)	2.6 (33)	2.6 (38)
Angola	1.7 (25)	3.4 (66)	4.1 (68)

Notes: (1) Blank cells indicate not available or very few; (2) figures in parentheses indicate number
of voyages in the sample; (3) data for 1791–97 are based on records of actual loadings and
turnaround times of ships at the places indicated, whereas those for 1750–75 and 1800–1805 are
estimated data derived from adjustments to slave arrivals in the Americas and sailing times from
Liverpool to the same as described in the source material. As explained there, the latter weights
estimates of loading times against the Bight of Biafra (and Angola). But the consistency of the
patterns by locality in 1750–75 and 1800–1805 with that for 1791–97 provides reassurance about
their reliability as indicators of such patterns and probably temporal trends.

Source: Paul E. Lovejoy and David Richardson, "'This Horrid Hole': Royal Authority, Commerce,
and Credit at Bonny, 1690–1840," *Journal of African History* 45, no. 3 (2004): 379.

merchants as a whole gained from faster turnaround times of ships in Africa than fifty years earlier. That, by itself, was indicative of slaving's continuing viability as a business even as British abolitionists sought to end it. What is also evident, however, is that Liverpool merchants were firmly locked into trade with African ports where daily loading rates for slaves in 1750–1805 were among the highest. These included Calabar, the Gold Coast (effectively Anomabu), and "Angola" (or ports along the Loango Coast south of Gabon as far as the Congo estuary). But the most striking evidence is for Bonny, where loading rates of slaves were consistently the highest of all in the Liverpool sector of the trade, often attaining levels two to three times those it achieved at other venues. Together with Calabar's, Bonny's performance made the Bight of Biafra one of the eighteenth century's most productive African slave-supply sectors, underwriting Liverpool's position as Europe's leading slave trading port in 1750–1807.

In a business in which, as noted earlier, those to whom responsibility for buying slaves in Africa were exhorted to make "dispatch," Liverpool merchants' predilection for trading with the Bight of Biafra, and especially Bonny, was hardly surprising. The fact that ships trading there could also do so with seemingly lower risks to their security from attacks from the shore or from rebellious slaves that threatened voyages to other places doubtless added to their attractions. Given such positive attributes as slave supply venues, indeed, it is perhaps surprising that so few slave merchants from non-British ports seemed to push for trade there. That may have reflected the region's unhealthy reputation historically. If that was so, it suggests that Liverpool, as well as Bristol before it, profited from looking beyond that reputation. But Liverpool's hold over the region's export trade in 1750–1807 was also perhaps testament to the economic importance of underlying, long-standing institutional factors such as commercial knowledge and networking in shaping differences in the geography of slaving among carriers of enslaved Africans from their homeland. Those factors gave Liverpool merchants access to a source of enslaved Africans almost unmatched in terms of efficiency of procurement and delivery before 1807. Understanding its roots is important in explaining the history of the Liverpool (and British) slave trade.

Located on an island in the Niger Delta, Bonny was seen as Africa's most proficient supplier of slaves at the time when British human trafficking reached its peak. Anticipating later historians' emphasis on how developments in its hinterland facilitated Liverpool's rise as a slave port, British contemporaries in the 1780s identified Bonny's status with its hinterland's productiveness in supplying slaves and its merchants' capacity to exploit it. The abolitionist Thomas Clarkson wrote in 1786 of Bonny's merchants going in a large fleet "into the inland country, to attend the fairs which are held there. They are mostly absent about nine days. They return frequently with fifteen hundred or two thousand slaves at a time, who are thrown on the bottom of the canoes, their hands and feet being confined in mats, and other ligaments of the country."[31]

Others elaborated on Clarkson's description. A leading Liverpool slave merchant, James Penny, suggested that goods to buy slaves were carried to markets eighty miles upstream from Bonny.[32] Another participant in the trade, Alexander Falconbridge, a former ship surgeon, claimed that slaves reaching Bonny came from fairs up to two hundred miles inland, with the fairs themselves receiving captives from places even farther away. The distances involved, according to Falconbridge, did not prevent the canoes from returning to Bonny "with full cargoes" in about ten or eleven days.[33] Yet another participant, Archibald Dalzel, would later acknowledge the strength of Bonny's (and Calabar's) links with their hinterlands when, in evidence to the African Association in 1804 on exploring the African interior, he underlined the virtues of doing so not through Dahomey, on which he had written, but rather via the Bight of Biafra ports. From these, he argued, there were "regular stages of one or two days journey" by which "European assortments are carried progressively" inland to slave suppliers, at each stage being "taken up by merchants who come no further from the interior, than to meet others nearer to the coast."[34] Other than for Bonny, there are few quite such explicit contemporary descriptions of how African merchants procured slaves for export at other African ports frequented by British ships in the 1780s or later. That, by itself, perhaps indicates the exceptional regard in which the efficacy of Bonny's slave supply network was considered at that time. It also offers an excellent example of how coalitions of elites in preindustrial societies could unite to exploit their power to promote international exchange.[35]

The descriptions of Falconbridge and others revealed the manifest elements of Bonny's slave supply system rather than the underlying dynamics or latent factors that animated them. Modern scholarship, however, has looked to shed light on them. Bonny increasingly emerged as the preferred outlet for Aro traders, an Ibibio-Igbo group, who came to dominate slave procurement and marketing across the Igboland interior of the Bight of Biafra in the age of the Atlantic traffic.[36] From their original base of Aro Chukwu, on an escarpment overlooking the Cross River on which Calabar was located, the Aro commercial network expanded westward inland during the eighteenth century toward the Imo River, along which Bonny gained access to the interior. There Aro diasporic communities forged blood pacts with local villages as bulking centers for slaves. Such pacts may

have happened as early as 1750, according to historians Kenneth Dike and
Felicia Ekejiuba. The westward movement of the Aro network matched
chronologically Bonny's rise as a slave port relative to its Cross River rival
farther east. Motivated by rent-seeking goals arising from bartering slaves
for trade goods, the Aro combined a fabled brutality and terror in slave acquisition with logistical sophistication and efficiency in marketing their
victims through inland fairs such as Uhuru and Bende. There they developed cultural ties as well as shared knowledge of slave markets with the
agents of coastal merchants they met. In many ways their commercial attributes paralleled those of the Liverpool traders with whom they ultimately
dealt, enabling Bonny in particular regularly to supply higher proportions
of the prime adult slaves that Liverpool merchants cherished than other
ports in the Bight of Biafra.[37]

The dealings of the Aro were increasingly with agents from Bonny,
whose share of imported trade goods into the Bight of Biafra rose from the
early years of the eighteenth century. They became regionally paramount
from the 1740s. Lubricating the flow of those goods inland was credit or
advances of trade goods by British and other traders to coastal merchants
against future slave deliveries. That credit fueled the deepening relationship between Bonny and the Aro. In its absence it is unlikely that slave exports in British ships in general and from the Bight of Biafra in particular
could have reached the scale they did.[38] The earliest evidence of credit in
British coastal slave transactions is to be found not for the Bight of Biafra
but for the Gold Coast in the later seventeenth century.[39] But evidence of
credit provision throughout the coast can be found thereafter, fueling
slaving activities at ports frequented by ships of British (and probably other
European) slave merchants.[40] Henry Thornton, the British banker and abolitionist, saw credit resting on trust between commercial agents.[41] Indeed, it became known specifically as "trust" at times in the Bight of
Biafra and elsewhere. Everywhere, however, its use involved risk, something that James Wallace overlooked in cataloging the hazards or uncertainties of the African trade. The risks associated with it were nonetheless
real, as some British shipmasters and merchants were able to attest in attempting to recover unsecured African debts.[42] As a result, the willingness or

eagerness of traders to advance credit to local African merchants commonly became dependent on protection mechanisms that incorporated indigenous practices. Their perceived quality, in turn, most likely determined how much credit was likely to be advanced and thus the amount of trade goods available to lubricate slave supply chains in ports' hinterlands.[43] Put another way, the intrusion of credit into coastal slave transactions everywhere exposed them to the classic agency dilemmas or principal-agent issues noted in the Introduction.

The practices that evolved in African ports to protect creditors against default varied. The most common were private order arrangements based on human pawning or hostage taking, often involving the kin of borrowers. Pawning was adopted, among other places, at Calabar, where local power remained largely decentralized, residing in effect within a series of separate and competing townships.[44] An adaptation of indigenous practice, pawning as a form of credit protection was not costless, since hostages were held on board ship for lengthy periods of time. It was known also to cause friction between creditors and debtors in practice, sometimes requiring intervention from local law enforcement bodies, at other times precipitating open violence.[45] In the political context of Calabar, however, it offered the only viable mechanism available locally to deter malfeasance in slave dealings based on credit. But, as contemporaries noted, pawning was not evident at Bonny, where it seems that a less complex yet ultimately more sophisticated and efficient system had emerged in tandem with Bonny's rise as a major slave exporting port. This system centered on the local office of *amanyanabo,* or elective military-political leader, whom Britons often referred to as the "king" and who served as guardian of the town's commercial interests and reputation. In that role he gained considerable wealth, but he also came to exercise a seemingly autocratic or absolute oversight of trade relations with outsiders.[46] The practice involved, when necessary, enforcing contracts, including repayment of debts, of local merchant houses with visiting traders. Evidence of the practice can be detected before 1700 and thus even before Bonny's rise to regional prominence, but its significance is evident in trade delays at the port during interregnums. A precursor of modern depersonalized mechanisms of contract adjudication, the centralization of contract enforcement at Bonny offered the prospect of speedier, author-itative, and more decisive resolution of commercial disputes there than at almost anywhere else in the Bight of Biafra and, indeed, probably in eighteenth-century Atlantic Africa. Efficiency in arbitrating disputes per-mitted Bonny to attract high proportions of Liverpool slave traders and in turn connected them through credit flows that underpinned river transport links with the Aro network, arguably the most dynamic and successful commercial diasporas to emerge in western Africa in the era of the Atlan-tic slave trade. The politics of Bonny may have introduced an unanticipated or fortuitous element into the port's export-trade credit arrangements, but their uniqueness and their adaptability to cross-cultural transactions en-couraged growth of such dealings. Bonny was not alone in adapting local governance practices to facilitate international exchange. It was, however, at the very summit in terms of creating an efficient contract enforcement system to enable external capital to fertilize inland commercial networks and to generate a major and regular supply of enslaved Africans to labor on British West Indian sugar plantations. By reducing uncertainty and risk in coastal transactions, institutional innovations of the sort that occurred at Bonny not only underpinned the security of Liverpool's connections with the port but also contributed to long-term growth of British slaving, with trade to the Bight of Biafra at its center.

One can easily overlook credit protection in Africa, as James Wallace did in 1795, when pondering the risks and uncertainties faced by British investors in slaving voyages. In important respects, however, it provides a valuable window on wider financial management issues, including principal-agent ones, relating to British slaving, and on how, as with the concentration of trade at Bonny, successful efforts by Liverpool slave merchants to address those issues allowed them to grow their business. In Africa, they built connec-tions with local sociopolitical elites to facilitate slave transactions and re-lied on the adaptation of local institutions to manage commercial risks, including default on debts. It is unclear how the indigenous merchants to whom British traders advanced credit then ensured delivery of slaves by those to whom they, in turn, entrusted imported goods to take to inland markets. It will probably never be fully known. One answer to that agency dilemma likely lay in indigenous debt collection practices, some of which rested on assumptions of collective responsibility for misdemeanors, with family or kinship groups being held accountable for malfeasance by individual members.[47] Possible insights into the working of such inland practices may be gained from cases similar to what was known as *panyarring*, whereby African coastal slave dealers held collectively accountable the fellow nationals of visiting British traders who misbehaved in dealings with them.[48]

Be that as it may, the situation in Bonny and in other leading African slave ports was in microcosm representative of the larger and complex financial arrangements that underpinned growth of British slave trading as a whole and the Liverpool trade in particular. Both were commercial edifices built on credit and debt recovery. Both involved merchant investors delegating responsibility for managing their affairs to other agents. Paper credit allowed British investors to outfit more slaving voyages than they might otherwise have done, but financial management of voyages still posed problems that, if unresolved, could prove ruinous for those involved in their outfitting. Scholars have shown, for example, how principal-agent problems and the accumulation of bad debts with British Caribbean planters fatally compromised the financial and commercial integrity of the Royal African Company, in the process contributing to opening the British slave trade to noncorporate groups.[49] The subsequent sustained growth of British slaving through 1807, however, suggests that that company's successors generally had more success in resolving the issues that had bedeviled its history. How they did so, and how far it reflected and affected changes within the British slave trade and its relation to the wider British economy, are the key issues addressed next.

THREE

The "Wheel of Unfathomable Commerce"

Credit, Incentives, and Sustainability

THE TRENDS AND STRUCTURAL change at the geographical points in Britain, Africa, and the Americas symbolized what is commonly known as the triangular trade. Growth in demand for slaves in such sugar-producing colonies as Barbados and Jamaica, Liverpool's eclipse of Bristol and London as Britain's slaving capital, and the Bight of Biafra's central place in supplying slaves to British ships were key structural features of British slaving that helped to determine and sustain its growth through 1807. Between 1750 and 1807 a commercial nexus linking Liverpool, Bonny in the Niger Delta, and Kingston, Jamaica, was at the core of British slaving endeavors, shaping the nation's success in their pursuit while reminding us, too, of their audacious, complex, and yet cruel and inhuman nature.

As a business endeavor, however, the slave trade was more than a movement of goods and people identified with a coercive system intended to repopulate British colonies in the Americas with enslaved African labor. Its very scale and success as an enterprise depended also on the capacity of those engaged in its pursuit to integrate in a sustainable way the financial needs and parameters of the business with the physical flow of ships, goods, and people that outwardly defined the infamous triangular trade. Like many other commercial enterprises at the time, slaving depended heavily on credit, whether to finance voyages, to lubricate slaving transactions in Africa, or to allow West Indian sugar planters to purchase slaves in anticipation of future income streams from selling the product of their labors. Credit, in turn, carried risk, a situation exacerbated when, as in the slave trade, the physical distances and time lags between creditors and borrowers were often large and investors in slaving voyages themselves depended on others to act overseas on their behalf, thereby precipitating issues of what economists call agency dilemma. That involved potential conflict of interest between investors (as principals) in an enterprise and those to whom they delegated responsibility (as their agents) to manage it in practice. Management of the relationship between slave merchants at home and their agents abroad was thus pivotal to harmonizing the material with the financial dimensions of slave trading as part of what one contemporary described as the "wheel of unfathomable commerce."[1] Failure to deal satisfactorily with potential conflict of interest could damage growth and sustainability of long-distance activities where supervision of agents was difficult if not impossible and action against any misbehavior on their part was essentially conceivable only sometime after the damage was done.

Historians have clarified how failure to address agency dilemma contributed to the steady decline of the Royal African Company's financial standing between 1672 and 1713. What is still lacking, however, is an understanding of how, albeit through a series of ports, investment in British slaving voyages grew on a seemingly sustainable trajectory across the eighteenth century and, implicit in that process, how merchant investors in such voyages addressed the issues of agency dilemma that had earlier undermined the Royal African Company. A focus on the issues of agency dilemma can lead us to understand how Liverpool in particular developed a credit and investment structure sufficient to sustain the exceptional levels of slaving activities it achieved in the second half of the eighteenth century.

In the two decades preceding abolition of the British slave trade in 1807, the nation's merchants invested more than £1 million annually in outfitting slaving voyages. Trade goods to exchange for slaves in Africa commonly accounted for two-thirds of that figure; the rest comprised investment in the ship, stores, and provisions. Annual totals around 1790 were several times the level of seventy-five years earlier, when London and Bristol controlled British slaving. By 1790 Liverpool merchants were easily the dominant investors. Credit helped to finance voyages throughout the history of

British slaving. In the era of Liverpool's dominance as much as a half to three-fifths of a voyage's initial outlays were commonly financed through borrowing, with dependence on credit to buy trade goods usually being significantly higher than in the case of equipping the ship for sea. Use of credit, usually identified in merchants' accounts as "tradesmen's notes," meant that Liverpool merchants, like their Bristol and London counterparts, could outfit more voyages for Africa than if they relied solely on their own capital. Its importance was elevated further by the length of slaving voyages, which often took twelve to eighteen months to complete and before therefore investors began to see a return on their investment. It is no surprise to find that voyage investors sought and often obtained credit of similar duration from those who furnished them with the goods they needed to outfit a slaving venture. The indications are that by the late eighteenth century British merchants in general and Liverpool ones in particular tended to secure better terms of credit when looking to outfit voyages for Africa than their continental European rivals, with Manchester textile manufacturers especially appearing at times to be more generous than most where Liverpool merchants were concerned.[2] Surviving merchant accounts also allow us to construct a broader picture of where that credit originated. Some came from suppliers of goods and services within the home ports of merchant investors, but investors in Bristol and Liverpool voyages, it seems, also relied heavily on suppliers of trade goods based in Birmingham, Manchester, and London to underwrite their ventures through credit.[3] At its peak in the late eighteenth century, therefore, British slave trading may have been centered in Liverpool. But its financing drew on lines of domestic commercial credit that stretched as far as the nation's capital as well as its emerging industrial heartlands.

As with other commercial ventures, the sustainability of the specific credit structure underpinning Liverpool's slave trade depended on the city's merchants to meet their obligations in good time. For those who had few or no other means to pay, that implied that to discharge their debts slave merchants were dependent on the speed of completion as well as the financial outcome of the voyages in which they invested. Success on both accounts yielded in theory the wherewithal to satisfy existing creditors and thereby renew the credit lines and associated supplies of trade goods with which to outfit fresh ventures. But the long-distance nature of the slave trade also meant that from its earliest days merchant investors in the trade were beholden to others to make local commercial decisions abroad that could fundamentally affect the outcomes they desired. Put another way, delivery of desirable outcomes to voyages had less to do with merchant investors' aims and ambitions and more to do with decisions made by those in whom they trusted to act for them during the voyages they financed. In eighteenth-century British slaving voyages the agents entrusted with such responsibility were the shipmaster, who was primarily responsible for day-to-day commercial matters from the time of leaving the home port until the arrival of his ship with slaves at an American market, and the slave factor, who took responsibility for selling the slaves, for determining the terms of their sale, and for forwarding the net proceeds arising from that sale. The returns might be made by the ship that delivered the slaves or by another. Either way, decisions made by shipmasters and slave factors helped to determine the financial outcome of slaving voyages. Their behavior, in turn, affected the capacity of merchant investors to deal with the domestic creditors on whom they relied to assist in financing their voyages. Accordingly the sustainability of the cycles of credit that fertilized British slaving was linked to merchant investors' abilities to navigate or resolve the issues of agency dilemma they faced.[4]

In looking at issues of agency dilemma in British slaving it remains important to recognize that levels of British investment in the trade were not immune to wider financial crises in the British economy such as those of 1772 and 1793.[5] Nor did successful efforts to resolve agency issues prevent bankruptcies occurring among British slave merchants. Indeed, some of the largest collections of merchant accounts relating to British slaving relate to bankruptcies. Financial success in slaving plainly did not depend solely on resolution of agency dilemmas implicit in its pursuit. Nonetheless, finding ways to resolve them—better still transforming them into mechanisms to identify agents' interests with those of the investors they served—could contribute to improved performance even in a business where, as James Wallace observed in 1795, there were always elements of uncertainty.

Particularly important were agents' roles as merchants' representatives in
commercial dealings in the African and American arenas of the trade and
in ensuring continuity in flows of credit linking British domestic suppliers
of trade goods through investors in voyages to African slave suppliers
and American buyers of slaves, and thence home, thereby maintaining financial liquidity in slaving operations. Other things being equal, the gains
accrued financially at least to those who most adeptly resolved agency issues. And the most adept, it seems, were Liverpool merchants, whose investment in slaving activities reached increasing heights as the eighteenth century
wore on. In examining how they did so, I begin with the evolving relationship of merchant investors to shipmasters and then at that with slave factors.

In their instructions to shipmasters about to sail to Africa, eighteenth-
century British merchants commonly reminded them of the need of ships'
"principal officers" to work together but were equally clear that within the
group it was to the master that they entrusted principal responsibility for
safeguarding their interests during the intended voyage.[6] Such instructions
were in effect a contract of employment. In addition to commanding the
slave ship, the master was typically given responsibility in the eighteenth
century for the conduct of trade negotiations in Africa.[7] He was in short
both commander of the ship and supercargo. In the latter role, he was offered guidance from the voyage investors about where to trade in Africa and
how many slaves to purchase. He was instructed to seek assistance from
his senior officers in managing purchases, not least from the ship surgeon,
who assessed the health of slaves before their purchase and subsequently
oversaw any medical treatment they received while on board ship. The master also assumed some responsibility for deciding where the slaves who
survived the Atlantic crossing would be sold, though in doing so he was
often guided by advice from employers either in his initial instructions or
through correspondence lodged with a nominated slave factor in the Americas, the second agent on whom voyage investors relied to assist in managing their affairs abroad.

However detailed the instructions issued to shipmasters were, they
could not cover all eventualities that might befall a slaving voyage. Nor,

given the lengthy time lags and uncertainties involved in communicating with shipmasters at sea could merchants easily update shipmasters' instructions once they sailed. Accordingly, some discretion was usually given them in interpreting their brief.[8] That in turn could expose investors to agency dilemma. Theoretically it could manifest in various ways. It could be linked to asymmetrical information (where the agent has more local and up-to-date information than the principal); to moral hazard (where the principal bears the risks for decisions made by the agent); and to conflicts of interest, such as the risk of an agent pursuing his own private trade or interest, possibly to the detriment of the principal. Of the three, moral hazard and conflict of interest potentially posed perhaps the greatest problems in the case of the slave trade. But in that respect, transatlantic slaving was no different from other long-distance trades.[9]

Examples of moral hazard for British slave merchants arising from ill-considered or mischievous behavior by shipmasters at the African coast are easily found. They arose even as British slaving under Liverpool's leadership was reaching new heights in the later eighteenth century and in places most frequented by the British. One source was entanglement of shipmasters in local African political or economic disputes and through which they hoped to profit. The most infamous case perhaps was at Calabar in 1767 when Liverpool shipmasters took sides with one township against another in looking to unblock trade. Their intervention helped to precipitate a local massacre, which, while yielding additional supplies of slaves, sowed distrust and bitterness in the damaged community that became linked to subsequent retribution against other visiting Liverpool shipmasters.[10] Elsewhere, in parts of Upper Guinea in around 1790, ill-judged, unsecured advances of credit by shipmasters to local resident white or mulatto dealers caused financial embarrassment for investors when the dealers failed to deliver the expected slaves, in one case at least because the dealer died before doing so, thereby raising alarms about debt recovery. Among those affected was the Liverpool merchant Robert Bostock, who in 1790 was prompted to complain about "a parcell of Rascally Captains" who having failed to recover debts exposed him, as the sole investor in the voyages affected, in meeting his obligations to his suppliers of African trade goods.[11] Other merchants' accounts show that Bostock was not the only one to suffer from such poor judgment by shipmasters.[12] Such instances demonstrate that though there was, as emphasized in chapter 2, discernible improvement in credit security arrangements in some of the places most commonly visited by British ships, gaps in such arrangements in some other places continued to expose investors in voyages to risks from unguarded decisions by shipmasters, even if compounded by unforeseeable events or uncertainties such as a local dealer's death.[13]

That said, where debt recovery was concerned, the problems that merchant investors in voyages encountered in Africa as a result of shipmasters' behaviors were likely much smaller in affecting their financial liquidity than those they encountered in British America. Local institutional safeguards for credit in most of the venues in which Britons traded for slaves perhaps mitigated the consequences for investors in voyages of poor decisions by their agents. In places like Bonny and Calabar by the 1780s, questions of the scale of local taxes on trade tended to overshadow those of debt recovery caused by "rascally masters." Other aspects of agency dilemma relating to shipmasters, however, consistently triggered anxiety on the part of investors in eighteenth-century British slave voyages, prompting them to action. The most troubling related to what is labeled theoretically as conflict of interest, which in this case revolved around issues of agents prioritizing their own interests over those of their employers. This issue had bedeviled the Royal African Company, particularly in managing its forts in Africa, where its local agents looked to pursue their own trade to the detriment of the company's business. It was still perceived as a problem even as entry into the slave trade was opened up to private partnerships and found reflection in instructions to shipmasters, which regularly included strictures against private trading on pain of financial penalty imposed on the master and senior officers should evidence of their illicit indulgence in it come to light. The penalties listed usually involved forfeiture of all emoluments payable to shipmasters and senior officers under the terms of the contract written into merchants' instructions. Such emoluments were potentially large, making the threat to confiscate them significant and underscoring how seriously merchants tended to view the potential risk to their ventures caused by conflict of interest and illicit trade. In their minds, senior officers had to be solely focused on safeguarding investors' interests, not distracted by others of their own.

It was not always easy for merchants to mitigate effects of moral hazard in a business where death was an integral part of its pursuit.[14] They did, however, attempt to tackle the issue of private trade by taking action other than words and threat of penalty to dissuade shipmasters from pursuing it. Their efforts to do so revolved around giving what came to be known as privilege slaves to senior officers over and above their standard pay rates. In the case of the shipmaster such slaves were one of a two-part package of such emoluments, the other, known as coast commission, being paid in recognition of his services in handling slave purchase in Africa. Such emoluments came to constitute in time sizable income sources for the parties receiving them, giving bite to threats of confiscation should evidence of engagement in private trade arise. Both privilege and coast commission became institutionalized in senior officers' contracts of employment in the eighteenth century, but in the case of privilege, there was an evolution in its structure that ultimately transformed what was initially a bribe into more of an incentive mechanism. As such it signaled a shift in principal-agent relations where ship officers were concerned, intimating perhaps a significant softening in investors' anxieties about conflicts of interest as the century wore on and as Liverpool assumed leadership in British slaving.

In 1759 the outfitters of a Bristol ship bound for Africa advised their shipmaster that, as part of his remuneration package, he was to receive an allowance of "privilege" slaves on condition that he undertook "no private Adventure of your own."[15] It was as clear a statement of the underlying rationale behind giving allowances of "privilege" slaves as one can find. The practice nonetheless had roots traceable at least to the late 1640s, when in 1646 and 1651 shipmasters of two slaving voyages were permitted to carry a specific number of slaves on their own account "over and above other wages." That was, according to the voyages' historian, the "customary practice" at that time.[16] It was also one that was continued some eighty years later, when, for example, the master of a London ship bound for Africa in 1730 was authorized to take out a specific sum on his own account to barter for slaves.[17] But a more common practice perhaps by that date was, as in the Bristol case of 1759, to give masters a specified number of slaves as privilege, with smaller allowances being offered to some other senior officers, each to be purchased out of the general cargo assembled by the voyage's outfitters. Other evidence from the 1750s indicates that recipients of "privilege" slaves were allowed to ship them freight free and to sell them separately from the main body of slaves landed in ships in the Americas.[18]

Efforts by such methods to deter shipmasters from pursuing illicit private trade did not, however, wholly resolve potential conflicts of interest. Those receiving privileges might, for example, prioritize the well-being of their own slaves over the whole shipload. Further innovation in privilege dispelled that possibility by both abandoning physical distinctions between privilege slaves and others and identifying instead the concept of privilege slaves with the well-being and value of a ship's whole human cargo. It was no longer primarily an instrument intended to discourage illicit private trade. Rather, it became a device to encourage shipmasters and other senior officers to attend to the well-being of the whole shipload of slaves. It was quietly transformed in effect into an incentive mechanism. Though no evidence of a coordinated process of change has surfaced, that transformation essentially involved either the calculation of privilege payments as a percentage share, usually 2 percent, of the total value of all slaves sold or a specific number, the value of which would be determined by the per capita mean value of the whole. Evident by the 1760s, the new methodology was associated with Liverpool's growing ascendancy in slaving.[19] Significantly, too, it increasingly aligned practices in determining the value of privilege slaves with that used to calculate the other major emolument received by shipmasters known as coast commission, which, like privilege payments, was usually paid where slaves were sold in the Americas. A recompense for the shipmaster's services in buying slaves in Africa, coast commission was typically paid throughout the eighteenth century at a rate close to 4 percent of the gross proceeds of the value of the sold slaves.[20] As such it was invariably the largest single component of a shipmaster's remuneration from a slaving voyage, easily eclipsing the monthly salary received as commander of the ship. Together with reforms to payments for privilege slaves, coast commission gave all shipmasters a powerful incentive to work to optimize the survival rate and sales revenues from their human cargoes while reinforcing, if necessary, the threat of merchant investors to confiscate all payments to ship officers should they pursue private trade. An indication of the value of a shipmaster's remuneration package exposes the severity of that threat. Equally importantly, it reveals, too, the value that merchant investors in slaving voyages placed on the skills and commercial judgment of those to whom they gave responsibility for the safeguarding and promotion of their own interests abroad.

Two examples illustrate the size and structure of earnings achieved by masters of ships that delivered 250 or more slaves to market, a figure close to the mean for British slaving voyages around 1790.[21] One concerns Captain Thomas Williams, who, following a voyage of seven months on the *Cavendish* from Liverpool, sold 287 slaves in July 1772 at St. Vincent in the West Indies. From the sale Williams was paid £350.40 sterling (or £4 in £104 of gross sales) as coast commission and a further £188.41 sterling (or 2 percent of gross sales) as privilege. With a combined total of almost £539 sterling, those payments were fifteen times his income from monthly salary to that point.[22] Thirty years later, in 1802, rising market prices for slaves ensured that the discrepancy between performance-related and salaried elements of Captain Charles Kneal's remuneration was even greater than Williams's, for when Kneal sold 305 slaves from the ship *Lottery* at Montego Bay, Jamaica, in December that year, also after a seven-month voyage from Liverpool, he received some £798.69 sterling as coast commission and a further £419 or so sterling in privileges, both at percentage rates against gross sales the same as those given to Williams.[23] The two combined in Kneal's case, however, were, at over £1,200, some thirty-five times his basic salaried income from the voyage to that point. It was also some fifty times the mean per capita income that the contemporary political economist Patrick Colquhoun estimated for England and Wales in 1801–3.[24] By that measure at least, Kneal's command of a Liverpool slave ship at that time was a highly lucrative business.

The financial gains that shipmasters such as Thomas Williams and Charles Kneal made from just one slave voyage offer insights into how as a result of a series of such voyages some shipmasters were able to retire from the sea and to join the ranks of merchant investors in the trade. It was evidently not unusual in Bristol and Liverpool. Their entry into the ranks of merchant investors offered firsthand practical experience of the trade, thereby helping to renew, reenergize, expand, and enrich the body's financial and knowledge bases.[25] Regardless of who financed voyages, however, the structure of shipmasters' pay clearly showed that, when it came to appointing those charged to manage voyages abroad, investors prized skills in buying, preserving, controlling, and even marketing human cargoes probably much more than navigational ones. That is not to say that, having appointed a shipmaster, investors trusted him to behave wholly responsibly in safeguarding their interests. Concerns about agency dilemma persisted, as regular warnings in merchants' instructions to shipmasters about private trade indicated. But the balance of shipmasters' emoluments, with coast commission consistently and significantly outweighing privilege slaves, and reforms to methods of paying the latter, increasingly evident from the 1760s, are indicative of a growing emphasis among Liverpool merchants in particular on the use of performance-related incentives rather than penalties to mitigate risks of agency dilemma such as conflict of interest.[26] Life-threatening uncertainties surrounding slaving voyages in Africa always held a danger of exposing investors in them to moral hazard, but the increasing rewards to shipmasters from aligning their interests with those of their employers were likely sufficient to eliminate most risks from private trading by at least the mid-eighteenth century. That did not, however, remove agency dilemmas for investors from transactions in slaves in the Americas. To the contrary, in a context in which reward systems for American-based slave factors were related to local market prices for slaves, the linking of ships' officer rewards to the same incentivized both shipmaster and factor to maximize prices wherever possible, even perhaps if doing so enhanced risks to voyage investors. Moral hazard and conflict of interest were not just confined to Africa; they were present in the American sphere of the trade, too, and how investors looked to manage them would have an even greater influence on the sustainability of British slaving activities.

Throughout the era of British slave trafficking, it was customary for shipmasters, as agents of investors in the voyages they commanded, to delegate the responsibility for selling the slaves they delivered and for recovering payment for them to specialist merchant houses, or factors, resident in the American colonies. The initial instructions to shipmasters on leaving the home port often specified the place and house to whom such responsibilities were to be given or from whom shipmasters might glean advice on where better prospects for sales and returns might be secured outside the first port of call. Growing British transatlantic commerce in general, with more and more ships in total crisscrossing the ocean, afforded expanded opportunities for investors in slave voyages to update their written instructions to shipmasters on where and through whom to sell their human cargoes pending their arrival in British America. The islands in the eastern Caribbean, notably Barbados, that lay directly on the route from Africa were a favored locality at which to lodge fresh instructions. Implementing any instructions, however, depended, among other things, on local market conditions and on the state of health of the cargo at the time of arrival in the colonies, thus obliging voyage investors usually to give some discretion to shipmasters on how to proceed in following them, thereby giving rise to moral hazard and creating scope for distrust and tension between investors and their agents.

Whomever a shipmaster chose to give responsibility for selling his human cargo, the process almost invariably involved some negotiation over the terms of sales and recovery of the proceeds therefrom. Two elements in that process were largely immune from negotiation, however. One was fees; the other was credit provision. Having accepted a consignment, factors would levy separate commissions on both the sale and the remittance of net proceeds arising therefrom.[27] Typical charges against the sales accounts would be provisions for feeding slaves pending sale, wages owing to crew discharged in the colonies, and emoluments to senior ship officers as well as the factor's commission on sales. Those against the return accounts would include the factor's commission on remittances, like that on sales deducted before the ship left for home. Individual rates of commission on sales and remittances were more or less standardized at 5 percent on each from the late seventeenth century onward and, with allowances for deductions from the sales, suggested that total fees received from the two sets of transactions were probably close to 9 percent on gross sales. That implied that factors might on average clear almost £700 sterling on each shipload of slaves they sold by 1790 and with some, such as those who sold Captain Charles Kneal's cargo from the *Lottery* in 1802, making considerably more.[28] Reflective of their importance to investors in slave voyages, for those regularly handling slave sales, factorage was plainly a lucrative business and one that attracted a stream of new entrants across the eighteenth century.

Through correspondence sometimes delivered by the shipmaster factors often received instruction from the owners of slave cargoes about the terms on which they expected them to be sold, but time lags between the issue and receipt of instructions and a recognition of the variety of circumstances that might affect slave sales at any time or place made it necessary, as noted, to give factors, like shipmasters, discretion in interpreting instructions. It was an acknowledgment of asymmetrical patterns of information, with factors on the ground having more up-to-date local information at the time of sale than those they were expected to serve, but it also gave scope for distrust or even tension in principal-agent relations, even provoking claims of factor malfeasance as contributing to the ruin of some British slave merchants. That aside, surviving correspondence of slave factors with eighteenth-century British investors in slave voyages is littered with explanations of why sales turned out differently from how investors expected or had been encouraged to believe they might do. Resolving or minimizing distrust and suspicion was pivotal to easing agency dilemma, no more so than on the question of the use of credit to lubricate colonial slave sales.

Among contemporary Caribbean planters, particularly those growing sugar cane, slaves were widely considered the most important part of the stock of a plantation.[29] But stocking plantations with slaves—and maintaining the stock—was costly, and planters typically looked to credit in purchasing slaves to grow or sustain their labor force. That was evident from the dawn of slave-based sugar cultivation in Barbados as planters looked to finance the acquisition of enslaved African labor through the future income streams its purchase was expected to yield them. And as plantation agriculture spread to new places, so demand for credit in purchasing additional slaves, or even slaves to replace those dying prematurely, continued to grow. It became an integral part of the flow of capital from Britain to the slave colonies that Adam Smith highlighted in his *Wealth of Nations* in 1776, annually reaching hundreds of thousands and cumulatively amounting to millions of pounds sterling by the time Smith wrote.[30] Though variable from one place to another and even from one year to another depending, for example, on the fortunes of the harvest, the length of initial credit that buyers of slaves demanded also tended to grow in the longer term, advancing generally from a few months or less than a year to as much as several years across the eighteenth century. As credit demands persisted, their financing and, even more, the recovery of the resulting planter debts became a central issue in factor-investor relations and associated agency dilemmas in British slaving.

Nowhere was the importance of credit to planter slave purchases and its potential to generate agency dilemma more clearly demonstrated than in its impact on market prices of newly arrived enslaved Africans in the Caribbean. And nowhere was it revealed more clearly than in a letter that William Woodville Sr. wrote in 1790 from Liverpool to the Bristol merchant James Rogers. In the letter Woodville invited Rogers, then one of Bristol's leading slave merchants, to consider sending a shipload of enslaved Africans to the French colony of Saint-Domingue. Woodville noted his own successful dealings with the French island since 1783, before observing "the different modes of selling Slaves in that Colony." The most common, he suggested, was to sell for part cash and part credit. The first was payable within three months of the sale and to be invested in produce to be returned with other freight by the ship; the second would run to twelve to fifteen months. An alternative, he suggested, was to sell to speculators for all cash or mostly cash with the balance in short-term credit of up to six months. But, he went on, it was "necessary to understand that great Sacrifices in the price must be made for ready money—perhaps as much as twelve or fifteen p[e]r Cent or as much as of[f] the price as would otherwise have been allowed twelve or fifteen Months for payment."[31] Put another way, without credit slave prices would suffer.

Rogers does not seem to have been tempted by Woodville's proposal. Its pertinence to the discussion here, however, is that in noting credit's capacity to hold up slave prices to a significant degree, Woodville failed to mention that slave factors, of which he had been one in Saint-Domingue, profited from the higher commissions resulting from credit-based slave sales. So, too, of course, would British shipmasters, such as his own son, in receipt of coast commission and privilege slaves. Nor did he dwell on the implicit risks that investors in slaving voyages would have to carry by giving credit to buyers in order to support slave sales and slave prices. In fairness, Woodville admitted that delays in repaying debts could often happen in Saint-Domingue, a point consistent with other evidence on remittance practices in the French slave trade.[32] He noted, too, that debts arising might attract interest when overdue. All of those points applied, of course, as doubtless Rogers recognized from experience, to slave sales in the British sugar islands. They had moreover applied for all of the time sugar colonies had been under the nation's rule. Implicit in that history were conflicts of interest in which, in their willingness to accede to planters' requests for credit and thereby boost through higher slave prices their own fee income, factors also exposed investors in slave voyages to the burden of supplying such credit and to the risks of delay and default that it entailed. Historians have recognized how, through its accumulation of unpaid planter debts, the Royal African Company as a trading organization became a victim through its dealings with slave factors of conflict of interest and moral hazard.[33] Our task here is to understand how its eighteenth-century successors looked to resolve that agency dilemma and thereby maintain growth of their slaving activities.

Although London merchants were prominent in driving investment in and growth of British slaving in the first quarter of the eighteenth century, Bristol and then Liverpool merchants sustained them thereafter. Bristol's period of ascendancy lasted until the mid-1740s, and the evidence suggests that the pattern of payments achieved by slave factors was not dissimilar to what Woodville described as standard at Saint-Domingue over half a century later, with a mix of ready money (produce, short-term bills, and specie) and deferred pay, but possibly with a higher ratio of ready money relative to deferred pay. Writing from Kingston, Jamaica, to the Bristol merchant Isaac Hobhouse in 1729, one firm of factors claimed that we "can't tell that we have been short in Remitting," observing that "the ⅝ of all our Guinea Men is made good with what we have advised, & are now Ship[p]ing" and that "the Aurora [slave ship] will carry ye ⅝ herself."[34] Assuming that claim was accurate, it probably included bullion arising from record numbers of reexports of slaves from Jamaica to the Spanish Main in that decade.[35] It still appears, however, that credit or deferred pay may have accounted for about a quarter of slave sales from Bristol ships even in those specie-rich years. That meant that the port's investors in slaving voyages depended on colonial factors to retrieve and forward a sizable part of returns on their original outlays in what the accounts of one major Bristol slave merchant labeled "after Remittance."[36] That implied, in turn, that the speed and completeness with which remittances were achieved could have potentially major repercussions for the sustainability of the city's slaving activities.[37]

In that context three observations are worth making. First, economic changes in the British Caribbean from the early 1730s may have handicapped debt repayment. Specie flows deteriorated as slave sales to Spanish America fell away, and because of losses of continental European markets for sugar due to rising competition from the French colonies, wholesale sugar prices in Britain tumbled to a century low in 1730–33, prompting political intervention in 1733 to protect British and Irish markets but in the meantime making debt clearance through sugar shipments less efficient. Second, any efforts by local slave factors to recover debts from recalcitrant planters were handicapped by difficulties in pursuing them through colonial courts that favored planter interests and most likely, too, the closeness of factors personally and socially with elements of the planter community.[38] Third, feelings that through local proximity slave factors were probably more sympathetic to planters' than distant investors' problems may have encouraged Bristol merchants to relocate junior family members to the colonies to oversee slave sales from their ships in a belief that family loyalties might prevail over other attributes in dunning planters to settle their debts. This strategy to manage slave sales persisted until at least the early 1750s.[39]

As a means of improving debt recovery from such sales, Bristol merchants' use of social capital was evidently far from foolproof. Surviving records reveal in fact fractious relations at times between Bristol slave merchants and kin who acted as factors for the disposal of their human cargoes in the West Indies. In 1754 one Bristol merchant charged a Jamaican house with which he had family ties of investing the proceeds from six slave voyages in other ventures rather than remit them home, thus threatening "your and our own ruin." He further observed how duplicity by other Bristol-related factors had caused misery for Bristol slave-trading families, mentioning specifically the major slave merchant Peter Day, who, broken-hearted by such behavior, had "died insolvent."[40] In that merchant's mind, misbehavior and selfishness by slave factors had ruinous consequences for those they were contracted to serve. In modern parlance, the merchant investors were victims of moral hazard.

Yet even as voice was being given to such concerns, changes to sale and remittance procedures relating to African slave imports into the West Indies were under way. They became identified with Liverpool's ascendancy in British slaving, and though the changes were not necessarily Liverpool initiatives in the beginning, the city's merchants were among the leaders in embracing them and the ones who benefited most from doing so. Their adoption involved a shift toward more impersonal principal-agent relations in managing slave sales that alleviated risks of advancing credit to planters from the shoulders of British slave merchants, thereby mitigating for them issues of agency dilemma in slave sales and helping to sustain and even grow investment in the business.[41] The new practices were not universally adopted in British slaving.[42] But they steadily evolved over a quarter century from the late 1740s and came to reconfigure the contractual relationship of slave voyage investors to slave factors in many instances and, as a result, the financial framework underpinning the credit structure of much of British slaving. Manifest in the last was a restructuring of the composition of remittances, allowing return by the slave ship of full rather than partial proceeds of sales of human cargoes that had previously characterized the trade. Variously known as the "bill in the bottom" or "guaranteed bill" system and unique, it seems, to British slaving in the later eighteenth century, it represented an institutional innovation central to slaving's continuing expansion and resilience under Liverpool's leadership in 1750–1807.[43]

A precise date when the alteration in slave merchant-factor relations began has yet to be determined, but traces of it can be found in the late 1740s and details of its more or less complete articulation as well as its geographical spread across much of the British West Indies and even to South Carolina by the early 1770s.[44] Its realization is also mirrored in slave merchants' accounts, which, in the case of the most comprehensive set of late eighteenth-century Liverpool slave merchant papers, reveal almost invariably the remittance, most commonly in postdated bills of exchange issued by slave factors, of the whole proceeds of the sales of slaves by the same ship that had brought them from Africa. The picture portrayed by those accounts covers the thirty years from the mid-1750s onward.[45] It is largely replicated in similar, if smaller, sets of accounts of other Liverpool slave merchants from the 1770s through 1807, though rather less so in surviving Bristol voyage records and merchant papers, thus suggesting differences in the enthusiasm among merchants at the two to embrace the new arrangements.[46] Where Bristol proved hesitant, Liverpool gained.

The core features of the new system as it became fully articulated were essentially twofold.[47] First, factors and masters sought to negotiate and specify conditions of the slave sale, including possibly a minimum mean price for slaves and related credit terms, before auction.[48] As in the past those negotiations were informed, among other things, by slave merchants' advice to masters, by factors' assessments of prevailing market conditions, and by perceptions of the general quality and attributes of the slaves delivered. Second, where credit was provided during sales, as it was in most instances, factors would receive, as normal, planters' credit notes and bills arising from sales. But rather than remit such bills and notes, factors would retain them for later personal settlement, remitting in their place bills issued on their own account either to the full value of the whole net proceeds of the slave sales or the balance not covered by other returns. Either way, the ship received the full value of the slave sales to take home "in the bottom." The factors' bills with which the ship returned home were, in turn, drawn against their own merchant correspondents in Britain, usually in London but sometimes in other cities. They became guarantors of factors' bills.[49] Those correspondents, in their turn, usually pledged in writing to known

slave merchants in Liverpool and other places to underwrite or endorse specific factors' bills on receiving them and to pledge payment of them when
due or, should early payment be required, at a discounted rate.

Effectively, therefore, the new slave remittance system introduced a
third-party underwriting of "slave bills" issued by factors and in which trust
in known and presumably reputable British finance houses became a substitute for the risk and uncertainty to investors in slave voyages of themselves advancing credit to planters and relying on the goodwill of factors
to recover debts. The system also introduced more predictability into the
timing of return payments, since the bills remitted by factors were typically
issued in sets of three, each with its specified date of maturity after reaching
Britain and being endorsed by the party on which they were drawn. The
length of credit supplied by finance houses under the new arrangements
extended considerably between 1750 and 1807, often reaching to several
years toward the end of the period. It was a scale of underwriting slave purchases that it was difficult to conceive British investors in slave voyages
alone sustaining in that period, underlining the wider implications of the
new arrangements. Under them, factors and their British correspondents
became de facto creditors of planters, releasing slave merchants from that
burden. They became local debt collectors on behalf of their own corresponding principals in Britain rather than, as in the past, on behalf of slave
suppliers. With changes in methods came changes in personnel, too, as
slave factors with links to British capital houses assumed increasingly more
importance in 1750–1807 than those with ties to particular slave merchants,
thus reinforcing the shift from personal trust to more impersonal arrangements implicit in the new remittance processes. And embodied in that shift
in personnel was a readjustment to the patterns of agency dilemma that had
characterized and hindered British slaving activities before 1750 but that,
once addressed, would allow Liverpool to prosper as a slave port.

In looking to explain how the change in remittance processes occurred and
their impact on long-run growth of British slaving, it is worth noting that
some established slave factors in British America were unsympathetic to
them. These included Henry Laurens of the firm of Austen and Laurens of

Charles Town, South Carolina, in the 1750s and 1760s. Pressed to agree to return the whole proceeds of slave sales in the bottom, Laurens remarked in 1755 that it was "a thing we could by no means agree to."[50] Laurens never relented from that position, retiring from the business before doing it, but others in South Carolina did so before 1776. They were perhaps tempted, as Laurens later wryly observed in 1764, by the possibility of retaining cash or earning interest from planters on debts arising from slave sales while simultaneously remitting postdated bills drawn on their London or other British correspondents in order to settle their accounts with slave merchants. For Laurens, the prospect of gaining earnings from slave sales over and above their standard fees was a powerful inducement for some to adopt the new remittance system.[51] He might also have added that insofar as increased credit availability boosted slave prices, as was happening in South Carolina in 1763–75, it elevated the fees as well. In short, colonial factors profited from having a strong banker-correspondent in Britain as guarantor for the slave bills they issued.

In the same correspondence in 1764 Laurens posed a related and in some ways even more critical issue, namely, why those backers in underwriting factors' bills were willing to "give Credit to their draughts by accepting them without effects in hand." His assumption was that, like the gains to factors themselves, the new arrangements yielded "some compensation" to "their friends" as guarantors. Most resided in London. And most were engaged in the West India produce trades that ultimately shaped the geography of British slaving and was the context in which the first moves towards the new bill remittance system occurred. By the time that system began to emerge in the late 1740s, Londoners had largely abandoned the outfitting of their own voyages to Africa. Some of those who continued to do so, like the London-born William Davenport, relocated to Liverpool. One can only speculate with Laurens about what induced other Londoners to enter the slave bill underwriting business around 1750 and to remain in it thereafter through 1807. The move exposed them potentially to more planter debt than they already held. But it allowed them also to consolidate through support for slave trading by others their own commercial and financial hold over the West Indian plantation sector and its related trades at a time of burgeoning national demand for sugar as well as territorial expansion in that sector in 1748–1775.[52] Indicative of inextricable linkages among credit, sugar, slavery, and the slave trade, the underwriting of factors' slave bills facilitated the continuation of London merchant houses' enrichment from West Indian commerce and finance without direct personal investment in what were widely considered risk-laden slaving voyages. Others, including former Glasgow tobacco lords, who were threatened with loss of their commercial interests in Virginia during the American Revolution, recognized the possibility of turning a profit from the West Indian commercial empire by sponsoring new firms of factors and underwriting their slave bills from the 1780s.[53] As they did so, some relocated to London. In the process they reinforced the capital's open and critical role in helping to sustain financially growth of British slave trafficking as an essential complement to their own commercial and business fortunes.

From the perspective of Liverpool slave merchants, who evidently supported and, with others, promoted the new remittance regime after 1748, what particular benefits did they derive from what in 1755 were called "full Remittance in the bottom" or "the whole in the Bottom in Bills"?[54] Two perhaps merit attention. The most obvious is that the burden and risk of providing credit to planters in slave purchases fell from their shoulders to the broader ones, financially speaking, of leading sugar houses and bankers in commercial houses identified principally with the imperial capital. Some indication of their size is provided by reports that in consequence of sales of some five thousand slaves in three months in early 1793 by the firm of Lindo and Lake of Kingston, Jamaica, "their Friends are now under security for them for an amount of 80,000 pounds."[55] Projecting from that to total arrivals in Liverpool ships in the same year, it is possible that Liverpool benefited from over £450,000 sterling of bill underwriting by others, with that figure rising to even higher levels in some years before the British slave trade was outlawed in 1807.[56] Most of the underwriters were almost certainly in London. Some paid a price of planter inability to repay debts arising from slave purchases. Others assumed ownership of defaulting planters' estates. Whatever the outcome for the guarantors of slave bills, it is improbable that any other slave port in the Atlantic world before 1807 gained such an advantage from third-party endorsement of slave bills as the London bill market offered to Liverpool at the peak of its investment in British slaving.[57] It eased the risk to Liverpool merchants of accumulating unsecured or bad planter debts. And together with institutional frameworks for credit protection that existed at the port's main slave supply sources in Africa, above all at Bonny, it fostered the circulation of Liverpool capital investment in the trade, thus mitigating the risk, in the merchant Robert Bostock's words, of "having nothing coming round."[58]

One other virtue of bills in the bottom where Liverpool's success in slaving was concerned may be discerned in the writings on paper credit, published in 1802, of the economist and abolitionist Henry Thornton. According to Thornton, bills, as written contracts issued by one party to pay a recipient or holder, were a form of money or medium of exchange. Those arising from foreign trade, he proposed, were especially important, providing one of the foundations of British paper credit, with bills on London, above all others, supplying the means, as one contemporary reviewer of his work remarked, "by which all the great payments of our foreign and domestic commerce are effected."[59] Unlike some later historians, Thornton did not attribute especial importance to slave bills in his general analysis of British credit, which, he asserted, set the British merchant "more at liberty in his speculations" while also providing "an indicator of the wealth of the [nation's] commercial world."[60] But since so many slave bills were drawn on London in 1750–1807 and, once endorsed for payment, became, in what the same reviewer of Thornton's work inelegantly labeled "transmissible documents," they seemingly proved exceptionally valuable to their primary recipients in Liverpool, enabling them to settle accounts with suppliers of African trade goods, particularly in Birmingham, Manchester, and London itself.[61]

According to one contemporary observer in 1789, bills on London were prized above those drawn on provincial ports, largely because of the relative ease with which they could be discounted.[62] That belief was underlined in 1774 by a London correspondent with a slave shipmaster, whereby the master was informed that when selling slaves at Jamaica, bills supplied by island factors associated with the firm of Hibberts and Co.

"would be Guaranteed" and would thus be "as good as the Bank and will tell well here" in London.[63] That remark, in turn, also helps to explain the advice a quarter of a century later of a Liverpool merchant that in dispatching voyages to Africa for slaves it was "always Custom[ar]y with us in that Trade" to get guarantees for bills in the West Indies drawn on London.[64] Other Liverpool slave merchants then and later clearly agreed, regarding bill settlements in and on London as a financial staple of their business.[65] Reinforcing that view, moreover, is evidence that suppliers of African trade goods in Birmingham and Manchester resisted acceptance of bills drawn on places other than London when settling accounts with those they supplied. In 1792, for example, Robinson and Heywood of Manchester advised the Bristol slave merchant James Rogers, when he looked to settle an account using a locally drawn bill, "that Bills on Bristol are not negotiable with us, & besides this inconvenience[,] they are attended with an expence of over ½ p Cent for redrawing upon London[,] Postages etc—which is a certain Loss to us, & w[hi]ch. We trust you will save us in future."[66] Looking beyond that specific response of Robinson and Heywood, who also supplied Liverpool merchants with textiles for Africa, we can discern an emergent integrated bill-based credit network and multilateral payments system among Liverpool's slave merchants, industrial capitalists, and London merchant financiers as components of a burgeoning national wealth tied to slavery.

Looking further still it is possible to identify evidence of financial practices that were probably peculiar to Liverpool and that allowed bills issued by slave factors to be used for more than settling accounts with suppliers of African trade goods. Once endorsed, they were used to expand the very credit base on which the financing of the port's slave trade rested. The key to that suggestion lay in Liverpool merchants' employment of slave bills as security for advances of goods and services on credit in the outfitting of new slaving voyages. In that regard the merchants of Liverpool may well have been more favorably placed financially than others in Britain. The point was clarified in 1790 by the Liverpool merchant Joseph Caton when, in correspondence with the slave merchant James Rogers of Bristol, he observed that banks in Liverpool operated "in a difirant [sic] way" to those in Rogers's city. More specifically, Caton noted that in Liverpool banks permitted merchants "to put in a bill that they [the bankers] know," against which "they will advance you for the amount[,] Charging you 5 p Ct till Due and al[l]owing you 5 p Ct after Due with ¼ p Ct Commissions."[67] Almost anticipating Caton's advice, another Liverpool correspondent advised Rogers a few months earlier that without the "arrival" or receipt of bills, that "being the custom of this place," a local iron dealer would "not give possession" of the goods ordered.[68]

Slave bills drawn on and endorsed in London almost certainly met Liverpool banks' demands. Moreover, the 5 percent charge for advances that banks reportedly chose to levy on bills until their date of maturity was about half the annual rate of "mercantile profit" investors in slave voyages anticipated earning from them when Caton made his observations. It made sense therefore, as the economist side of abolitionist Henry Thornton would probably reluctantly have acknowledged, for Liverpool merchants with endorsed or "guaranteed" bills in hand to employ them as collateral to fund new slaving voyages.[69] Furthermore, knowing that slave ships were most likely to return home with bills to be endorsed in London may have assisted the port's merchants with multiple simultaneous investments in slave voyages to calibrate more efficiently their schedules. Even as the locus of eighteenth-century British slaving operations shifted northwestward from the capital, London would thus continue to play a pivotal role financially in the nation's success as a slave-trading emporium.

The bill in the bottom system that evolved after 1750 was seemingly unique to the British slave trade. It found no obvious equivalents in the French trade or the Portuguese trade out of Brazil, the other two major sectors of the eighteenth-century transatlantic slave traffic. Its ramifications for growth of the British slave trade in general and Liverpool's in particular were multifold. In tandem with developments in credit protection regimes in Africa, notably Bonny, and in shipmasters' changing remuneration packages, it eased agency dilemmas facing British slave merchants. But the bills in the bottom did more than mitigate exposure of such merchants to planter debts or allow them to repay their debts at home. In Liverpool's case especially, they refreshed the cycles of credit and investment on which

growth of the nation's slave trade depended. Its development did not eliminate bankruptcies among slave merchants or, as in 1793, their exposure to
the dangers of more general financial crises. But as an important element
within a series of institutional reforms surrounding eighteenth-century
British slaving that eased issues of agency dilemma, it contributed to the
expansion of that "Great Wheel of Unfathomable Commerce" that mysti-
fied some contemporaries and of which Britain's and more particularly Liverpool's successes in slave trading were such a conspicuous part.[70]

Seen from a slave's rather than a slave merchant's perspective it was, of
course, a deadly wheel, described by the poet Thomas Cowper as a "diabolical" business as the abolitionist challenge to Britain's continuance in it
began to mount in the 1780s. By 1786, some Liverpool merchants were evidently aware that some of their commercial correspondents were unprepared
to "advocate for the African Trade," even while such merchants reminded
them that it was "the principal business of this port."[71] Unconsciously or
otherwise, such correspondence reflected an emerging tension between the
alleged economic importance of the trade and its perceived and, in some
quarters, openly stated inhumanity. What the merchants of Liverpool and
elsewhere, however, probably failed to appreciate was the extent to which
public antipathy in 1786 toward the "deadly wheel" on which the city's, and
in some minds even the nation's, prosperity rested would so quickly erupt
into a social movement capable of encouraging Parliament first to debate its
future and then finally to outlaw it in 1807.[72] Ultimately, the human costs of
the trade, described by the editor in 1789 of a long-standing work on commerce "as disgraceful to an enlightened age," would be among the primary
factors in provoking and sustaining that movement.[73]

Few seem to have understood better than the Liverpool merchant Joseph
Caton the importance of credit to the city's performance as a slave port.
Frustrated and angry in 1790 that Manchester suppliers of cotton textiles
were demanding "ready money" or cash for their wares, Caton protested
that "if a man was to pay ready money for all his Cargoes he must Either
have 3 Capitals or Lett his Ships Lay up Two years out of three[,] for a ship
was one year out and the Remittance Two years."[74] Caton was quite right:

without commercial credit from Manchester and other suppliers of trade goods, Liverpool merchants could not have invested as much in slaving voyages as they evidently did, whether in 1790 or during the thirty or more years Caton himself spent in the business. His career largely overlapped Liverpool's rising ascendancy in the Atlantic slave trade. Implicit in his 1790 comment, however, was a recognition that other domestic factors contributed to Liverpool's expansion of its slaving capacity. They included the growth of the Manchester textile industry and, aided by changes in remittances for slaves, the financial triangulation of Liverpool, London, and Manchester as part of the precocious growth of the nation's paper credit. To the factors to which Caton directly or indirectly alluded, I have added others, such as the enterprise and foresight of Liverpool merchants in investing in their port's commercial infrastructure. Whatever the merits of any of these specific explanations were, however, it is impossible, as the thrust of Caton's own remarks in 1790 implied, to account for the sustained growth of British slaving and Liverpool's role in it without reference to wider changes in the British economy of which it was a part.

That said, it is likely that if Caton were to have reflected on his own long involvement in slave trafficking, he would have recognized that the scale of the city's investment had been dependent also on circumstances and events remote from Britain's shores. As an investor in some thirty-five voyages to Africa through 1790 and some fifty in total during his business career, Caton would have surely perceived the desirability of finding creative solutions to issues of agency dilemma in the slave trade. Indeed, as master of at least ten voyages from 1764 onward he would have benefited from the performance-related pay that such solutions afforded and that doubtless contributed financially to his own elevation from shipmaster to merchant investor.[75] As shipmaster, he traded almost completely to the Bight of Biafra, an experience that probably gave him insights into the region's productiveness as a source of slaves and of its value to Liverpool merchants, even if, like his contemporaries, he did not fully understand the internal causes of it. Equally, as a voyage investor he seemingly saw the value of exploiting slave supplies at Sierra Leone and Windward Coast that were largely neglected before Liverpool sought to tap them. Similarly, his keenness to deliver slaves to Dominica and Grenada, newly acquired by Britain from France in 1763, could well have prompted him to ponder the intimacy of British imperial expansion to growth in demand for slaves, while simultaneously underscoring planters' hunger for credit in populating new lands with slaves and thus the benefits to Liverpool merchants of the new remittance procedures then coming into vogue in the British Caribbean. Perhaps most importantly of all, his homeward voyages to Liverpool with remittances for slaves in sugar or, more likely, in bills drawn on London sugar houses may well have impressed on him the intimate connection between slavery and his fellow citizens' craving for sugar as the driver of long-term demand for enslaved Africans in British America and of the role of merchants in cities like Liverpool to meet that demand. As we try to explain why the British slave trade became so large, reaching unprecedented and internationally remarkable levels under Liverpool's leadership in 1783–1807, it is appropriate to locate its growth within the complex, expanding, and yet increasingly interconnected and integrated British Atlantic world of which it was a part. But it is also necessary to recognize that the ambitions, behaviors, beliefs, and social capital of merchants such as Joseph Caton shaped its long-run growth trajectory and, in doing so, tragically reshaped, too, the lives of millions of unknown Africans.

PART TWO

Opinions

FOUR

"Vulgar Error"

Questioning Transatlantic Slavery in the Age of Locke

IN JUNE 1783, Adam Jema enrolled as a seaman on the Liverpool slave ship *Essex,* commander Peter Potter. Taking in slaves in Upper Guinea, the *Essex* proceeded to St. Vincent, where 291 enslaved Africans were disembarked in early July 1784. Jema reached the island, but on 12 July he was discharged from the ship's muster roll.[1] Such discharges of crew of slave ships in the West Indies were not unusual. They allowed merchant investors in voyages to reduce ships' running costs once the need to manage slaves on board ship ended while retaining a smaller crew to sail the vessel home. Jema's discharge might be considered then as a typical cost saving adopted by British slave merchants. What made it unusual was that Adam Jema was an enslaved African. His employment as a slave was not unique among the many thousand British slaving voyages, but cases such as his were probably less common in the British trade than in, say, the Portuguese Brazilian one.[2]

Adam Jema's discharge nonetheless exposed the harsh transactional and racial realities of British slaving, particularly because his owner was Peter Potter, the ship's master. In his voyage wage book, Potter described Jema as a "Black boy"; noted that wages owing him, amounting to £7.19s.4d, were "brought to the Cr[edit] of the Captain's Wages account"; and recorded that Jema, "being a blackman his own property," was "sold at St. Vincent." Whether Jema counted as one of the 291 Africans sold from the *Essex* in July 1784 is unknown. I suspect he was not. But having been one of those responsible for their delivery to St. Vincent, he was, presumably unknowingly, destined when leaving Liverpool seemingly to spend his remaining days among them.

Adam Jema's experience was just one of the many millions of tragic personal histories associated with the Atlantic slave trade, described by David Brion Davis as "one of history's greatest crimes against humanity."[3] It underscores, too, David Eltis's remark that "ordinary people could and did trade in slaves, as well as the fact that ordinary people became slaves," and that acknowledging both represents a "beginning of comprehending the enormity of the forced migration" that constituted transatlantic slavery.[4] Underlying the enormity of that gruesome business was the racially defined notion of property rights in people that Potter displayed in 1784. As a mentality that saw and treated enslaved Africans as merchandise, it was commonplace, though not universally accepted, within British commercial circles before and during Peter Potter's lifetime. The trade's banality within such circles was manifest in many ways. It surfaces in a standard British accounting text that first appeared in 1736 and underwent numerous editions through 1769 and beyond, in which regularly updated accounts of "negro slave" sales were used to illustrate bookkeeping principles in a "factory" in the West Indian "sugar islands."[5] It appears in marine insurance policies, in which enslaved Africans in transit were considered akin to livestock, a view endorsed in an infamous lawsuit brought in 1783 on appeal before the Court of King's Bench, whereby the jettisoning of slaves alive at sea from a ship in 1781 was said to have been "the same as if Horses had been thrown overboard."[6] It resurfaces in a ship officer's correspondence with his wife in December 1786 in which he describes "our very disagreeable Cargo" from New Calabar as "Black Cattle" and observes how he had "almost Melted in the Midst of the five or six Hundred of them."[7] And it appears in published contemporary histories of slave ports such as Liverpool, in which, to underscore Potter's sale of Adam Jema, "the gains of an African voyage" were said to be always subject to "probable calculation."[8] Potter's sale of Jema, in sum, reflected a mind-set that, in viewing enslaved Africans as commodities to be considered like any other in purely transactional terms, guided British slaving to new heights in the quarter century after Adam Jema was so heartlessly discharged and sold in 1784.[9]

Yet even before Adam Jema embarked on his fateful voyage, actions challenging British involvement in enslaving Africans were being mounted, some of them achieving success. In 1772 an enslaved African, James Somerset, won a landmark decision in the Court of King's Bench, preventing his owner from deporting him to the West Indies from England against his will.[10] The case was widely reported in England and its American colonies.[11] The chief justice in the case, William Murray, Lord Mansfield, based his decision purely on legal argument, offering what has been seen as a "narrow holding" concerning a "conflict of laws." In it Mansfield confirmed that once in England, enslaved Africans had rights under English law, which he extended to prevent forcible deportation. But in reaching his decision, Mansfield described slavery as so "odious" that it could not be introduced by reference to "mere reasoning or inferences from any principle, natural or political," but could be established only by "positive law." Seen as an unnecessary remark where Somerset's particular case was concerned, his statement represented a legal novelty, its intention being, according to one recent study, to shift consideration of the slavery issue from the courts to Parliament, which might be better placed to resolve its "inconveniences."[12]

Inspired by reports of the *Somerset* case, an attempt that began in Scotland in 1774 by the enslaved African Joseph Knight to recover his freedom culminated four years later in a decision of Henry Home, Lord Kames, in the Court of Session in Edinburgh in which slavery was deemed to have no legal status in Scottish law, thereby removing the conflict of national and colonial laws governing slavery with which Mansfield had grappled and ensuring Knight's liberation. Prompting one Edinburgh newspaper immediately and enthusiastically to declare that "the rights of humanity" had been "weighed in the scales of justice," the Kames decision was also pronounced by one eminent Scottish professor of law in 1781 as "an authentic testimony of the liberal sentiments entertained in the latter part of the eighteenth century."[13] It was a decision, too, with which Mansfield probably privately sympathized, encouraging some to posit that when he had passed down his judgment in 1772 he did more than extend domestically English ideas of freedom and rights to enslaved Africans: he knew, too, that his decision would have adverse legal, political, and economic consequences for colonial slavery.[14]

These landmark legal cases referred primarily to the status and rights of Africans brought to Britain as slaves, but in the interval between the lawsuits the slave trade itself was formally challenged politically. The challenger was David Hartley, MP for Kingston upon Hull, who moved a resolution in 1776 in the House of Commons condemning the slave trade as "against the laws of God, and the rights of man."[15] Sir George Savile, MP for Yorkshire, who, with Hartley, was noted for his benevolence, seconded it, but it was easily defeated as Britain descended into what one contemporary called civil war with its American colonies.[16] The phrasing of Hartley's resolution, nonetheless, was important, blending religious doctrine with a growing secularization of liberal ideas that marked the age. Together they would subsequently underwrite British abolitionism.[17] In retrospect and even to some contemporaries, as noted elsewhere, Hartley's move in 1776 was doubtless premature, even naive, but in combination with the landmark legal judgments in England and Scotland that largely reversed earlier ones favoring slave owners, the temerity Hartley displayed in openly questioning the slave trade was yet another sign that a wind of change in public attitudes toward slavery had begun to blow in Britain as political differences with its North American colonies deepened in 1763–76.

Further important challenges to the moral legitimacy of British slaving immediately arose at the conclusion of the war that broke out in 1776. Two in particular merit attention. They bookended the fateful journey of Adam Jema on the slave ship *Essex* in 1783–84.[18] The first in June 1783, the month Jema left Liverpool, was a petition to the House of Commons by some 273 Quakers, calling for the "humane interposition of the Legislature" on grounds of Christian faith and "principles of humanity and justice" to end the exporting of "Negroes" from Africa by "all persons whatsoever."[19] The petitioners considered the "many thousands" of victims of British slaving to be "our fellow-creatures, entitled to natural rights of mankind," but under "the laws of this country" they were held as "personal property, in cruel bondage." The second appeared, also in London, coincidentally just days after Jema's discharge and sale in St. Vincent. This was a pamphlet written by James Ramsay, an Anglican clergyman and sometime resident of St. Kitts. In it, he, too, demanded Britain's withdrawal from the slave trade.[20]

Motivated by comments accusing him of failing sufficiently to condemn the "horrid trade" in Africans in an earlier published work hostile to British West Indian slavery, Ramsay insisted that "the distinction between master and slave never was meant by the God of nature to be an object of society."[21] He went on to explore the human costs of slave trafficking before presenting a series of intriguing counterfactuals intended to allay potential concerns about the "shock" that ending the slave trade might inflict on Britain's economic well-being and national security. In doing so, Ramsay, more perhaps than the Quakers, exhibited an acute political awareness of how calculation of economic and political interest would become intertwined with ethics in shaping the landscape of future debates about British slave trade abolition. In particular, he observed "the utmost importance to the state" of the sugar trade "with which that for slaves is connected at present."[22] With such remarks, he not only identified a political conundrum for abolitionists but also gave public voice to what some West Indian planters, nervous about emerging challenges to British slaving on ethical grounds, were already thinking in private.[23] Among Britain's West Indian planters concern over the slave trade's future was palpable after 1783.[24]

The interventions of James Ramsay and the Quaker petitioners of 1783, like Hartley's motion in 1776, were symptomatic of shifts in British ideas about the ethical, legal, and economic arguments that had been deployed to justify British participation in enslaving Africans from at least the mid-seventeenth century. Their moves, like Hartley's, gave political meaning to the growing hole in such justifications that religious leaders and intellectuals had been systematically creating over several previous generations.[25] My primary task in this chapter is to uncover the roots of that questioning of views supporting the enslavement of Africans. As they themselves acknowledged, Hartley, Ramsay, and later Thomas Clarkson were, among others, heirs to a prolonged and widening theoretical and evidence-based intellectual critique of slavery and slave trading that emerged in Britain at least from the late seventeenth century, paralleling the very growth of trafficking itself.

An intellectual critique of slavery, inspired in part by religious beliefs, was not unique to Britain from the late seventeenth century onward, but

in terms of intellectual rigor, sustained energy, and ultimately scale what
happened there hugely exceeded in importance what some late eighteenth-
century British writers identified as having occurred briefly in Spain over
250 years earlier.[26] In Britain's case, the emergent antislavery intellectual
discourse united theology with philosophy and social science; combined
emotion and sensibility with reason; and through its inescapable engagement with related issues of personal freedom, of rights, of sociability, and
of a shared humanity, gathered exceptional and enduring political traction
during and after the last third of the eighteenth century. It became a vital
constituent part of what psychologist Steven Pinker has labeled the humanitarian revolution that accompanied other fundamental change in British
society at that time.[27] For some historians it would increasingly shape the
nation's international identity.[28]

Whatever its resonances in Britain, reflecting on the meaning of
slavery and its application to Africans was not just an Anglocentric oc-
cupation from the late seventeenth century. It was integral to transatlantic and European enlightenment thinking that developed during the
following century. The British Quaker petitioners of 1783 were far from
being the first within that denomination in the Atlantic world openly to
question the morality of slavery. In many respects, they took their lead
from North American brethren. Similarly, although English and Scottish
philosophers were among the earliest critics in northern Europe of slavery, including the enslavement of Africans, French philosophes were also
criticizing the institution by the mid-eighteenth century, deploying religious, rationalistic, or satirical arguments to make their case and seemingly inspiring a rise of academic prizes in France on the subject of slavery
over the century.[29] As with Britain, much of that discourse pivoted
around the universality of rights. Domestically important, the French
Enlightenment's precise influence on British antislavery thinking is more
open to debate. But abolitionists such as Ramsay and Clarkson did acknowledge French as well as British, especially Scottish, philosophers,
while some Scottish as well as such English jurists as William Blackstone
in the second half of the eighteenth century were evidently well versed,
as one might anticipate, in French writings such as Montesquieu's *De*

L'Esprit des lois. This treatise rapidly gained international attention after its anonymously authored publication in 1748.[30] Conversely, however, English novels such as Samuel Richardson's *Pamela* and *Clarissa,* published in the 1740s, influenced subsequent discourses over human rights in France, while later in the century British philosophical discourses helped to reshape German thinking on the ethics of slavery.[31] It is evident, therefore, that British intellectual discourses on slavery were, at least from the mid-eighteenth century, part of an increasingly concerted, assertive, and cosmopolitan tapestry of thought. In that respect, the humanitarian revolution was transnational, not just Anglocentric.

British antislavery ideas were unquestionably enriched and reinforced from the 1740s by developments in France. But challenges to ideas supporting the enslavement of Africans that the philosopher William Paley described in 1785, in an unveiled attack on Aristotle's justification of slavery, as founded on a morality "built upon instincts" that allowed one to find "reasons and excuses for opinions and practices already established," evidently arose in England a century or more before Paley wrote those words.[32] They were not, moreover, utterances of isolated moralists. Rather, they were interwoven into seventeenth-century defenses of English liberties, which also infiltrated contemporary thinking about the nature of the nation's emergent empire long before, as some have claimed, they surfaced as a British "crisis of liberty" following defeat in the War of American Independence.[33]

Antislavery impulses in Britain relating to Africans had a protracted, century-long gestation period. They began to assume academic credibility from the early eighteenth century and gathered in time a widening domestic audience before gaining a renewed and even more urgent political resonance and symbolism in the decade preceding the war with the American colonies. French writings gave encouragement and reassurance to architects of the philosophical foundations of such impulses after 1748, but in Britain the intellectual driving force behind them was always primarily homegrown. It was to be found in a rich, and ultimately globally significant, mix of philosophical discourses surrounding rights, sociability, and national identity and values, on the one hand, and a growth of British transatlantic religious nonconformity and evangelicalism, on the other.

The historian Quentin Skinner has argued that in the seventeenth century the English often defined their sense of personal liberty by reference to slavery, where slavery was understood as a state of dependence on the arbitrary will of others.[34] Identified with Thomas Hobbes, who linked freedom to the absence of hindrances on what one "has a will to do," the juxtaposing of freedom and slavery in the philosopher's *Leviathan* that Skinner noted resurfaced in later English writings. In a series of essays published in the London press on liberty and tyranny in 1720–23, known as Cato's Letters, one of their authors, Thomas Gordon, proposed that liberty is "to live on one's own terms" whereas slavery is "to live at the mere mercy of another" and thus to be in "a continual state of uncertainty and wretchedness, often an apprehension of violence, often the lingering dread of violent death."[35] Such arguments also accord with Samuel Johnson's *English Dictionary*, first published in 1755, where a slave was defined, among other things, as "not a freeman." To that basic definition, Johnson added two others. The first was "mancipated to a master" and the second "a dependant."[36] To slave, he suggested, was to drudge, to moil, or to toil.

In revealing multiple meanings of the noun "slave," Johnson reflected the reality of its practical usage in language in 1755 and in earlier periods in British history. For most English before 1660 the words "slave" and "slavery" were most synonymous with threats to English liberties, whether from Barbary corsairs or from perceived tyrannical behaviors of Charles I and his Catholic allies before and during the civil wars of the 1640s.[37] Such fears did not dissipate with Parliament's victory in the wars. They informed John Locke's *Two Treatises of Civil Government* of 1689, which rationalized the people's right to resist oppressive rule and thus the Glorious Revolution of 1688–89; the subsequent wars with Louis XIV's Catholic France; and the Jacobite uprisings of 1715 and 1745.

English fear of enslavement found a voice, too, in the fiction of the early Hanoverian age. It surfaced when in Jonathan Swift's satirical novel, Lemuel Gulliver, enslaved in Brobdingnag (or the Land of the Giants), was said to consider his enslavement "laborious enough to kill an Animal of ten Times my Strength."[38] The "Continual Drudgery" that Swift attributed to that experience followed that of Daniel Defoe's Robinson Crusoe, whose temporary captivity in North Africa was said in 1719 to be "the most miserable of all conditions of life."[39] The drudgery that Swift described anticipated Johnson's later definition of the verb "to slave" as being "to drudge." In all these contexts, enslavement of freeborn Britons was considered totally unacceptable and, where it occurred, the product of some "Misfortune" or "Unfortunate Accident."[40] To avert it, the English authorities from 1684 onward were prepared to pay, at least where preventing Barbary corsair seizures of crew and passengers on English shipping were concerned.[41] The rights of the freeborn English, later British, to protection from enslavement (or tyranny) that were implicit in that policy persisted throughout the whole era of British transatlantic slavery and beyond.

The refusal of English voyager Richard Jobson to buy enslaved Africans offered to him in the Gambia in 1623, noted in chapter 1, might seem to suggest that, to English eyes, that viewpoint extended at that time to Africans. To assume so would be wrong, for in claiming that the English did not enslave others, Jobson totally overlooked the slaving activities in Guinea the Elizabethan state had endorsed sixty years earlier under the direction of Sir John Hawkins. Reported in Richard Hakluyt's voyages, published in 1589 and 1598–1600, Hawkins's ventures were unsuccessful financially but, seen in the context of mercantilist-inspired national rivalries, demonstrated that the English were willing to enslave others in pursuit of enhancing overseas trade and enriching the nation. In that regard they followed where the Spanish and Portuguese had led. The earlier Elizabethan ventures focused on tapping into the slave-based production of precious metals flowing out of Spanish America. The potential of bullion to enrich European nations continued to fascinate some English mercantilist writers of the early Stuart period.[42] And accessing Spanish bullion would remain an economic objective of English enterprise and diplomacy where the slave trade was concerned for another century and a half. From the 1640s, however, it was not so much Spanish American trade but rather the national wealth-enhancing potential of sugar production in its own West Indian colonies that reanimated English interest in enslaving Africans even as the nation itself fell into bloody civil war against Stuart tyranny. Established by 1660, the sugar-slave nexus would continue, as James Ramsay saw in 1784, to drive that interest into the abolitionist era.

From the 1660s the African trade became firmly embedded in ongoing mercantilist reinterpretations of the concept of the balance of trade and more specifically the contribution of slave-using colonies to the nation's treasury and its international status.[43] Pivotal to that process was the political elevation of mercantile interests consequent upon the civil wars. That in turn strengthened nationally a civic epistemology of commercial knowledge in which self-interested merchants combined with others to shape economic thinking and trade policy.[44] In some cases it included extolling the African trade's material benefit to the nation. The economic virtues of enslaving Africans were highlighted from early in the Restoration period and remained a central feature of British writings on economics and trade long into the eighteenth century. They were to be found in the works of Sir Josiah Child, of Charles Davenant, and, perhaps most famously, of Malachy Postlethwayt. Together, in various tracts published between 1668 and 1746, they severally underscored the importance of the nation's successful pursuit of trafficking Africans to its colonial enterprise, its wealth, and its power.[45] In 1745 Postlethwayt hinted that direct trade with Africa might grow without prejudice to the slave trade before taking by the 1760s a more radical stance, advocating in some publications to "rouse some noble and benevolent Christian spirit to think of changing the whole system of the African trade," based, he contemplated, on "a friendly, humane and civilized commerce" that might replace slaving.[46]

Seemingly oblivious to any moral scruples in the mid-1740s, however, Postlethwayt's early tracts, like those of his mercantilist predecessors, spoke to and endorsed a viewpoint that, as the London slave trader William Snelgrave noted in 1734, justified the enslavement of Africans almost exclusively in terms of economic advantage.[47] For the mercantilists, at least, the core issue was not whether slaving benefited the nation but how to maximize its rewards. Discussion of the last, as historian William Pettigrew has shown, became entangled under the later Stuarts in political controversy, including arguments over royal prerogatives and British liberties in the context of decision-making about imperial expansion.[48] The second of those embraced ideas of free trade, or allowing open entry to those who, to quote one contemporary writer, "by their birth-rights are equally intituled [sic] to all Trade."[49] Ideas of British liberties therefore could not be wholly disentangled even from the nation's pursuit of the enslavement of Africans.

It may seem ironic that a nation that saw itself as singularly committed to protecting personal liberties at home chose so purposefully to legitimize its subjects' right to buy and sell enslaved Africans.[50] The irony, however, was not totally lost on contemporaries. Among them were some slave traders. One was the shipmaster Thomas Phillips, who, when his officers pressed him during a voyage in 1693–94 to mutilate some unruly slaves, sternly refused to do so. He recorded in his voyage journal published years later that he could not "entertain the least thought of it, much less put into practice such barbarity and cruelty to poor creatures who excepting their want of Christianity and true religion (their misfortune more than their fault) are as much the works of God's hands, and no less dear to him as ourselves."[51] More tellingly still was the statement of the former London trader William Snelgrave, who in prefacing his book on Guinea and the slave trade, published in 1734, wrote that "as I love Freedom myself, so I readily leave the Reader to judge and believe as he pleases, concerning what is here related."[52] That comment perhaps betrayed signs of the "managed discomfort" or the "uncomfortable part of educated consciousness" that historians have sometimes identified with British involvement in slaving by the 1720s.[53] Another interpretation, however, may be that, with such remarks, Snelgrave was practicing the "Habit" of "modest Diffidence" in expressing himself that Benjamin Franklin claims to have learned around 1720 from reading Xenophon and Alexander Pope, and which, as he went on to note, permitted him to present himself as a *"reasonable Creature"* enabling one "to find or make a Reason for everything one has a mind to do."[54]

It is unsurprising to discover that, while economics were fundamental to mercantilist approaches to enslaving Africans, Christian participants in or supporters of the slave trade often looked to find moral justification for the practice. Unable to contemplate lifelong and hereditary enslavement of fellow Christians, they drew nonetheless on scripture or other sources of moral authority to legitimate their actions. In the early Restoration period, they needed to look no further than John Milton's *Paradise Lost,* published in 1667, or in other of his works, to find moral reassurance. Though he staunchly defended English liberties against threats of Stuart absolutism, Milton did not extend his belief that slavery was unacceptable for Englishmen to Africans, whom he saw as naturally inferior and tainted by the sin of Ham.[55] In referencing the curse of Ham, Milton reflected conventional though not necessarily universal wisdom at that time.[56] Within a few decades, however, though notions of their savagery or heathenism persisted, reliance on the curse to justify enslaving Africans had diminished, even among some slave traders.[57] And when in 1734 Snelgrave resorted to moral arguments to buttress the economic in order to legitimate enslaving Africans, he did so not by reference to biblical injunction or even ethnicity. He chose instead to argue that the export slave trade improved Africans' general survival prospects compared to their likely experience in their homeland.[58] In invoking that argument, with its Aristotelian notions linking slavery with human progress, Snelgrave was neither the first nor the last to paint the Atlantic slave trade as beneficial for its victims.[59] This argument was in fact a staple among eighteenth-century British traders and even some planters.

Long before the 1730s, however, some had begun to ask searching questions about the legitimacy or lawfulness of British slave trading. And by the 1730s some leading practitioners of the slaving business in London such as Snelgrave knew it. In two separate works published in 1713 and in 1732, Alexander Pope, one of the principal poets of the Augustan period, identified slavery with conquest, not Christian humanity.[60] And in 1735 John Atkins, a naval officer and, like Snelgrave, a voyager to Africa, launched a fierce assault on the "Pretences" that he alleged underlay rationales to justify the enslavement and deportation of Africans.[61] Acknowledging Snelgrave, Atkins highlighted the "Robbery of inland, defenceless Creatures" on which the trade rested; chastised Britons for being "Accessaries [*sic*]" through trade "to all that Cruelty"; and emphasized how, when removed "from their Countries and Families," Africans were subsequently exposed "to the worst of Christian Slavery" in the West Indies, where, animal-like, they "have a Property in nothing, not even their Wives and Children." Dismissing the "Nakedness, Poverty and Ignorance of these Species of Men" as justifying their enslavement, Atkins unhesitatingly condemned the trade as against "natural Justice and Inhumanity." Whether or not Snelgrave knew in 1734 of Atkins's intended broadside, his admission in that year that "Several Objections have often been raised against the Lawfulness of this Trade" suggests that he recognized that attitudes toward the trade's legitimacy were shifting in some quarters.[62] That conclusion is strengthened by the fact that, as one who chose to emphasize the economic motives underlying all trades, including slaving, the former London-based trader conceded that "to traffick in human Creatures, may appear at first sight barbarous, inhuman and unnatural." As Snelgrave saw it, by the 1730s, if not earlier, a moral lens was evidently beginning to be focused on a trade previously viewed by those with influence and power primarily in narrow mercantilist terms.

Like Snelgrave's acknowledgment that some saw trafficking as unnatural, Atkins's denunciation of it embodied a dismissal of cultural or racial ideas to justify enslaving Africans. Put more positively, implicit in his argument, as in Pope's poetic vision, was a sense that instead of depicting Africans as a race apart one should see them as part of the human race and, as such, naturally entitled to share in the liberties, rights, and justice that God in his wisdom had bestowed on all humanity. Though Atkins did not spell it out, his moral code almost certainly was one that could envisage Africans, enslaved or otherwise, being embraced within the Christian community. In common with others in the 1730s, Atkins still did not consider slavery wholly unthinkable.[63] But his writings did reflect new strands of post-Restoration English thinking about the immorality or illegitimacy of aspects of the nation's trafficking of Africans. They were ideas of which Snelgrave was seemingly aware in 1734. It is important then to examine the sources of such concerns. Doing so enables us also to identify the contributions of others in Britain who, even as Snelgrave's book was being published, were building on late Stuart foundations in ways that extended, theoretically enriched, and ultimately made irresistible the intellectual case against the nation's slaving practices during the succeeding two generations.

Milton may have drawn on cultural-historical interpretations of the story of Cain and Abel to morally justify enslaving Africans, yet while he was doing so Christians of different denominations in England had begun to question the curse and the slavery practices it helped to legitimate. The mildest form of questioning pivoted around mistreatment of the enslaved as God's creatures. A more ideologically pregnant one concerned the right of enslaved Africans to Christian baptism, provoking resistance from those who saw enslavement as incompatible with those professing Christianity.[64] A third strand found aspects of slavery and slave trading as practiced by the English toward Africans so objectionable and of such dubious legitimacy as to merit outright rejection or condemnation. Such a range of views existed within and across Christian denominations, reflecting both individual personalities and nuances in scriptural interpretation and religious practices within Protestantism itself. Beneath such variations, however, it is possible to detect some intellectual movement toward a more unified perception of Africans, notwithstanding differences in cultural backgrounds and behaviors, as part of a larger humanity created by God. In that context, the savage treatment of enslaved Africans at the hands of white owners, and even, for some, the processes of their actual enslavement, came to be considered incompatible with Christian theology. Implicit in that viewpoint was a questioning of the so-called curse of Ham that was already dismissed in some scientific writings as "vulgar error."[65]

Among the earliest English Christians to reveal discomfort about slavery and the slave trade were the Quaker George Fox and the reformist preacher and Presbyterian Richard Baxter. Their public utterances encompassed the full spectrum of late seventeenth-century English Christian criticisms of slavery just outlined. In 1657 George Fox urged brethren "in all those plantations" in the West Indies who owned African and Indian slaves "beyond sea" to be merciful toward them, since, citing Acts 17:26, God "hath made all nations of one blood to dwell upon the face of the earth."[66] Subsequent travels to the islands only reinforced Fox's concerns, which by the late 1660s were shared by other nonconformists, including some in New England.[67] A less restrained assault on slavery was to be found in Baxter's writings. A noted controversialist and a believer in the immortality of the soul and in universality of Christ's atonement, Baxter in 1673 described the buying and selling of Africans "as one of the worst kinds of theft in the world" and claimed that those involved in it were "the common enemies of mankind" and to be "as fitter to be called incarnate Devils, as Christians." He had no better opinion of planters, whom he accused of denying slaves access to Christianity, treating them as beasts, actuating their bodies to "worldly drudgery," and making "profit their treasure, and their God."[68]

Baxter was not alone in his contempt of the slave trade and British plantation slavery. Echoes of his feelings, including ideas of slave trading as theft, appeared in the writings of others, including Quakers and Anglicans. In 1688 in Pennsylvania four recently arrived Dutch-German Quakers were as stern as Baxter in denouncing what they called "the traffik in men-body" as well as Christians' collaboration in promoting the enslavement of "negers" and their descendants for life. But their protest, known to historians as the Germantown petition and sometimes considered emblematic of Quaker feelings toward slavery, almost immediately and quietly disappeared into the Pennsylvania Quaker archives for a century and a half.[69] It was left instead to others publicly to sustain Baxter's assault on the institution. Prominent among them were the Anglican clergyman Morgan Godwyn and Thomas Tyron, a merchant, promoter of vegetarianism, and follower of the German mystic Jakob Böhme. Both Godwyn and Tyron had spent time in the slave colonies before separately publishing tracts in London in the period 1681–85 that condemned what they had seen, largely on grounds similar to those adopted by Baxter. In Tyron's case, his arguments were interlaced with, in other works, pleas for the humane treatment of all animal species.[70] Of the two, Tyron's writings almost certainly reached wider audiences, but in the Baxter tradition, Godwyn's offered the more profound and sustained theological case, as one would expect. Admitting to being provoked by Quakers when visiting Barbados, Godwyn went further in some ways than Baxter, openly dismissing the identification of slavery with black skin and underlining Africans' natural humanity by urging their right to share in Christian baptism.[71] In the decade after Baxter's intervention in 1673, Anglican voices thus began to join other, nonconformist ones in robustly challenging their English countrymen to reflect on how they treated enslaved Africans, urging in particular that Christian values be given precedence over what Tyron labeled "a false conceit of *Interest*" and Godwyn the addiction to mammon.[72] If the Germantown petition of 1688 is an indication, some colonial Quakers shared that feeling, too.

It is important to acknowledge that, Tyron apart, none of the other contemporary religious figures who publicly challenged England's enslavement of Africans queried slavery per se. Baxter and Godwyn questioned, for example, the means by which the English acquired slaves and the unchristian way in which they treated them as fellow creatures but did not condemn slavery in principle. Neither did George Fox or even his silenced Germantown fellow Quakers, who in their remarkable petition of 1688 denounced the enslavement of Negroes against "their will and consent" and insisted that, as with whites, there "ought to be likewise liberty of the body, *except of evil-doers.*"[73] Among some of the most radical late seventeenth-century Christians in the English Atlantic world, therefore, it was not automatically assumed that, even though human beings were all naturally born free and equal in the eyes of God, slavery itself was wrong. They saw it, in fact, as justifiable in some circumstances.[74]

That does not mean that Baxter, Godwyn, and others were immaterial to the planting of English seeds of antislavery ideas where Africans were concerned. Bearing in mind that at the time they were writing English slaving was conducted under the aegis of the Royal African Company, Baxter's and Godwyn's association of English slaving with theft and their comparison of traffickers with sellers of "souls to the Devil" had political significance. Their personal celebrity added weight to the theological burden of their interventions, turning them into dangerous, even seemingly seditious, gifts.[75] The timing of their messages was also important, coinciding as it did with a growing debate nationally about the relation between the company's trading monopoly and slavery, on the one hand, and the values and nature of an emergent empire built on a mix of free and coerced labor, on the other. That debate, in turn, constituted an important subplot of an even larger, ongoing domestic political discourse centering on personal liberties, Parliament, and royal prerogative dating from the time of the Civil War and to which the use of prerogative in shaping the development of empire in post-Restoration England gave renewed energy.[76]

Ideas of natural law and social contract, typically associated with the writings of the contemporary lawyer, philosopher, and public official John Locke, are commonly seen to lie at the heart of that discourse's revitalization. Locke's position on slavery, which emerged out of debates over political sovereignty and empire, has proved controversial. It was, however, in many ways congruent with that of Baxter and Godwyn, thereby helping not only to foster a growing accord between their strands of thinking about the legitimacy of slavery but also to ensure that ideas of moral philosophy would inform debates over the state's approach to organizing the English slave trade in the decades following the Glorious Revolution of 1689.[77]

Locke's formal views on slavery arose in the context of what he saw as the right of free people to resist tyrannical rule, which threatened politically to enslave them and to break the contract that existed between a ruler and the ruled.[78] Accordingly his most forthright statement on slavery arose in a riposte to Sir Robert Filmer, who, in works written around 1650 but reprinted posthumously in 1680, defended the principle of Stuart divine right. Rebutting Sir Robert, Locke opened his first treatise on government in 1689 with the declaration that slavery is "so vile and miserable an estate of man, and so directly opposite to the general temper and courage of our nation; that it is hardly to be conceived, that an Englishman, much less a gentleman, should plead for it."[79] The robust tone of that remark was similar to that of Locke's contemporary Algernon Sidney, whose thoughts on slavery were written in 1682–83 but published only posthumously in 1698.[80] Their depictions of slavery's intrinsic misery were later repeated in fictional works of the Augustan age such as Defoe's *Robinson Crusoe*.

Despite Locke's forthright statement of 1689, some have accused him of hypocrisy, citing his help in drafting slavery-accommodating constitutions of the Carolinas in 1669 and 1682 as well as his early shareholdings in the Royal African Company after 1672.[81] Such actions seem difficult to reconcile with his later philosophical tenets advocating universal and inalienable rights and his reported acknowledgment, like Baxter and Godwyn, of Africans' (and Native Americans') humanity.[82] Scholarly interpretations of such findings and their implications for evaluating Locke's historical contribution to thinking about slavery continue unabated, having become embroiled in what has been seen as "the mutually constitutive relationship between liberalism and colonialism" and developments within natural rights theory.[83] But in pondering Locke's relevance here, we should recognize that for him slavery was not unthinkable in principle, notwithstanding his damning indictment of it in practice. In that regard he was, with the exception of the sixteenth-century French philosopher Jean Bodin, not unusual among his ilk.[84] That did not mean, however, that in his philosophical writings Locke sought to justify African slavery and slave trading in the Americas; to the contrary their association with violence and conquest were anathema to him and inconsistent with what he considered legitimate as opposed to illegitimate enslavement.[85] In looking at Locke on slavery, it is always useful to see the lawyer in him as well as the philosopher. Still, in his treatises, he made a telling philosophical intervention at the very moment that Baxter and Godwyn were challenging the nation's slavery practices from a theological standpoint.

Two points about Locke's thinking about slavery need to be noted. The first is that Locke saw slavery, like liberty, rights, and property, not as socially or, pace St. Augustine, divinely ordained but as originating in nature and thus before and outside the social contract between people and ruler. As David Brion Davis observes, in taking that position Locke overturned traditional Stoic and Christian ideas of bondage as being the product of "a sinful society"; it was part, instead, of natural law and, as such, as universally valid as private property.[86] The second is that Locke saw slavery as legitimate only in very specific circumstances. Defining them put him in partial agreement and disagreement with other early modern philosophers such as Bodin and the Dutch thinker Hugo Grotius.[87] Unlike Grotius he thought voluntary slavery inconceivable, believing that "he that cannot take away his own life, cannot give another power over it."[88] Locke admitted biblical stories of Jews selling themselves into slavery but saw their resulting condition as drudgery, not slavery, for "the person sold was not under an absolute, arbitrary, despotic power." For Locke, all slavery was involuntary, implicitly involved such despotic power, and was essentially linked to conflict, violence, or war. Like Jean Bodin, who rejected "war slavery" in any form, Locke regarded slavery based directly on conquest as illegitimate but, unlike the Frenchman, believed it legitimate in a situation where an individual was seen to forfeit his or her life to another through an unsuccessful act considered worthy of punishment by death. Under those circumstances, to Locke, bondage represented commutation of a death sentence, and in his telling it was particularly relevant to "just war," a concept not unlike one deployed by Grotius, whereby those defending themselves against aggressors were entitled to enslave the vanquished. Those defeated, in short, were enslaved through debt to the mercy of their captors.[89] Theirs was, in Locke's words, the "perfect condition of slavery, which is nothing else, but the state of war continued, between a lawful conqueror and a captive."

Scholar Brad Hinshelwood has proposed that in the real-world transatlantic context Locke was perhaps more mindful of Native Americans than of Africans when pondering slavery in policy terms.[90] Yet in defining the circumstances under which slavery might be deemed legitimate, Locke's writings placed him alongside Baxter and other contemporary theologians in opening avenues by which England's enslavement practices toward Africans could be held up to scrutiny. Baxter's and others' allegations that English traffickers were robbers or thieves were reminders that to the English, as Locke intimated, the processes by which people became enslaved mattered equally with the nature of the misery they were forced to endure in bondage. Because English slaving in Locke's day was officially under royal charter, how slaves were obtained in Africa and subsequently offered for sale at the African coast assumed legal, moral, and political significance, reflecting on English integrity, virtue, and use of power.[91]

Locke's writings also exposed, with Baxter and others, similar issues with regard to expansion of slavery in English America, in which ambitions of territorial conquest, accompanied by African slaves, vied politically with concepts of an English maritime trading empire modeled on the Dutch but without the domestic land borders that militarily exposed the republic.[92] Together with continuing squabbling over the management of the nation's slaving system, the rivalry that consumed Tory and Whig factions at home over the nature of the empire and that in 1710–20 pivoted around royal control through the South Sea Company of the potentially lucrative Spanish slave *asiento* ensured that even beyond Locke's death in 1704 transatlantic slavery regularly insinuated itself into the ongoing power struggles over political sovereignty in England that had begun decades earlier.[93] It was, moreover, a contest that played out at the highest level of politics and reverberated through the political classes more widely. Images of political slavery as well as African slavery began to appear in the works of playwrights in England through the 1690s.[94] There is also evidence that issues of empire permeated the nation's poetic language, with Pope's outburst about conquest and slavery in 1713 reflecting what has been seen as rising concern about the violence, inhumanity, and social destructiveness of imperial expansion found in the works of other poets in England from the Restoration onward.[95] And for yet others, it featured in the satirical and other writings of some of the leading novelists of the Augustan age.[96]

As measured by his philosophical writings and post-1689 interventions in public life, Locke's anxiety about the drift of the politics of English colonialism and slavery now seems clear.[97] So, too, was his respect for African humanity as well as his understanding of the very limited conditions under which slavery could legitimately exist. Those conditions placed him closer to Bodin and Grotius and more distant from the early seventeenth-century English philosopher Francis Bacon in his views on slavery. Bacon's endorsement of "war slavery" or conquest, and his conflation of it with chattel slavery, was according to one scholar, "no doubt serviceable to English colonial settlements in the New World."[98] Compared to him, Locke's views offered philosophical comfort and even perhaps a sense of legal reassurance to those among his contemporaries who queried English slavery practices from a Christian perspective. But unlike Bacon, they also put him with the clerics on a potential collision course with greedy, territorially hungry, and racially insensitive English planters, committed to hereditary chattel slavery for Africans as part of a worldview shaped by the age's mercantilist ideology.

On any reckoning of their contribution to growth of English foreign trade after 1660, planters and their slaving allies seemed a vital, unchallengeable economic and political force.[99] Despite that, in tandem with the writings of other contemporaries, Locke's ideas on slavery fed into from 1690 onward a concern among some theologians about the legitimacy of English slaving practices under the aegis of Stuart patronage. That in turn was part of, and helped nurture, an emerging consciousness of African humanity and a questioning of how to reconcile orderly and virtuous expansion of the English Atlantic empire with the nation's own historical and, some believed, exceptional devotion to freedom. Cato's Letters in 1720–23, written in the aftermath of the South Sea Bubble, gave public expression to that conundrum.[100] So, too, a decade later did Pope in his celebrated *Essay on Man;* Snelgrave in prefacing his account of the Guinea trade; and Atkins in his sharp response to it. Without demanding slavery's or the slave trade's abolition, their interventions embodied signals that slaving was considered inhuman, disreputable, and, as practiced, often against natural law. There was, in short, an uncomfortable sense by the 1730s that how the country was treating enslaved Africans was contrary to what Locke had called "the temper of the nation" when rebutting Sir Robert Filmer's support of Stuart absolutism and describing slavery's vileness. Over the following two generations that sense would deepen and widen intellectually.

Contrary to "the Laws of God, and the Rights of Man"

The Intellectual Roots of the British Anti–Slave Trade Movement

IN 1734 the former slave ship captain William Snelgrave published a study of the Guinea trade in which he underscored the economic advantages that Britain derived from shipping enslaved Africans to the Americas. He also recognized, however, that some Britons harbored reservations about such activities, and in seeking to address them he suggested that the trade saved its victims from barbarism and premature death in their homeland.[1] Snelgrave's efforts to ascribe virtue to enslaving Africans repelled some, prompting another voyager to Africa, the naval officer John Atkins, to denounce them as "pretences" that exposed Africans to "the worst of Christian slavery."[2] In his intervention Atkins did not wholly condemn slavery. In that respect he followed others in Britain who had questioned the ethics and practice of British slaving from the 1660s onward. Those concerns, which Atkins evidently shared, and of which Snelgrave was seemingly aware, have been discussed. I now look to see how they began from around 1730 to transmute into an antislavery intellectual discourse and ultimately into an antislavery and anti–slave trade ideology.

That process had begun even before the exchange between Snelgrave and Atkins in 1734–35. It involved a morphing of the issues surrounding Britain's participation in slavery that exercised Atkins and his predecessors into a more profound theological and secular intellectual critique of the slave trade's morality and economic value. An evolving intergenerational process, it was sustained through the outbreak of the War of American

Independence in 1776. It reflected more than antislavery sentiment: it was a shift of major intellectual significance and was foundational to the rise of British abolitionism, ultimately legitimizing ideologically the movement to outlaw British slaving. Its essence was captured in the language of MP David Hartley's resolution in 1776 condemning the British slave trade; it was, he declared, "against the laws of God, and the rights of man."[3] Though Hartley's motion was easily dismissed by Parliament, in its blending of religious doctrine with a growing secularization of liberal ideas, it established the intellectual principles or ideology underlying the effort to end the slave trade that he started and which would revive as soon as the Revolutionary War ended. Historians have, of course, pored over the intellectual roots of that conflict and more recently its impact on British abolitionism. Less well studied is how, in fact, the unfolding conflict in 1763–76 helped to inject into the domestic public and political spheres the intellectual challenges to British slaving that had accumulated during the preceding half century.

The intellectual questioning of the morality of slavery and slave trading that had emerged in Britain by 1776 evolved out of the theological and philosophical tenets that had informed challenges to practices of English slaving under the Stuarts. It included a widening of religious groupings, mostly of nonconformist or evangelical leanings, as well as of philosophical thinkers, the most important being the Scottish Enlightenment school, whose influence on British philosophical ideas grew in the decades following Scotland's union with England and Wales in 1707. That influence signaled a notable shift away from the primarily London-centered querying of English slaving practice that had existed under the later Stuarts. It was reinforced by the increasing range of nonconformist critics of slavery, most of them with followings in provincial Britain as well as mainland North America. The emerging national and transatlantic inputs into British intellectual ideas about slavery mirrored their own spreading economic penetration of eighteenth-century British society. They ensured that by the time of the American Revolution Britain was home to probably the most energetic, open, and disciplinarily diverse intellectual discourse about slavery in the

Western world. Theology and philosophy were far from separate elements of that process, but at the risk of simplifying I begin with critiques advanced by religious practitioners before turning to the arguments of philosophers.

Among eighteenth-century religious objectors to slavery, the Society of Friends has gained particular prominence in the historical literature, not least because of the brethren's disproportionate representation in the first 1787 London slave trade abolition society. Not all British Quakers abstained from slavery even in the 1780s, but by that date the slave trade was anathema to probably the vast majority, as indeed was slavery itself. That in large part was probably owing to a strong statement of a London society in 1761 against participating in slave trading. That occurred almost three-quarters of a century after, as noted in chapter 4, the Germantown four in Pennsylvania had urged in 1688 the ending of the traffic in "Men-body" or "negers" and three years after the Pennsylvania brethren finally chose to implement that plea. The close chronology of the moves in Philadelphia and London to urge Quaker abstention from trafficking in Africans is testimony to what David Brion Davis defines as an eighteenth-century Quaker internationalism. It suggests, too, that the impetus for the London move came from the American side, which was home before 1776 to two of the most notable and influential Quaker campaigners against the slave trade in the Atlantic world: New Jersey–born John Woolman and the French-born Pennsylvanian Anthony (Antoine) Benezet.

Some see Woolman as the greatest eighteenth-century Quaker and "the channel through which the antislavery impulse flowed."[4] His journal, published posthumously in 1774, revealed an early antipathy to buying and selling Africans.[5] Subsequent writings, in which he proclaimed Africans "to be of the same species" as whites, despaired about unjustly depriving them of "the Sweetness of Freedom," and acknowledged the shame attached to the nation that was "the Cause of their being here," are commonly thought to have encouraged Pennsylvanian Quakers' moves to end the slave trade.[6] To Woolman is also attributed a campaigning model that combined public lectures, petitioning, and the sponsorship of publications with the intention of translating righteous conviction into social action.[7] It was one that would eventually transfer to Britain, informing Quaker-initiated British abolitionism from 1783 onward.

John Woolman died while undertaking a proselytizing mission to Britain in 1772.[8] But by that date other American Quakers, notably Anthony Benezet, were heavily engaged in promoting Woolman's anti–slave trade message in the mother country.[9] A teacher of Blacks and young women in his local community from the early 1750s, Benezet began his public crusade against slavery when in 1760 he published a brief tract in which he denounced the "vain pretences" used to justify the slave trade. Drawing on evidence of European traders' and travelers' accounts, he further charged the trade with being "inconsistent with the Gospel of Christ, contrary to natural Justice and the common feelings of Humanity, and productive of infinite Calamities to families and nations."[10] In a series of other works published between 1762 and 1771, Benezet elaborated on and underlined those arguments, looking to reach a wider audience as he condemned as "vulgar prejudice" claims by "their lordly masters" that Africans were "inferior in their capacities," sentiments he had held since he began teaching them years earlier.[11]

In his wish to reach out, Benezet was eminently successful. Though published in Pennsylvania, his writings soon gained a religiously diverse audience in Britain, his readers being evidently attracted by his willingness not just to underline his spiritual message but also to rely on published historical studies to sustain his essentially moral case against enslaving Africans. His use of travel and other accounts relating to Africa proved exemplary and was followed, and in some cases even plagiarized, by others. A regular correspondence with specific individuals in Britain helped him to promote his work and its message. Among his correspondents was the Anglican Granville Sharp, who championed James Somerset when winning his landmark case in Lord Mansfield's court in 1772 and otherwise distributed copies of antislavery literature such as Benezet's as well as corresponding with him on related issues.[12] Others included the Methodist leader John Wesley, who drew heavily on Benezet's writings in his own, and Benezet's fellow American Benjamin Franklin, then resident in Britain, to whom Benezet wrote in April 1772, noting some interest in North America in curtailing the slave trade and urging Franklin to join with others in England to bring the issue of slave trade abolition to Parliament.[13] His timing elicited a remarkable response from Franklin, who, reflecting on

evidence of the demography of British slaving Benezet had sent him, exco-
riated in the *London Chronicle* newspaper "the Hypocrisy of this Country
which encourages such a detestable Commerce by Laws, for promoting the
Guinea Trade, while it piqu'd itself on its Virtue[,] Love of Liberty, and the
Equity of its Courts in setting free a single Negro." He followed that reference to the *Somerset* case by observing to Benezet that "Several Pieces here
have lately printed against the Practice" and hoping that "in time it will be
taken into Consideration and Suppress'd by the Legislature," Benezet's
"Labours" having "already been attended with great Effect."[14]

Another of Franklin's close correspondents was the MP David Hartley, who put a motion to Parliament in 1776 to end the British trade. What
influence, if any, Benezet's plea and Franklin's response had on Hartley's
action remains unclear, but the exchange throws light on Benezet's impact
in British antislavery before 1776. It continued after the American Revolution, with the Anglican Thomas Clarkson citing in 1786 the Pennsylvanian
Quaker's writings as being valuable to his own Cambridge thesis on slavery.[15] As a colonial advocate, like Woolman, of Africans' innate, demon-
strable humanity, the gregarious and intellectually acute Benezet was
instrumental in building bridges across British religious denominations,
and between religious and secular groupings, in support of the antislavery
cause that shaped his own and Woolman's life's work. He was, in short, a
pioneer of an informal and embryonic English-speaking transatlantic anti–
slave trade network before 1776.[16]

It is important to recognize that American Quakers' involvement in
stoking antislavery ideas in Britain occurred during an Atlantic-wide religious revivalism that had its origins in the Great Awakening of the 1740s.
The last is often identified with Jonathan Edwards, Charles and John Wesley, and George Whitfield (or Whitefield). It precipitated new fissures
within the Protestant communion while simultaneously prompting a mul-
tidenominational evangelical upsurge that penetrated both nonconformist
(or dissenting) and Anglican communities. Not all the revivalist leaders
questioned slavery. Edwards, indeed, owned slaves while Whitfield encouraged slavery's adoption in Georgia, where it was legalized in 1751.[17] But
Charles Wesley registered his personal antipathy toward slavery before 1750

and went on to reaffirm it in poetry in 1758.[18] By the early 1770s his older brother, John, had followed suit. Referencing Benezet's work, John Wesley described the slave trade in his journal in 1772 as "the execrable sum of all villainies," which he considered "infinitely exceeded" in its brutality "whatever Christian slaves suffer in Mahometan countries." It was a view he held in terms of slavery's villainous nature until his dying days.[19] Within two years of that diary entry, he also published a damning indictment of slavery itself. His tract was rapidly reprinted several times and soon reached American audiences.[20]

As leader of an emergent Methodist movement sometimes under assault from Anglicans, John Wesley's tract carried a potent message. Echoing earlier sentiments revealed by his brother, Charles, Wesley's antislavery position reflected his belief in Africans' shared humanity under God, measured, among other things, by their natural talents and indigenous societal achievements. It also underscored Charles's early observations on the "horrid cruelties" that Africans suffered under white legal jurisdictions at every stage of their journey from Africa to plantation life and premature death in the Americas. For John as well as for Charles Wesley, however, as doubtless for many of their fellow Methodists, public intervention against slavery was more than a personal choice. It was a duty dictated by both their own interpretation of the gospel and their role as self-appointed practitioners of "God's grace to all humankind." That role required individuals outwardly to live their own lives—and to treat others—in accordance with the gospel story.[21] A hallmark of the Wesleyan movement, it involved dealing empathetically with others seen to be cast as outsiders in ways not dissimilar in principle to how nonconformists themselves at the time felt marginalized in terms of their liberties and rights as members of British society.[22] Inwardly significant for many nonconformists, as well as in time for Anglican evangelicals, Wesley's public espousal of antislavery ideas ensured that, as a leading figure within the rapidly growing Methodist community, questioning of slavery in Britain's religious quarters would quickly extend beyond the readership of Benezet's works in the decade before 1775.

If "inwardness" was the foundation of Benezet's and Wesley's routes to antislavery, their writings had wider intellectual and political significance.

Wesley's tract, for example, has been interpreted as supplying a rhetorical sentimentalism based on the relation between sensibility and sympathy typical of some contemporary novels, bringing "private feelings into the public sphere" and anticipating subsequent abolitionist debating strategies.[23] Equally significantly, however, in the current context is the extent to which Wesley's pamphlet, as well as Benezet's writings from which it borrowed, chose to privilege evidence-based historical, judicial, philosophical, and other writings over religious doctrine in their public questioning of African slavery.[24] Wesley, like Benezet, recognized that the gospel was a necessary but, in the wider public's mind, not a sufficient justification for slave trade abolition. Adopting the posture of "public theologian" and putting "the Bible out of the question," he drew on empirical evidence and on theories of natural law and freedom to arraign slavery and the slave trade.[25] He used evidence from European travelogues and the journal of the trader Thomas Phillips to paint pictures of an idealized Guinea and of the grim demography of transatlantic slavery. It allowed him to charge that it was an "entire mistake" to think it were "a kindness to deliver" Africans to the Americas as slaves. Wesley portrayed the slave trade itself as rooted in fraud and, in an echo of Locke's writings, dependent on provoking illegal wars. He referenced the English jurist William Blackstone to question the Roman Code of Justinian as legitimizing the practice of slavery. He noted the claims of Montesquieu, among others, regarding slavery's degrading effects on the social consciences or "moral values" of traffickers and masters. He cited at length the arguments of the Scottish academic John Millar, published in 1771, on the stunting effect of slavery historically on socioeconomic development. And perhaps most strikingly, as Britain was descending into war with its American colonies, when remarking on slave rebellion, he defended enslaved Africans' prerogative in "asserting their native Liberty, which they have as much right to as the air they breathe."[26] In sum, John Wesley, like Benezet, insisted not only that Africans were entitled to the same liberties as Britons but also, transcending Locke, that slavery itself was contrary to natural justice and law.[27]

By distilling a range of nondoctrinal arguments into their own antislavery tenets, John Wesley and Anthony Benezet widened the appeal of the case they made beyond their own particular religious constituencies. Through their publications, indeed, they may have countered in some ways the despair of the Scottish academic John Millar, whom Wesley cited, about "how little the conduct of man is at bottom directed by any philosophical principles."[28] Their writings, in effect, reflected a growing cross-fertilization of intellectual ideas pertaining to slavery, involving a shifting balance of argument between the religious and the secular, between the emotional and the empirical and scientific, that the Scottish Enlightenment itself embodied and to which Millar was both an heir and a contributor. Within the growing intellectual assault on slavery before 1775, it became increasingly difficult to disentangle religious impulse from philosophical and economic reasoning.[29] But even though the Scottish Enlightenment evolved in a society where the principal centers of learning lived in the shadow of the kirk, the elite, it has been argued, "cherished and encouraged ideas and intellectual activity," ensuring, in turn, that in Scotland at least, "the Enlightenment came to be an integral part of the establishment."[30] Developing a critique of slavery within a growing sense of progress from rudeness to refinement in the human condition, ideas associated with the Scottish Enlightenment, as Wesley showed in 1774 and Clarkson acknowledged in 1808, reinforced the intellectual case against the slave trade that arose in part, possibly even primarily, in the initial stages, from religious convictions.[31]

The roots of the Scottish, or more accurately Scottish Hibernian, revulsion philosophically against slavery lay in the early eighteenth century. It would ultimately embrace natural law, ethics, culture, demography, history, and political economy, drawing by the mid-eighteenth century on English and French philosophical sources. Where Benezet is often depicted as the religious inspiration of antislavery in Britain, that accolade in philosophical terms is commonly given to the Ulster-born Presbyterian and Glasgow University's professor of moral philosophy, the Reverend Francis Hutcheson, whom Benezet acknowledged to have been an influence on his own thinking. Hutcheson, in turn, counted among his students David Hume and Adam Smith, who met while Smith was delivering lectures at Edinburgh in 1748–50 and remained close thereafter until Hume's death in 1776. In 1751 Smith would follow the deceased Hutcheson as chair first in logic, then moral philosophy, at Glasgow, where John Millar, Smith's own student, would become professor of civil law in 1761–1800. Through a succession of students who went on to claim academic distinction, therefore, Hutcheson became father of a strain of intellectual thinking that, embraced and refined by Hume, Smith, and Millar, among others, would take in new directions the philosophical discourse about slavery inherited from Locke. Put another way, developments in eighteenth-century Scottish moral philosophy were heavily university-based, with a strong educational focus and supportive of a moderate Presbyterian (and Whig) outlook on life.[32]

Hutcheson's writings were published over forty years, beginning in 1725. Some, including his most systematic treatise on moral philosophy published in English, only appeared in print a decade or so after his death in 1746 but were probably written during the 1730s and were evidently known to his students. Hutcheson doubtless shared Locke's views on the vile and miserable nature of slavery but, unlike Locke, found little reason to justify the institution. In his posthumously published work of 1755, he challenged the so-called doctrine of Aristotle, whereby some were "naturally slaves," proclaiming that the "natural sense of justice and humanity abhors the thought." He proposed instead that the natural and inalienable rights to life, liberty, and decision-making "belong equally to all" and could not be taken away without individual consent.[33] Elsewhere, when writing of masters and servants and commenting on slavery, he argued, that "no cause whatsoever can degrade a rational creature from the class of men into that of brutes or inanimate things, so as to become wholly the property of another without any rights of his own."[34] That appeared to dismiss Locke's notion of enslavement through just war, with Hutcheson arguing that it could not be "justly pleaded here, that captives would be put to death if they could not be made slaves and sold as such," thereby owing "their lives and all to the purchasers."[35] In these last respects Hutcheson acknowledged in the study in which such arguments were made his own intellectual debt to his predecessor and tutor at Glasgow, Gershom Carmichael. In 1724, he had insisted in print that "men are not among the objects over which God has allowed the human race to enjoy dominion" and that "the consent of nations" (or just wars) could not deprive innocent individuals of their personal liberty.[36] On these and other grounds, Carmichael, not Hutcheson, is sometimes considered the founder of the Scottish Enlightenment.[37]

It is important to acknowledge that Carmichael's and Hutcheson's thoughts on slavery arose in the context of their rethinking of a system of moral philosophy that entailed a movement away from Locke's libertarian individualism and rationality toward one in which social relationships and human emotion played a more prominent role. It is true that Carmichael was among the first in the Scottish school to embrace a natural rights philosophy, but he embedded it within a set of ideas of self-love, human sociability, and "the common good" that distanced him from Locke. Carmichael's student Hutcheson continued that pattern, extending his mentor's beliefs in ways that had major repercussions philosophically and practically in terms of national perceptions of what was ethically right and wrong and of how the pursuit of self-interest could be considered compatible with society's and mankind's general happiness and well-being.

Two tenets of Hutcheson's thinking were fundamental to that process, providing the basis of subsequent eighteenth-century arguments about moral philosophy and, within its remit, the enslavement of Africans.[38] One was the notion of an innate, God-given, moral sense rooted not in reason but in emotion. The other was that in exercising that sense humans were guided less by self-love or self-interest than by benevolence, a search for social approbation in which through their behavior individuals had regard for the public good, making their actions' contribution to the happiness of others the standard of moral behavior. That did not mean, as scholars have noted, that Hutcheson was hostile to self-love; to the contrary it helped to make individuals industrious, thereby adding to accumulation and general welfare. But in emphasizing human sociability, it placed affection, benevolence, and social interdependence, not individual autonomy, at the heart of Hutcheson's moral philosophy while leaving room for the pursuit of individual industry capable of producing outcomes considered socially desirable and beneficial. Seen through the lens of the "impartial spectator," which helps to distinguish right from wrong, Adam Smith later drew on notions of conscience, sympathy, and humanity's social nature to lay the foundations for an imagined harmonious and beneficial moral order.[39]

The social turn of Carmichael and Hutcheson's moral philosophy influenced their followers' approaches to slavery within civic society, widening ultimately the challenge to the institution beyond the boundaries the two proposed. Sympathetic to Hutcheson's vision of a society based on benevolent principles, and despite clouding his intellectual contribution by some racist remarks, David Hume, Hutcheson's student, conjoined an economic assault on slavery to the moral one his teacher presented.[40] In his essay on "the populousness of ancient nations," first published in 1752 and later revised, Hume prefaced his analysis with the belief that "wherever there are most happiness and virtue, and the wisest institutions, there will be the most people."[41] He then went on to attribute the larger populations of contemporary European nations compared to the ancient world to the "cruel and oppressive . . . civil subjection" embodied in slavery systems that featured so widely in ancient civilizations. Seeing slavery as "in general disadvantageous both to the happiness and populousness of mankind," Hume attributed such effects to the greed of slave owners, who, he argued, with remarkable prescience where abolitionism was concerned, preferred to recruit fresh slaves rather than encouraging their reproduction, thereby inhibiting general population growth. For Hume, history's lesson was clear: human happiness (and progress) was better served by the practice of hired labor than by slavery.

Though less of a ringing moral condemnation of slavery than others espoused, Hume's clinical, evidence-based, exposé of the human and social costs of slavery anticipated further assaults on the institution from Adam Smith and John Millar. Both found reasons to condemn slavery, and in Millar's case actively to campaign by 1790 to end Britain's slave trade. But, contrary to Hutcheson, both couched their opposition as much in historical sociological terms as in some divinely inspired innate human psychology. In his *Lectures on Jurisprudence* at Glasgow, some surviving student notes on which were only made publicly available between 1896 and 1978, Smith left his audience in no doubt about "the miserable life the slaves must have led." Identifying the origins of slavery with tyranny and violence, he reminded them of the arbitrary and cruel punishments and the sociodemographic burdens inflicted on enslaved people throughout history.[42]

Millar's academic utterances on slavery largely appeared in the second (1773) edition of his writings on social distinctions and ranks in history, first published in 1771. As with some of Smith's writings, Millar's reflected the influence of Hume's experimental methodology, applied it to human experience, and placed the evolution of liberty, sensibility, and labor relations in comparative long-run perspective. Similar to Smith's, Millar's analysis entailed a four-phase historical model of social relations that embodied progressive change in manners and structures of authority and within which rights and values evolved in response to changing human need. His schema, like Smith's, began with hunter-gatherers and concluded with the contemporary commercial world. Within that schema Millar depicted slavery's inherent brutality not just as inhuman, as evinced in his later campaigning, but as "inconvenient and pernicious" in the context of the opulence, politeness, and humanity of a commercial society such as the Scotland of his day.[43] As the recent editor of his work has argued, in Millar's mind, "slavery and brutality toward inferiors" had "no place in progressive societies because authority has legitimacy when it is used to efficiently satisfy need."[44]

For his part, Smith had come in his work on moral sentiments to a similar, if broader, conclusion, perceiving a direct connection between levels of human civilization and of social empathy or benevolence, with contemporary western Europe at the apex of such a relationship. As he remarked in his 1762–63 lectures, the "greater the freedom of the free, the more intolerable is the slavery of the slave."[45] Such remarks were consistent with Montesquieu's work on law, published in 1748, which both Smith and Millar knew well, with Millar in particular joining the French philosopher in emphasizing slavery's hurtful impact on "the good morals of a people," with slaves, as he saw it, being deprived of "the most powerful incitements to virtue" and masters tempted "to abuse by that absolute power" with which they are invested.[46] The tensions implicit in Millar's and Smith's historically rooted theories relating to social values and slavery contained potentially profound ideological import, allowing later British abolitionists to proclaim the institution's capacity "to vitiate the human mind" and to besmirch the country's sense of self-identity.[47]

For Millar and Smith, however, slavery's presence was more than a test of moral or national character; it was, as Hume had argued, economically costly, too. Of the former two, Millar was the first in print to insinuate slavery's economic implications, observing in 1771–73 that "men will commonly exert more activity when they work for their own benefit, than when they are compelled to labour merely for the benefit of another." For Millar, the "introduction of personal liberty" had "an infallible tendency to render the inhabitants of a country more industrious," thereby "producing greater plenty of provisions" and, echoing Hume, supporting increased "populousness" as well as national security.[48] Smith anticipated Millar's views in his Glasgow lectures in 1762–63 and then a decade later offered a more trenchant critique of slavery economics. In *Wealth of Nations*, published in 1776, he proposed that the "experience of all ages and nations . . . demonstrates that the work done by slaves, though it appears to cost only their maintenance, is in the end the dearest of any." Such inefficiencies, he argued, arose from slavery's disincentives to effort and innovation, among other things.[49]

Not all Scottish political economists at the time that Smith and Millar were writing were hostile to slavery. Nor was Smith the first to extol the virtues of freer trade.[50] But Smith's *Wealth of Nations* incorporated a more brutal assessment than Millar's of slavery's economic inefficiency into a wholesale rejection of mercantilist ideas that since the mid-seventeenth century had considered British America's slave plantation agriculture as vital to enhancing national wealth. Where mercantilists through the 1740s identified slavery and trafficking Africans as promoters of British prosperity, Smith and Millar saw them as hindrances to it, indeed incompatible with a commercial society's continuing advancement. Personal liberty and freer trade were considered fundamental to that process. Elsewhere, signs of a softening of the traditional grip of mercantilist thinking on British policy toward dealings with the outside world appeared in the writings of Malachy Postlethwayt, who twenty years after observing in 1745 British colonial agriculture's dependence on African slaves, was imagining new trade relations with Africa premised on other, more humane forms of commercial exchange. But it was Smith who produced the intellectual coup de grace to a mercantilist ideology that held slavery close to its heart. And he did so to advance further British commercial prosperity. Whether or not enslaving Africans had contributed to raising Britain's commercial standing in the world, Smith's (and Millar's) message was clear: progress and slavery were separable. Previously they had seemed inseparable. That view was one also shared by English philosophers such as William Paley by the 1780s.

The backcloth to the politicization of opposition to the British slave trade that began on the eve of the War of American Independence included a transformation in views within Britain's intellectual elite about the acceptability of slavery compared to a century earlier. It embodied, among other things, an acknowledgment of Africans as part of humanity, untainted by superstition or prejudice as being peculiarly suited to enslavement; of contradictions between defense of British liberties and imposing slavery on others; and, perhaps often overlooked where slavery was concerned, of the historicizing of slavery, with a recognition that social values might shift in tandem with a society's development.[51] Where Locke in the late seventeenth century could still contemplate legitimating slavery—and English clerics remained prepared to accept it—by 1776 slavery and slave trading were increasingly seen philosophically to be wholly inconsistent with British values in an emerging era of civilization and enlightenment. At the same time, the proportion of British clerics willing to endorse it was likely in rapid decline. Eighty years on from Locke's treatises of 1689–90, though some still harbored forms of racism, slavery had become wholly repugnant on moral and economic grounds to probably the vast majority of British intellectuals. That revulsion was one shared by 1776 by increasing numbers of thinkers about slavery in western Europe and British America north of Maryland.

How a tide of intellectual ideas transmutes into a political ideology capable of delivering social change remains a complex and controversial issue. It has not, however, stopped historians from speculating on the subject where the rise of British abolitionism is concerned. In fairness, some of the contemporaries involved in critiquing slavery in Britain remained highly skeptical of the power of their ideas to reshape the nation's policy landscape. Among the more notable was Adam Smith, whose writings have often been at the center of historical discourses on the meaning of abolitionism. In probably his first-known public statement about slavery's future, in 1762–63 Smith posited that the institution might never be totally or generally abolished.[52] Noting the "tyrannic disposition which may almost be said to be natural to mankind," he argued that a "love of domination and tyrannizing" made it "impossible" even in free societies for slaves "ever to recover their liberty." He went on to underline the political difficulties of depriving those invested in slavery "of the most valuable part of their substances" and the security risks of doing so when the enslaved vastly outnumbered the free.[53] Lest it be thought that in later years he changed his mind, it appears that Smith still harbored similar thoughts about the barriers to ending slavery in practice when he published the *Wealth of Nations* in 1776.[54] Others followed Smith in expressing reservations about the capacity of their ideas to reshape society. I have already noted how in the early 1770s Smith's student John Millar bemoaned how little emerging liberal philosophical principles seemed to influence public policy, and he was joined a decade later by the cleric and abolitionist advocate James Ramsay, who in 1784 expressed pessimism about the ability of "speculative men" to propose "any thing, however just and practicable," that "will operate at once on the public." The "utmost that reasoning can be expected to do," he added, "is gradually to correct and inform public opinion, and change insensibly the popular way of thinking."[55]

Smith revealed great prescience in recognizing the economic and political barriers that those seeking to end British engagement in slavery would face, but in the final analysis his personal pessimism about the possible eradication of it was overstated. Historians, moreover, have proved less reticent than he was about discerning the impact of "the useful speculations of philosophy" on the course of abolitionism, though their choice of strands of thinking to emphasize has varied considerably, thereby provoking sustained and seemingly irresolvable debate. The stage was set by the Anglican cleric Clarkson, who in the opening chapters of his history published in 1808, presented a résumé of antislavery writings by British and other authors. Its message was overwhelmingly a humanitarian one, supported in part by reference to Glasgow professors, including Smith. Significantly, Clarkson focused primarily on Smith's writings on moral sentiments, published in 1759, rather than *Wealth of Nations,* which he described simply as showing "in a forcible manner . . . the dearness of African labour, or the impolicy of employing slaves."[56] Clarkson's treatment defined the perceived intellectual roots of abolitionism for well over a century until it was vigorously challenged by Eric Williams, who relied less on Smith's theory of moral sentiment and more on his antimercantilist *Wealth of Nations,* with its stress on enterprise and free markets, to redefine the purpose of abolitionism and, looking beyond its intellectual roots, integrate it into a class-driven theory of social change in the age of British industrialization.[57] Where Clarkson ignored the Industrial Revolution, Williams placed it center stage in seeking to place Smith's views on the economics of free labor and slavery at the heart of his interpretation of the relation between philosophical ideas and British abolitionism. In his telling, economic calculation replaced charity or benevolence in explaining British abolitionism. *Wealth of Nations* mattered more than *Moral Sentiments.*

Smith's analysis in *Wealth of Nations* admitted the possibility of tensions between individual pursuit of ambition and the social good, thereby creating space for what has been called "unsociable sociability."[58] But both he and Millar identified stage theories of history in which moral values adjusted in tandem with levels of commercial development, rendering in their view slavery as incompatible with Scotland's contemporary standing. The binary divide between morality and economics that emerged in the Clarkson and Williams interpretations of the abolitionist impulse was not therefore one that either Smith or Millar would easily have understood. Nor does it meet with the approval of some historians. Notable among the dissenters was David Brion Davis, who argued that antislavery and Smith's political economy reflected the needs and values of an emerging capitalist order. Each was committed to showing that "all classes and segments of society share a natural identity of interest," even in the pursuit of humanitarianism, and in doing so transformed "a sincere humanitarianism" into "an integral part of class ideology, and thus of British culture." For Davis, then, abolitionism transcended collective motivation; it reflected a paradigmatic shift in thought and values, thereby redefining "new conceptions of social reality" as well as policy and political action.[59]

Locating ideas at the heart of abolitionism, Davis, like Clarkson and Williams before him, firmly identified it with Scottish Enlightenment thinkers such as Adam Smith. They provided the intellectual rationale for an assault on an institution and a commercial policy that were together firmly entrenched in the mind of the body politic with promotion of the national interest. Davis found support for his argument not only at a theoretical level, adopting Gramscian ideas of hegemony, but also in noting the sympathy for humanitarian beliefs among some other leading political economists of the day. He also observed the incorporation of antislavery thought in imaginative literature, particularly the work of the poet William Cowper, whose poem *Charity,* published in 1782, he cited at length. Primarily read by society's educated clite, the poem contained lines that united spirituality with humanitarianism, depicting a God-made "social plan, [which] by various ties attaches man to man," and condemning those driving "a loathsome traffic" and who "buy the muscles and bones of man."[60]

By such means, Davis began to articulate transmission mechanisms through which intellectual ideas on slavery started to shape an ideology of abolitionism by the 1780s. Moreover, research since he wrote has further enriched our understanding of the processes involved, revealing, among other things, references to Smith's ideas on both moral sentiments and political economy in the correspondence, speeches, and writings of religiously inspired abolitionist leaders such as William Wilberforce.[61] Regardless of whether one accepts Gramsci's theory of hegemony, the two-way flow of ideas concerning ethics and economics that became part of the political world of abolitionism from the 1780s only reinforces Davis's argument on how the Scottish Enlightenment, among other sources of intellectual ideas, shaped Britain's emergent antislavery ideology. His intuition was right: unscrambling economic, religious, and philosophical ideas about slavery when pondering the rise of British abolitionism makes little sense historically. It was interrelationships among those ideas that made the intellectual assault on slavery so profound and ultimately impossible to resist. The mix of sources of ideas also potentially widened the pool of possible enthusiasts for the cause.

While the works of Clarkson, Williams, and Davis agree that views opposing slavery and the slave trade were commonplace and respectable in British intellectual circles by 1776, they still offer at best only limited explanations of how such views translated into political intervention against the slave trade from 1787 onward. Some like Williams and more recently Christopher Brown have seen the American Revolution as critical to that process. Williams saw the loss of the thirteen colonies as weakening the position of the British West Indies; Brown argued that it precipitated a crisis of empire and of British national identity out of which moves to abolish the slave trade emerged as part of a reevaluation of Britain's international position.[62] But neither properly explains why efforts to outlaw the slave trade were launched in 1787 and even more importantly why such efforts were accompanied by a mass petitioning movement unprecedented in British history and unmatched elsewhere at any time in the rest of the world. To varying degrees the same critique can be made of both Clarkson and Davis, neither of whom fully engaged with the issue of why large swathes of British society were so repulsed by the nation's involvement in the slave trade as to become committed to campaigning against it. A top-down approach that largely focuses on the circulation of intellectual ideas among an educated elite fails to appreciate the breadth and depth of antagonism toward slaving felt by large sections of British society by the 1780s. It also fails to address the issue of how articulation of that opposition through mass petitioning of Parliament and other means created the circumstances in which Parliament by 1788 was forced actively to engage with the question of the slave trade's compatibility with Britain's values and interests from 1788 onward.[63] Intellectual shifts over a century in attitudes toward British involvement in slavery clearly offered a rational justification for abolitionists to challenge the slave trade by 1787. But only public opinion and its mass mobilization allowed them to claim the political legitimacy they needed to build and sustain a parliamentary campaign to try to outlaw it.

"Tumults of Imagination"

Literature and British Anti–Slave Trade Sentiment

IN HIS AWARD-WINNING book *Moral Capital,* the historian Christopher Brown claims that it was "politics, more than public opinion, that placed slave trade abolition on the public agenda." He acknowledges early criticisms of slavery but views them as "distant antecedents," to be seen as "sincere but inconsequential protest," not part of some larger narrative of cultural progress building, "block by block, to a higher stage of moral consciousness" capable of releasing "abolitionist fervor across the cultural landscape."[1] The trigger for that abolitionist outburst, Brown argues, was a crisis of British liberty awakened by the nation's defeat in the conflict with its mainland North American colonies. Heavily dependent on contingency to explain timing, Brown's narrative places, like Eric Williams's *Capitalism and Slavery* before it, fallout from the American Revolution center stage in the story of British abolition. In Brown's case, the nation's political leaders are characterized as wrestling after 1783 to reestablish the nation's moral purpose as an imperial power. He follows Williams in placing political leadership and national interest at the forefront of the politics of early British abolitionism.

We have seen that before 1776 there had emerged within Scottish Enlightenment thinking a moral vision of British society that was consistent with the nation's changing commercial standing and that involved a dismissal of slavery and slave trafficking as consistent with that vision. It drew on and gained support from others, including English and French philosophers, as well as leaders of several religious denominations. The American Revolution arguably accelerated political interest in that vision; it did not give birth to it, however. In searching for that vision's roots it is important to recognize that though it emerged publicly from the formal musings of clerics and philosophers, it was not simply an intellectually constructed signpost to a future society. Rather, it incorporated social values more widely held in Britain based on individuals' own emotions and experiences, on a range of other sources of personal knowledge, or on both. In his "History of Astronomy," published posthumously in 1795, Adam Smith saw as one of the philosopher's tasks the reordering of the "jarring and discordant" elements of British society embodied in its natural "tumults of imagination."[2] Far from being detached, the philosopher took inspiration and motivation from observation and experience of the social world. Philosophers were catalogers as well as imaginers of social change. How that public imagination was articulated with respect to slavery and the slave trade is worthy of examination.

Scholars have recently shown a growing interest in imaginative literatures as a vehicle of cultural change. This approach involves looking at such literatures less in terms of their genre and more in what they do: what, in effect, their social impact was. In this scenario, imaginative literatures such as novels, to the development of which the eighteenth-century English are considered to have been innovators, widened their readers' cognitive experiences. That contributed psychologically through extrapolation and self-reflexivity to the enrichment of individual and even collective senses of shared humanity and empathy toward others.[3] In doing so, novels and other forms of imaginative literature such as poetry might be seen as reinforcing ideas that lay at the heart of the moral philosophy of Francis Hutcheson and his students. Scholars have identified other of such literature's influences. Historian Edward Thompson, for example, saw it as helping to redefine individuals' notions of rank and class, the last, as historical categories, being "defined by men as they live their own history."[4]

A more recent and immediately pertinent example in this context is provided in Lynn Hunt's study of the invention of human rights. In it she explores how novels written by Samuel Richardson and Jean-Jacques Rousseau contributed to a growing awareness of personal rights in mid- to late eighteenth-century France. Hunt focused principally on how the

Richardson and Rousseau novels depicted women's status and their efforts to assert personal autonomy within an unfavorable sociolegal environment. And in a critical passage relevant to my analysis, she insisted that any account of transformative historical change "must in the end account for the alteration of individual minds." That process reshaped the social and cultural context, reflecting not just the ideas of great thinkers and writers but the "shared experiences of many individuals," whether through their interactions, their reading, or their observations.[5] It allowed the diffusion across widening boundaries of secular imaginings of what was considered moral.

Hunt's study extends into the public or social sphere a connection within individual affections between "the power of imagination" and the "violent eager embracings" of an object or objective that Daniel Defoe articulated in 1719 in *Robinson Crusoe*.[6] One scholar has responded to Hunt's argument by urging recognition of rising antislavery sentiment as being more politically potent in inventing the rights agenda than the more feminist-oriented one that she emphasized.[7] Regardless of such criticism, her work reveals the potential insights that might be gained from examining the changing incidence of references to slavery in eighteenth-century British imaginative literature and other media forms and the interrelationship between the information and ideas they contained and their readers' or observers' feelings toward them. They both mirrored and informed such feelings. Scholars have shown that imaginative literature pays "attention to particularity"; it focuses on "personal psychology and social context," on immediate and recognizable human experiences and interactions, rather than abstract theorizing.[8] Others have underlined the eighteenth-century novel's increasing literary realism and emphasis on speaking truth to individual experience.[9] Seen from that vantage point, it is not accidental that imaginative literature and other print media such as newspapers helped to take people out of what Steven Pinker sees as their "parochial stations," widening the marketplace of ideas to which they were exposed. That he sees as an essential ingredient in fostering the humanitarian revolution he claims emerged in the later eighteenth century.[10]

Moves to end the British slave trade were an important, indeed fundamental, aspect of such a revolution, entailing empathy for peoples from substantially different cultures. They occurred against a background of sustained and exceptional growth and enrichment of British print culture that proved critical in inspiring a latent but mounting national public spirit against the trade. Concerns about the slave trade began to be evident during the deepening conflict with the thirteen colonies through 1776, when they became entangled with arguments over colonial liberties and British tyranny. They erupted publicly, dramatically, and with immediate political repercussions in 1787–88. To highlight that effusion of public outrage is not to dismiss or marginalize the role of leadership in the long-run evolution of the politics of British abolitionism. It is, rather, to recognize that changing the political conversation or agenda where slavery was concerned depended on more than intellectual or spiritual guidance and authority. It required also—and critically in 1787–92—the willingness of people, in J. R. R. Tolkien's words, "with good hearts" to "arise from their quiet fields" and begin to "shake the towers and counsels of the Great."[11] The petitioning campaign in those years signaled antislavery's fusion into a social movement. As far as the slave trade was concerned, it ensured that a political Rubicon was crossed in 1787–88. The crossing was signaled by Prime Minister William Pitt and opposition leader Charles James Fox. When faced with an avalanche of petitions, Pitt and Fox agreed publicly in 1788 to launch an investigation into the slave trade on the pretext that the status quo was not an option and that Parliament, not the Privy Council, which was already conducting an investigation, was the proper body to conduct it.[12] As some West Indian planters and slave traders quickly realized, a decisive and permanent shift in the nation's mood toward the trade had occurred.

In reflecting on the launch in 1787 of the anti–slave trade campaign, Thomas Clarkson noted the congruence between public sentiment and political intervention to end the trade. To "coincide with the wishes of the people," he proposed, "appeared to those in authority a desirable thing."[13] Reflective of Pitt's and Fox's actions, Clarkson's remark was insightful. It anticipated by half a century Abraham Lincoln's famous observation during a slavery-related debate in Ottawa in 1859 that leadership was necessary but rarely sufficient to effect change. Public sentiment, he argued, was everything. "With public sentiment," he proposed, "nothing can fail; without it nothing can succeed."[14] Such propositions anticipated one modern political theory relating public opinion to policy change. Known as the Overton window, after political scientist Joseph Overton, the theory has gained notoriety through association with modern-day populist nationalist politics or fictional conspiracy themes.[15] Its basic tenets, however, are pertinent here. They include a belief that an idea's political acceptability depends on whether it falls within the window or range of policy options the public is prepared to accept at any particular point in time. The theory also recognizes that the range of such options can change to reflect shifts in social norms or values, with ideas once considered near impossible to contemplate becoming politically more acceptable as the mood changes. One of the skills of political leaders is to recognize and adjust to changes in mood.

Though usually applied to contemporary politics, such propositions render Overton window theory relevant here. Indeed, the theory draws on ideas articulated in 1828 by the political scientist William Alexander Mackinnon in his reflections on public opinion, the growth of the middle classes, and the facilities of communication in a civilized society.[16] In doing so, it urges us to listen to Clarkson's refusal to see a dichotomy between public opinion and political intervention where slave trade abolition was concerned. Pitt and Fox endorsed action in 1788 because, Clarkson averred, the public wished it. The central question we need to answer is why the public did so.

What Clarkson meant by "the people" when he reflected on the desire of politicians to accommodate its wishes is uncertain. In quantitative terms it was undoubtedly less than the total adult population and probably less even than the male half of it. It was, however, almost certainly greater than the 220,000 people—all of them men—entitled to vote around 1790, and perhaps closer to the 400,000, mostly men, estimated to have signed petitions against the slave trade in 1792 or possibly the 1.7 million who did so in 1787–92.[17] That did not mean that elections were unimportant in offering a sense of the public mood about the slave trade; as the *Belfast Commercial*

Chronicle observed in late 1806, "Friends [of] the oppressed African race will be pleased to learn, that during the course of the Elections in various parts of the kingdom, the popular sentiment has been strongly expressed against the continuance of that traffic in human flesh."[18] Nonetheless, the weight of numbers signing petitions evidently mattered when Pitt and Fox decided to endorse an inquiry into the trade in 1788, and it continued to do so to the leaders of abolitionism through 1792 and beyond. As one abolitionist put it in 1792, "Those who have no vote" were "nevertheless comprehended in our idea of the public mind."[19]

Four years earlier, in 1788, however, Fox had intimated that it was the apparent respectability of those signing petitions as much as the numbers that was vital in swaying his decision to intervene. For Fox, the concept of the people was more than a numerical calculation; it also had qualitative dimensions, with the character of those expressing views carrying in some ways more weight in influencing the conduct of affairs of state than other factors.[20] While numbers were never unimportant, therefore, it was just as likely that the perceived social standing of the owners of the voices protesting the trade—their capacity to behold, to feel, and to judge "for themselves," as another writer observed—that Clarkson had in mind when defining them as "the people."[21] And in doing so, he largely followed tradition. Respectability was critical. So, too, was personal autonomy.[22]

Self-possession or independence was a vital attribute of those seen as providing a barometer of moral values in eighteenth-century Britain. Voluntarily given, signatures on petitions declaring the slave trade to be wrong could be seen to reflect a judgment by what the eighteenth-century British jurist William Blackstone saw as "free agents, endowed with discernment to know good from evil" and who looked benevolently to extend their own sense of "moral autonomy" toward their fellow creatures.[23] Some contemporaries of Blackstone help one to flesh out those qualified to make such judgments. Ironically, one was the West Indian planter and one-time London mayor William Beckford, who included "the manufacturer, the yeoman, the merchant, the country gentleman" within what he called the "middling people of England."[24] Another was the novelist Oliver Goldsmith, who in *The Vicar of Wakefield,* published in 1766, referred specifically to "the people." He saw them as outside "the sphere of the opulent man's influence," as the "middle order," wherein resided "all the arts, wisdom, and virtues of society." They were, he declared, "known to be the true preserver of freedom, and may be called the People."[25] As well as those identified by Beckford, the membership of Goldsmith's definition included tradesmen, artisans, and representatives of the learned and other professions. Self-possessed or "independent," they were arbiters of the nation's moral pulse, those on whom the power of the great in society largely rested. Many of them, depending on where they lived, were qualified to vote, but some were doubtless disenfranchised by a growing mismatch between geographic patterns of population growth and parliamentary representation. It is, nonetheless, quite possible that the philosophers John Millar and Adam Smith had in mind the groups identified by Beckford and Goldsmith when in the early 1770s they contemplated incongruities between slavery and the shifting values of the commercial society in which they lived. And insofar as they constituted a major body of supporters of the petitioning campaign against the slave trade in 1787–92, they were doubtless important, too, in imbuing it with the political respectability and force that Fox and others acknowledged.

Such arguments are consistent with the ideas of Mackinnon, who in 1828 defined public opinion as "that sentiment on any given subject which is entertained by the best informed, most intelligent, and the most moral persons in the community, which is gradually spread and adopted by all persons of any education or proper feeling in a civilized state." Pivotal to Mackinnon's thesis was, in an echo of Millar and Smith, the rise of the middle classes, whose capacities to expand property and wealth through commerce and industry, and whose identification with educational improvement and with facilities of communication, including the press, allowed them increasingly to overshadow the landed aristocracy and gentry in shaping public opinion and state policy.[26] Mackinnon's thesis anticipated not only the reformism of the period in which he was writing but also the weight that historians of different theoretical persuasions have subsequently placed on the influence of the middle classes on British abolitionism. It is difficult to deny that middle-class males were a core constituency of the anti–slave trade campaign, but that should not distract from recognizing that they were not the only party to become involved in the social movement that underpinned it. A review of some evidence relating to those involved in the movement clarifies the picture.

Apparently reliable estimates of numbers of petitioners in 1787–92 do exist, but detailed data allowing us to identify them individually are lacking. There are, however, lists of signatories of two petitions from Manchester dated in May 1806. One was signed by about two hundred merchants and manufacturers of the town, who came together under Sir Robert Peel, then MP for Tamworth in Staffordshire, to oppose a bill restricting British slave deliveries to foreign colonies; the other, which attracted many times as many signatures from the "inhabitants" of the town, supported it.[27] Drawing on local directories, an analysis of the signatories to the two petitions, however, reveals a broad spectrum of occupations supporting them both, with a much larger range of supporters favoring restriction than not.[28] They included cotton spinners, various artisan and professional groups, petite bourgeoisie such as shop owners, and some manufacturers. Though opponents of the bill seemed strongly motivated by self-interest, with some textile producers and merchants in particular fearing disruption to raw cotton imports, the known occupations of signatories do not suggest a simple or clear class division in attitudes toward the slave trade. They reveal, instead, patterns of opposition and support that transcended class but that were especially evident where views sympathetic to the enslaved were concerned. They also expose, however, a clearer gender-based division, with female signatories overwhelmingly favoring restriction of slave supplies, rather than the opposite, suggesting that among those Manchester women willing and able to make a public statement, antislavery views predominated. In that regard, their position was not unlike that of some male groups such as spinners, joiners, some professionals, and churchmen. If Manchester is a guide, by 1806 public opposition to the slave trade comprised a wide spectrum of social and occupational and other categories largely embracing men but including some women as well.

Manchester sent other large petitions to Parliament favoring abolition in 1787 and 1792, a move that found favor with Charles James Fox, who congratulated at that time Thomas Walker, a cotton merchant in the town, himself instrumental in organizing both petitions. Contrary, it seems, to William Wilberforce, whom Fox accused of throwing "cold water upon petitions," Fox thoroughly endorsed them, believing that it was "from them and other demonstrations of the opinion without doors that I look for success," and he was thus "happy that the town of Manchester sees the matter in this light."[29] Sadly, however, the signatories to the two early Manchester petitions, widely seen to have numbered ten to twenty thousand, are unknown, and in their absence we must turn to other sources to identify whether the pattern of support in 1787–92 nationally was similar to that found in the Manchester evidence some fifteen to twenty years later. That earlier evidence suggests that some support then, and possibly later, came from groups who may not have troubled to sign petitions. In other words, the occupational backgrounds of petitioners, where known, do not give a comprehensive picture of the anti–slave trade movement's full range of supporters.

One particular group was aristocrats, which in the 1780s and later included ardent abolitionists. They were unlikely petitioners but reinforced through ancestry, rank, and title the campaign's identification with respectability that Fox and others admired. Their support was evidence of novelist Kazuo Ishiguro's assertion that distinguished households in England built reputations through "furthering the progress of humanity" or "alleviating the great problems of the day."[30] Among the earliest to protest the slave trade was the household of Sir Charles Middleton (later Lord Barham) and his wife, Margaret, whose residence at Teston in Kent gave its name to an abolitionist circle in 1785–87. Its intent, according to the antislavery poet Hannah More in an allusion to Magna Carta, was to make Teston "the Runnymede of the negroes [sic]."[31] There were others, including women, among the elite of the English landed classes to offer public support to that objective.[32] Yet more indications of the support for antislavery among the peers of the realm is to be found in subscribers to the narrative of the former slave Olaudah Equiano (aka Gustavus Vassa) published in 1789. Some 309 named individuals sponsored the first edition of this antislavery tract that rapidly went through multiple editions. They included thirty peers of the realm. That was slightly more than the churchmen, among them bishops, who are more commonly identified as supporters of abolitionism.[33]

Further evidence of those who sympathized in 1787–92 with slave trade abolition arises from a project accompanying the founding of the London-based Society for Effecting the Abolition of the Slave Trade. The project involved relocating mainly destitute Africans then in Britain to Sierra Leone to create "a new model settlement in Africa for former slaves who would govern their own affairs and demonstrate their capacity for economic independence."[34] It represented, in effect, an application of British values to the rebuilding of Africans' lives. Organizers included prominent abolitionists who looked to fund the project through subscription, the minimum sum being £50 per person. That was roughly double per capita annual income in England and Wales at that time, which naturally restricted enrollment to those with sizable income or wealth.[35] By 1792, there were some 1,833 subscribers whose names are known.[36] The personal histories of many of those named remain to be traced, but among the better known were London banker and economist Henry Thornton; engine-builder Matthew Boulton of Soho, Birmingham; porcelain maker Josiah Wedgwood of Etruria, Staffordshire; and textile factory magnate Sir Thomas Arkwright of Bakewell, Derbyshire. Collectively they linked antislavery with what one contemporary called the Age of Experiments.[37] Of the remaining subscribers for whom we have some information, a few were clerics and sizable proportions were urban dwellers. Names and titles show that the vast majority were male, but by 1792 some 10 percent of the project's share capital was owned by women, some of them unmarried. Women subscribed a similar proportion of the funding used in 1789 to assist publication of the first edition of Equiano's narrative, which also attracted financial support from churchgoers.[38] Because of the minimum subscription requirement and higher risk of the Sierra Leone project, the mean wealth of those involved in financing it was doubtless much higher than that of those who funded Equiano's book. There were nevertheless noticeable similarities in the gender, religious, and, possibly, residential composition of the two groups. From what we know of them, all were likely to be considered at least middle class and respectable, though with a generous sprinkling of ancestry and nouveaux riches to add social luster.

Inspection of the provenance of anti–slave trade petitions in 1787–92 supplies yet further evidence of signatories' backgrounds, reinforcing the picture just described. In the most detailed analysis of the petitions, historian John Oldfield has revealed their nationwide provenance.[39] Petitions against the slave trade came from civic bodies and religious and other groups. They came from rural as well as urban communities, though city dwellers substantially outnumbered rural petitioners. Since urban centers had a greater diversity of trades, professions, and service activities, it suggests a pattern consistent with historians' traditional identification of middle-class and artisan groups with the anti–slave trade movement. It is a picture, too, that the occupational breakdown of the 1806 Manchester petitioners endorses. Size and growth rates of towns and cities seem to have made little difference as to whether they submitted petitions, though they did affect the number of signatures attached. Nor did geography, as smaller, seemingly sleepy and genteel civic communities across southern England and elsewhere joined burgeoning industrializing communities in other parts of Britain in petitioning against the slave trade. Such rich variegation in the provenance of petitions to Parliament suggests a movement based more on ideas of nation and culture than simply on class. It raises serious questions for those who see antislavery protest as a cloak for the interests of industrial capitalists. The movement was, rather, more consistent with notions of the people—independent-minded individuals—as Clarkson and his contemporaries such as Mackinnon likely understood.

Women's financial support for the Sierra Leone project and Equiano's narrative reminds us that from the beginning the anti–slave trade movement was not a male preserve. For some affluent women the movement created opportunities for political participation; it even offered the possibility of influencing policy. Such women were part of Clarkson's people. Once opened, however slightly, it was a door they and their followers refused to see closed where slavery was concerned. According to some historians support for the anti–slave trade cause also quickly extended beyond "the middling rank" of people to more working-class groups.[40] The petition from Manchester in late 1787, seen to have been "from the people at large" and signed by an estimated one-fifth of the cotton textile capital's populace, may have been an early sign of such involvement. Within a month of the Manchester petition, the London Society was praising "the spirited

exertions" of towns such as Manchester, Birmingham, and other principal manufacturing centers.[41] One was Sheffield, where a local newspaper
in February 1788 mentioned a petition signed by two thousand of the town's
residents.[42] Within a year of the Manchester petition Parliament had received petitions condemning the trade from no fewer than twenty-four other
boroughs and towns. Two-thirds were from northern England, and especially from towns that had "strong artisan and working class cultures and
were at the forefront of the Industrial Revolution."[43] The pattern continued thereafter, with some seven to eight hundred metalworkers from Hallamshire, near Sheffield, joining the petitioning campaign in 1789, while
Leeds later looked to submit one, its compilers explicitly encouraging "the
roughest sons of lowest labour" to sign up.[44]

Such petitioning activities may often have originated in public meetings, though how many were attended by working-class people who then
signed up is unknown. But boosted by the relatively high proportion of the
population known to have signed petitions in places such as Exeter, Manchester, and Sheffield, the equivalent of almost one in six of the adult male
population of England, Scotland, and Wales in 1787–92 may have endorsed
in writing the anti–slave trade movement. In overall social composition the
movement may well have prefigured that found in the Manchester inhabitants' petition of 1806. More certainly, it was, as Oldfield observes, "a movement of quite staggering proportions," ultimately joining together places
as far apart as Edinburgh in Scotland and Redruth and East Looe in Corn-
wall, and being conducted, it seems, as observers of an Edinburgh petition in 1792 noted, "with the most admirable decorum."[45] Regardless of its
precise social composition, creating and sustaining that public profile was
a key objective of the leaders of the anti–slave trade movement.

With a middle-class core but a support that embraced landed gentry
and captains of industry as well as artisans and other workers, the anti–slave
trade coalition was the most socially diverse protest movement to emerge
in Britain during the Industrial Revolution. It often involved ordinary
people looking to do something extraordinary. Women's and former African slaves' involvement enriched its diversity. It was not the small electorate of the time but the "sense and virtue" of a much larger coalition of voices

of people who had "a mind to comprehend, and a heart to feel," let "their situation" in the nation be what it might, that gave the movement to abolish the slave trade its political leverage.[46] It facilitated the movement's capacity publicly to empathize and speak on behalf of those whose voices were otherwise unheard but who were seen, in the words of historical sociologist Charles Tilly, as "deprived, excluded, or wronged," or, in the case of enslaved Africans on board British ships, all three.[47]

That so many felt the need to protest suggests that by 1787–92 knowledge of the slave trade was widespread and that many in Britain considered it an exceptional evil. The extent to which such an expression of outrage was spontaneous rather than manufactured is a question to which Tilly's analysis of the rise of mass politics in Britain from the mid-eighteenth century is relevant and which I explore later. But suggestions that petitions were a direct outcome of public meetings and evidence of voluntary subscriptions to African narratives are indicative of some spontaneity in behavior. Public meetings, in turn, were symptomatic of continuing evolution through the politics of organized protest of the redefining of the political nation that historian John Brewer discerned as having taken root a generation earlier in the 1760s. As a relatively early manifestation of that process, the anti–slave trade movement was one of the largest and most multifaceted socially. It also possessed clarity of humanitarian messaging that allowed it successfully to transcend class, gender, and even ethnic boundaries in appealing to the underlying libertarian and patriotic instincts of the British people.

One of the factors Brewer identified in redefining the British political nation was an information explosion linked with what one observer in the 1760s called an "epidemic Frenzy of reading News-papers" and another labeled a "raging thirst for news" at coffeehouses. Such developments, Brewer believed, reduced the level of "political sophistication" between the capital and the provinces.[48] Contemporaries, however, identified social as well as geographical effects arising from growing print media. Samuel Johnson in 1758 saw newspapers as "the rivulets of intelligence, which are continually trickling among us, which every one may catch, and of which every one partakes." They ensured that "the knowledge of the common people of England is greater than that of any other vulgar."[49] Nearly forty years later, in 1795, the Scottish moral philosopher Dugald Stewart extended Johnson's analysis. Referencing the diffusion of wealth among the "lower orders," which afforded them the independence and leisure to benefit from "the important effects of the printing press," Stewart went on to extol the "extensive propagation of light and refinement arising from the influence of the press."[50] Stewart's emphasis on the press's influence on the social diffusion of enlightened thinking had arguably much wider import, extending beyond Mackinnon's noted earlier. Uniting Stewart's comments with those of Johnson suggests, indeed, the probability that widening humanitarianism was an integral part of the changing political nation during Stewart's lifetime. As Joseph Gales, a radical Sheffield newspaper editor sympathetic to antislavery, suggested in 1787 as abolitionism was being born politically, the function of the press was to make "known the wants and necessities of individuals" and to form "a link in the vast chain which connects mankind to each other."[51] If debate over the slave trade constituted a key element in the articulation of humanitarianism, the press was in some newspaper editors' minds an important instrument in promoting that debate.

Two features of the press's role in enriching of public knowledge of the slave trade should be noted. The first is that newspapers were not the only print-based medium through which public discourse about the trade was conducted. Imaginative literature and the theater were involved, too. In the former case, poetry rather than novels was particularly important, the philosopher Francis Hutcheson remarking on the epic poem or tragedy as giving "vastly greater Pleasure than the Writings of Philosophers, tho' both aim at recommending virtue."[52] If poetry was pleasurably instructive, so were the writings of playwrights, old and new. The number of commercial theaters in London rose from two to seven across the eighteenth century, while outside the capital there was a veritable surge in playhouses, prompting one modern scholar to write of a "dizzying growth" in provincial theater.[53] Furthermore, audiences at theater productions were seemingly socially inclusive. It was a characteristic that carried implications for drama of "audience's self-representation" as well as for theater's need to accommodate patrons' demands in terms of spectacle and content.[54] These demands included the fashion for moral sentimentalism following publication of Samuel Richardson's novels *Pamela* and *Clarissa* in the 1740s. As Samuel Johnson observed in 1747, "The drama's laws the drama's patrons give."[55] It was an indication that, as with writers of imaginative literature more generally, playwrights were both tutors and students of public sentiment.

Theater's surging eighteenth-century popularity exposed a second issue relating to the influence of the press, broadly conceived, on public sentiment. It concerned access to the printed word at a time when large sections of the population were illiterate. As measured by the dissemination of "the capacity to decode a text across most of their population," literacy levels in late eighteenth-century Scotland were among the highest in Europe, and those in England were "nearing that level of competence."[56] That was one of the factors encouraging growth in commercial print media during the period, with newspaper output at the forefront. But literacy rates in England around 1805 were up to 50 percent higher for males than females and varied widely across social classes, being largely dependent on family wealth and access to education. In practice that meant a very high proportion of the burgeoning middle classes probably had at least substantial degrees of literacy, that some within the artisan classes were relatively proficient where literacy was concerned, and that many working-class people had very limited, if any, literacy.

Such social disparities in literacy did not inhibit Britain's continuing evolution as an information- or knowledge-based market economy and society.[57] But neither, it seems, did they preclude the rise to prominence of humanitarian instincts across social classes. That, in part, was a reflection of structural change in society, notably the growth in manufacturing and service activities that fostered urban-centered expansion of middle-class and artisan groups. It was also, however, a product of the vocalization of ideas and knowledge within the expanding urban settings that helped to redefine the political nation to include artisan and other working people. Theater was one vehicle for such processes. So, too, were the nonconformist chapels and churches that grew in tandem from the 1740s with urbanization. And so, according to Brewer, were organized public readings of newspapers and other texts that constituted an institutional part of the evolving political nation.[58] Such developments ensured that, despite much continuing illiteracy, moral sentimentalism and related ideas that surfaced in print media could gain widespread social traction in eighteenth-century Britain, helping to foster antislavery beliefs as part of a nationwide humanitarian revolution.[59]

One of the most striking features of early British abolitionism is the degree to which its leaders recognized the value of the printed word to mobilize public support. In its initial years, the London Society heavily subsidized the circulation of thousands of copies of texts, pamphlets, reports, and even woodcuts supportive of slave trade abolition, thereby making such materials free of access to potential supporters.[60] During his earliest tours of the country, Thomas Clarkson visited newspaper editors and proprietors in several towns, seeking their support for abolition. It was Clarkson's belief that the British people needed only to be made aware of the evils of the trade in slaves to be convinced to support the cause.[61] The speed and scale with which the London Society was able to produce pro-abolition materials betokened the existence of a large publishing industry in London and elsewhere in Britain by the 1780s. Parts of it were Quaker-led and were embodied in the early membership of the abolition society. At the same time, while perhaps important from a campaign perspective, Clarkson's efforts to enlist newspaper support for abolitionism should not deflect attention from the extent to which imaginative literature, journals, and newspapers had already primed public concern about the nation's involvement in slaving some time before Clarkson sought newspapers' assistance. It was evident and mounting before the 1780s and continued to develop even before Clarkson toured the country.[62] It grew in tandem with urbanization and with a related and vibrant publishing industry that while looking to inform and entertain its reading public had itself a direct commercial interest in reflecting as much as shaping attitudes. Where slavery was concerned, experience horizons had been broadened and "memory engines" activated among a growing number of Britons at least a quarter of a century before Clarkson solicited newspaper support.[63]

In seeking to understand Britons' embrace of antislavery ideas, it is important to recognize both the vibrancy and social reach of the nation's publishing industry and the images of slavery and the slave trade it presented to its readers and audiences. There seems little reason to doubt that by the last third of the eighteenth century, if not earlier, Britain had a print culture unmatched in the Western world. Publication figures give some indication of its potency. By the 1770s London and Dublin publishers, London being much the larger, regularly had around five hundred works described as literature, classics, and belles lettres on their title lists, a figure largely sustained through 1800 and probably larger than a quarter of a century earlier. It included works of poetry, some in the 1760s relating specifically and in the fashion of belles lettres or "polite culture," to planter life in the West Indies. It also included a rising number of novels, which by the end of the century accounted for 15–20 percent of the whole.[64] Costs of books probably restricted their purchase to middle- and upper-class buyers, but increases in lending or circulating libraries, in which women as well as men enrolled, extended the social reach of imaginative and other writings.[65]

Impressive though the lists of books in print and in circulation were, even more striking was the scale of publication and distribution of newspapers and journals in Britain by the 1770s. It seemingly attracted increasing shares of readers and resources of a burgeoning publishing industry by that date. Estimates of British newspaper output vary, but all point unequivocally in the same direction. By the early 1770s total newspaper issues were running at 12–14 million a year. According to some estimates, that was 5 million (or 70 percent) more than just two decades earlier and up to fourteen times the number of issues before 1700.[66] During the ninety years from 1680 to 1770, the British population grew by less than 100 percent, suggesting therefore a growth in newspaper consumption in the same period six to seven times faster than the population as a whole. It was, moreover, geographically widespread, with growth in titles outside London moving more or less in harmony with that in the capital and the total reaching well over a hundred by the early nineteenth century.[67] That growth was insufficient to ensure that every British town had a local newspaper by 1800, but it is evident that some papers circulated well beyond the locality where they were published, so it seems likely that residents of most British communities could satisfy their appetite for news should they have wished to do so.[68] In that respect, the British reading public was likely better served than any other in Europe.

What is also clear, however, is that, as Samuel Johnson asserted in 1758 and historian John Brewer affirmed, the appetite for news transcended class boundaries. That was particularly so in urban places, the intrinsic functions of which, according to one historian, were "the creation, circulation, and dissemination of news and information."[69] Another has noted the awareness and mental sharpness that living and working in towns helped to promote as part of the "functional dynamism" that urban society inculcated.[70] With their increasing diet of local as well as national and international news, newspapers were central to such processes, as indeed were such urban institutions as taverns, assembly rooms, chapels, and increasingly libraries in disseminating and sharing the information they offered. Rising urbanization was instrumental in transforming Britain into a nation of newspaper readers. The prelude to a humanitarian revolution, urban life began to redefine the nation's political culture and power as well.[71]

The integration of books, newspapers, and other print material into eighteenth-century Britain social life was largely driven by such demand-side factors as the rising incomes, urbanization, and expanding membership of what Goldsmith in 1766 defined as "the People." Some artisans and others among the so-called lower orders also shared this thirst for information and news and the resulting moral and political concerns it raised. Demand alone, however, did not fully explain the process. The liberalization of licensing newspapers in 1695 is usually seen as foundational to subsequent press expansion. Even more important was the fact that newspapers, publishing, and theaters were commercial ventures as well as sources of information and creative ideas.[72] And in their search for audiences and for advertising and other income to maintain their financial viability they had to be innovative in terms of product improvement, of marketing, and of growing their public appeal. The newspaper industry, in particular, exhibited much volatility, reflected in turnover of titles, but overall proved

sufficiently attractive to new investors and adaptable to new opportunities to sustain long-term growth.[73] If the writers and performers of
imaginative works as well as newspaper editors were peddlers of information and ideas capable of inspiring social change in eighteenth-century
Britain, they could do so in large part because of those adept in developing financially sustainable businesses through which to articulate them.
It is difficult, in sum, to conceive of the humanitarian revolution implicit
in the British anti–slave trade movement without acknowledging the
commercial acumen of Britain's theater impresarios, publishers, and
newspaper proprietors. That was, moreover, precisely what the London
Society and Clarkson understood in 1787.

In 1752 the lexicographer and critic Samuel Johnson wrote admiringly of
the writings of the novelist Samuel Richardson, whose best-selling and
widely translated books *Pamela; or, Virtue Rewarded* (1740) and *Clarissa;
or, The History of a Young Lady* (1748) have been considered as infused with
"tremulous language of feeling" and "suffering sensibility," encouraging
moral reflection.[74] For Johnson, as his biographer James Boswell later reported, Richardson's writings "taught passions to move at the command
of virtue," and a reading of the sentiments embodied in the novels was di-
dactically more significant than their specific story lines.[75] They elevated
the value of imaginative literature as a contribution to emerging intellectual
and public discourses on human virtue and moral sentiment, turning novels, among other forms of literature, into what one recent scholar has called
successful commodities and efficient cultural agents, encouraging social
change through their public reach more than how they are written.[76]

　　Such ideas permeate Lynn Hunt's study of the invention of human
rights, which uses Richardson's novels as vehicles to focus on ideas of female autonomy as part of that process. Though some scholars see Richardson's novels as portraying women's gendered sensibility in ways that are
"impossibly angelic," there is little doubt that they questioned the overbear-
ingly male, transactional, and misogynistic images in some contemporary
writings, and that the artist William Hogarth satirized in his *Marriage
A-la-Mode,* painted in 1743–45.[77] Richardson portrayed his novels' heroines,

as Hunt observes, as independent-minded and morally autonomous. When Johnson reflected in 1752 on Richardson's work, however, he was as much preoccupied with Britain's enslavement of Africans as he was with British women's status. It was quite likely as an antislavery advocate that Johnson could see in Richardson's work an example of how to harmonize passion with virtue in pursuing a moral cause.

It is possible that, among Richardson's readers, his novels' underlying sentimentalism inspired some to ponder and embrace the antislavery cause. His work did contain some passing, though sobering, references to slavery, as indeed did that of earlier novelists such as Daniel Defoe.[78] But neither Richardson nor Defoe matched earlier or contemporary playwrights and poets in the depth and range of their questioning of slavery and whose reflections on it were, in turn, increasingly overshadowed by those of the generation of imaginative writers after Richardson. Johnson's words in 1752 appear in retrospect almost like a call to arms to British novelists, poets, and playwrights to use their pens to mount further challenges to slavery, drawing on the values implicit in Richardson's novels. Some evidently ignored it, as evinced in the belles lettres of James Grainger and John Singleton, who in the mid-1760s depicted in generally approving tones sugar planters' exotic lifestyles in the British West Indies.[79] But Johnson's call, if such it was, was answered by increasing numbers of British authors of imaginative works, some of whom enjoyed wide popular appeal and thereby ensured that the modest trickle of criticism of British involvement in slavery evident in imaginative works from at least the 1690s would become by 1770 a steady and growing stream, if not a flood. In that respect developments in imaginative writings paralleled and arguably intersected with philosophical and religious intellectual discourses.

Among the earliest pieces of imaginative literature relating to British transatlantic slavery was Aphra Behn's novella *Oroonoko,* published in 1688.[80] In her subtitle and preface Behn identified her work as "a true history," containing "enough of Reality to support it." It related the story of an African prince, Oroonoko, tricked into slavery and taken to Surinam, under English rule before 1667, and his African-born lover, Imoidra. Variously interpreted since with creating the trope of the noble savage or identifying

women's ideological attachment to antislavery, Behn's tale was drama-
tized in 1696 by Thomas Southerne, in what has been seen by some as a work
exploring parallels between the social conditions of slaves and women.[81]
Be that as it may, the play contained some caustic observations on what it
called the "Man-destroying Trade" and enjoyed enduring popularity,
achieving no fewer than 315 performances in London alone during the
century after its debut.[82] Some historians entertain doubts about its educational impact on audiences, highlighting its mixed messages regarding
who might or might not merit enslavement, but at least one has suggested
that if London theatergoers learnt anything about African slavery from the
stage, "it would most likely have been from *Oroonoko*."[83]

Within half a century of *Oroonoko*'s first performance opportunities
for Britons to learn more about slavery through exposure to imaginative
writings grew noticeably. There were, as noted earlier, references to slavery in Defoe's and Swift's writings, but the most thoroughly documented
source of observations relates to poetry, then still perhaps more important
than novels in the lexicon of British imaginative literature. In his anthology James Basker has identified no fewer than forty references to slavery in
published English-language poetic works between 1696 and 1750. Many offer stories of what might be called the suffering sensibilities of the enslaved. Equally, they sometimes followed *Oroonoko* in portraying that
suffering and its tragic outcomes in personal terms rather than in the more
abstract, even theoretical, ones found in the intellectual discourse favored
by philosophers. In doing so they created images of slavery's cruelties and
violence with which readers could identify and empathize. Basker's anthology exposes how in the 1720s, for example, more than one poetic work
drew on a specific slavery-related tale dating from the 1650s. It concerned
the betrayal of Yarico, variously described as an "Indian" or "negro [*sic*]
virgin," by a white sailor, named Inkle, whom she rescued from shipwreck
and by whom she became pregnant, before she was then sold into slavery
with her unborn child. Thereafter the story figured much less prominently
in British poetry but resurfaced again in 1787 when it informed a new
London-staged tragicomic opera that ended more happily with the two lovers marrying.[84] From a vehicle used to expose the inhumanity of racially

based slavery éarly in the century, the story of Yarico and Inkle became one to point more optimistically toward interracial cooperation at the political birth of British abolitionism.

Stepping outside the specifics of such tales one can discern a key feature of imaginative literature's early contribution to British popular antislavery thinking: its focus on the personality and lived experiences of individual enslaved people as a mechanism for attracting public sympathy for their plight. Defoe, among early eighteenth-century novelists, saw in "others"—in his case, Friday—"the same affections, the same sentiments of kindness and obligation, the same passions and resentments of wrongs, the same sense of gratitude, sincerity, fidelity, and all the capacities for doing good, and receiving good" with which God had imbued Christians.[85] Seeing Friday as his servant or "man," Crusoe did not consider him a slave, even though he had rescued him from death at the hands of cannibals. Defoe's contemporaries among imaginative writers held a similar view where enslaved Africans were concerned, commonly depicting them as innocent human beings victimized by evil deeds of others: theft, trickery, or tyranny were terms frequently associated with their fallen state. Such language both anticipated and later reinforced naval officer John Atkins's denunciation in 1735 of what he saw as British slave traders' participation in illegal enslavement practices, as noted in chapter 4. But in personalizing the consequences of such actions for those seen as fellow human beings, poetical interventions also introduced to lovers of verse a sense of the incongruity between enslaving Africans and notions of human sociability to be found in the deeper recesses of the contemporary philosophical works of Hutcheson and his students. Poets humanized abstract principles. Moreover, they began to comprehend and articulate how the pain and anger that some enslaved Africans felt toward their captivity might translate into passive or violent resistance as a natural reaction to their condition. As Samuel Johnson noted in 1749, "An envious Breast with certain Mischief glows / And Slaves, the Maxim tells, are always Foes."[86] In exposing the brutal realities of slavery in often graphic and personal terms, poets invited their readers instinctively to reflect on and even to imagine how they would have felt and reacted emotionally in similar circumstances. To empathize was, after all, to be human.

In the quarter century after Johnson seemingly sought to legitimate slave resistance—a position he sustained until his death in 1784—critical commentary on slavery in British imaginative literature swelled to new heights, finding expression even among those born in or residents of slaving ports such as Bristol and Liverpool.[87] Basker's anthology of poetry provides one measure of its growth. His listing of poetry materials in 1750–75 with slavery-related content may be incomplete, but at fifty-six published items, it was some three times greater than the annual rate of output of the previous half century.[88] It was, moreover, noticeably higher around 1770 than two decades earlier. There was also by that stage an increasing commentary on slavery in other imaginative literary works. The comic opera *The Padlock* in 1768, coproduced by Isaac Bickerstaffe and Charles Dibdin, was the first of a series of new works with slavery-related content that appeared on the London stage over the following decade; most were written by Dibdin and, if performance numbers are a guide, were very popular.[89] Beginning with Sarah Scott's *History of Sir George Ellison,* published in 1766, and Laurence Sterne's *Tristram Shandy,* published serially in 1759–67, novels with more explicit slavery-related content than that evinced in Richardson's *Pamela* and *Clarissa* also began to appear from the 1760s onward, seemingly reflecting, like poetry, a growing public appetite for stories about slavery in general and West Indian slavery in particular.[90]

It is not difficult to find messages in comic operas and novels consistent with antislavery ideas. In the conclusion to his comic opera, *The Islanders,* first performed in 1780, Dibdin urged his audience to remember that "all mankind are brothers" and that "the name of Master and Slave be forgotten."[91] Such sentiments were anticipated by Sterne's writings in the 1760s. In volume 9 of *Tristram Shandy,* written in 1766, Sterne questioned on grounds of religion and shared humanity racial gradations of human beings, identifying the "fortunes of war" and the racialization of Africans as a means used to justify slavery's whip.[92] In his *Sentimental Journey through France and Italy,* published in 1768, Sterne challenged slavery more widely. Perceiving in Paris a caged bird pleading for freedom as a metaphor on slavery,

Sterne described slavery as "a bitter draught," which, "though thousands in all ages had been made to drink" it, was "no less bitter on that account."[93] Likewise, in *Sir George Ellison*, published just two years earlier, Sarah Scott intimated her subject's natural abhorrence of slavery and went on to insist, on his acquiring through marriage a slave plantation in Jamaica, on his determination, if not to free the enslaved, to at least treat them benevolently. In doing so, he reminded his less benevolent wife, in an echo of Richardson's words in *Pamela*, that in the grave "the lowest black slave will be as great as we are; in the next world perhaps much greater; the present difference is merely adventitious, not natural."[94]

Despite such evidence, historians have been cautious in ascribing antislavery impulses to British theatrical works and novels. Some agree with historian Wylie Sypher that, where the eighteenth-century was concerned, there was "no drama of anti-slavery" but only "a number of plays in which the Negro plays his part"; even then a blackened actor played the African character.[95] As for references to slavery in novels, one scholar has claimed that they were "never as sustained as in the response in poetry and polemic," while another has insisted in seeing in some British novels, including *Sir George Ellison*, where the novel's thrust focused on amelioration not abolition or prototypical proslavery arguments.[96] Yet others have chosen to remind us that although Sterne clearly opposed slavery and was doubtless aware of emerging antislavery sentiments in Britain, his fiction's approach to slavery remained abstract, ahistorical, and decentralized. It failed, they opine, fully to engage with the specifics of slavery's racism or the economic and legal structures underwriting British black servitude.[97]

Some, nonetheless, have seen drama as providing ties to humanity where British concerns over slavery were concerned.[98] Endorsement of that viewpoint is found in more recent interpretations of the character of Mungo, the pivotal enslaved African figure in *The Padlock*, whose comedic persona in the opera is counterbalanced by an open willingness to challenge his master. One scholar has accordingly considered Mungo as toggling uneasily between "acceding to society's assumptions about black inferiority and honouring his essential humanity."[99] That observation, in turn, is consistent with one contemporary epilogue on the opera, published in 1787, urging, among other things, that Mungo be seen as "a man by Britons snar'd and seiz'd, and sold."[100] For whatever reason, Dibdin and his ilk may have been reluctant to confront slavery head-on, preferring to approach it for comedic effect, but their work still fueled arguments concerning enslaved Africans' inherent humanity. In similar fashion, though some doubt the value of Scott's or Sterne's novels as a "political tool" in changing attitudes, the authors' engagement with the subject of slavery, regardless of their specific views of the institution, was indicative of its being actively in the public's mind.[101]

There were, moreover, contemporaries who believed that reputable novelists such as Scott or Sterne could shape opinion. Nowhere was that more evident than in a private correspondence, later made public, between the London-based former slave Ignatius Sancho and Sterne himself, wherein Sancho, seized by Sterne's comments in his *Sermons of Mr. Yorick* in 1766 on slavery's historic bitter draught and encouraged by the "humane" writings of Sarah Scott, implored him specifically to condemn West Indian slavery.[102] Handled in Sterne's "striking manner," Sancho asserted, such an intervention would "ease the yoke (perhaps) of many"; but even if just one was helped, he believed, "what a feast to a benevolent heart" it would be. Sterne, in response, referenced his forthcoming comment on slavery in volume 9 of *Tristram Shandy* while privately indicating his opposition to Caribbean slavery and to racial justification of it. Revealing on Sancho's part at least a belief in a power of sentimental novelists to effect change somewhat greater than some later historians have tended to assume, the correspondence would go on to attract considerable attention when it appeared in Sterne's letters published by his daughter in 1775 and then in Sancho's own letters published in 1782.

Beyond individual works, it appears that imaginative literature's commentaries on slavery from at least the 1750s not only shared the sentimental values that informed enlightened philosophical ideas but reflected also the latter's deepening moral critique of slavery and trafficking of Africans. It typically echoed the assumption that, notwithstanding cultural differences, Africans were fellow human beings, with ranges of emotions and other qualities similar to the rest of humanity. It focused on the brutal treatment—and resulting loss of life—of enslaved Africans in British America, with its repercussions for British human trafficking. And it began to reflect tensions between Britons' attachment to personal liberty and imposing slavery on fellow human beings abroad. One recent study has shown how Hannah More, in her poem *On Slavery*, published in 1788, parodied James Thomson's famous work *On Liberty*, published fifty years earlier in order to make that point, reminding us that it was difficult to reconcile Britain's insistence on being a place where, in More's words, "the soul of freedom reigns" with its willingness to "forge chains for others she herself disdains."[103] It was a message that others were advancing in the generation before Hannah More so poetically encapsulated it.[104]

Trends in imaginative literature carried, however, a broader message in terms of British attitudes toward the slavery question by the third quarter of the eighteenth century. For many in Britain before that date there was possibly an unspoken assumption of the banality of African slavery, even an acceptance of its essential value to the nation's well-being. In the world of portrait art, slavery existed in plain sight; it was part of the architecture of well-heeled, respectable families, with Black servants, often children or juveniles, appearing on the margins of white family portraits.[105] The appearance of "Africans" or "Negroes" in works of composers, playwrights, poets, and novelists increasingly lifted a veil on slavery's acceptance or respectability. It transformed often static, often shadowy appendages to respectable, middle-class British family life into human beings within a larger, more dynamic, transactional social history canvas, with backstories, emotions, and lived experiences to which readers or viewers of such works might relate, thereby giving them ideological purchase. Put another way, imaginative literature, with its sentimental orientation and growing public audience, accelerated the breakdown of an often unconscious popular acquiescence in British promotion of slavery overseas that had largely prevailed before 1750 and that Scottish philosophers and some spiritual leaders were increasingly questioning. It was a process that crossed the nation's religious and even political divides, as antipathy toward slavery found within the ranks of some arch social conservatives and Anglicans blended with that of nonconformist groups.[106] In a nation steeped in a commitment

to personal liberty, by the middle of the eighteenth century slavery could
no longer be quietly ignored: for increasing numbers of Britons, it appeared
not just inhuman and tawdry but even unpatriotic to continue its pursuit.
For some, the sheer scale of the involvement simply compounded the national disgrace.[107]

The precise social reach of those beliefs before 1775 is difficult to
gauge, but there are signs that it was wider than is sometimes supposed.
Theater, it is claimed, attracted socially diverse audiences in Britain in the
eighteenth century, and the number of productions with sentimental story
lines increased as the century wore on. That said, it is still possible to question the extent to which the sentimentalist, antislavery leanings of some
poets and novelists reached beyond upper- or respectable middle-class audiences, for books likely remained prohibitively expensive to lower-class
households.[108] Other print media, however, maybe reduced the cost barriers to the wider circulation of their musings. Prominent among them were
journals and newspapers. We have seen that as early as 1720–23 the London press offered an outlet for reflections on British freedom in the aftermath of the South Sea Bubble. But it was one of the century's most famous
newspaper proprietors, Benjamin Franklin, who articulated the press's
value in conveying philosophical ideas—or "the Wisdom of many Ages and
Nations"—to a wide readership. In 1732–57 he offered his colonial readers
an annual almanac in which news items were interlaced with "Proverbial
Sentences" offering instruction on the virtues of industry, among other
things, to "the common People, who bought scarce any other Books."[109]
When in England before 1775, Franklin was not averse to using the letter
columns of the London press to promote antislavery ideas, anticipating in
that respect Clarkson's efforts in 1788 to mobilize newspaper proprietors'
support for the same.[110]

By the time that Franklin was using the British press to urge the ending of British slaving, others were doing so through imaginative writings.
One anonymously authored poem in 1775 published in the *London Magazine* and entitled "Remarks on the Slavery of the Negroes," pondered the
"wretched exiles, bath'd in briny tears, / Forc'd from their country by some
ruthless hand, / And sold for captives in a foreign land." Its publication

without apparent controversy in one of the capital's most widely read contemporary magazines, it has been argued, was testimony to "the degree to which the literate public either shared or at least acquiesced" in the sentiments expressed.[111] In 1775–76, excerpts from the Sterne-Sancho correspondence noted earlier also appeared in other London journals. Moreover, the reprinting of such excerpts was not restricted to the London press. There was one in Edinburgh, and in England in December 1775, the *Chester Chronicle, or, Commercial Intelligencer* carried one.[112] In Franklin mode, therefore, by 1775 at least, the press was plainly seen by some proponents of antislavery as a valuable ally in articulating the ideas of the educated elite's published and private thoughts to a larger, nationwide audience. Among them were those whom Samuel Johnson had identified in 1758 as "the common People."

Items appearing in newspapers of imaginative literature opposing slavery or of the potential of such literature to shape opinion are testimony to their editors' sense of what was of interest to their readers. They exposed a shifting attitude toward the enslavement of others that more conventional forms of imaginative literature of the day was indicating, bringing discourses about slavery based on personal stories or emotions to a much larger audience than those found in works affordable only by middle-class households could achieve. In both cases, the emotional appeal of such writings mirrored philosophers' growing emphasis on feelings, sentiment, and sociability in shaping human interaction, broadening readers' experiences and inviting them to reflect on the stories they embodied and how they themselves might have reacted in the circumstances depicted. In that respect the appearance before 1776 of poetical and other items in the press condemning slavery and the slave trade was a foretaste of how the power of the press would later be mobilized to build demonstrations of public support for abolitionism.

The circulation of opinions on the slave trade and slavery was, however, not the only information about them that newspapers supplied in the course of the eighteenth century. They also supplied a regular and increasingly full diet of factual data relating to British slaving voyages. This included details of ship itineraries but significantly, too, reports of the slaves themselves, their survival rates, and their resistance to enslavement. Such reports increased in detail from the mid-eighteenth century, offering brief insights to those who read them of life on board such ships and the reactions of the enslaved to it. Accordingly, just as Basker's anthology of poetry provided insights into the trajectory of British imaginative writers' feelings about slavery, so the cataloging of the details of slave voyages found in newspapers may offer a barometer of their editors' perceptions of what they thought their readers might wish to know or perhaps should know. I turn next to examine the impact of their decisions.

SEVEN

Reaching "the Common People"

Newspapers, African Voices, and Politicizing
the Slave Trade

A CELEBRATED CORRESPONDENCE in the late 1760s between the former slave Ignatius Sancho and the famous novelist Laurence Sterne, published in 1775 after Sterne's death, revealed a mutual belief in a shared humanity, with Sterne ascribing African enslavement to racism, not intellectual or cultural difference.[1] Both agreed about its immorality and illegitimacy. The correspondence also exposed on Sancho's part, however, an assumption that shifting British perceptions about slavery as a prelude to its ending rested primarily on interventions—or what he saw as "epicurean . . . acts of charity"—by the nation's white literati and intellectual elite. That position perhaps reflected Sancho's own experience of regaining freedom, which depended to a large degree on his association with members of Britain's high society. Nor was it a wholly misleading assumption. In the decade following the correspondence, support from well-placed individuals in British society committed to antislavery principles was important in allowing the slaves James Somerset and Joseph Knight to press their court cases to regain their freedom in England and Scotland in 1772 and 1778, respectively. And members of the aristocracy added luster to the list of those prepared publicly to endorse abolitionist works such as Olaudah Equiano's narrative, published in 1789.

But not all former slaves living in Britain in the late eighteenth century saw the possibility of change in the same way. Some believed that change in public perceptions of African humanity and slavery extended well beyond the nation's social or educated elite. And they identified more than books and pamphlets as instruments for effecting change. They saw, too, a vital role for newspapers with their wider circulation and social reach. One striking example occurred on 25 April 1789, a few days before William Wilberforce formally launched the parliamentary campaign against the slave trade, when a group of liberated Africans, or self-styled Sons of Africa, published a letter in the London-based publication *The Diary; or, Woodfall's Register.* It was addressed to William Dickson, formerly private secretary to the governor of Barbados and author of *Letters on Slavery,* published in London in early 1789. In it they complimented Dickson on including in his book "accounts of some Negroes eminent for their virtue and abilities." They also applauded his revelation of the "but too just picture of the Slave Trade, and the horrid cruelties practised on the poor sable people in the West Indies" to the detriment of Christianity. Praying that a bill to abolish the trade would soon be passed, they argued that it was "the duty of every man who is a friend to religion and humanity . . . to shew his detestation of such inhuman traffick," recognizing that "thanks to God *the nation at large is awakened to a sense of our sufferings*" and that those "*who can feel for the distresses of their own countrymen, will also commiserate the case of the poor Africans.*" Echoing Sancho's urging of benevolence toward slaves, the nine writers in 1789 clearly drew an emotional interconnection between distress of people at home and the plight of enslaved Africans overseas, thereby casting the potential domestic social net of antislavery sentiment much wider than that which Sancho assumed. Moreover, it was a net that slavery-related column inches in newspapers could appear to play a part in shaping.[2]

The relation between newspapers and public opinion in the eighteenth century remains a contentious topic. Some echo Dugald Stewart's remarks of 1795 that depicted the press as a "potent force in the gradual enlightenment which characterizes the eighteenth century," or, more specifically, as an influencer of debates on issues such as antislavery in the 1770s and 1780s, thereby "affecting the course of English history."[3] Others appear more ambivalent, acknowledging that newspapers educated "their readers in the significant national issues" but suggesting that it was the consumer or reading public who "called the tune" where newspaper content was concerned.[4] Wherever the balance between the press as mirror and

shaper of opinion lay, however, newspaper content likely reflected an evolving, ongoing conversation between editor and reader similar in many ways
to that in imaginative literature, except that in the case of newspapers it involved a much larger and socially more diverse audience. Assuming this
to be true, then content analysis of collections of British newspapers should
offer insights into the timing and scale of shifts in the public's interest in
issues pertaining to slavery and the slave trade during the eighteenth
century.

The online British Newspaper Archive (BNA) contains electronically
searchable digitized copies of British newspapers from the seventeenth
century through the present day.[5] It offers the largest collection of newspaper materials worldwide for the British Isles, covering, among other things,
eighteenth-century London, English provincial, Scottish, and Irish newspapers. It is not a comprehensive collection of eighteenth-century newspapers, some of which had very short lives, but it has long runs of a sizable
number. There is no reason to assume the collection's content has any inherent bias where slavery and the slave trade are concerned, suggesting that
key word searches such as "Africa" and "slave" should offer a reasonable
indicator of trends in their coverage of issues pertaining to the slave trade.
    Slave trade searches of the BNA based on the key words "slave" and
"Africa" reveal that citations of such words rose fifteen- to twenty-five-fold,
respectively, between the first and second halves of the eighteenth century.[6]
A search of a separate online version of the British Library's Burney Collection, now subsumed within the BNA but in which the search program
offers breakdowns of types of information reported, suggests that such citations were essentially news or business related.[7] Some early eighteenth-
century "slave" citations relate to Europeans held in Africa, but increasingly
"slave" became synonymous with enslaved Africans.
    Overall, the growth of citations for "slave" and "Africa" is similar to
that of estimated total newspaper output in the century after 1690. This may
suggest that it was growth of the industry as much as a predilection for
reporting African enslavement that largely explains the trend in citations.
That suggestion, in turn, finds corroboration in tendencies of editors

outside London to reprint news previously reported in the capital's press. The trend may have been linked also to the timing of entry of new titles into the industry, some of which regularly carried over many years Africa- or slave-related content from the date of their launch.[8] Such findings still imply, of course, that more readers of newspapers were exposed to news of the slave trade and slavery as the range of newspaper titles increased across the nation.

Despite such cautions, there remain grounds for assuming that rising newspaper reporting of Africa- or slave-related events reflected more than simply changes in the scale of press output. There are signs, indeed, that from the point of view of newspaper editors the slave trade became increasingly newsworthy. One indicator is that, overall, press reporting of the slave trade across the eighteenth century expanded faster than the actual trade in slaves itself. Another was the increasing specificity used in identifying places of trade in Africa, which suggests that the use of the key word "Africa" in content analysis likely understates shifting reporting levels of slaving activities.[9] The pickup in the complexity of reporting seems to have been particularly noticeable in the third quarter of the century, significantly perhaps at the same time that critiques of slavery and the slave trade in imaginative writings and philosophical works were intensifying. It becomes apparent when, instead of searching newspapers using the key words "Africa" and "slave" separately, one does so with them combined. The search produces fewer hits overall, as one would expect, but even with the caveat about the "Africa" designator noted above, the trend is striking. Whereas there were 75 references to "Africa" and "slave" combined in 1700–1749, there were 2,862 in the following sixty years. Allowing for differences in length of time periods, that was a thirty-fold increase in citations. Moreover, the number increased in each decade from 1750–59 through 1800–1809, reinforcing the impression that "Africa" and "slave" were increasingly inseparable in editors' and therefore readers' minds. A similar pattern emerges when using the search term "slave trade." That reveals 299 references, or around 6 a year, in 1700–1749. The figure then rose almost sixfold to 35 a year in 1750–79 and to 175 a year in 1780–89, both significantly higher than growth of the trade in those periods. It continued to rise thereafter.[10] Compared to the first half of the eighteenth century, when a story specifically on the slave trade appeared in the British press on average every two months or so, by the 1780s one was appearing more or less every other day. Even before, therefore, Thomas Clarkson reported in his history of abolition published in 1808 appealing twenty years earlier to the humanitarian instincts of those in the newspaper industry to support the anti–slave trade campaign, the slave trade had become an increasingly regular topic of conversation between newspapers and their readers in the previous decades. Clarkson's approach to the press perhaps gave it further impetus, but it was from a base that was already substantial by 1787.

If there seems little doubt that newspaper proprietors and editors evinced growing interest in reporting on British slaving from 1750 onward, it is important to acknowledge that much of the coverage before abolitionism related to seemingly routine business matters: sailing schedules, specific ports of arrival and departure in Africa and the Americas, and losses of ships abroad. Much of it was included in the "maritime news" section of the papers and was likely culled in many cases from *Lloyd's List* and other London news outlets. The apparent banality of the reporting, however, should not be allowed to disguise its wider significance, not least in relation to trading locations in Africa, which helped to enlighten readers' understanding of the continent. Perhaps of greater import was that the more standard news items were accompanied from midcentury onward by increasing reports of numbers of slaves shipped and "buried" at sea as well as of shipboard slave revolts and the efforts of crew, sometimes unsuccessful, to suppress them. The growth in reporting of insurrections reflected to some extent an increase in their incidence, linked in part to shifts in the geography of British commercial activities in western Africa.[11] Nonetheless the growing incidence of such reports begs questions about why newspaper proprietors elected to publish such information and how those who read them chose to interpret them. What is evident is that, as a result of such reporting, the suffering of Africans as well as African resistance to enslavement most likely became part of public conversations about the British slave trade, whether in the London coffeehouse, in the provincial inn, on the street, or even in the homes of artisans and middle-class professionals.[12] Newspapers widened and enriched public understanding of how the slave trade worked and, equally important, how its victims reacted to it. It was one of the marketplaces of information that abolitionists such as Clarkson sought to exploit from 1788 onward.

In April 1753 the *London Magazine: or, Gentleman's Monthly Intelligencer* published a story of a slave uprising on the Bristol ship *Marlborough*.[13] One of the few to have survived the uprising was evidently a prime source, his version appearing in a letter to his father published in the preceding weeks in Bristol and London newspapers.[14] It followed a more cryptic statement on the loss of the ship and crew that appeared in the February issue of the *Gentleman's Magazine* and that concluded with the proclamation, *"How sweet is liberty!"*[15] As related in later reports, the *Marlborough*'s story was clear. According to the *London Magazine,* the ship's captain had taken on some slaves at the Gold Coast with the intention of using them as "guardians" for the main body of enslaved Africans he proposed to buy at Bonny in the Bight of Biafra. Later, on leaving Bonny, the ship experienced an insurrection, the prime instigators, it seems, being the Gold Coast slaves, who gained control of the ship and killed all but a few of the crew. It was further reported that "the Negroes" being "so expert at the [ship's] great guns and small-arms," they succeeded in repelling efforts by another Bristol ship, the *Hawk,* to recapture the *Marlborough,* whereupon the leaders of the revolt set ashore at Bonny 270 of the "Bite Negroes . . . that chose it," before setting sail "with intent, as is supposed, to go to their own country, tho' the undertaking was extremely hazardous, as they had no one to navigate the ship." The report failed to indicate what happened subsequently to the ship's former slaves, but the vessel may have been retaken and reached the Americas.[16]

Newspaper reports of the insurrection on the *Marlborough* were exceptionally detailed. They also arose during a period in 1749–78 when shipboard insurrections on British slave ships reported in the press reached a historic high. Overall, there are records of slave insurrections during 153 British voyages in 1698–1808—an average of some 1.4 a year—but that figure rose to around 3 a year in 1749–78, with 3–6 being reported per annum in eleven of those years.[17] While reflecting to some degree changing patterns of British slaving in Africa, the rise in such reports, it has been suggested, mirrored a shift "in the interests and preoccupation of the literate public," which helped to ensure that incidences of rebellion were "more likely to be reported—particularly in the published record."[18] Support for that argument is to be found in evidence of increased press reporting from the 1760s of slave losses—or "burials"—as well as slave loadings and deliveries on British ships. They suggest a growth in public curiosity and interest in slaving voyages and their outcomes, particularly concerning the fate of their human cargoes. Chronologically, that matched mounting criticisms of British involvement in slaving in other print media such as philosophical and religious treatises and imaginative literature, implying some possible linkage between them.

There is evidence that, as with the printing of antislavery poetic pieces, publicizing shipboard insurrections and other slave-related aspects of voyages may have been a deliberate choice or calculated act on the part of some journal and newspaper editors. Its intention, if such it was, was probably to fuel public awareness of the human and other costs of Britain's continuing pursuit of slavery and slave trafficking. The suggestion gains credibility when one notes that in 1753 Samuel Johnson was closely involved with the *London Magazine* at the time it carried the initial *Marlborough* story in February 1753. A high church Tory outlook shaped Johnson's general views on slavery by the 1750s, but a belief that it was legitimate for slaves to rebel set him apart from many in the mid-eighteenth century. As such, his radical position on slave rebellion may have become embedded in the journal's editorial policy over many years. According to one count, between 1737 and 1773 the journal included no fewer than fifty articles covering some forty-three slave revolts at various stages of transatlantic slavery.[19] One was the *Marlborough* story; another was Tacky's Rebellion or War in 1760 in Jamaica, the largest slave uprising in the eighteenth-century British West Indies.[20] Both involved "Coromantee" slaves, often seen as among the most rebellious by contemporaries.[21] The extent to which the *London Magazine*'s policy encouraged editors of other journals or newspapers to do the same is unclear. Be that as it may, whether journals and newspapers were following or shaping demand for information, from 1748 onward there was an unusually rich diet of reports on shipboard and other slave insurrections in the British press for their readers quietly to ponder and discuss.

Outside journals and newspapers, the propensity of Africans to rebel or at least to resist by other means their enslavement was regularly referenced in the private correspondence and other records of slaving voyages. Its frequency was testament to slave traders' recognition that, as the French marine insurance expert Balthazard-Marie Émérigon put it in 1783, where slaving was concerned, "insurrection was always a peril of the sea" since "enemies will be brought on board."[22] Not surprisingly, since insurrection could potentially destroy a voyage from a financial point of view, investors took precautions to mitigate the risk. Human error and other factors resulted in as many as perhaps 10 percent of slaving voyages experiencing a shipboard insurrection, but their precautions seem to have been largely effective as far as owners were concerned.[23] Very few British ships experienced the disaster that confronted the *Marlborough* in 1752. Nonetheless, resistance by slaves—and fear of it—was an ever-present reality and could manifest itself in ways other than insurrection. It was a constant reminder that at least some among the enslaved Africans on board British (and other) ships were unprepared quietly to accept their fate. Some planned rebellions; others seem to have reacted spontaneously against their status. In doing so, they anticipated calls by others who suffered under slavery and oppression to resist, by force if necessary.[24] They became in the words of Nelson Mandela, written in another context, "heroes who acted as curtain raisers to the major conflicts that subsequently flamed out, and who acquitted themselves just as magnificently."[25] By protesting their enslavement, they were, in effect, early "outriders" of British abolitionism.

For those with sympathy for antislavery, however, the reporting in journals and newspapers of slave insurrections was not without its concerns. Particularly troublesome were reports of heavy losses of British seafarers during such events. Gauging how readers of the revolt on the *Marlborough* reacted to its crew's slaughter is difficult to judge from this distance in time, but for the public of a maritime nation to read of such

peacetime losses of seamen other than through natural causes was doubtless horrific to many. Notwithstanding the fact that the ships' crews were
the enslavers, it possibly stirred or reactivated in the minds of some readers images or feelings of African savagery or vengefulness that still existed
in the later eighteenth century. For example, in his *Theory of Moral Sentiments,* published in 1759, Adam Smith commended Africans for their command of passions but also discerned a preoccupation with "their own
wants and necessities," which inhibited them from giving "much attention
to those of another person." Such characteristics, he went on, nurtured a
"heroic and unconquerable firmness," which disguised "a vengeance" that
when they "give way to it, is always sanguinary and dreadful."[26] Four years
later, in 1763, and in an eerie echo of the *Marlborough* story, and with perhaps an eye on reports of Tacky's Rebellion in 1760 in Jamaica, the poet
James Grainger urged West Indian planters not to buy Gold Coast or "Coromantee" slaves, since they "Chuse death before dishonourable bonds,"
or, "fir'd with vengeance," seize "thine unsuspecting watch, / And thine
own poniard bury in thy breast."[27] Though many envisaged Africans as
victims of slavers, some may well have seen evidence in the *Marlborough*
case of a familiar stereotype depicting Gold Coast slaves in particular as
uncontrollable and brutish.[28]

Despite Smith's observation on Africans' vengeful character, he nevertheless opposed slavery in principle and did not consider them worthy
of enslavement. To the contrary, he wrote, "Fortune never exerted more
cruelly her empire over mankind than when she subjected those nations of
heroes to the refuse of the gaols of Europe."[29] It is also interesting that while
Grainger painted in 1764 a damning view of Coromantee slaves, he prefaced his views by observing that "they were born to freedom in their native land."[30] He was not alone among Britons by the 1760s to make such an
observation. Several other poets, as James Basker's anthology of their work
shows, made the same point.[31] Ideologically, it was an acute and very potent observation. For whereas some at that time, including Grainger, focused on *how* Africans' alleged character defined the violent nature of
their reactions to being enslaved, Grainger's observation that they had been
born free and Smith's perception of their heroism begin to reveal *why*

Africans incarcerated on slave ships or held as plantation slaves ob-
jected, seemingly with some persistence and sometimes with violence, to
their captivity.

In his study *Black Jacobins,* historian C. L. R. James reminds his
readers that "on no earthly spot was so much misery concentrated than on
a slave-ship."[32] Contemporaries saw the same. In verse written in 1788 but
not published until forty years later, the poet William Cowper compared
slaves on board ship with "sprats in a gridiron, scores in a row."[33] A year
later, in 1789, James Field Stanfield, who had sailed on a slave ship, wrote in
verse of the enslaved, "In painful rows with studious art comprest, / Smok-
ing they lie, and breathe the humid pest," while William Wilberforce in his
first speech on the subject in Parliament in May 1789 saw the middle passage from Africa to the Americas as "the most wretched part" of the whole
business, with "so much misery condensed in so little room" and which was
"more than the human imagination had ever before conceived."[34] Surrounded by the ocean's "intimidating vastness" and subject to the whims
of strangers whose diet, language, culture, and motives they did not understand, for enslaved Africans the middle passage must have been a harrow-
ing, at times literally suffocating, experience with potentially profound
psychological consequences.[35]

The misery that Africans were forced to endure on slave ships doubtless contributed to their determination to fight back against their oppressors, transforming rebels into savages in the eyes of slave ship crews. It has
encouraged comparisons with the reaction of the mob in Britain, the violence of which has been equated with misery rebelling or the pinch of famine turning people into "monsters."[36] Yet it is a mistake to see shipboard
insurrections only in such reactive terms. They were a reflection, too, of
slavery's assault on humanity. It was Africans' "sassiness" in the face of their
loss of freedom, the desperate sense of a lost autonomy or control over their
own lives, reinforced perhaps with morbid fears of what the future held,
that ultimately drove some to rise up.[37] As the Russian novelist Fyodor
Dostoyevsky wrote when reflecting on his own political incarceration a
century later, "no brands, no fetters" could make him or his fellow inmates
forget they were human beings.[38] There is no reason to assume that

enslaved Africans felt any differently. Accordingly, though portraying rebelliousness as reactive, situational, opportunistic, and personality driven
may help explain its timing and form, the underlying motivation for rebellion was primarily political or ideological. Just as historian Quentin Skinner
saw threats of slavery as allowing Britons to define their own notions of
freedom, so the experience of being sold into British or European slavery
gave Africans actually suffering that fate a grievous and, for some, intolerable sense of what they had lost. It took away their humanity. Consciously
or otherwise, depictions of slave insurrections in the British press and
elsewhere sometimes supplied affirmation of that point, portraying Africans as devoted to personal freedom as much as Britons.

The circumstances that led Africans to be forced into the export
slave trade to the Americas are unlikely ever to be fully understood.[39]
Slavery evidently existed in Africa, and it is possible that some born to
that condition entered the trade, though if it happened it was more likely
inadvertent rather than deliberate, since selling those born into slavery
breached conventions in some African societies and was thus a potential
source of resistance.[40] But most studies agree that in the precolonial era
slaves accounted for no more than a third and in most cases less than a
quarter of most African societies' populations. Together with proscrip-
tions against selling slave-born Africans, such findings suggest that the
vast majority of those entering the export slave trade were born free and
were forced into it against their will. Some were victims of climatic
changes, but most were almost certainly enslaved through violent means,
including kidnapping, slave raiding, and warfare. The extent to which
such activities escalated as export demand for slaves in Atlantic Africa
grew and the consequences that flowed from them continue to be debated.[41] Regardless of the trend, there is nonetheless mounting evidence
of internal resistance within Africa to the activities of indigenous enslavers who sought to profit from supplying domestic and export markets.[42]
By whatever means, therefore, that they came to be sold into such markets, Africans almost certainly resented it, and some acted on their resentment. It was a resentment, moreover, rooted in loss of family and
freedom, not simply material conditions.

Historians can easily overlook the degree to which shipboard insurrection was a product of Africans' anger at loss of their personal freedom and its implications for those from whom they were forcibly separated. Ironically, it was an African slave dealer at Calabar, Duke Ephraim, who offered a glimpse into the resentment felt by free Africans taken into the export slave trade when in 1789 he wrote to two Bristol merchants to protest the behavior of one of the merchant's ship captains in kidnapping two of his canoe men, whom he labeled "free men." Duke Ephraim threatened retribution should they not be repatriated.[43] He was not the only Calabar merchant to resent the illegal seizure of associates deemed free.[44] Such cases reveal that notions of freedom, sociability, and responsibility toward others within communities plainly existed in Africa, even in places where enslaving and selling for gain people from outside was pivotal to their economies. And they also reveal that anger and violence might easily follow among those who saw themselves or others as unjustly enslaved and sold. That could apply to those who, having previously been involved in supplying African captives to British ships, were themselves through chance or the fortunes of war deported from their homeland to British America. That, indeed, was the fate of the leader of Tacky's Rebellion in Jamaica in 1760.[45]

Reports of shipboard insurrection in journals and newspapers paid little or no attention to notions of African resentment at loss of freedom to explain such events, but as noted earlier, poetical writings referred to African freedom. So, too, did narratives written by former slaves who lived in Britain and North America. Among the first to be published in Britain was that of Albert Gronniosaw, whose narrative has usually been overshadowed in historical studies by the later Afro-British works of Ignatius Sancho, Ottobah Cugoano (aka John Stuart), and Olaudah Equiano (aka Gustavus Vassa).[46] Equiano's narrative was a literary sensation following its publication in 1789. Published seventeen years earlier in 1772, coincidentally the year of the *Somerset* case, Gronniosaw's short work is now considered the least antislavery in tone and in content of the works published by Africans in Britain before 1790.[47] It went, nonetheless, through multiple editions and, according to historian Philip Gould, "apparently sold quite well," though not enough apparently to alleviate its author's poverty. Gould attributes its appeal, like that of similar texts after 1772, to being "able to combine multiple genres—spiritual autobiography, travel narrative, ethnography, political commentary—as well as religious, sentimental, and gothic discourses." Such attributes, he believes, made African narratives "flexible enough to appeal to various readerships simultaneously," giving them increasingly wide audiences. Sancho's letters, published in 1782, attracted some two thousand subscribers, a total later easily eclipsed by Equiano's unashamedly antislavery narrative.[48] Seen in literary terms, the African texts of the later eighteenth century may have tended to offer a black message in a "white envelope," as is sometimes alleged, but beginning with Gronniosaw the published writings of the four Afro-Britons revealed significant compatibilities between their values, as former slaves, and those of most other Britons.[49] It was not a character difference but enslavement that triggered African resistance or, as Cugoano insisted, became a responsibility for those enslaved. Still, though culturally different, Africans, when free, seemed as humane and civilized as Britons.

Yet, twenty years before Gronniosaw published his narrative, similarities surfaced between the reported behavior of self-liberated African slaves and British values in the *Marlborough* insurrection narrative published in the *London Magazine*. Like imaginative literature and African narratives, the *Marlborough* story invited its readers to judge African reactions to captivity relative to their own values. In doing so, it offered them a complex, multifaceted behavioral picture, particularly on the part of the Gold Coast "guardians," the reported instigators and organizers of the insurrection. The narrative depicted them initially as ruthlessly determined to reassert and then defend with violence their autonomy and that of their fellow slaves. Having overcome and destroyed their captors and fiercely resisted reenslavement, they then displayed a charitable or benevolent disposition to allow those among the "Bite" former captives who wished it to land again near Bonny, before looking to return home. As written, therefore, the *London Magazine*'s narrative anticipated elements of Adam Smith's vengeful, yet heroic Africans as well as of his larger theory of moral sentiments in depicting the actions of the Gold Coast insurrectionists of 1753.

Readers who glanced briefly at the article may have missed its ideological content or thrust, but more careful readers—and perhaps those who read or studied philosophy—may well have appreciated it. Its message is open to interpretation but carried an antislavery tone. It contained several elements. The first, implicit in the insurrection itself, was that violence and bloodshed were inseparable from slavery, not least when its intended victims chose to resist or rebel. In that respect published reports in the press of shipboard revolts (and slave "burials" at sea) opened a public window on the human costs of slavery that had previously been largely focused on Africa itself but thereafter centered on the middle passage as well as on the trade's cost in white and African lives. When deaths from disease were added subsequently to those from other causes, the fate of crew on British slave ships would later provide an important early line of assault on the trade for abolitionists from the mid-1780s.

The second element was that, having escaped captivity, the Gold Coast insurrectionists revealed sentimental and other emotions akin to those identified by British philosophical and imaginative writers as markers of human beings' natural sociability and sympathy. Moreover, in tandem with personal freedom, such attributes were considered elemental in informing British manners and the nation's identity in the world. If insurrection was an indicator of the Gold Coast guardians' determination to recover their freedom, what the press report also exposed to its readers was that, despite their different cultural habits, Africans were self-evidently as much part of the human race as defined by philosophers, poets, and others. Britons' acquaintance with the personal histories and sentiments found in published African narratives and other works from around 1770 onward reinforced that perception.

To portray insurrections as political statements, a view consistent with Johnson's perception of slave revolts, is to identify a third, perhaps more subliminal, element in the *Marlborough* story that ultimately gave it and other press reports of shipboard revolt in 1750–75 wider ideological resonance in the changing context of the time. If such insurrections were to be perceived as personal or collective struggles or even wars of liberation, press reports of them by implication painted as oppressors those who

fought against them. To see their fellow countrymen in that light was uncomfortable for Britons nurtured on stories of how the nation itself had historically resisted political enslavement by Stuart kings. That irony has not
been lost on historians. But it was also something to which contemporaries
alluded when they argued around 1770 that Britain's continuing role in
transatlantic slavery was incompatible with its status as a civilized nation—
that is, one based on values of personal freedom and benevolence.[50] African slave resistance and reports of its brutal repression were not easily
reconciled with that self-image.

On the evidence of philosophical and religious works, of imaginative
writings, and of newspaper content, negative attitudes toward the slave
trade had become much more commonplace in Britain by the third quarter of the eighteenth century. Even as the nation's investment in the slave
trade was reaching then unprecedented levels in 1763–75, in consequence
in part of the acquisition of more potential sugar colonies in 1763, intellectual and public opinion appeared to be hardening against Britain's continuing involvement in slave trafficking. The root of that opposition was
fundamentally ideological: trafficking was increasingly seen as both inhuman and inconsistent with the values of freedom and sociability that permeated British literature and newspaper output in the emerging age of
sentimentalism. The political economist Malachy Postlethwayt's shift from
arch-defender to skeptic of Britain's role in the slave trade in the twenty years
before his death in 1767, as noted elsewhere, was instructive and a sign of
the times. So was evidence of mounting public sympathy for antislavery
even among writers on the West Indies.[51] Fewer and fewer Britons were prepared publicly to advocate for the slave trade as the century wore on. Of
those who did, most had a personal stake in its continuance.[52]

To infer from the above that early moves to outlaw the British slave
trade, such as MP David Hartley's motion in 1776, mentioned in chapter 5,
reflected extraparliamentary pressure would be an exaggeration. The motion was essentially impromptu; there was at that time no known pressure
group outside Parliament to coordinate or mobilize opinion or action. But
that did not mean that Hartley's motion was of such little importance as is
commonly assumed. To the contrary, despite its heavy defeat, the motion

placed the issue of the slave trade on the political agenda. It did so moreover at a time when civil war within the Old British Empire was about to
break out between mother country and its mainland North American colonies. As is well known, that was occasioned ostensibly by colonists' resistance to efforts by the British government to impose taxes on them as a
contribution toward covering the nation's rising debt burden caused by the
French and Indian (or Seven Years') War of 1756–63. Those moves provoked accusations of oppression and "political enslavement" among white
colonists conscious of their rights to traditional British liberties as well as
of their lack of representation in Parliament.[53] Such allegations, in turn,
were sharpened by British efforts to coerce colonists into acquiescing to
their demands in measures that divided British opinion by 1775, with some
sympathizing with the colonists' stance. Among them were individuals and
groups who combined such sympathy with antislavery attitudes. Significantly in the current context, the British authority's coercive measures in
the thirteen colonies encouraged some to see parallels between the nation's
slaving history and its actions to subdue white colonists prepared openly
to challenge them. The imperial crisis thus propelled public antislavery
sentiments on to the political stage. It is important to look at how that happened and what its implications were for the rise of abolitionism as a political cause and as a social movement after 1783.

In a study based on Newcastle-upon-Tyne and Norwich, historian Kathleen Wilson highlighted the capacity of eighteenth-century English towns,
with their taverns, assembly rooms, and street theater, to be instruments
"of cultural and political struggle that both mirrored new social hierarchies
and refashioned the parameters of political debate."[54] In support of her arguments, she drew heavily on newspaper materials, which, among other
things, revealed imperialism's influence in shaping the nation's changing
sense of identity. It, in turn, became interlocked with what she described
as an "anti-corruption critique of authority that identified national, social,
and moral ills with the distribution and exercise of political power."[55]
    Evident before 1750, that critique assumed heightened intensity,
greater social inclusiveness, and an expanded political agenda in the age

of the American Revolution. Domestically, several developments contributed to that process. Among them was religious revivalism centering on a
mix of Protestant dissent or nonconformity and Anglican evangelicalism,
which raised the profile of leaders such as John Wesley as well as some Anglicans. The latter included William Warburton as a standard-bearer of
changing social norms and values.[56] But research by James Bradley and
others has shown that, by the time that, for example, Wesley was putting
to paper his thoughts on slavery, religious nonconformists were engaged
with a range of contemporary political issues, thereby enriching the local
urban political cultures that Wilson explored. Nowhere was that more evident than during the crisis with the mainland North American colonies.
Widely covered in the press, the crisis animated occasionally fierce political debate in some towns and cities. That was particularly evident in places
with contested parliamentary constituencies, where elections exposed local divisions over the colonial strife. Focusing on religion's "social nature"
and links between "the experience of the material world and religious
views," one study relating to Bristol, a city with a substantial material interest in the crisis, identified an underlying "rhetoric of political and economic inequalities and their connections" in the city's election contest in
1774.[57] More specifically, the study located some Bristol dissenters' identifying politically with the American colonists' defense of their personal liberties within a larger context in which, aware of their own inferior social
and legal status in Britain, they supported the rights of the disadvantaged
as a counterweight to the power of the rich. If that outlook was more widely
shared, it suggested that in the heat of the crisis of liberty that deepening
colonial conflict engendered, religious dissent added a new layer to Wilson's
depiction of an evolving English, maybe British, urban political culture. It
involved a critique of the misuse of power to perpetuate legal, moral,
and social ills, including inflicting slavery on others. And it followed that
religious dissent became another component of a British politics capable of
discerning, in Wilson's words, "the possibilities of a libertarian or virtuous
imperial polity and the nature of its links to the 'nation.'"[58]

Transatlantic slavery itself did not figure directly either in Wilson's
analysis or in that of the Bristol election of 1774. But by that date dissenting

groups were inclined to be sympathetic to colonial political rights as well as to antislavery. It is probable therefore that the plight of African slaves was not far from the thoughts of dissenters when they pondered the American crisis or indeed their own disadvantaged standing in British society. Some may indeed have been alarmed when in the same year, 1774, an American congress argued that the British government's coercive measures might presage the diminution of Britons' own liberties. That idea soon elicited a stinging rebuke in 1775 from Samuel Johnson, who, while defending government policy toward the colonies, famously queried why it was that "the drivers of negroes" in mainland British North America were among those making "the loudest yelps for liberty."[59] Casting doubt on whether British liberties were at risk, Johnson's vitriolic intervention contrasted with that of others more sympathetic to the colonists' cause who chose to remind the world of Britain's historic role in promoting transatlantic slavery. One of the more notable was Tom Paine, who in an article in the *Pennsylvania Journal and Weekly Advertiser* in early 1775 denounced the "wicked and inhuman ways" by which "the English" pursued the slave trade. While acknowledging the colonists' complicity in enslaving "multitudes" of Africans, he urged Americans to reflect that they themselves "now are threatened with the same" and to renounce their association with "Traders in MEN."[60]

Despite their differences over the legitimacy of American resistance to Britain's tax and other measures, Johnson and Paine were nonetheless firmly on the same side where ending trafficking in enslaved Africans was concerned. Their positions underscored the existence of a broad coalition of voices hostile to slavery and human trafficking even as the nation was dividing over the colonial crisis. Their public exchange also revealed how the stain of association with African slavery could be used to damage reputations of defenders of whites' liberties. An unanticipated outcome therefore of the colonial crisis was by 1775 the entanglement of African enslavement with transatlantic ideological and political debates about the rights of white subjects under the British crown. Thereafter it was impossible to separate such debates, and the springs of insurgent consciousness they embodied, from the question of African slavery.

In the intensifying heat of the colonial crisis in 1774–75, antislavery rhetoric on both sides of the British Atlantic began to transition toward political action. Within weeks of publishing his 1775 article on British slaving, the exiled Paine became a founding member of America's first antislavery society.[61] Located in Philadelphia, it was Quaker dominated but in addition to Paine included among its founders Benjamin Franklin, an associate and correspondent of the MP David Hartley. The society met with understandable hostility among whites south of the Mason-Dixon line. But southern planters came to accept Paine's subsequent arguments in favor of independence laid out in *Common Sense* in 1776 following the extraordinary decision in November 1775 of Lord Dunmore, then British governor of Virginia, to offer freedom to any slave prepared to enlist in the British forces once military skirmishes between British and colonial troops had occurred farther north.[62] Formal outbreak of war in July 1776 sucked the air out of America's earliest abolitionist society. The issues the society highlighted continued nonetheless to influence politics and the law in emerging states north of the Mason-Dixon line during and after the war and to bedevil American constitution making and politics nationally following independence.

If the Philadelphia antislavery society was one outcome of the rhetorical exchanges between Johnson and Paine in 1775, another was David Hartley's motion to the House of Commons in early 1776 condemning British slaving on grounds of religion and natural rights. A philosopher's son educated at Oxford, Hartley developed a liberal outlook that saw him embrace antislavery and the need for reconciliation with the colonies by the 1770s.[63] Both surfaced during a lengthy and detailed correspondence with Franklin, who shared Hartley's antislavery beliefs as well as his efforts to reconcile the colonies and mother country until late during the developing imperial crisis. As noted elsewhere, they corresponded over slave trade abolition before the Johnson tirade in 1775. As late as November 1775 Hartley saw the eradication of slavery in mainland North America, which he described as a "vice" and as "contrary to the laws of God and man, and to the fundamental principles of this Constitution, and from which yours [that is, the colonists'] are derived," as a first step toward the British and Americans jointly "establishing the fundamental right to liberty of all mankind."[64] To further that ambition, he contemplated the possibility of giving colonial slaves the right to trial by jury, a measure unlikely to be considered favorably in the slaveholding colonies. Against that background, however, it seems very likely that Hartley saw moves to outlaw British slaving as part of the same liberal agenda.

Considered politically inconceivable by his fellow parliamentarians in 1775–76, Hartley's hopes on all accounts were fatally undermined even while he was penning them by, among other things, Lord Dunmore's cynical and desperate efforts to encourage Virginian slaves to support the British cause. As with the American antislavery society, the deepening conflict and resulting war ensured that a political silence fell over the future of the British slave trade until the mid-1780s, with Hartley's motion in 1776 becoming for some at least a distant and faint memory.[65] The motion marked nevertheless the first step in giving political form to antislavery ideas. Both literally and figuratively it was a child of the American crisis that erupted in 1763–76 and in which ironically for those in power the central issue in question was the liberties of free whites within the British Atlantic Empire. It also signaled that some in Britain, including politicians, had reached a stage of personal moral reasoning to undertake a course of action regardless, in words that Wilberforce would use in 1789, "the consequences be what they would."[66] But the embryo from which the Hartley motion emerged had been conceived and nurtured over decades, and its personality reflected the moral and religious content of the groundswell of public antipathy toward slavery and the slave trade that had been building for decades. Once properly marshaled by the "assiduous and affecting eloquence of . . . new pleaders in the cause of humanity," as Granville Sharp later put it, "the naturally reflective disposition" of the nation would become an impossible force politically to ignore.[67]

In 1783 his friend Benjamin Vaughan urged Benjamin Franklin to finish the autobiography he had begun before the War of Independence, noting that during "the immense revolution of the present period," it was vital that "good people" not "cease efforts deemed to be hopeless" and not take instead "their share in the scramble of life, or at least of making it comfortable principally for themselves."[68] Vaughan's remarks to Franklin were pertinent to steps to end the British slave trade at that time, a move that Franklin evidently favored in correspondence with David Hartley before 1776. The House of Commons overwhelmingly rejected Hartley's motion in that year. Writing in 1792, another abolitionist, the philosopher and parliamentarian Edmund Burke, also acknowledged that around 1780 "an abolition of the slave trade would have appeared a very chimerical project."[69] But by 1792 Burke recognized that something fundamental had changed and that a real possibility of achieving abolition existed. That he attributed to the "popular spirit" which he saw as evident outside Parliament "and which has carried it through" to the House of Commons at that time. For Burke, slave trade abolition was no longer the chimera it might have appeared twelve years earlier or when Hartley put down his motion in 1776. For him the change was linked to the management of public opinion, or the "perseverance and address to excite the spirit" he detected. He was not alone in thinking that way. As an opponent of abolition noted in 1790 when reflecting on the strength of the anti–slave trade agitation, "The minds of most men are in some degree prepossessed upon the subject."[70]

Ten years after Vaughan wrote to Franklin, the planter and British historian of the West Indies Bryan Edwards offered a stern defense of British Caribbean slavery but conceded that "nothing is more certain than that the Slave Trade may be very wicked" and that the "age itself is hourly improving in humanity."[71] First published in 1793, such words spoke to the underlying disposition of the British people on which Sharp commented and which he assumed others, including himself, had helped to agitate. There was some truth in that. Yet neither Edwards's nor Sharp's earlier commentary should induce one to assume that in 1776 public opinion in Britain wholly or even largely acquiesced in the nation's slaving or that there was a sudden burst of national enlightenment after 1783. The fact was that a seismic shift in attitudes toward the slave trade had been taking place in Britain from at least the 1730s. It found expression in philosophical and religious treatises, in imaginative writings, and in the press. It was more than isolated or disconnected observation. It had internal intellectual coherence and logic. And it excited latent public sympathy. The problem was that in 1776 it lacked formal coordination; it still remained to be politically mobilized. As Burke observed in 1792, however, the situation had changed radically from the mid-1780s, transforming the idea of slave trade abolition that Hartley had placed before Parliament in 1776 into an active public campaign to deliver it. That involved, as Sir George Savile, a sponsor of the Hartley motion, observed in 1783, recognizing that "nothing in this world is to be done by solitary efforts" but rather by sometimes accepting as accomplices those with whom one might not always be "sentimentally nice."[72] What Savile and Hartley still failed to appreciate, however, is that effecting political change required more than bringing accomplices together. It depended, as Burke acknowledged in 1792, on mobilizing public feelings around "a simple method" of action and, equally importantly, on building an organization capable of channeling those feelings in ways sufficient to give them effective political leverage or will.[73] How that was achieved is our next subject.

PART THREE

Politics

EIGHT

"To Interest Men of Every Description in the Abolition of the Traffic"

Mobilization and the "Take Off" of Abolitionism

THE FOUNDING IN May 1787 of the London-based Society for Effecting the Abolition of the Slave Trade can be seen as a pivotal moment in the history of British abolitionism. It represented the formal establishment of an extraparliamentary body with a specific remit to pursue the eradication through law of the nation's trafficking of Africans to the Americas.[1] The founding may be considered as the initiating event of a remarkable social movement, the seeds of which had been sown in the preceding decades. Just four years earlier Quakers had petitioned Parliament to end the trade, so it is unsurprising that the majority of the society's twelve founding members were Friends. Among the others was Granville Sharp, who had pursued through the courts the freeing of enslaved Africans in England. Another was Thomas Clarkson, a Cambridge graduate who had written a prize-winning essay while at university on trafficking of the "human species." He published it in 1786, and thereafter, like Sharp earlier, devoted his energies to ending the enslavement of Africans. Often in the shadow historically of William Wilberforce, who from 1789 championed the anti–slave trade cause in Parliament, Clarkson presented an essential bridge between the people at large and Parliament in growing the anti–slave trade campaign in 1787–92. Over that same period, the membership of the London Society, in tandem with the leadership of the campaign in other towns and cities, quickly expanded to include more non-Friends, thus building a more broadly based ecumenical body and movement.

Quakers were few in number and politically ostracized, so it was immediately evident that the London Society would need to broaden its wider public appeal to achieve its goals. The minutes of one of its meetings in July 1788 emphasized that goal while linking it to the society's political ambitions. The society's aim was "by diffusing a knowledge of the subject, and particularly the Modes of procuring and treating slaves, to interest men of every description in the Abolition of the Traffic; but especially those from whom any alteration must proceed—the Members of our Legislature."[2] The statement embodied an agenda for social change that by that date replica committees or societies founded after May 1787 in Manchester and elsewhere in Britain had also embraced. Some but not all of them were Quaker inspired. Together, they looked to mobilize local resources and sympathy in order to continue to press elected and other politicians nationally into acting to rectify a perceived social injustice or evil. As such, their collective approach anticipated the theoretical ideas behind the Overton window, noted in chapter 6. Their objective was clear, as was their strategy for achieving it. Moves to mobilize resources and opinion reflected an understanding of where between abolitionist activists and the British slavery interests the balance of political power lay in 1788. It was heavily weighted in Parliament in favor of slavery. Accordingly, a coordinated, ecumenically diverse, and sustained expression of public disquiet about the immorality of the trade in African slaves was required to reweight that balance, to give, in short, antislavery ideas and sentiments political legitimacy and thus enhanced and continuing political traction. As measured by the flood of petitions to Parliament in 1788–92, the resulting upsurge in public antagonism toward the slave trade was both unprecedented and historically unmatched in not only British but also global history. It almost certainly exceeded the initial expectations of the predominantly Quaker founders of the London Society. Its scale was testament to the breadth of the long-standing growth in public nervousness about the trade's compatibility with British values that accompanied the nation's successful pursuit of slaving over the previous century. Its outpouring in 1788–92 changed the country's political mood irrevocably, even if the actions of the nation's legislature failed to endorse that shift in law until 1807.

The anti–slave trade campaign was one of a series of organized pro-
tests in Britain between the 1760s and 1830s in what historical sociologist
Charles Tilly has labeled the age of mass politics. Among other issues to
excite such protest was Catholic emancipation, parliamentary reform and
the franchise, and trade unionism. Some individuals became activists in
the pursuit of more than one cause, but of the various issues to prompt campaigning, the one relating to slave trade abolition achieved the earliest success; none of the others realized their objectives, wholly or in part, until at
least twenty years after the slave trade was outlawed. That, by itself, is perhaps testimony to the peculiar opprobrium that became attached in British minds to the nation's identification with trafficking Africans. It may be
testimony, too, to the exceptional skill, resources, and strategic insight with
which those who organized the campaign against the slave trade, outside
and inside Parliament, brought to bear in developing it from the late 1780s
onward. Tilly went on to describe those exhibiting such skills as "political entrepreneurs."[3] Insofar as that term applied, it seemed especially so
to those who managed the successful anti–slave trade campaign.

That campaign offers an early British example of what Tilly and other
sociologists consider a social movement. Tilly defined "social movement"
as "a sustained organized challenge to existing authority in the name of a
deprived, excluded, or wronged population."[4] As a definition it accorded
with those of other sociologists when he was writing; it still commands
broad agreement. Scholars also agree, however, that analysis of social movements requires an understanding of specific aspects of them. Analysis of
those leaves room for interpretive disagreement, thereby giving rise to differences in theories of social movements. The differences largely revolve
around issues of timing, of sociopolitical context, and of motivation on the
part of participants.[5] Tilly recognized the importance of some of them as
he explored relations among structural change, growing affluence, and the
rise of mass politics in industrializing Britain as well as between spontaneity and "imposed consciousness" in motivation.[6] Putting aside for the moment the details of Tilly's arguments, resolving issues of timing, context,
and motivation lies as much at the heart of analyzing the social movement
surrounding slave trade abolition as of any other.

My task is to explain why and how the anti–slave trade movement in Britain in 1787–92, unique as it was in the international history of abolitionism, arose when it did. It involves looking for answers to several key questions. Why did a small group of committed abolitionists launch in 1787 a campaign to mobilize public support to end the British slave trade? What resources did they harness and direct in doing so? And why did so many people, apparently from diverse backgrounds, respond so positively to the campaign leaders' call to arms in 1787–92? Providing answers to such questions involves looking at issues such as the campaign strategy, timing, social capital, and self-reflexivity on the part of those who enlisted in the movement. Those answers, in turn, shed light on the leadership qualities of the anti–slave trade campaign and on the wider relation between antislavery and British industrialization, both of which have been the subject of prolonged and as yet unresolved historical discourse.

Embodied in the London Society's minutes of July 1788 were two key ideas that had informed the anti–slave trade campaign from its formal initiation just over a year earlier. The first was to focus the campaign solely on ending the slave trade, not on challenging slavery itself. Given the then prevailing intellectual beliefs, which abolitionist leaders doubtless knew, about the immorality of slavery, electing to focus only on slave trade abolition was clearly a deliberate strategic choice. It had implications for the campaign that need to be recognized. And it requires some explanation. The second idea was to elevate public awareness of the evils of the slave trade with a view to bringing moral pressure on legislators, as "those from whom any alteration must proceed," to revoke the right of Britons freely to engage in trafficking Africans by sea. Put together, the two ideas or principles suggested an agenda for a social movement that was both conservative in tone and respectful of British constitutional protocols in practice. In that respect, from its earliest days, though addressing a practice that itself was inherently violent, the anti–slave trade movement assumed a mantle of peaceful protest that distinguished it from some other forms of collective action in what was a revolutionary age. That was implicit to some extent in the movement's early Quaker leadership. But it was an aura that the movement was able largely and successfully to sustain even as the cause faced international challenges beyond its control from 1789 onward to its political respectability. In sum, early decisions about strategy allowed the campaign against the slave trade to avoid being tarnished with notions of radicalism linked to overt attacks on the property rights of British West Indian planters. It retained throughout a demeanor or sense of moral righteousness, humanity, and political legitimacy. Moderate in terms of its objective, and courageous and virtuous in pursuing a "worthy" principle, the campaign would still require adaptability to "shifting political contexts" to effect delivery in 1807 of its primary goal.[7]

There is little doubt that members of the London Society of 1787 and its later incarnations tended to favor abolition of slavery. Its founding was in fact preceded by published works condemning the institution. One was that of the Anglican clergyman James Ramsay, whose pamphlet protesting the slave trade followed his critical reflections on the treatment of slaves in the sugar colonies.[8] The choice of campaigning against trafficking of Africans rather than Caribbean slavery itself was likely based largely therefore on a political rather than moral judgment, a feeling or calculation of what the society believed parliamentarians at that time might be persuaded to countenance.[9] It was also in tune, however, with a growing tendency to see the slave trade as more than just an appendage to a distant system of colonial slavery; it came to be a pursuit capable itself of repulsing those made aware of its practices. From at least the 1730s, the legality of some British slaving practices, notably in Africa, had been questioned. Against a background of increasing and more detailed newspaper stories about British slaving activities from around 1750, concerns over the trade then became embroiled in public discourses during the crisis with the thirteen colonies in 1763–76. That was the context for David Hartley's motion in Parliament in 1776 against British slave trading. Moreover, the process by which slaving was being subjected to open questioning resumed as soon as the war with the former colonies ended in 1783. Quakers petitioned Parliament in that year to outlaw slave carrying. Their petition was followed by James Ramsay's pamphlet in 1784 condemning the trade, by the protracted judicial case in 1783–85 over an insurance claim for slaves jettisoned alive from the ship *Zong* in 1781, and by the publication in 1786 of Thomas Clarkson's Cambridge dissertation on the trade in the human species.[10] The last painted a grim picture that identified the slave trade with planter indifference to the consumption of enslaved Africans in Caribbean sugar production as long as new supplies of captive Africans were available. Clarkson would later confess to a belief that ending the slave trade might quietly lay "the axe at the very root" of slavery itself.[11] But in choosing to target the trade in slaves, rather than slavery, the London Society in 1787, of which Clarkson was a member, was doubtless aware of the accumulating, unfavorable image of the trade by then in vogue and the possibilities that created of exciting a public outcry against it. Political considerations thus almost certainly determined the London Society's decision to focus on African trafficking in 1787, but it was a rational choice made easier by the growing catalog of severely damaging trade-related stories in the public domain that some of its members had helped to identify.

Within a year of the founding of the London Society, the abolitionists' strategy had begun to bear fruit. From December 1787 petitions against the slave trade began to reach Parliament, with a petition from Manchester condemning the trade being one among the first substantial wave in early 1788. A signal perhaps of the wider public mood from a city closely connected with Liverpool slave trading, the Manchester petition has assumed major symbolic significance among some historians of British abolitionism.[12] Together with other petitions in early 1788, as well as evidence on conditions on British slave ships supplied by the London Society to parliamentarians, such representations evoked a positive response from some members of both Commons and Lords, exposing in the process disharmony within elite political circles over how to react to public pressure to end British slaving. Though no guarantee of the cause's political success, it gave the effort political legitimacy and its leaders grounds for optimism in their strategy's capacity to deliver change. One immediate and unanticipated outcome was the passing in July 1788 of the Dolben Act, named after Sir William Dolben, MP for the University of Oxford, the purpose of which was to regulate slave-carrying capacities of British ships and thereby reduce shipboard slave mortality as part of "the cause of humanity."[13]

Though the measure was decried by at least one ministerial opponent in the Lords as the product of a "five days fit of philanthropy," one supporter reaffirmed its legitimacy by reminding his fellow legislators that the issue of conditions on slave ships "had been before the public a year, during which time evidence and petitions were presented to Parliament."[14] More significantly still, however, Dolben's intervention, which Prime Minister William Pitt supported, arose against the background of Pitt's own decision, endorsed by opposition leader Charles James Fox, in May 1788 to respond to petitioning against the slave trade by establishing a formal parliamentary inquiry into the trade and its future. Upstaging one then under way by the Privy Council that Pitt had previously endorsed and that would finally report in April 1789, the parliamentary investigation launched in late 1788 might have been considered a delaying tactic intended to defer or postpone consideration of abolition. Seen from the abolitionists' perspective, however, it cemented the political legitimacy of their cause. Though success was far from certain, by July 1788 the future of Britain's slave trade was assuredly on the nation's political antenna, and the strategy adopted by the London Society and reaffirmed in its minutes of the same month had, with assistance from politicians' disunity on the issue, helped to put it there. The society's primary task from that date was to mobilize the embryonic movement's resources to maintain the political momentum for abolition it had begun to establish in the preceding year.

Between 1788 and 1792 the anti–slave trade movement sustained the twin-track, but interconnected, approach—people and Parliament—that it had developed before July 1788, though adapting it to changing circumstances, notably in the context of the opening of the parliamentary investigation into the slave trade that Pitt had authorized in May of that year. The idea behind the campaign remained the same: to appropriate public opinion in ways consistent with constitutional proprieties and to provide evidence on the slave trade sufficient to persuade enough parliamentarians to accept the righteousness of the cause and to act accordingly. Each strand of the approach was intended to maximize exploitation of the political space opened up in May–July 1788 by the speeches of Pitt and Fox and the ensuing Dolben

Act, even though the act could be construed as endorsing rather than damning the trade. Each strand, too, required the mobilization of resources to educate potential supporters and to enlist the widest possible expression of public sympathy for the movement.

From what we know of the leadership of the anti–slave trade movement inside and outside Parliament—from the designated parliamentary leader, William Wilberforce, through the membership of the London and other committees that formed the backbone of the movement from 1787 onward—it is evident that it drew inspiration and commitment from spiritual conviction. For many, investing energy and time in the movement was a sacred duty dictated by a need to express in their personal lives instructions on how to conduct themselves as Christians that they took from reading and reflecting on scripture. Within that mentality they had a duty as Christians to save Africans, as fellow human beings, from enslavement and, in freedom, to help them take responsibility for their own spiritual and material well-being and for the manner of their dealings with others. Manners and morality were inextricably interlinked. But spiritual beliefs or instruction alone were insufficient to build a social movement capable of convincing others who did not share so deeply the same divinely inspired purpose to act. Indeed, it may have been only those with sufficient personal wealth or income and thus possibly time and other resources to commit heavily to the anti–slave trade cause that were in a position actively to play leading roles in shaping the movement in which it became embodied. It is important, in other words, to look at leadership of the anti–slave trade movement in the round, to look beyond the spiritual values from which it drew energy and commitment and to appreciate the financial and other resources, including contact tools and professional and marketing skills, on which it could call in its determination to build a political case for abolition and that brought public pressure to bear on parliamentary decision-making. The anti–slave trade movement was, in effect, more than ecumenical. It was shaped, too, by wealth and class as well as by emerging and related questions of empowerment in later eighteenth-century industrializing and urbanizing Britain.

The historical record offers a number of examples of how leaders of the anti–slave trade campaign at national and other levels used the resources available to them to try to influence Parliament. For instance, the majority of the earliest members of the London Society were more than just Quakers; they were mainly in business, too, offering the campaign both financial means and talents essential to its promotion.[15] The society's assets in those respects expanded as others with business skills joined it within the two years after it was founded. Its accounts suggest that the society distributed, often free to recipients, thousands of copies of reports, texts, and even woodcuts of slave ship models throughout the country in 1788, using Quaker networks and the skills of Quaker publishers such as the London-based James Phillips to do so.[16] It commissioned works, including poetry, condemning the trade and financed lecture tours and research trips, notably by Thomas Clarkson. Intended, like publications, to spread the campaign's messages, the last unearthed first-hand witnesses with knowledge of the trade as well as objective data pertinent to its human costs to present to the parliamentary inquiry on the trade established by Pitt after May 1788. It was also while on one such tour outside London that Clarkson related in 1808 attempting to elicit support for the cause from newspaper proprietors and editors in various towns across the western counties of England from Cheshire south. Evidence of a surge of newspaper reports on the slave trade in the period that Clarkson identified offers some support for his initiative's success.[17] But newspaper coverage of the trade was already growing before 1788, and there is strong evidence, too, that Manchester-based and other campaigners had approached newspaper publishers in their own areas to assist in publicizing anti–slave trade activities, including petitioning drives, before Clarkson made his approaches.[18] From the outset, abolitionists inside and outside London realized the value of vigorous, evidence-based propaganda in building and sustaining their campaign and mobilizing a mass audience or constituency, and were prepared to invest money, personal skills, and time in order to do so.[19]

Clarkson's and others' efforts to enlist support from newspapers can also be seen as an element in contact arrangements critical to building a social movement. Newspapers were conduits of information and ideas essential to broadening individual experiences, activating public discourse, and even facilitating group action, including petitioning. In that respect, they reinforced other contact tools that brought together like-minded people within particular localities or across regions, creating, in turn, through co-ordinated petitioning and other public activities the appearance, indeed the reality, to observers of a well-orchestrated, highly integrated national campaign. Recent local studies have shed important light on how that campaign was built not just from the top down but also from the bottom up, often drawing on existing social capital and institutional practices. A study based on the prosopography of learned professional activists in Plymouth has shown how they relied from 1788 onward on local traditions of petitioning, on associational cultures, and on a thickening set of local institutions to mount and sustain local antislavery activities that ultimately transcended denominational and partisan boundaries.[20] Similarly, a study of the signing of anti–slave trade petitions has shown how in Manchester its spatial distribution or clustering was shaped by the physical layout of neighborhoods, voluntary associations, religious institutions, clubs, inns, and taverns, suggesting that patterning of relations based on kinship networks and other forms of associational activity that cross-cut class lines were as much part of shaping community engagement with the anti–slave trade cause as wider shifts in collective consciousness.[21] In both cases, they add substance to theory that indicates how social movements can build on or emerge out of "pre-existing social ties, habits of collaboration and zest for collective action that comes from common life."[22]

While it is possible to claim that in local contexts abolitionism was unexceptional in emerging organically alongside other causes and appeals and in drawing on existing institutional protocols, it remains difficult to disconnect, where slave trade abolition was concerned, local activities from the wider national movement for change of which they became a part. Historians offer insights into how grassroots activity evolved into a broader social movement. Richard Huzzey, author of the Plymouth study, observed how antislavery activists there were innovative in directing associational culture towards national political pressure, while Kinga Makovi, who wrote the Manchester study, noted the part played by inns and taverns as places where visitors and itinerant merchants with knowledge of the larger campaign interacted with local communities. Such examples are consistent with more broad-brush studies that identify Quaker and other religious knots of networks that acted as conduits or contact tools within, and equally importantly, between communities, ensuring widespread and coordinated flows of literature, public information, and news of events and meetings pertaining to slave trade abolition.[23] They, in turn, played a part in promoting regionally or nationwide other activities designed to reinforce the anti–slave trade message.

Among such activities was the consumer boycott of slave-produced sugar launched at the height of anti–slave trade petitioning in 1791–92. Estimates suggest that at the boycott's peak one in thirty Britons, or around three hundred thousand, participated in it. Seemingly largely female led, it appears also to have been principally urban based.[24] The boycott coincided with publication of Mary Wollstonecraft's *Vindication of the Rights of Women* in 1792, which might be seen as legitimating female involvement in abolitionism, an issue to which I return later.[25] But it was the writings of others, notably the Dublin-born poet and Quaker Mary Birkett and the London Baptist, printer, and pamphleteer William Fox, who most likely stirred the abstainers from sugar, reminding them of how, in Birkett's words, "sweetened tea" made them complicit in "th'extremity of misery" suffered by enslaved Africans.[26] Of the two, Fox was probably more influential, with his widely circulated pamphlet going through no fewer than twenty editions within a year of publication in 1791.[27] Together with Birkett's poetry, the pamphlet offered evidence of the power of literature to stir individuals' moral conscience, illustrating, as the Quaker abolitionist Elizabeth Heyrick noted in 1824 in reflecting on the 1791–92 acts of personal abstinence, how "greater moral revolutions have been accomplished by the combined expression of *individual resolution,* than were ever effected by acts of Parliament."[28] An endorsement of collective action, Heyrick's observation may also be seen as retrospective testimony to the perceived intensity and public reach of the anti–slave trade movement by 1792, a movement in which women had found a way to participate.

Underlying the contact tools and the sugar boycott accompanying that movement one may discern elements of what Tilly saw as the identification of mass politics with structural changes in later eighteenth-century

British capitalism. The general thrust of his work had echoes of arguments linking British slave trade abolition to industrialization, aspects of which, posited by Eric Williams and others, have been addressed elsewhere in this book. But that still leaves open issues about industrialization's impact on the social movement underlying abolitionism that Williams, with his specific focus on ideology, conspicuously failed to address and that later historians still labor to resolve. In terms of organization, one can observe such linkages. They were implicit in the occupational structure and skill sets of the London and other committees that from 1787 onward looked to advance the anti–slave trade cause. They were evident in the production and sale of Wedgwood porcelain items intended to popularize images associated with the cause. And they appeared in the associated growth of religious and other social networks that accompanied rapid urbanization as an essential, but sometimes neglected, component of the Industrial Revolution from the mid-eighteenth century. That revolution, historian Patrick O'Brien has urged, was "quintessentially industrial, commercial and urban."[29] It has also been seen to embody an emergent knowledge-based economy and society, with burgeoning towns and cities and their mix of professional, skilled, and unskilled occupations and new associational activities forming its core.[30] That transformation, which arguably included a humanitarian revolution, was clearly firmly under way by the time that the so-called take off into industrialization in 1783–1802 is said to have occurred.[31] The fact that mobilization of public opinion in Britain against the slave trade occurred within that same period was surely not accidental. Beginning in the third quarter of the eighteenth century and accelerating thereafter in tandem with the nation's population growth, urbanization was synonymous with developments in marketing and other services, social networking, and knowledge production and dissemination that were themselves fundamental to the organization of the movement to end the slave trade.[32] The leaders of that movement were more than just what Tilly labeled "political entrepreneurs." They were "business" leaders able to perceive latent possibilities for organizing social change in the age of industrialization and urbanization in which they lived. They were, moreover, often prepared to sink denominational and other differences to pursue a shared and, in this case, moral objective.[33] In that respect they pioneered a novel form of targeted collective action that would help to change history.

Growth of organizational capacity and skill were necessary but not sufficient to explain the large influx of people drawn into the anti–slave trade movement in 1787–92. We need also to understand why so many people felt sufficient empathy toward the desperate—and increasingly well publicized—plight of Africans packed on British slave ships to behave as they did. Why did so many sign petitions condemning the trade? Why did hundreds of thousands abstain from consuming sugar in 1791–92? Why did women choose openly to wear jewelry carrying images of enslaved Africans? The answers lie in individuals' personalities as well as in the feelings and beliefs that guide human action. They involve a complexity that embraces personal experience, imagination, and psychology, including individuals' capacities for self-reflexivity and extrapolation. They are precisely the issues that motivated historian Lynn Hunt's study of the invention of human rights, in which she argued that historical change results from individuals changing their minds and, through sharing their experiences, altering the social context.[34] In altering that context, the mobilization of anti–slave trade opinion changed irrevocably the political framework in which British slaving was debated from 1787. Yet why so many individuals felt compelled to join others to protest its continuance at that time and in the way they did still remains to be fully explained. With the distance of time, it becomes more difficult to do so.

Religious teaching that saw trafficking of Africans as dehumanizing and incompatible with Christian values was doubtless fundamental for some, maybe many, who supported the cause. That was almost certainly true of national and even many local leaders of abolitionist bodies. It may well have applied also to some of those who signed petitions, abstained from consuming slave-grown sugar, or otherwise took action to protest the trade. There still remains some room for doubt about that proposition, not least because the identities of so many of those who engaged in extraparliamentary anti–slave trade activity in 1787–92 and beyond are, like the enslaved Africans with whom they empathized, lost to the historical record. Nevertheless, insofar as those guided by religious instruction took their guidance from the pulpit or preacher, it is perhaps tempting to identify their behavior as reflective of a form of imposed consciousness. Commonly associated with class-based theories of history, that approach may be unfair to those supporters of abolitionism who did so, in part at least, as a result of self-reflexivity about their own status and lived experiences in a society in which their own political influence was at best highly circumscribed and in some cases almost nonexistent. It is likely that British industrialization and urbanization helped to create the personal circumstances under which such self-reflection might occur and even expand socially. In that respect active engagement in the anti–slave trade movement perhaps represented an act of self-empowerment as much as one of natural or religiously inspired empathy for Africans thought to be unjustly and cruelly treated.

Some historians identify anti–slave trade mobilization with assertiveness in the public sphere on the part of an emergent middle class, but what lay behind that characteristic, even if true, is not wholly clear.[35] The imperative of sacred duty, particularly among dissenters and evangelical Anglicans, offers one explanation. But it is possible to suggest at least one other that complements rather than challenges that largely spiritual one. It concerns lack of empowerment at a time of revolutionary socioeconomic change. Its roots may be traced to several sources linked to British urbanization. Towns and cities were often epicenters of British religious revivalism from the 1740s. Rising levels of urbanization also brought rapid growth of professional and other middle-class occupations, some of which attracted religious dissenters. That combination can be seen to have underlain middle-class leadership in the anti–slave trade movement.

Yet, even as structural and religious developments were strengthening the potential voice of middle-class dissent in British society, an emerging disconnect between the contemporary geographies of political representation, which still favored the south and east of England, and of demographic change, which saw absolute and relative increases in population overall and urban centers particularly in other parts of Britain, tended to hinder its expression politically. Discontent with that situation began to find outlets from the 1770s in demands for constitutional change and parliamentary reform. For dissenters such demands were reinforced by discrimination against nonconformists in British social and political life, and they were further sharpened by the disenfranchisement in practice of many within the middle-class dissenting community through residence in burgeoning urban communities without actual representation in Parliament before 1832. Unsurprisingly, perhaps, among the early supporters of political reform were some who embraced antislavery ideas, exposing a sense of identity among dissenters excluded from or deprived of formal political influence at home with Africans whom they saw as being brutally and unfairly wronged in the name of the British state and the national interest. That underlying pattern would persist through the early nineteenth century but moves for constitutional and political reform stalled in the 1780s and remained largely unthinkable politically in Britain in 1789–1815. In its absence, therefore, political empowerment for many British middle-class dissenters anxious to influence national policy but effectively denied representation in Parliament entailed challenging through other available means a palpable wrong they saw as wholly inconsistent with their own ethical values. The social movement against the slave trade to which middle-class dissenters contributed in 1787–92 was in part an expression of their personal anxieties and political frustrations.

Personal anxiety, experience, and frustration of other sorts were perhaps instrumental, together with religious convictions, in explaining why some others joined that movement. Take, for instance, the apparently sizable involvement of women in the sugar boycott campaign of 1791–92. Again religion may have played its part, as some of those urging abstention highlighted sugar's connotations of sinful overindulgence as well as its associated costs in terms of African lives.[36] Some historians also identify the boycott as an expression of "female virtue," notably feelings of compassion and sympathy, as well as reflecting assumptions about sugar's polluting effects on the body as a symbolic representation of larger society.[37] But it is worth noting, too, that, like most men, women had no voting rights in 1792 and, even more, within marriage at least experienced other major forms of legally sanctioned discrimination that in effect denied them the personal autonomy and financial independence enjoyed by their spouses. Mary

Wollstonecraft's famous work on the rights of women, published coincidentally during the sugar boycott, contained references to slavery, but her
work seemed more of a commentary on female subjugation in general than
an overtly antislavery text.[38] Nonetheless, in referencing slavery, *A Vindication of the Rights of Women* was reflective of earlier publications dating
from the 1730s onward, in which marriage and assumptions about female
character became vehicles for denying women rights and thereby rendering them, like slaves, naturally exploitable and ultimately expendable.[39] It
was thus not difficult for women such as Mary Wollstonecraft by 1792 to
discern parallels between their own status in British society and the stories and images in newspaper cartoons of sexual predation and other abuses
of women slaves on British slave ships or on Caribbean sugar plantations.

Despite the evident sensitivity of some, mainly middle-class and self-
educated, British women to their oppressed status, there was nevertheless
one area in which married women generally still retained a modicum of personal autonomy similar to that of spinsters or widows. It was in managing
household budgets: it remained, it seems, largely their own "private sphere"
or domain.[40] And it opened up possibilities for all women, but especially
for married women sensitive to their status, to deploy that limited power
for a noble social and political end. Household management gave women a
not insignificant choice, given the long-standing and growing British use
of slave-grown sugar: to refuse on behalf of their own families to endorse
consumption of a product so clearly destructive in its production to the lives
of the enslaved and thus so central to sustaining British slaving with all of
its own destructive consequences.[41] Boycotting sugar seemed to provide a
means to checking slavery's inherent cycle of destructiveness. To adopt it
as a family policy represented in 1791–92 an act of empowerment and humanity on the part of legally and socially disadvantaged women in British
society. Through the writings of Elizabeth Heyrick a generation later, female abolitionists would continue proudly to celebrate it. Abstention was
virtuous at several levels.

Complex elements of self-reflexivity and of issues of power, albeit in
different combinations and guises, may also be detected when considering
why some groups of artisans or workers opted into the social movement that

succeeded in placing the slave trade on the nation's political agenda. As with middle-class men and women, the identification of artisans with nonconformity and their sympathy for the colonial cause in the imperial crisis before 1776 were indicative of a latent, spiritually based empathy for those who, like enslaved Africans, they believed to be wronged. But precisely why they and perhaps other working people elected to sign petitions condemning the slave trade in 1787–92, as some evidently did, and what impact their own life experiences had on that decision are still issues worthy of study.

The symbolism that some historians have attached to the Manchester anti–slave trade petition of late 1787, said to have been signed by as many as one-fifth of the town's fifty thousand residents, should not distract attention from why so many of those in a town with such direct economic ties to transatlantic slavery felt compelled to denounce British slave trading on grounds of morality and justice. A similar argument applies to the Sheffield metalworkers that collectively produced knives and other trade goods exchanged for slaves in Africa yet chose in 1788 to petition against the slave trade. Neither Manchester nor Sheffield had elected representatives in Parliament at the time, so, in common with some other industrial towns, petitioning likely remained their residents' principal option to make their voices heard politically on the national stage. As in the other cases discussed earlier, for some petitioners religious scruples likely trumped perceptions of economic self-interest. When informed of what slaving entailed, they felt unable to condone an activity that offended their moral principles. Yet even among those whose objections rested on religious principles, their understanding of the conditions that enslaved Africans had to endure may well have intersected with anxieties they themselves felt about trends in the condition of labor in their own communities, thereby reinforcing moral concerns about slaving practices. Assuming that to be the case, then one needs to explore the material or social circumstances of their community's life that encouraged some individuals or groups in places with vested interests in British slaving publicly to express empathy for enslaved Africans. Religious or fundamental moral scruples aside, part of the answer in northern industrial towns such as Manchester and Sheffield lay in technological and other changes in the local economy that precipitated

deteriorating conditions of labor of some groups, thereby giving rise to public concerns on their behalf. It was human fallout from economic change
as much as its productive consequences that mattered.

The timing of the Hallamshire metalworkers petition of 1788 perhaps
owed much to the founding in that year of the *Sheffield Register,* a newspaper that regularly reported on the local anti–slave trade petitioning effort
and had a radical editor who pronounced that "the rights of mankind are
better defined and understood than at any former period."[42] That pro-
nouncement reflected a pattern of growing political radicalism in the Sheffield region that, as historian Julie MacDonald pointed out, culminated in
1791 in the formation of a local society for constitutional information that
adopted a reform agenda modeled on that of Tom Paine. Within a year of
its founding the society had a membership of some two thousand. It was
said that its members were mostly from "the lowest order," thereby making it, according to another historian, Albert Goodwin, "the first working-
class reform association of any consequence."[43]

The emergent political radicalism from within which the Hallamshire
anti–slave trade petition arose was probably in part linked to religious revivalism in which South Yorkshire shared, but for some, including metal
grinders in the cutlery trade, it may also have been a mask for wider concerns about threats to their status within the local Sheffield community by
the late 1780s.[44] That threat arose out of changes in the cutlery industry
and its local political influence that had begun at least two decades earlier.
Cutlery grinders were traditionally leading members of the Cutler's Society, which oversaw the cutlery trade and played a prominent role in politics in Sheffield, but their local status declined in the later eighteenth century
as technical and product innovations in the cutlery business prompted
greater diversity in the society's membership. By the 1780s new cutler masters were seeking to refuse entry into the society of journeymen and ap-
prentice grinders, thereby curbing their power. Further moves to dilute it
through renegotiating contracts of employment intensified division within
the cutlery trades, provoking grinders to strike and unionize in an effort to
protect their traditional autonomies and privileges. It seems likely that,
against that background, grinders were prominent among the signatories

to the Hallamshire metalworkers' petition against the slave trade in 1788. Perhaps more than any other constituency of metalworkers in the Sheffield region at that time, they had good reason collectively to respond to appeals to the rights of man and to empathize with the misery viewed as unjustly inflicted on enslaved Africans. Seen from another perspective, their support for the petition may be construed as part of a process of redefining their own sense of community within a changing and, from their viewpoint, more uncomfortable, even oppressive, social environment.[45]

It is possible to discern similar forces in play in the background to the first Manchester anti–slave trade petition that was launched in December 1787. Just as in Sheffield, where the new editor of the *Sheffield Register* was seemingly instrumental in promoting the Hallamshire metalworkers' petition, so a visit from the outsider Thomas Clarkson may have helped to stir the Manchester community to action. In October 1787 Clarkson addressed a heavily attended public meeting at the Collegiate Church in Manchester, where, he later reported, the pulpit from which he spoke was surrounded by some forty to fifty Black people. The biblical text on which he based his lecture related to oppressing strangers. Christians, he argued, knew the "heart of a stranger," having once been strangers in Egypt. Thus, he believed, Christians should comprehend how deporting Africans from their homeland to an alien place "must be productive of pain to the ear of sensibility and freedom."[46] Clarkson's speech doubtless touched an emotional nerve with his congregation, thereby contributing to local moves to launch the petition that landed in Parliament two months later. As one would expect, it was not a movement with which local manufacturers and merchants dealing in cotton textiles sympathized. To the contrary, they joined Liverpool slave merchants whom they regularly supplied with such textiles for export to Africa in consistently opposing slave trade abolition through 1807.[47]

As with the Sheffield anti–slave trade petition, the names of those who signed the first Manchester one are unknown. But for at least some who did sign, the sensibility toward strangers that Clarkson evoked may have extended to growing numbers of new arrivals within Manchester's community whose lives were increasingly being blighted by cycles of human misery associated with British transatlantic slavery. Their experiences offered their observers in Clarkson's audience possible insights into the suffering of enslaved Africans far away. Moreover, the Africans attending his lecture supplied a visual human connection to them. Prominent in the audience's mind perhaps were cotton textile workers, for Manchester had become by the 1780s the hub or principal gateway of the national cotton textile trade, of which a sizable proportion was devoted to supporting Britain's slave trade. Consequently outdoor (or home-based) spinners and weavers, cotton spinning mills, and textile-related machine production figured prominently in the economic landscape surrounding the town.[48] Whether any of those textile workers attended Clarkson's lecture or signed the subsequent petition is now impossible to say with certainty. But among the many who did attend or among others living in or near the town who shared the mounting public interest in the trade, it was surely impossible for some at least not to have reflected on evidence of degrading conditions of labor observable or encountered on their own doorsteps as they pondered and protested the treatment of enslaved Africans. Industry-based human misery was a growing presence among the population of Manchester and its surrounding towns by 1787. At its heart were technological changes in spinning and weaving cotton that fostered the factory system and revolutionized the structure and growth of the British cotton textile industry and the working conditions of those employed in it. By 1787 that revolution was well advanced where cotton spinning was concerned. And, as historian Jane Humphries has urged, "the new view of industrialization," with its emphasis on aggregate output and other measures, "does not dispense with the spectacular changes in technology, labour processes, industrial relations and industrial organization that drove the old industrial revolution."[49] That old view placed humanity and trauma at the heart of the economic history of industrialization.

The rise of factory-based cotton textile production would ultimately undermine traditional outdoor spinning and weaving activities that had earlier supported the industry's growth. As early as the 1780s, however, it was already prompting concentrations of spinning operatives and machine minders in mill towns or villages where hundreds of men, young women, and children came together to live close to and to labor in cotton mills. The children included some as young as seven to ten years old who were recruited from workhouses; their reward for their labors was sometimes employer-supplied board, lodgings, and Sundays of instruction in Christianity. Others among the juvenile workforce were from single-parent families, forced to seek employment to boost the family income.[50] Young or adult, male or female, all employees were subjected to a work regime of unremitting toil over long hours, of brutally repetitive task-centered activity, and of unbending discipline as mill owners strove to make a return in a competitive environment on their sizable investments in buildings, equipment, and stocks of materials. Historians have seen parallels between plantation slavery and factory work, where it has been said that as a booming sector the West Indian plantation economy produced "a paradoxical model of the factory complex, with its mix of modern technologies and ancient mode of labor domination."[51] If, as has been claimed, "there is no mystical attraction between pain and humanitarianism," then seen from the perspective of observers of Lancashire's emergent factory methods, practices there may have appeared superficially as familiar as what they knew of experiences of enslaved African men, women, and children in British America.[52] Unlike slavery, factory labor offered adult workers potentially higher annual earnings, largely from a combination of increased weekly wages and more year-round employment. That was its primary attraction. But with it came significant human costs in terms of individual autonomy, of pride in work, and of personal physical and mental well-being. Overcrowded and unsanitary living conditions compounded the last, increasing labor turnover and thereby encouraging regular recruitment and training of new "strangers" to work the mills.[53] In common with other British urban centers at the time, growth of mill town populations (and thus working people) depended, like Caribbean sugar plantations, on in-migration, not natural reproduction. Persistence of such migration was an indication of the fateful mix of hopeful yet commonly unfulfilled dreams of those who elected, or were obliged by circumstance, to enter the then unregulated labor market that fed growth of the early factory system.

Nineteenth-century commentators were often damning of life in British textile mill towns, which provided rich source material for theories of alienation and wage slavery, among other things. But thoughts on the inhumanity or soulless nature of the factory system surfaced even as it was first emerging. Adam Smith extolled the economic benefits of the division of labor he identified with it, yet he also attributed a mental mutilation or deformity that could afflict workers subjected to seemingly unending, mindnumbing, repetitive task work. It revealed a tension between his "abstract theory of capitalism" and real-life experiences of labor conditions.[54] His views were also shared by other Scots, among them Adam Ferguson and John Millar as well as by the editor of Smith's unpublished essays, Dugald Stewart, who in 1795 saw a need for growth in education and other forms of knowledge-based "intellectual improvement" in society to mitigate the socially damaging effects of the "subdivision of labour accompanying the progress of the mechanical arts."[55] Later writers would compare that process to "slave work," or what the late Victorian age socialist William Morris would see as "useless toil" or "mere toiling to live, that we may live to toil."[56] But long before Morris distinguished between pleasure-giving work and useless toil, the dehumanizing influence of factory work was vividly captured in William Blake's celebrated remarks, probably composed in 1804, on mentally fighting back against England's "dark, Satanic Mills."[57] Such sentiments were in turn reminiscent of an even earlier observation by one of the factory system's pioneers, the hosier Jedediah Strutt of Belper in Derbyshire, who pronounced in 1765 that, contrary to what "some Divines wou[l]d teach," the "getting of Money" was "the main business of the life of Man."[58] Factory masters themselves, some of them dissenters like Strutt, did not, of course, inhibit workers' pursuit of Christianity. To the contrary, some insisted that child laborers receive religious instruction, perhaps with a view to instilling discipline in their lives.[59] But Strutt's chilling, unemotional words offered an insight into a brutally exploitative state of mind that from the late seventeenth century onward was more commonly identified with British sugar planters. From at least the 1680s they stood accused of being willing to subordinate Christian values or humanity to their Godlike pursuit of mammon. Recognizing their susceptibility to being seen as barbarous savages on account of their neglect of slaves' well-being, some planters sought by the 1780s to diffuse that suggestion by emphasizing their British imperial roots and cultural ties and to distinguish their behavior from that of Creole white "slave-holders," a term by 1789, according to one planter, identified with repression and bloody-mindedness.[60] As a line of defense it failed, but insofar as it invited listeners to compare life on sugar plantations with that in factories or other industrial venues, it probably only reinforced within those knowledgeable of the lives of textile mill workers a sympathy for Africans, who, as a former sailor on a Liverpool slave ship claimed in 1787, "arise from friendly sleep to pining pain; . . . to Slav'ry, hunger, cruelty, and toil."[61] And if any of Clarkson's audience in Manchester in October 1787 wanted assistance in discerning parallels between the two, the presence of some fifty Africans in the Collegiate Church at the time he spoke perhaps afforded it.

Manchester and Sheffield were, of course, just two of many places that forwarded anti–slave trade petitions to Parliament in 1787–92. Even if we assume, however, that my interpretation of the mix of feelings and motives underlying the petitions is broadly accurate, we cannot be sure that it reflected that of people nationwide who joined the movement. As historian John Oldfield has rightly observed, towns and places distant from the epicenters of the British Industrial Revolution petitioned Parliament too.[62] It would, nonetheless, be premature to dismiss the circumstances in industrial towns as unusual or exceptional as we seek to uncover the emotions that made people feel so hostile nationally toward the slave trade. Industrial towns were probably disproportionately engaged in the very early petitioning campaign against the trade. They were some of the earliest, too, in which newspapers, a major and growing source of public knowledge of the slave trade, began actively to encourage or support those campaigns, tapping into local feelings in doing so. And they were home to a large segment of the expanding nonconformist urban or metropolitan middle-class groups that some historians see as a key component of the anti–slave trade movement, bringing to it an energy derived from religious principles as well as from a sense of personal injustice and of empathy toward others they saw as being treated unjustly. That sense was perhaps implicit in their religious training but was likely reinforced by experience or perception of political and social injustices identifiable with an emergent industrial-urban landscape that, in its human consequences, challenged increasingly prevalent ideas of sympathy and sociability.

Historian Lynn Hunt has argued how through enlarging human experiences imaginative literature encouraged personal processes of self-reflection, the outcomes of which, when shared with and by others, altered social contexts and thereby helped to promote change historically. Similar processes involving multiple forms of literature, including newspapers, contributed from the mid-eighteenth century at least to some rethinking of the nation's role in slave trading and slavery as part of an emergent humanitarian revolution in ideas. I maintain, however, that the rethinking process concerning slavery, which was not confined to Britain alone, became embedded in other larger transformative changes in British society, thereby giving it a peculiar and more dynamic social resonance nationwide. Pivotal among those other changes were nonconformist religious revivalism and economic changes identified with the Industrial Revolution. They intersected in various ways to ensure that in 1787–92 emergent industrial towns across the nation joined London, its commercial capital, to become principal arbiters and drivers of growth of the anti–slave trade movement. Geographies of petitioning and other collective action associated with that movement indicate, it is true, that the residents of such towns were not alone in feeling the pain and sense of injustice inflicted on Africans by the nation's commercial and imperial ambitions. It was ultimately a nationwide movement. But it is difficult nonetheless to imagine that the movement that emerged in 1787–92 could have developed on the scale and with such fervor without acknowledging the human emotions stirred by experiences resulting from the onset of the Industrial Revolution. In that sense, the anti–slave trade movement cannot be seen in isolation; it was, instead, a symptom of wider forces of social change in early industrial Britain.

In terms of petitioning and other forms of collective action, the social movement to end the nation's slave trade reached its height in 1792. Thereafter such activities subsided but did not totally dissipate, as another though less intense burst of anti–slave trade petitioning occurred in the years before the outlawing of the trade in 1807. It would be misleading, however, to assume that public interest in the slave trade's future waned after 1792. The opposite, in fact, may have been the case. There is indeed good evidence that while agitation for slave trade abolition abated as Britain became preoccupied with international affairs from 1793, nationwide public interest in the trade and its legal standing remained at least largely unchanged between 1792 and 1807. One measure of such interest lies in newspaper reports. When we track interest through newspapers in the slave trade before 1788 beyond that date, we find that public interest continued to accelerate from 1788 onward, reaching levels in 1804–7 higher than in 1788–92.[63] Interest also appears to have expanded geographically, with a growth of press reports in Ireland, which united politically with Great Britain in 1801, matching that of other parts of the enlarged kingdom. The nationwide interest established by 1792 was at least maintained then through 1807, with an Irish voice being added politically to the cause from 1801. Though the number of newspaper titles represented in the British newspaper archive expanded through 1807 and beyond, growth of reporting about the slave trade in specific publications suggests that in the commercial judgment of their editors and proprietors there remained a strong, even mounting, public appetite for news of the slave trade and its future from 1788 through 1807. Politicians who regularly read the press would, moreover, have probably gained the same impression, while leaders of the abolitionist campaign in Parliament would seek as late as 1804–7 to test and demonstrate the strength of continuing public sympathy for their cause, recognizing its value to maintaining its legitimacy politically.

If the breadth of newspapers' coverage of the British slave trade offers a measure of the public's continuing interest in it, the persistence of their coverage from 1788 through 1807 also provides an indication of the prolonged and intense political struggle that arose in Parliament to determine its future. The mobilization of public opinion in 1787–92 placed the issue of Britain's involvement in trafficking Africans by sea firmly and decisively on the nation's political agenda. But as the minutes of the London Society of July 1788 recognized, only by convincing legislators of the wisdom of outlawing the trade could the society and its followers achieve their objective. Faced with a long history of parliamentary approval of British slaving, abolitionists' efforts to build a social movement to question its practice was necessary to gain political attention for their cause; without it, parliamentary consideration of the trade's future, as the MP David Hartley had discovered in 1776, was impossible to contemplate.

Gaining Parliament's attention, however, was no more than the first step toward winning approval for abolition. With structurally unrepresentative Houses of Commons and Lords and with administrations unwilling for internal reasons to embrace the future of the slave trade as a government measure until very late in the long parliamentary process, winning proved to be an uphill task. The private member bills through which abolitionists sought to advance their case were always open to attack or delaying strategies from various quarters. Some in Parliament had vested interests in the continuation of slave trading; they regarded it as an essential pillar to the growth and prosperity of the British Caribbean colonies and thus the nation's wealth. Others, perhaps greater in number, though less committed directly by personal interest to slaving and slavery, were cautious about pursuing a seemingly radical course or remained to be convinced that abolishing the slave trade, though morally right, was consistent with defense of the national interest. Energizing both of these constituencies from 1789 onward were concerns about the security of the nation and its sugar colonies at a time of outbreaks of slavery-related conflict and violence in the Caribbean basin in 1791 and of war in Europe two years later, each directly linked, in turn, to the French Revolution and its aftermath. Such concerns merged with political factionalism at home to pose immovable obstacles to enactment of abolition before 1805 but which, against a background of demonstrably sustained public interest in the issue, were then addressed and defused through imaginative strategies by abolitionist leaders in 1806–7, thus allowing passage of slave trade abolition on grounds of morality, justice, and sound policy. Still, in a period of nation-threatening conflict abroad and of entrenched and sometimes deeply reactionary conservatism at home, the parliamentary politics of slave trade abolition remained complex, fraught, frustrating, and time-consuming. How they were navigated from 1789 onward and finally brought to a successful conclusion in 1807 are subjects for the next chapter.

NINE

Finding *"a Pathway for the Humanities"*

The Politics of Slave Trade Abolition, 1791–1807

IN HIS *Address to the People of Great Britain, on the Propriety of Refraining from the Use of West India Sugar and Rum,* published in 1791, the radical dissenter and bookseller William Fox accused the nation's consumers of British Caribbean sugar of being complicit in slavery and, given sugar production's costs in terms of African life, in supporting the nation's slave trade. The *Address* is widely seen as the most influential of the many and various pamphlets Fox wrote and published in his lifetime. It rapidly went through multiple editions and, though estimates vary, may have sold between seventy thousand and two hundred thousand copies in Britain and the Americas. It is credited with helping to stimulate the sugar boycott that occurred in Britain in 1792 as one element of the extraparliamentary campaign to end the slave trade that peaked in that year. Even as he sought, however, to challenge people to change their behavior, Fox recognized that getting them to do so would not be easy, noting in the pamphlet's conclusion that "hardened by habit, the mind is with difficulty accessible to the convictions of guilt." He went on to observe how "actions are not easily influenced by the force of moral principle, when counteracted by custom" and when "the greatest violations of duty may be practiced by the conduct of our associates." In effect, tensions within individuals or groups could exist in reconciling actual behavior, rooted in habits or customs, with doing what was morally right. For Fox, change represented "the test of our virtue," requiring individuals "to investigate [their] conduct with the most anxious solicitude."[1]

Viewed through a society-wide rather than an individual lens, Fox's remarks take on fresh significance in the politics of abolitionism. Metaphorically, they are a reminder that the anti–slave trade campaign, driven by its religious attendants or feelings of guilt, was confronted, even at a time of revolutionary domestic industrial and social change, by powerful conservative, even reactionary, forces deeply committed to what Fox labeled prevailing customs and associations, whether in defense of an established identity, an ideological outlook, or a vested interest. Those invested in Britain and in the West Indies in slavery were the most obvious parties to oppose abolitionism. Tensions between the two opposing groups were sometimes exposed when abolitionist campaigners lived in or visited Bristol and Liverpool, which had continuing strong connections with transatlantic slavery and its products. Understanding the strength and representation of slave power in late eighteenth-century British society, with its historic sense of connectivity and identity with that society, is important therefore if we are to examine the contested politics of abolitionism after 1790. By itself, however, it is not enough. For, just as from the 1780s the anti–slave trade campaign attracted support from various social groups or classes, so those who, for reasons of identity and vested interest, resisted calls in Parliament for abolition found support during the 1790s among other legislators unwilling to countenance on moral grounds the proscription of an activity customarily considered as pivotal to Britain's commercial, maritime, and national well-being. In addition to those directly associated with West India interests, parliamentary opposition to the anti–slave trade campaign arose from members of the court and administrative factions close to George III as well as from some Tory and Whig faction leaders, among them government ministers. The reasons behind the stance of such parties varied, but the outright hostility or skepticism of government ministers toward slave trade abolition was particularly significant, making its adoption as formal government policy inconceivable before 1806–7. That was so even though William Pitt, who was sympathetic to abolition, was prime minister for all but three of the twenty-three years before his death in 1806. In their efforts to resist moves to outlaw the slave trade, therefore, West Indian interests found invaluable parliamentary allies among deeply conservative elements firmly embedded in structures of government and political power. An appreciation of their role, as well as that of the West India lobby, is critical to understanding the complicated and tor-tuous parliamentary politics surrounding the anti–slave trade campaign in 1791–1807.

The campaign against the slave trade was one component of a larger mass politics of reform in Britain, against which conservative forces ulti-mately coalesced in the unstable international climate unleashed by the French Revolution. Against a background of growing violence and terror in France and its spread through war beyond French borders, the initial sympathy that some abolitionists evinced for French revolutionaries' goals combined with fears that political debate in London and Paris could pro-voke slave uprisings overseas, realized in 1791 in Saint-Domingue, only strengthened conservative forces' resistance to slave trade abolition from 1792. The mood swing in Parliament associated with shifts in the interna-tional and national environment was mirrored in the changing reception given to abolition bills that William Wilberforce regularly introduced into Parliament from 1791 onward. Following the outbreak of war with France in 1793, slave trade abolition, if not regulation, drifted down the national political agenda through 1799 and fell out of it altogether in 1800–1803 as circumstances dictated. To adapt the argument of the abolitionist and philosopher-politician Edmund Burke, rules of prudence rather than pro-cesses of metaphysical abstraction or logic would ultimately assume pre-cedence over "lines of morality" where outlawing British trafficking was concerned.[2] It would take a revision of international circumstances for Brit-ain in the continuing struggle with France and a corresponding recalibra-tion of abolitionists' arguments and parliamentary strategy after 1803 to reenergize the anti–slave trade campaign in 1804–7 in a way sufficient to allow it to overcome the forces of conservatism that had held abolition in abeyance for over a decade.

In 1862 the Irish professor of law and political economy John Elliott Cairnes described "Slave Power" as "the system of interests, industrial, social and political, which has for the greater part of half a century directed the career of the American Union [the United States]." At the time he wrote, this power was geographically embodied in the Southern Confederacy, which was seeking "admission as an equal member of the community of civilized nations."[3] When Cairnes was writing, there were some four million slaves in the Confederacy, equivalent to one-third of its population and to two in fifteen of the US population as a whole. Historian Moses Finley would later see the antebellum US South as one of three slave societies in the modern world, the others being the Caribbean and Brazil.[4] Cairnes's analysis highlighted the despotic tendencies of slave power in the South, which he identified with a wealthy minority who worked in concert politically to favor their own interests and to give "the tone to the public morality of the nation."[5] For Cairnes it was "this Power, which has directed [the nation's] public policy; which has guided its intercourse with foreign nations, conducted its diplomacy, regulated its internal legislation, and which, by working on its hopes and fears through the unscrupulous use of an enormous patronage, has exercised an unbounded sway over the minds of the whole people."[6]

Cairnes's analysis of the roots of the US Civil War anticipated in its basics that which the West Indian scholar Eric Williams would offer eighty years later to explain abolition of the slave trade and ultimately British Caribbean slavery in 1807 and 1833, respectively.[7] Though different in form, both were seen in essence as outcomes of power struggles between a social order linked to coerced labor and an emergent one based on industrial capitalism and associated with an ideology of free labor. There was, however, one crucial difference between the two story lines: whereas Cairnes depicted US slavery as still vibrant and politically and militarily aggressive through 1861, provoking civil war, Williams saw the British Caribbean planter class (and, by implication, the "slave power" in Britain identified with it) as a declining force, with the ending of the slave trade in 1807 being a measure and product of their retreating economic and political influence in the face of an increasingly powerful industrial capitalism in Britain. The fact that antislavery in Britain was one element within a larger mass politics associated with shifts in the industrial-urban balance of British society may offer some support for Williams's interpretation of why Parliament outlawed the slave trade. But the teleological components of Williams's argument probably understate the continuing power of the British Caribbean planter class and their British allies to resist and frustrate the call for slave trade abolition after 1787. The evidence suggests, indeed, that, though many planters complained in the 1790s of living by treading on the heels of their income, the British West Indian slave economy remained expansive and productive through 1807.[8] Moreover, its commercial and financial importance to the British economy, though perhaps not so great as some imagined at the time and since, showed no sign of abating before 1807.[9] As in the rest of the eighteenth century, therefore, the defense and security of the West Indian slave colonies continued to be a high priority in 1793–1807 for deployment of the nation's military resources, even as Britain was engaged in war with revolutionary France in nearby continental Europe.[10] Against such a background, Williams's interpretation of British slave trade abolition rests on a false prospectus of a diminished slave power in Britain through 1807. The West India interest and its power were, in fact, far more resilient than he seemed to imply. Put another way, the prosperity and security of the British West Indies still mattered to Britain in 1807: the key issue was, would continuance of the slave trade help or hinder their achievement?

The West Indian colonies may have been jewels in the crown of the eighteenth-century British Atlantic Empire, but the slave power to which they gave rise came to reside primarily in Britain, with London at its center. Transatlantic commerce was a key driver of eighteenth-century British overseas trade, and within it, sugar produced in the West Indies by enslaved Africans was the single most important export from British America from 1650 through 1807 and beyond. In return, the West Indies became major markets for British exports as well as the principal destination for slaves carried across the Atlantic in British ships. If the persistence and intensity of British imports of sugar in return for exports of manufactures and other goods underwrote the growth of West Indian slave power, that power's location in Britain resulted from increasing flows of human and capital resources from the sugar islands to the metropolis. Sugar planters frequently bought estates in the home country, becoming absentee planters. Those who lived in the islands commonly sent their sons to Britain to be educated in private schools and Oxbridge or to train at the Inns of Court.

Many of them subsequently returned to the islands, but others stayed in Britain, where, together with the growing numbers of resident absentees, they came to constitute a central component of a socially well embedded yet distinctive and very wealthy West India interest in British society from at least the mid-eighteenth century.[11] Other, equally embedded, British stakeholders in continuing West Indian prosperity and security were London-based agents of British Caribbean colonies as well as sugar merchants, slave traders, bill discount houses, and suppliers of trade goods and services to the plantation economies and slave traders.[12]

Some indication of the collective wealth and influence, locally and nationally, of absentee West Indian planters was provided by the one-time prime minister the Earl of Shelburne, who four years before assuming that office in 1782 declared, "There were scarcely ten miles together throughout the country where the house and estate of a rich West Indian was not to be seen."[13] Though doubtless exaggerated, Shelburne's statement nonetheless underscored the extent to which slave-based wealth was seen to permeate British society. That point has been reinforced by evidence arising from back-projection from slave compensation records of 1834–38, which themselves show how a surprisingly large and variegated range of middle- and upper-class people of different political and religious persuasions across the length and breadth of Britain were custodians of such wealth.[14] Moreover, both Shelburne's remarks and the 1834 compensation accounts excluded the many properties and estates owned by British West India planters and slave merchants before 1807, the construction of which underlay, it has been argued, Bristol's eighteenth-century urban renaissance as well as contributing to the gentrification of parts of Glasgow, Liverpool, and London in the same period.[15] Together with absentee planters, those same groups became important patrons of the arts and education, holders of mayoralties and other offices in local government, and, after 1783 especially, investors in major urban development projects, some of them in support of the West India interest.[16] In short, slave power extended deeply and widely throughout British society at the time abolitionism emerged as a political force.

From 1787 onward the West India interest in its various forms predicted calamitous consequences for the British economy were the slave trade to be outlawed to British subjects. The chief justice of Jamaica declared in 1788 that "stopping further supplies [of slaves] will in a rapid progression destroy the English sugar islands." A year later, a leading planter of the island saw abolition as "the maddest piece of work that was thought off [*sic*] since the Croisades," while in 1792 the agent of the Codrington plantation in Antigua claimed it would be "totally subversive to our ancient System of Colonization," precipitating an "overset" of the British islands.[17] The claims persisted in private and public until the eve of abolition itself. Historian Seymour Drescher has noted, however, that, in opposing abolition, British slave interests from the outset "made no attempt to initiate a broad counter-petition drive or to reach out beyond their traditional interest network."[18] For each petition in favor of the slave trade between 1787 and 1792, there were more than a hundred against it. Petitions in its favor, moreover, tended to attract on average far fewer signatories than those opposing the trade. Unlike the anti–slave trade movement, therefore, advocates for the slave trade eschewed, even decried, mass politics. They chose, instead, to organize their efforts through established or newly created planter and merchant associations in cities such as London, Bristol, Glasgow, and Liverpool with close connections to the West Indian slave plantation complex.[19] And they focused, in Drescher's words, "their collective political energies on pamphleteering, parliamentary lobbying and private appeals to sympathetic government officials."[20] That strategy was consistent with historical interpretations that see parallels between Britain's eighteenth-century mercantilist state and models of political economy and rent seeking, whereby vested interests exploit political connection and influence in order to maximize economic gain or to protect existing advantage.[21] But the Lewis Namier–like view of politics implicit in that interpretation, with its privileging of faction and interest over principles or ideas, perhaps needs to be qualified by recognizing that behind the methods used by the West India interest to advance its case was a shared sense among slaveholders of their role, as free-born Britons, in protecting white liberty, security, and identity in the face of "the oppression, destitution, and dependency that characterized the lives of the enslaved majority" among whom they resided.[22] Seeking to defend their own vested interests, they portrayed themselves, in short, as architects or even the embodiment of Britain's national interests abroad.

Against that background, London agents of West Indian colonies such as Stephen Fuller, who represented Jamaica, were key advocates of the status quo where slave trading was concerned. They were one of several means by which West Indian planters made their feelings known to British political circles.[23] They delivered long experience of personal and formal dealings with relevant government bodies as well as legislators favorable to the proslavery cause. They were assisted in the last respect by strong representation in Parliament of West Indian and related interests. It is estimated that in the third quarter of the eighteenth century some forty to sixty members of the House of Commons at any one time had West Indian interests.[24] That figure may have risen to as many as seventy-four following the general election of 1780, at which time perhaps, with support from planters in island colonial assemblies, the absentee planter group in Britain represented a powerful transatlantic Westminster lobby or even what historian Trevor Burnard has described as being a "ruling class at the peak of its power."[25] Whether or not that was the case, the representation of West Indian interests in the Commons remained strong through the last quarter of the century. Recent estimates suggest that the West India lobby, while falling somewhat after the end of the Parliament elected in 1780, still seemingly numbered around fifty-five MPs when William Wilberforce famously launched in May 1789 the parliamentary campaign to outlaw the slave trade.[26] Such levels of representation reflected, among other things, the ability of those with West India connections to outbid others in elections for parliamentary boroughs, in the process reaffirming the sustained wealth of Britain's slave power in the emerging age of abolitionism.

It has been pointed out that MPs with West Indian interests did not operate wholly as a united block.[27] Moreover, numbering forty to sixty for the most part, those with a personal connection to the sugar colonies, constituted no more than a tenth of all members of the Commons at any time. In that respect, even if it worked as a unified group, the West India interest's capacity by itself to frustrate efforts to outlaw the slave trade might seem to have been limited. That, however, is to overlook the frequent absence from the Commons of many country MPs, thereby ensuring that, as the London agent for Massachusetts Bay pointed out in 1764, the West India interest could "turn the balance [of the House] on which side they please."[28] That comment was not without relevance at the time of abolition bills in the 1790s, when with support from others a modestly united West India interest could defeat such measures in thinly attended sessions of the Commons. Its power was acknowledged as early as 1789 when Wilberforce saw that, with a few exceptions, the great majority were opposed to abolition, since the trade "was absolutely essential to their property," and it was manifest even when as in 1794 moves to curb the trade were confined to precluding the nation's traders from supplying slaves to British planters' competitors, a move that saw "the whole force of the West India interest" arrayed against Wilberforce's proposal.[29] What such reactions showed was that in order to succeed ardent abolitionist members of Parliament had to enthuse and convince uncommitted members to embrace their arguments. Without their support, the West India lobby remained, with support from conservative elements of the political establishment, a formidable obstacle to the abolitionists' achievement of their goal. In short, abolitionism may have been born in the towns and shires of Britain, but its political achievement depended on devising a strategy to win votes in Parliament.

The political framework within which the West India interest and its allies traditionally functioned ensured that their lines of argument against efforts to outlaw the slave trade were conventional, even predictable.[30] Many were embodied in pamphlets, some of which circulated widely.[31] Some chose to attack the credentials of abolitionists, but the principal line of defense for the trade offered by planter, merchant, and other of its advocates was the ruination that abolition would visit on the sugar islands (and the nation) and the advantage that rival powers such as the French would gain by Britain acting alone.[32] Pragmatic economic and political arguments were sometimes complemented by claims that the slave trade was positively beneficial to Africans, improving their temporal and even their spiritual lot relative to what they experienced in their homeland.[33] Designed to counter suggestions of slavery's immorality, such arguments were amplified by claims that, contrary to abolitionist assertions, the slave trade was not

inconsistent but rather consonant with "the principles of the LAW OF NA-
TURE, the Mosaic Dispensation, and the Christian Law, as delineated to
us in the Sacred Writings of the Word of God."[34] Despite such efforts, the
arguments advanced by supporters of the trade were insufficient to halt the
shift in the "cultural playing field" that accompanied and underwrote abolitionism.[35] Indeed, acknowledgment of that shift was at times reflected
in proslavery publications that openly accepted the need for trade regulation and improved treatment of slaves in the colonies.[36] But, as content
analysis of debates in Parliament reveals, economic and political concerns
dominated the arguments of the West Indian interest in 1787–1807, with
up to two-thirds of contributions from opponents of abolition emphasizing national economic and security issues above all others. Among abolitionists, by contrast, moral considerations dominated contributions in
almost exactly the same proportion.[37] That polarization of arguments
persisted, moreover, largely unchanged from 1787 through 1807, as the
West India interest and its allies sought politically to deflect increasing
public moral discomfort about the nation's involvement with slaving by
underscoring the potential economic costs of abandoning it.

To underscore abolitionism's costs was to appeal to more conservative and uncommitted elements in Parliament. It reminded them of both
the trade's long-standing political legitimacy and its identification with assumptions, seemingly grounded in historical experience, that associated
national power with expansion and security of the empire and its connections with property rights in enslaved Africans. Sustaining that position
sometimes involved challenging claims by some like Thomas Irving, inspector general of British exports and imports, who in evidence to Parliament followed Adam Smith in casting doubt on the value of colonies and
slavery to the nation's prosperity.[38] For its defenders, debate about the trade
involved more than the future of the West India interest; in a revolutionary
age at home and abroad, it was a referendum on the existing economic and
political order. That did not mean that allies of the West India interest were
wholly oblivious to the shifting moral sentiments of the time or were unprepared to make concessions, even if grudgingly. Though Liverpool slave
merchants vehemently opposed them, for most there was a willingness to

accept restrictions on British ships' slave-carrying capacities, such as those endorsed by Parliament in 1788 and 1799.[39] Seemingly endorsing the trade's continuing legitimacy, such regulation was charitably construed in 1788 as "an honourable commemoration of [Parliament's] humanity," less charitably, as a "sudden fit of philanthropy, which was but a few days old," and "should not be allowed to disturb the public mind."[40] But from the West Indian interest's perspective, the principal challenge always lay in measures to abolish the trade, whether wholly or in part. For abolitionists the goal was to transcend regulation, reassuring in some ways though that was, and to win outright abolition.[41] Doing so would ultimately require transforming debates over the morality of the slave trade into a question of its compatibility with national security, or, in other words, to fight the West India interest on its own terms. That would, in turn, entail aligning abolitionists' moral objections to the slave trade with concerns about the defense of the nation's interests in the West Indies in the context of changing international circumstances.

Parliament was always the primary focal point of proslavery interests' opposition to slave trade abolitionism. In 1788–90 they largely concentrated on prolonging and influencing the outcome of the investigations into the trade undertaken by both houses of Parliament. Assuming this was, at least in part, a procedural device to delay, potentially indefinitely, other parliamentary moves to end the trade, it had some immediate success. But it was insufficient to prevent Wilberforce in April 1791 from introducing an abolition bill in the Commons. This was the first of nearly a score of measures proposed in Parliament in 1791–1807 to end British slaving, whether wholly or partially, immediately or gradually (table 9.1).

The parliamentary struggle over slave trade abolition can be divided into three phases of voting patterns relating to these various measures, particularly in the Commons. The first and shortest of these covered 1791 and 1792 and was a high-octane period when petitioning of the House reached unprecedented levels. In these two years, not only were some of the highest numbers of votes cast in the Commons on both sides of the slave trade debate, but there was also a sharp reversal from disapproval to approval of abolition proposals in the Commons. This reversal prompted opponents

Table 9.1. Sequence of anti–slave trade measures and their fate, 1791–1807

(1)	(2)	(3)	(4)
Apr. 1791 (B)	A	Lost 88:163	
Apr. 1792 (B)	A	Won 234:87	A+B
Feb. 1793 (M)	A	Lost 53:61	
June 1793 (B)	C	Lost 29:31	
Feb. 1794 (B)	C	Won 56:38	B
Feb. 1795 (M)	B	Lost 61:78	
Mar. 1796 (B)	B	Lost 70:74	
May 1797 (M)	A	Lost 74:82	
Apr. 1798 (M)	A	Lost 83:87	
Mar. 1799 (M)	A	Lost 54:84	
May 1799 (B)	C	Won 38:22	B (61:68)
June 1802 (M)	A		C
May 1804 (B)	A	Won 124:49*	B
May 1805 (B)	A	Lost 70:77	
May 1806 (B)	C	Won 35:13	D (43:18)
June 1806 (R)	A	Won 114:15	D (41:20)
June 1806 (B)	D	Won**	D**
Feb. 1807 (B)	A	Won 283:16	E (100:36)

Notes: * First reading vote; second reading, 100:42; third reading, 79:20. Clarkson, *History,*
2:492–94. ** The measure was unopposed.

Column (1): Date of Bill (B), Motion (M) or Resolution (R).

Column (2): Proposed outcome: (A) immediate abolition; (B) abolition within a year; (C) geographical restriction on trade, either in delivery (1793 and 1794 to foreign colonies) or sourcing supplies in Africa (as 1799); (D) restriction on new ships entering the trade.

Column (3): Vote in Commons: first number represents votes in favor (where known), second number votes against.

Column (4): Fate: (A) The Dundas amendment (see text) to the original bill approved in the Commons, including gradual abolition and immediate restriction on British slave deliveries to foreign colonies, passed 230:85 (the 85 were against any abolition) (Clarkson, 2:449), with a compromise date for ending the trade in 1796 approved 151 to 132; (B) blocked in Lords, e.g., 1799 bill lost in Lords by 68 to 61 (Clarkson, 2:484); (C) no progress; (D) passed the Lords in a vote; (E) voted through in the Lords before the Commons.

Sources: History of Parliament website for member William Wilberforce, https://www
.historyofparliamentonline.org/volume/1790-1820/member/wilberforce-william-1759-1833;
Thomas Clarkson, *The History of the Rise, Progress, and Accomplishment of the Abolition of the Slave Trade by the British Parliament,* 2 vols. (London: Longman, Hurst, Rees, and Orme, 1808): 2:463 (Feb., June 1793); 2:467 (Feb. 1794); 2:472 (Feb. 1795, which suggests that support for the motion was 57); 2:479 (Mar. 1799), which has voting of 74:82 and may be a confusion with May 1797; 2:508 (May 1806), which was later described by Clarkson as the first bill "which dismembered this cruel trade" (2:509); 2:525 (June 1806).

of abolition to make adjustments in their parliamentary strategy to frustrate it, with the House of Lords being pivotal to that process in 1792 and in the following decade.

The second and longest phase, from 1793 to 1803, was defined by much lower, if more even, levels of Commons voting. The low-level equilibrium of voting in these years favored West Indian slave power and its conservative allies, with defeats for abolition proposals in the Commons outnumbering approvals by seven to two. As Thomas Clarkson observed in 1808, however, "after 1791 no one of the defeats, which [abolitionism] sustained, was disgraceful," with majorities against being "so trifling, that the abolitionists were preserved a formidable body, and their cause respectable."[42] In these years, moreover, measures to regulate insurance practices in the slave trade and to curb carrying capacities of British slave ships gained parliamentary approval in 1794 and 1799, respectively.[43] The third phase of the parliamentary struggle, which began in 1804, culminated in the passing of the Abolition Act of 1807. This period of abolitionist triumph witnessed some resurgence of petitioning to Parliament, though far from the scale of that between 1787 and 1792; newspaper reports of public support for abolition at the general election of 1806; levels of support in the Commons for abolition similar to and, in 1806–7, greater than 1792; and, perhaps most remarkable, unprecedented and decisive majorities in the Lords in the same two years for abolitionist proposals. Faced with Clarkson's "formidable body" of abolitionists, the seemingly well-orchestrated parliamentary campaign of resistance to slave trade abolition mounted through 1803 disintegrated three years later.

Almost two-thirds of the proposals introduced in the Commons in 1791–1804 to outlaw the British slave trade (wholly or partially) were immediately voted down. On the four occasions when a majority in the Commons supported such a measure, the opposition found other means to thwart its passage into law (see table 9.1). The 1792 bill for immediate abolition, which passed the House of Commons by a majority of 147 votes, was subject to what in effect was a wrecking amendment, proposed by Home Secretary Henry Dundas, First Earl of Melville, in favor of gradual abolition, the date for the final ending of the trade being set in 1796. Seemingly reconciling sympathy for abolition with moderation in its implementation, Dundas's amendment secured majority support in the Commons but, in slowing the bill's passage through the House, gave opportunity to members of the Lords to stall it completely. A similar fate in the Lords befell bills passed in the Commons in 1794, 1799, and 1804. In 1794 their lordships used the stalling tactic of demanding new evidence or inquiries; in 1799 and 1804 they simply voted down the bills.

These procedural barriers underlined the difficulties of navigating through Parliament what were in effect before 1806 private member bills to outlaw the slave trade. They are a reminder, too, of the difficulty of detaching the issue of slave trade abolition, including opposition to it, from adjustments in the broader British political landscape after 1783 connected to radical change at home and abroad. Attitudes toward the slave trade in effect became entangled in or identified with wider and growing fears relating to mass or popular politics, radical reformism, social order, and, following revolution in France in 1789, national security. Perceptions of abolitionism's populist or radical tendencies reinforced beliefs in some parts of Britain's political establishment of the risks to order posed by the emergence of the anti–slave trade movement in tandem with other reform impulses, some of which were supported by abolitionists. But reactions in Britain to the French Revolution, with its radical messages, its dissolution into bloodshed and civil war, its association with the 1791 Saint-Domingue slave uprising, and its envelopment in international conflict across the English Channel from 1792 onward, raised existing alarms about the movement in some domestic quarters to new and politically more acute levels. In some ways, in fact, they deepened fault lines in British political identities and allegiances that had emerged during the American Revolution, in the process fostering the consolidation, at least until 1806, of the position and power of those hostile to abolition. In sum, the global fallout from demands for liberty, equality, and fraternity in France in 1789 strengthened the hand of the West Indian interest and its allies in resisting efforts to outlaw the British slave trade for most of the period through 1807.

Excluding those with an immediate stake in the slave trade's continuance, the high politics of opposition to outlawing it pivoted around groups generally committed to defending the status quo. One such group was the court and administrative faction attached to George III. Hostile to Charles James Fox and distrustful of William Pitt, the king was a consistent and outspoken opponent of abolition through 1807. Though not all the court opposed abolition, as late as May 1805 the king, when faced with the possibility of restrictions on British slaving, continued to decry the "ideas of false phylanthropy [sic]" that he believed threatened the future of the British Caribbean islands.[44] He yielded ultimately only when faced with decisive votes in favor of slave trade abolition in both Commons and Lords. The monarch's stance on the issue reflected racist views as well as his status as the religiously and politically sanctioned head of state of a property-based, socially hierarchical nation founded on the rule of law and the defense of personal liberty, and the international standing and national security of which was seen to rest on a maritime empire linked to the enslavement of Africans. But white colonists in British North America directly challenged the king's authority when they successfully rebelled in 1776–83 against his rule, helping to instill a deep paranoia in the king and his friends toward populist agitation and its threat to social order. Events in France from 1789 and in Saint-Domingue from 1791 compounded that paranoia, in the latter case through linking revolutionary change in France to slave insurrection, huge loss of life and property, and economic collapse in the Caribbean's richest sugar colony. Even before the Saint-Domingue uprising, however, fears that agitating the issue of the slave trade in Parliament could provoke unrest, possibly even rebellion and social disorder, in the British Caribbean were articulated, sometimes to those with access to the king's ear.[45] In revolutionary times, those fears ensured that George III and his entourage would become consistent allies of the West India interest in resisting slave trade abolition.

The king's party was not alone in aiding West India interests in such resistance. There were elements within the ranks of both Tory and Whig politicians, too. Critically, they included important office holders within the four Tory-dominated administrations that governed the nation from December 1783 to January 1806, a period moreover in which, other than in 1801–4, Pitt was prime minister. It included one coalition administration with the Portland Whig faction in 1794–1801. Even before that administration, however, Henry Dundas, then home secretary, played a leading role in killing the abolition bill that passed the Commons in 1792. And he was not the only Tory minister in the period before the coalition to resist outlawing the slave trade. Another was the deeply conservative, even reactionary, Edward Thurlow, later Lord Thurlow, who was lord chancellor through 1792. Yet another was Charles Jenkinson (or Lord Hawkesbury), who was said to be close to the king, was president of the Board of Trade in 1786–1804 and joined Pitt's cabinet in 1791. Elevated to the Lords in 1796, Jenkinson would assume the hereditary title Earl of Liverpool, which would pass, on his death in 1806, to his son, the MP Robert Banks Jenkinson, Lord Hawkesbury (1796–1806). Like his father, the younger Jenkinson opposed abolition. A future Tory prime minister, he was foreign secretary in the 1801–4 Tory administration of Henry Addington (later Lord Sidmouth), who was himself hostile to abolition, and then home secretary in Pitt's short final administration through January 1806. Another leading Tory office holder at that time, John Fane, Tenth Earl of Westmorland, took a similar stance. From Thurlow through Westmorland, therefore, there were powerful Tory opponents in Pitt's cabinets to slave trade abolition, thereby inhibiting its adoption as government policy.

That ministerial opposition was strengthened in 1794–1801 by the entry of Portland Whigs into government in coalition with Pitt. Reflecting divisions within the Whigs that had roots in the American war, the realignment of the Portland faction was precipitated, among other things, by what one contemporary labeled Fox's "dashing so deeply into the slave trade" and by his "unfortunate encomium of the French revolution."[46] The second of those issues ultimately induced Edmund Burke in 1793 to describe his former mentee as the enemy of "the order of things long established in Europe."[47] Comprising what some saw as "Whig grandees," the Portland faction included some natural allies of the more reactionary elements in the Tory party hostile to slave trade abolition.[48] The most prominent was its leader, William Henry Cavendish-Bentinck, Third Duke of Portland, whom one historian has described as one who revered "the traditional social order," was "intrinsically suspect" of innovation, and disdained popularity as "almost always a false guide."[49] His family also had West Indian connections reaching back to the early eighteenth century.[50] Assuming the position of home secretary in the coalition administration in 1794–1801 on Dundas's appointment as war secretary, Portland not only joined Dundas and others in helping to stall abolition but, as disorder mounted in nearby Europe and fear of the same spread to Britain, also introduced deeply reactionary measures at home, notably suspension of habeas corpus in 1794 and the passing of anti-association legislation (or combination laws) in 1799–1800.

In the context of slave trade abolition, the importance of these successive, overlapping phalanxes of ministerial allies of Britain's slave power through Pitt's death in January 1806 is difficult to understate. They were key elements of the political environment constraining leading political champions of slave trade abolition such as Pitt and Fox from achieving their ambition in their own lifetime. Contemporaries acknowledged ministers' capacity to stall abolition, if not regulation, before 1806. Referring to Lord Chancellor Thurlow's hostility to the Dolben Act of 1788, which was seen by some as a "favourite measure" of Pitt, Clarkson suggested that Thurlow's behavior had "a mischievous effect, on account of the high situation in which he stood," allowing him to influence "some of the Lords" and, "in taking the cause of the slave-merchants so conspicuously under his wing," emboldened them "to look up again under the stigma of their iniquitous calling."[51] Ministerial opposition on that occasion did not prevent the passing of Dolben's regulatory bill. But the capacity of leading ministers to block *abolition* measures was underscored by Dundas's behavior in 1792 and by splits in Pitt's other cabinets thereafter. Indeed, in 1799 Fox reportedly refused Wilberforce's request to support another attempt to pass an abolition bill, believing that "it stood no chance while the present ministry lasts."[52] The ministry in question was Pitt's Tory-Whig coalition, during which Wilberforce's bills to end or restrict Britain's slave trade suffered regular defeats in thinly attended debates in the Commons. Fox's pessimism, moreover, likely infected others, including ultimately Wilberforce, who elected not to introduce further bills between June 1799 and April 1804, a period which saw Pitt resign in January 1801 over the king's resistance to

Catholic emancipation, to be replaced by an administration even less sympathetic to abolition led by Henry Addington through April 1804. Only when Pitt returned to office as prime minister in that month did Wilberforce resume his parliamentary campaign to end the slave trade. But it was less Pitt's reinstatement as prime minister and more changes in the national and international scene that prompted him to do so. And ultimately it was neither Wilberforce nor Clarkson but others, including new members of the London Society, reformed in 1804, who would oversee the parliamentary campaign that resulted in the abolitionists' triumph in 1807. The new committee included evangelicals from Wilberforce's Clapham Saints, such as Zachary Macaulay, James Stephen, Henry Brougham, Henry Thornton, and Thomas Babington, who were united through marriage ties and the pursuit of "practical Christianity."[53] Equally significantly, though Clarkson resumed his travels to promote public awareness and reported finding in July 1805 that the ardor of "former friends . . . to remain unabated," with "all ranks of people [being] warm in the cause and desirous of lending their aid," it was on "parliamentary action" more than in "the earlier phase of the campaign" that the committee devoted most of its attention from 1804 onward.[54] In doing so they could, nonetheless, increasingly draw reassurance from the continued lively newspaper coverage of the parliamentary proceedings in 1804–7, reflecting, in turn, the popular sympathy for the cause that still prevailed or that, as Clarkson later saw it, could be rekindled and "turned into enthusiasm," thereby furnishing the cause "with endless sources of rallying."[55]

In 1808 Clarkson described the hiatus in parliamentary campaigning from June 1799 through April 1804 as Wilberforce's "deliberate choice." Intended to give "members [of the Commons] time to digest the eloquence" of the abolitionists' case, the pause was expected to last "till some new circumstances should favour its introduction."[56] Whether or not Clarkson portrayed Wilberforce's motives accurately, his interpretation was consistent with Fox's pessimism in 1799, suggesting indeed that at that time Wilberforce had come to share it, notwithstanding the positive gloss that Clarkson sought to place on his behavior. A more telling implication of Clarkson's remarks, however, is that by 1804 circumstances more favorable to abolitionism existed. If Wilberforce assumed such, he was not alone in that opinion. Wilberforce was a member of the London abolition society that was reconstituted in 1804 with a view to planning the relaunch of the parliamentary campaign. Among the most recent supporters of the cause was Henry Brougham, founder of the *Edinburgh Review,* who in 1804 invited members of the Commons that had previously voted on abolition before 1800 "to enquire whether any of the events which have taken place during the interval, are such as to change the nature of the case" for abolition.[57] Together with another lawyer and Wilberforce's brother-in-law, James Stephen, Brougham would make a profound contribution to reshaping the intellectual content and policy focus of the reenergized parliamentary campaign for abolition from 1804 onward, allowing Wilberforce, Clarkson, and their fellow abolitionists finally to make history in 1807.

For Clarkson the relaunching of the parliamentary campaign in 1804 had its roots in the union with Ireland. A response to the 1798 Irish Rebellion and intended, among other things, to remove the threat of French intervention in Ireland to which it had given rise, the union took effect on 1 January 1801, adding 100 new MPs to the existing 551 of the Commons. It also increased the membership of the Lords. The first formal election of new Irish MPs to Westminster after the union occurred in 1802, those taking their seats in 1801 having previously been elected to the Irish Parliament. Clarkson ascribed the relaunch of the abolitionist campaign to a belief that, among the newly elected Irish members to take their seats, "most of them were friendly to the cause."[58] Based on moral grounds, that was a common contemporary view that seemed to be confirmed when Wilberforce gained a comfortable majority for the bill he presented in the Commons in 1804. Though that vote remains to be closely studied, the sense was that Irish MPs largely supported the measure, though there was also a sizable fall in the anti-abolition vote compared to 1796–99. Despite fears among some British slave merchants in June 1804 that "the Affrican Trade . . . will go this time," the 1804 bill failed to make further progress for reasons to which historian Roger Anstey has alluded.[59] When it was reintroduced in the following year, however, it was narrowly and unexpectedly voted down.

Ignoring the perhaps unexpected increase in Commons votes against abolition compared to 1804, Clarkson's explanation for the reverse in 1805 largely focused on the Irish members whom he saw as being heavily lobbied "by those interested in the continuance of the trade." That pressure, he alleged, persuaded all but a few not to vote. What the "dismal representations" were that Clarkson ascribed to the pro–slave trade lobby is unclear. But if we can assume that his account is broadly accurate, whatever ideological and logistical support it was felt that the Irish union might have given to "the friends" of abolitionism in the "infancy of their renewed efforts," it was evidently insufficient to move the cause forward decisively in 1804–5.[60] To explain abolitionism's advance from 1804 onward, therefore, we need to look elsewhere.

For some historians the answer to the conundrum lies outside Britain. More specifically it lies in suggestions of an overproduction crisis in the British West Indies in the years immediately preceding slave trade abolition. First raised publicly as a subject of debate just before the Abolition Act passed in 1807, the historian Eric Williams resuscitated it in the 1940s as a primary explanation of the timing of the measure.[61] His suggestion that overproduction of sugar drove abolition continues to resonate with some historians, primarily with respect to 1799–1807.[62] That short-term overproduction, if that is what it was, might be seen, of course, as a measure of the British West Indies' relative economic success internationally and therefore at variance with Williams's other claims regarding the islands' decline before 1807.[63] Be that as it may, the rationale for the overproduction theory lay in claims of a conjuncture of burgeoning sugar output in the British islands in the aftermath of Saint-Domingue's spectacular collapse and of increasing war-induced constraints on demand for British reexported sugar in continental Europe. The alleged crisis is thought to have reached its height as economic warfare between Britain and Napoleonic France intensified during and after the third wartime coalition of Britain, Austria, and Russia in 1804–5. That, in turn, so the argument runs, instilled sympathy for abolition among some older British West Indian planter communities anxious about market competition from foreign and captured colonies then being supplied with slaves by British and other traders. As noted earlier, the argument found some support in at least one West Indian pamphlet issued in 1807 highlighting concerns of underconsumption of sugar just as others with Caribbean interests were publicly denouncing moves to outlaw British slaving.[64]

In an important intervention five years earlier in 1802, entitled *Crisis of the Sugar Colonies,* the abolitionist James Stephen acknowledged that Saint-Domingue's collapse as a sugar exporter had opened up European markets to British sugar producers.[65] That, in turn, encouraged a surge in sugar output and exports from the British Caribbean and elsewhere after 1791 that continued largely unchecked through 1807. Prices of newly imported slaves in the British sugar colonies remained high in real terms through 1807, reflecting productivity gains in sugar production and underwriting buoyancy in demand for additional slave labor supplies.[66] A third or more of that demand for new slaves arose in colonies outside the British West Indies or in colonies conquered by the British during the wars with France from 1793 onward.[67] In *Crisis,* Stephen bemoaned "the spirit of speculation that lately poured millions of British capital into the soil and the slave markets of colonies soon to revert to an enemy," and went on to suggest that from a wartime imperial perspective, such investment posed "a calamity far more fatal than even the dreaded progress of negro-liberty."[68] It raised the specter indeed of "that defamed monster the Slave Trade" becoming a source "of our humiliation and ruin."[69] Focusing specifically on Trinidad, Stephen claimed that while the West India interest "strenuously and successfully opposed a suppression" of any part of the slave trade, it saw "without an audible murmur, three-fourths of the whole existing Slave Trade of this country poured into the conquered Colonies, to open new lands there upon British account, and raise by their future produce a powerful rivalship in the sugar and cotton markets of Europe."[70] That claim, which, insofar as it concerned the proportion of British slave deliveries to conquered colonies before 1802 was exaggerated, may still be seen as consistent with suggestions of an emergent overproduction crisis in the British islands, with a particular focus on the older colonies.

It is important to note, however, that Stephen himself dismissed any suggestion that such a crisis (even if it were to materialize) might enhance sympathy for abolitionism among planters. To the contrary he observed that "no possible advance in the price of negroes or depreciation of West India produce" would be sufficient to induce them "to coalesce with any opposition to the Slave Trade."[71] For Stephen, attachment to slavery and the slave trade that helped to sustain it easily trumped among planters any short-term market crisis. His fellow abolitionist Henry Brougham made a similar point two years later, when he observed that, if given the option, colonial assemblies would not choose abolition.[72] Equally, those directly involved in the business viewed the prospect of abolition with alarm and trepidation. In the third letter in his Mercator series, John Gladstone, who had West Indian plantation interests, openly denounced the policy on the eve of the passing of the final abolition bill. He issued a "warning voice against that blind enthusiastic zeal, which, in alliance with selfish policy, threatens our colonies with desolation." For him the slave trade was "but the means of which slavery is the end," and as such the risk of sugar output "exceeding the consumption," as one planter had argued, was minor when compared to "the dreadful hazard that awaits the abolition, as the fore-runner of attempts at emancipation," and, with its identification publicly with notions of humanity and justice, its likely encouragement of insurrection among Creole slaves in the colonies.[73]

Such denunciations of abolitionism were not confined to the public sphere by 1806-7. They surfaced in private correspondence, too, as planters and merchants reflected on the concerns among planters on events in London. The Jamaica planter Simon Taylor fretted constantly about the repercussions of Wilberforce's efforts to end the slave trade for the stability and future of the islands.[74] The same applied to island correspondents of British slave merchants right up to the moment of the passing of the Abolition Act in 1807. Writing from Kingston, Jamaica, in September 1806, one slave dealer commented that "if Our present ministers are really serious in their attempt to Abolish the Slave trade, they are giving the Death Stroke to Great Britain, for should it take place, We consider it most impolitic & dangerous a measure that could have been adopted as the West Indies will be ultimately lost to the Mother Country."[75] Six months later, in early March 1807, the same correspondent, in ruminating on the fact that

"Our Ministery [sic] seem determined on the abolition of the African Trade," considered it a measure that "if adopted will We are afraid bee too severely felt not only by the Colonies but the Mother Country." Significantly, he went on to note that "the unexampled success of Buonaparte on the Continent and the want of Vent for West India Produce makes every thing at a perfect stand here, but hope 'ere long things will wear a more pleasing aspect."[76] Viewed through the private correspondence of slave dealers such as the Kingston-based John Hinde and Co., marketing problems for West India produce in wartime were no more than a temporary distraction for British Caribbean fortune hunters. The real danger to their fortunes lay, as planters and merchants saw it, in slave trade abolition.

For Stephen, such opposition to abolition was hardly surprising. His primary purpose in writing in 1802, however, was to highlight British slave traders' penchant for stocking foreign or conquered colonies with slaves as part of a wider threat to Britain's imperial and national interests. His task, as he saw it, was to expose how the "particular interests of Liverpool" put "those of the empire at large" at risk.[77] Addressed to Prime Minister Henry Addington, the *Crisis* was Stephen's response to Napoleon's dispatch in December 1801 of a sizable military force to Saint-Domingue, formerly the greatest Caribbean sugar island before its slave uprising in 1791. Napoleon's move was, Stephen believed, among the "leading motives with France in the recent pacification," a mutual search for peace with Britain that resulted in the Peace of Amiens in March 1802. In Stephen's eyes, Napoleon's action posed a direct challenge to British security founded on the Royal Navy's "wooden walls."[78] To his mind its sinister intent was doubtless compounded in May 1802 by the French emperor's sudden reversal of France's revolutionary decree of 1794 outlawing slavery in the nation's Caribbean colonies. Napoleon seemed set on challenging Britain's position in the West Indies.

A core element of Stephen's 1802 publication was a forensic-like theoretical analysis of several possible outcomes of Napoleon's West Indian venture, of which the most likely and, from Britain's perspective, the most comfortable outcome would be its defeat by the rebel forces. France's failure and the subsequent independence of its former colony, renamed Haiti, from 1 January 1804, revealed, historian John Oldfield suggests, remarkable prescience on Stephen's part. Oldfield also emphasizes that Stephen's analysis had wider ramifications, not least in recognizing that "the slave rebellion of 1791 had radically changed black expectations and, at the same time, had created a rising tide of black consciousness" that was impossible to repress and could prove infectious, thereby threatening British interests.[79] The fear of slave rebellion was particularly noticeable among British planters as abolitionist arguments raged at home, but in assessing the motives and meaning of Napoleon's Caribbean venture in 1802, Stephen firmly located the protection of the nation's West Indian interests closer to the center of the geopolitics of the ongoing Anglo-French struggle for global hegemony. In doing so he initiated a reimagining of the slave trade's role as a strategic policy, and therefore government, issue. Put another way, *Crisis* created the foundations for translating moral concerns about the slave trade into a rational policy choice favoring abolition in the context of the intensifying economic warfare with Napoleonic France and its satellites that would emerge in 1804–7.

Publications of Henry Brougham in 1804 and of Stephen again in 1805 carried that process forward. Where Clarkson identified union with Ireland in 1801 as critical to the relaunch of the anti–slave trade campaign, Brougham saw Haitian independence from France in 1804 and Stephen neutral trade in wartime from the West Indies to Europe as reenergizing politically the abolitionist cause. A Scottish lawyer, Brougham was probably influential in getting Stephen's 1802 book reviewed in the Edinburgh journal he founded that year. In 1803 he himself published a lengthy tract on comparative colonial systems.[80] But his most immediately important intervention was a tract on slave trade abolition published in early 1804 in anticipation of the issue being brought again to the House of Commons. The tract began by dismissing some standard tropes of slave trade supporters, including claims that abolition would be ruinous to Britain economically. Adopting what today are seen as small ratio arguments, he suggested that, relatively speaking, investment in the trade was a "small pittance" or "extremely trifling" and could easily be rechanneled profitably toward other branches of commerce, which were "understocked with capital."

Unsurprisingly, he claimed that no "tenable grounds" existed for asserting that the "African trade" was "directly necessary either to the commercial interests or maritime power of this country."[81]

As Brougham emphasized in the preface to his 1804 tract, however, his main focus was on "the interests of the West Indies," and his primary objective was to examine links between "the late changes in St. Domingo and the continuance of the Slave Trade," or, more specifically, "the new arguments which the advocates of Abolition derive from the present state of St. Domingo." These explained the timing of his intervention. In it he acknowledged how the "fruit of our iniquity" in being involved in slavery "has been a great and rich empire in America." But in an accompanying striking passage he urged that we be "satisfied with our gains, and being rich, let us try to become righteous—not indeed by giving up one sugar cane of what we have acquired, but by continuing in our present state of overflowing opulence, and preventing the further importation of Slaves." For Brougham, the threat to the "present condition of the Colonies" came not from eliminating slave imports but rather, in what was an extension of Stephen's 1802 argument and, with the example of Saint-Domingue's history in mind, from a "sudden and violent increase of the Slave Population."[82] Particularly significant was the surge in slave deliveries by Britons to conquered as well as foreign colonies and Brougham's association of human trafficking from Africa with increased propensity for slave rebelliousness in the West Indies. He noted especially an identification of the shattering rebellion in Saint-Domingue with the huge slave imports into the colony in the preceding decade. Whether or not Brougham was wholly justified in making the last connection, it was a refrain sufficiently heard at the time to give it credibility. Most importantly, it allowed Brougham, aware of the high levels of British slaving activity in 1793–1804, to paint the slave trade itself, not its abolition, as the real and imminent danger to "the existence of the western wing of the British Empire" and to its "splendid state of current opulence."[83] For Brougham, the example of Haiti, "a commonwealth of savage Africans" located in the middle of slave colonies, was a reminder that in deferring what morality and imperial self-interest dictated, Britain risked the probability of the slave trade being abolished "by the utter destruction of the colonial system" itself.[84] Brougham, in effect, created a narrative in which opponents of the slave trade were friends rather than enemies of the British West Indian imperial project. In doing so, he began to transform an earlier nervousness among some abolitionists about the propensity of enslaved Africans to rebel into an argument they were prepared to advance in favor of not just ending the slave trade but also ultimately slavery itself.[85] In Brougham's telling, by 1804 planters had to choose between surrendering the slave trade and sacrificing their possessions.[86]

Brougham may have been the first but was not the last to discern the significance of Haitian independence for the abolitionist cause in 1804–7. Another was Marcus Rainsford, who had direct personal experience of the former colony and had come to admire the skill and fortitude of its rebels. In a lengthy work published in 1805 he noted "the danger of a community of manumitted slaves in the American Archipelago," before going on to identify rebelliousness with slave imports and warning that "if the black population of the other colonies of the Antilles combine to increase as it has done during the last fifty years, and overbalance that of the whites, no power but that of the exercise of humanity, can preserve them to their possessors."[87] Another to reference Haiti was the abolitionist Zachary Macaulay, who, like Brougham and Stephen, was a member of the rejuvenated London Society. Macaulay's comments appeared in a pamphlet published in 1805 as a response to reports previously submitted from the sugar islands to the House of Commons.[88] The burden of the commentary was an excoriating attack on West Indian planters in which Macaulay used evidence from the reports to silence the claims of "the most determined stickler for West Indian humanity" and to condemn the "detestable traffic which is the main prop of colonial despotism."[89] Drawing on reported cases of murdered slaves, in which the perpetrators escaped punishment, Macaulay challenged the efforts of planters to present themselves to the outside world as civilized and law-abiding people, proposing instead that "a state of society exists in the West Indies, of which an inhabitant of this happy island can form no adequate conception" and going on to denounce the "mere mummery of legislation" in the islands intended to protect the slaves.[90] Not content just to denounce the inhumanity of West Indian planters, Macaulay also remarked on how the "reporters labour to keep out of view the dangers which threaten Jamaica from the example and proximity of St. Domingo, and from an increase in the Negro population in the island." And he proceeded to ridicule claims that "the more the Negro population is increased, the greater will be the security of the West Indies" before challenging assertions that slave trade abolition threatened the economic viability of the older British islands. With respect to the latter, he reiterated arguments first made by Stephen in 1802 that, infatuated by opposition to abolition, planters "in the old islands" had remained silent while British traders supplied slaves to Trinidad and "the fertile plains of Guiana."[91] For Macaulay, outlawing the slave trade offered "the only safe and practicable, and at the same time effectual remedy, which can be applied to the dreadful evils of our colonial system."[92]

Through Brougham and Macaulay in particular, abolitionist literature in 1804–5 built on Stephen's *Crisis in the Sugar Colonies,* published in 1802, to argue that, given the example of Haiti, the intransigence of the British West India interest's continuing predilection for slave imports posed a direct and immediate threat to the colonies' security. Only abolition of the slave trade could remove that threat. Whether those arguments by themselves would have been sufficient ultimately to convince parliamentarians to outlaw British slaving is unknown, but they were unquestionably strengthened in 1805 by another intervention from James Stephen that identified continuance of slave trading as a major risk not just to West Indian but also to national security. Stephen's critical contribution was his *War in Disguise: or, The Frauds of the Neutral Flags,* published in October 1805 and reprinted in 1806.[93] In it, Stephen addressed the conundrum of why, despite the economic collapse of Saint-Domingue as a sugar producer and Britain's seizure of other West Indian colonies, the "commercial and colonial interests of our enemies [in which he included Holland and Spain under French control], are now ruined in appearance only, not in reality."[94] Appearing coincidentally at the time of Trafalgar in October 1805, which ensured Britain's dominance at sea and facilitated its blockade of European ports from the Elbe to Brest from mid-1806, Stephen's answer centered on France's continuing capacity to draw on "trans-marine sources of revenue"

242

POLITICS

through the relaxing in wartime of its traditional mercantile regulations governing trade between colony and mother country in favor of opening its ports to neutral flags.[95] Such "relaxation of the national monopoly," commonplace within mercantilist systems, including Britain's, allowed neutrals to import directly the produce from what Britain saw as hostile colonies before reexporting it to European ports under French control.[96] Because of its geographical location, the United States, in Stephen's eyes, had an exceptional advantage in facilitating such commerce, enabling it to grow and profit from flows of goods and commercial settlements from "former fountains" to "former reservoirs."[97] Research has since confirmed that assessment.[98] Depicted as a "protection unduly imparted to our enemies, in respect of their colonial interests, their trade, and commercial revenues," Stephen saw the "abuse of neutral trade" as more than just a means of "sustaining the French exchequer"; it was also "highly dangerous to our future safety," providing the financial means "to nourish a monster that threatens desolation, not to England only, but to Europe."[99]

Written by a notable maritime lawyer with personal experience of working in the Caribbean, this analysis doubtless carried weight in determining more aggressive British attitudes toward "neutral trade" after 1805. That would culminate in increasing economic warfare by 1807 between Britain, on the one hand, and the United States and Napoleonic Europe, on the other. His analysis, however, also added a strategic dimension beyond that which he, Brougham, and Macaulay earlier applied to British traders' predilection for supplying slaves after 1793 both to foreign colonies and to colonies conquered (and in some cases retained) by Britain. An affirmation of British slave merchants' enterprise and vitality in response to market opportunities, such activity assumed a more sinister and pressing aspect politically when viewed through the prism of *War in Disguise*. In supplying labor to West Indian colonies with historic or ongoing connections with France and its political satellites, British slave traders came to assume an unpatriotic aura, offering succor to the enemy in wartime. Paraphrasing Stephen's comment in 1802, their greed elevated Liverpool's profit seeking above combatting the Napoleonic threat. *War in Disguise*, in short, redefined slave trade abolition as a national security issue as much

as a humanitarian or even an imperial one. It justified abolitionism on mercantilist grounds.[100]

There is evidence that the interventions in 1804–5 by Brougham, Macaulay, and Stephen advanced the political traction of slave trade abolition
through 1807. As early as the summer of 1804, Pitt and his cousin William
Wyndham Grenville, First Lord Grenville, and foreign secretary under Pitt
before 1801, encouraged Wilberforce to postpone a motion on abolition he
proposed to put to the Lords until the next session of Parliament, when, in
an allusion perhaps to Haitian independence, it might be "regarded as a
new question, on the ground of the danger to the colonies."[101] Firmer evidence of Haiti's impact is provided by Wilberforce's letter to the freemen
and other inhabitants of Yorkshire on slave trade abolition, published just
before the abolition bill of 1807. In it he encapsulated for his electorate and
for the purpose, it seems, of influencing the House of Lords, the thrust of
the policy principles offered by the three abolitionist authors just noted,
referring directly at one point to Stephen's *Crisis in the Sugar Colonies* of
1802. Adumbrating the considerations other than "abstract right and duty"
that he felt had "commanding force" in dictating abolition, he emphasized
the "regard for the well being of our West Indian colonies themselves, and
the prosperity of the British Empire." More specifically, Wilberforce noted
"the lesson which the Island of St. Domingo has taught those most unwilling to receive it," highlighting "the immense disproportion between Blacks
and Whites in our islands . . . [as being] a subject of most just and serious
dread" and heightened "by introducing that very description of persons
which has been acknowledged by the most approved West Indian writers
to be most prone to insurrections."[102] For the parliamentarian to whom outlawing the slave trade was a sacred duty to prioritize policy imperatives
during the final push toward that goal testified to the political power of his
allies' own publications in the preceding years.

The greatest testament to their power, however, lay in the manner and
means through which abolition was accomplished politically in 1804–7.
Specific issues relating to imperial and national interests identified directly
with Haiti or with the ongoing war with Napoleon advanced incrementally
the abolitionist agenda, drawing into the process growing support from

previously uncommitted parliamentarians. The sequence of measures by which the trade's fate was finally sealed is clear. It began with Pitt's August 1805 order in council, which Stephen and fellow evangelist Attorney-General Spencer Perceval helped to draft, banning British slave deliveries to Dutch Guiana, recently seized by Britain following the resumption of war with France and its allies in May 1803.[103] It continued in May 1806 with parliamentary legislation, which, it appears, Stephen also helped to draft, that in effect extended the scope of that order, banning British slave trading to both foreign territories and colonies surrendered to Britain "during the Present War" (46 Geo III c. 52). Introduced at the same time that the British blockade of continental European ports under Napoleonic control was being instituted, that ban deprived the colonies concerned of many of their slave imports, thereby weakening the growth and potential export of their commercial crops, while simultaneously cutting off "a really large part of the British slave fleet."[104] Two months later, in July 1806, in a measure sometimes neglected by historians, a two-year ban on the clearing out from British ports of ships not previously employed in the slave trade was instituted (46 Geo III c. 119). Finally, in March 1807, a total ban on British slaving was approved, effective from 1 May 1807 (47 Geo III Sess. 1 c. 36). Another law in August 1807 brought the Sierra Leone Company, launched in 1787, under crown control, banning slave trading in the territory it controlled (47 Geo III Sess. 2 c. 44). In the case of the two key legislative measures of 1806 and 1807, arguments in their favor focused overwhelmingly on the national interest or the inexpediency of British slaving activities, not their immorality.[105] That line of argument—captured in the phrase "sound policy"—raised the profile of other abolitionist supporters in Parliament relative to that of Wilberforce in the final stage of the campaign. It also accounts for the fact that each of the four measures approved between August 1805 and March 1807 were government sponsored, with the coup de grace of March 1807 being delivered by Prime Minister Lord Grenville as head of the Ministry of All the Talents. In that sense, formal abolition of the British slave trade in 1805–7 was a policy-driven political act rather than a moral one.

If the manner by which abolition was achieved is clear, the relative importance of factors shaping its final accomplishment in 1804–7 remains open to discussion. To return to a theme implicit in C. L. R. James's aphorism, noted in the Introduction, about great men making history, what made abolition possible and achievable at that particular juncture? Contingency certainly played its part. Admiral Nelson's victory at Trafalgar in October 1805 gave Britain mastery of the seas, helping to sustain continuing access for British merchants to global markets even as economic warfare with Napoleonic Europe deepened and, in the case of Liverpool, as slave trade abolition took effect.[106] One might argue that the confidence gained from Trafalgar was an antidote to any lingering national commercial fears associated with slave trade abolition. At the same time William Pitt's unexpected and premature death in January 1806 prompted the formation of a new government led by Lord Grenville and that included Charles James Fox, long-standing Whig sympathizer of abolition, and would, as historian Judith Jennings reminds us, have more friends of abolition than Pitt's final one.[107] For so long out of government, Fox's unanticipated reentry into it with Grenville in early 1806 provided a political impetus for abolition probably inconceivable under Pitt and one lasting beyond Fox's own death in September 1806. Yet another contingency, particularly pertinent to the passing of the abolition bill in March 1807, was the imminent and unrelated decision of the US federal government to outlaw foreign slave carrying by its nation's ships, effective from 1 January 1808. Foreshadowed at the US Constitutional Convention twenty years earlier, that intervention, together with the collapse of slave carrying in wartime by French and Dutch ships and the final outlawing of the Danish trade from January 1803, effectively undercut suggestions made by some sympathetic to British slavers that, in ending its own slave trade, Britain would leave an open market to other carriers.[108]

While contingencies such as those just mentioned cannot be ignored, neither can the role of human agency or personality in the final push to end the slave trade. One should not forget, for example, the Haitian rebels (and other slave insurrectionists) on whose courage and sacrifice Brougham and Stephen built their arguments about the perils posed by continuing slave imports from Africa to Britain's West Indian Empire. Historians have reminded us of how shipboard insurrections curbed the number of slaves carried across the Atlantic; insofar as it contributed to ending British slaving, the Haitian Revolution had a similar effect.[109] Closer to home, it is important to acknowledge the role of personal connections, whether old, more recent, or even new, in furthering the process of abolition. Among the first was Pitt's friendship with Wilberforce, which arguably contributed to Pitt's issuing of the order in council relating to Dutch Guiana in 1805. The more recent included Wilberforce's with Brougham, Macaulay, and Stephen, the last cemented by marriage, and collectively bringing an imperial perspective to the anti–slave trade campaign to reinforce Wilberforce's humanitarian or moral one. And the last, and in terms of the timing of abolition possibly the most significant, was Wilberforce's embrace of the leadership of Grenville, following Pitt's death, in seeking to move abolition on to the statute book. That new alliance was based on a common belief in the righteousness of the anti–slave trade cause. It was forged by regular correspondence between Grenville and Wilberforce in the year or so before March 1807. Committed to an agreed strategy that related ministerial leadership to tactical improvisation, policy focus, and a more self-effacing Wilberforce presence in parliamentary debates, that alliance played a central part in guiding the abolitionists' legislative agenda to a successful conclusion in 1806–7.[110]

The formal campaign to end the slave trade, which Quakers were primarily instrumental in launching in 1787, was driven by religious and humanitarian principles. Its legislative victories in 1806–7, however, essentially rested on concerns over the trade's compatibility with imperial and national security, or sound policy. Those victories were also largely the product of political maneuverings in Parliament by evangelical Anglicans who shared Quaker antipathies to the trade in human species. To point to these shifts is not to imply that humanitarianism was largely a disguise for more Machiavellian calculations driving the anti–slave trade cause through 1807. A refusal to take oaths was, of course, always a barrier to Quakers joining Parliament. More generally, however, it is worth recalling that while sound policy became the dominant motif of abolitionism in 1806–7 there remained, as Thomas Clarkson observed, a real and powerful, even if for tactical reasons more muted, undercurrent of sympathy for and commitment to humanity and justice inside and outside Parliament as the anti–slave trade campaign reached its climax. It follows, too, that, while contingency and personality played their parts in shaping the culminating moments of that campaign, allowing abolitionists to make history, scruples about the legitimacy of Britain's continuing involvement in the trafficking of enslaved Africans on grounds of morality and national security ultimately defined its rationale and purpose. Contrary to Oscar Wilde's reference in another context (cited in the introduction), ethical principle as much as personality moved the age in the case of British slave trade abolition.

With a background of industrial revolution at home and military maritime conflict abroad, it is unsurprising that some historians have identified economic calculation based on perceptions of national interest as part of that process. Eric Williams famously identified abolition of the slave trade as the first stage in an industrial-capitalist inspired shift from a slavery-related mercantilism toward free trade. At the same time, Williams associated the precise timing of slave trade abolition with an overproduction crisis in the British sugar islands. Though both propositions have attracted support from other historians, there are strong grounds for questioning each of them. That does not imply that economic factors were unimportant in shaping the rise and outcome of the campaign to end the slave trade. To the contrary, I have argued that industrialization and urbanization contributed to the campaign's emergence as a mass social movement and thereby its acceptability as a legitimate object of concern, moral or otherwise, for Parliament. It is also necessary to recognize how the return of war with Napoleon in 1803 brought to the fore perceptions of the damaging impact of slave-trading practices on Britain's imperial and national interests. Rather than look for capitalist plots or at overproduction crises to explain the outlawing of the slave trade, historians would do better, I would argue, to envisage it as integral to British policy choices in the intensifying economic war with France that followed Haitian independence and Trafalgar.

An important corollary of such arguments is that between 1787 and 1807 debates over the slave trade moved from the periphery to the mainstream of British politics. The process by which that occurred was not even through time. It developed rapidly through 1792, stagnated in 1793–99, almost atrophied in 1799–1803, and then resurged dramatically from 1804 to 1807. The underlying pattern was consistent not just with Edmund Burke's famous argument about lines of morality and mathematics varying but also with C. L. R. James's dictum about how circumstances dictate the capacity of individuals to make history. It highlights, too, the importance of extraparliamentary activity in building the campaign in the first place and of the political skills of its parliamentary advocates in 1806–7 in redefining the balance of arguments in favor of abolition in the context of changing domestic and international circumstances. It is to those skills that we should ultimately look in searching for the greatness of the principal anti–slave trade campaigners. Saying that, however, is not meant to understate the leading campaigners' humanitarian instincts or the part played in the wider movement by the humanitarian revolution that Steven Pinker has discerned. Both are commonly and rightly seen, contrary to Williams, as foundational to abolitionism. One may, indeed, go further and urge that the humanitarian impulse be considered as implicit in an interpretation of the events of 1806–7 as the first critical achievement of a longer-term process that would redefine Britain's national and imperial identity. The process arguably began even before the precocious onset of Britain's industrialization or the loss of the nation's thirteen colonies in 1776–83 on which historian Christopher Brown has placed much emphasis. It found practical, political expression in challenging the slave trade in 1787–1807. And it would continue in the century after 1807 with a hegemonic industrial Britain's commitment to practical moves to suppress the international slave trade and ultimately slavery itself. In that larger, long-term scenario, the act of 1807 marked the political coming of age of abolitionism and the values it espoused.

On the "Heroism of Principle"

Reflecting on the British Slave Trade
and Its Abolition

I BEGAN THIS book with a quotation from Oscar Wilde's *Picture of Dorian Gray,* published in 1890, which highlights the importance of human personality relative to principle in shaping the world in his time. I conclude it with a quotation from Jane Austen's *Mansfield Park,* published in 1814, in which the author alludes directly to the slave trade and later comments on the "heroism of principle" and equally importantly the need or even "obligation" to do one's duty by it.[1] From very different perspectives, the two quotations speak to this book's core theme concerning the relative importance of agency and ideology in shaping the history of the British slave trade. That trade first emerged on a continuing basis during England's mid-seventeenth-century rivalry with the Dutch for European maritime supremacy and in tandem with the nation's initial imperial expansion in the Americas, itself a major ingredient in that rivalry. It matured as an integral part of Britain's burgeoning Atlantic maritime empire in 1660–1776, a period in which European, particularly British, demand for sugar and other products of empire expanded almost inexorably and, given the human cost of their production, helped to ensure that Britain became the world's leading slave carrier from 1750 to 1807. But the nation's attachment to the slave trade came increasingly to be questioned before and during the age of revolutions in the last quarter of the eighteenth century. Some historians see the British crisis of empire triggered by the American Revolution as pivotal to that process. Others focus on slave resistance, notably during the Haitian Revolution in 1791–1804. Still others stress radical social and ideological change at home associated with the Industrial Revolution, an event

linked ironically in the minds of some historians with the nation's enrichment from Caribbean slavery. Yet others still locate it in a largely
home-based humanitarian revolution rooted in emergent philosophies of
benevolence and humanity and a growing revulsion at state-sponsored violence. With some exceptions, a vital attribute of these various sources of
debate about Britain's slave trade is that they originated outside the trade
itself. The business of slave trafficking, as far as British investors were concerned, remained profitable to the end, a fact reflected in the scale of their
continuing participation in it, notwithstanding parliamentary measures to
regulate its conduct from 1788 onward. Why the British proved so adept
at slave trafficking and why Parliament chose in 1807 to outlaw a business
widely considered since the 1640s as a pillar of Britain's national and imperial interests are among the central issues this book has addressed.

Assuming consumer sovereignty, we may plausibly argue that responsibility for Britain's eminence in slave trafficking through 1807 ultimately lay
with the increasing number of Britons who developed a sweet tooth for a
crop that slaves cultivated. Some abolitionists acted on that assumption
from 1791 by encouraging the boycotting of Caribbean sugar, thereby recognizing and underscoring the linkage between the human cost of its cultivation and ongoing demand for imports of enslaved Africans into Britain's West
Indian colonies. But supplying that demand was not without challenges,
risk, and even uncertainty, and without British carriers' ability to address
and manage them, the British Caribbean demand for new captives could not
have been so readily accommodated. To ascribe responsibility for the scale
of the nation's trafficking of Africans to sugar consumers, necessary though
they were, is to neglect the adaptability and efficiency of British slave carriers themselves. Those attributes, I would argue, underwrote Britain's leadership of slave carrying in the century before 1807. In tandem with the
nation's emerging naval supremacy and with trends in productivity in Caribbean slave labor, it allowed the British sugar islands to grow in number and
to prosper. That, in turn, has naturally provoked historical debates over
why Parliament chose in 1807 to outlaw British slave trafficking.

The challenges facing slave traders were rooted in the business's
Atlantic-wide multipolar nature as reflected in the pattern of British slaving

voyages. Laden with trade goods sourced from both home and abroad, including the East Indies, ships sailed from their port of origin to western Africa and then crossed the Atlantic with their human cargo before returning home after its sale in the Americas. Atlantic wind and ocean current systems facilitated their voyage patterns, but voyages were not without risks from natural hazards, from the international conflicts that punctuated the period from 1640 through 1807, from competition from other carriers for slaves in Africa, and from disease and resistance among the enslaved Africans during the infamous middle passage from Africa to America. To those risks were added agency dilemmas inherent in the pursuit of such a long-distance trade, challenges in expediting turnaround times of ships in ports during and between voyages, and issues relating to recovery of credit advances used to lubricate transactions in Africa and America. Each had the potential to destabilize the harmonizing of movements of capital, ships, slaves, and trade goods across time and Atlantic spaces that was pivotal to the business's sustainability and growth. Not all British slave traders rose successfully to the trade's formidable challenges, but the growing scale of their activity and the trade's continuing profitability as a business through 1807 were testament to the success of many in doing so. That success was founded on the competitive framework within which the British slave trade developed during the so-called free trade period that followed the ending between 1689 and 1712 of the Royal African Company's monopoly of British commerce with Africa. Central to its delivery, however, was a series of other, primarily institutional, innovations that addressed questions of agency dilemma, credit security, and capital turnover that had proved irreparably damaging to the Royal African Company's own commercial performance. They were manifested in changing contracts between investors in voyages and ship officers charged with their management overseas; in improvements in Anglo-African credit protection arrangements in regions where British traders congregated; in the evolution of new remittance procedures that alleviated slave traders from the risks of underwriting credit to planters in their purchase of newly imported enslaved Africans; and in the use of slave bills endorsed by London to sustain capital circulation and growth in the British slave trade. After 1770, changes in ship technology such as copper sheathing reinforced institutional innovation.[2] Liverpool merchants were the main instruments and beneficiaries of that catalog of innovations. Investment in local port infrastructure and locational advantages in wartime allowed that city's merchants to attract new capital into the trade from the 1740s, enabling them to build commercial and financial axes with established as well as new British slaving venues in Atlantic Africa and the Americas. None were more important in 1750–1807 than Liverpool's ties with Bonny in the Niger Delta and Kingston in Jamaica, but underpinning Liverpool's success, too, were deepening domestic ties with Manchester, Birmingham, and London, all sources of essential trade goods for Africa and, in London's case, the clearinghouse for slave and other bills. While the fortunes of British, particularly Liverpool slave traders, depended on building networks overseas and developing institutional practices to reinforce or supplement trust, they also had domestic roots. They included the opening of the African trade to free entry, a national political commitment to maritime empire, and a growing integration of the country's slaving capital with its principal industrial and financial ones. In brief, the exceptional scale of British slaving reflected a blending of individual and collective enterprise with a sympathetic, expansive, at times aggressive, and overall successful national and imperial mercantilist outlook.

Emerging against this background of British commercial achievement in slaving, the anti–slave trade campaign launched in 1787 shared some of its underlying characteristics. Just as slave trafficking was ultimately linked to growing and widespread British sugar consumption, so the campaign to end the trade quickly became identified with substantial nationwide public sympathy, thereby gaining political legitimacy. As a result, just as slaving operations were multipolar in nature, so campaigning to end them assumed a similar, if geographically more circumscribed but not simply national or British, multipolarity. British antislavery was part of an international movement.[3] As the seat of national government, London was the ensuing British campaign's political epicenter in the same way that Liverpool was by the 1780s the country's slaving one. But like Liverpool's merchants in their commercial pursuits, the London-based leaders of the anti–slave trade movement drew support and inspiration from networks of people and groups across the country and beyond. Those networks included prominent members of Britain's burgeoning urban-based industrial and tertiary sectors, whose association with the campaign contrasted with the linkage of Manchester textile manufacturers, Birmingham gun makers, and London East India traders and sugarhouses with slaving. British business thus assumed a Janus-faced position toward slave trafficking, based on the relative weighting on the part of its leaders of motives of commercial self-interest, on the one hand, and of religious and ideological convictions, on the other. It follows that antislavery, like sugar consumption and the pursuit of the slave trade, was more than a class-based phenomenon; it transcended class, religion, gender, and even race. Moreover, just as Liverpool merchants and their allies at home and abroad were innovators in their pursuit of commercial profit, so those who campaigned to end the trade drew on their own experiences in business and politics to harness skills of advertising, of knowledge dissemination, and of social networking to promote their cause inside Parliament and beyond. If the slave trade helped to promote revolutionary domestic commercial, financial, and industrial change, as some historians allege, those seeking to abolish it also showed an acute awareness of how to adapt the commercial practices of their age to their political ends. Accordingly, connections between the slave trade and economic change in Britain were more multifaceted and multidirectional than is sometimes supposed. Innovation was in effect as much part of the politics of the anti–slave trade movement as it was of Britain's successful pursuit of the trade itself. Without such "political entrepreneurship," to use historian Charles Tilly's felicitous phrase, the campaign would not have attracted the nationwide sympathy that it did.[4]

One cannot explain, however, the nation's success in slave trafficking or the anti–slave trade movement's public appeal solely by reference to entrepreneurship or other forms of *British* agency. Essential to the success of British trafficking was African agency, or, more specifically, the preparedness of coastal African ethnic groups to sell people from mostly other ethnic backgrounds into overseas slavery, to contract with British traders to supply them, and to engage with dealers at inland markets in order to satisfy those contracts. The slave export trade from Africa involved integrating external demand for captives with indigenous African supply networks. African enslavers and dealers were pivotal to that process. The relations among the political economy of slave supply, social disorder, and long-run African underdevelopment, first highlighted by late eighteenth-century British abolitionists, continue to be a source of historical debate.[5] But African dealers in slaves, often working in tandem with local political leaders, were seemingly largely oblivious to any pain and social costs inflicted on others as they sought to profit from the trade. We know of at least one dealer who in 1806 threatened to kill a British missionary newly arrived in Calabar if it was evident that William Wilberforce was involved in sending him. As that was not the case, the missionary survived that threat but sadly died soon after from disease.[6] Nonetheless, the incident underscored the point that some Africans were just as heavily invested ideologically and economically in the Atlantic slave trade as Liverpool merchants were before 1807. Some remained so after that date.[7] Their control of supply combined with pressures on carriers to achieve dispatch in slave transactions ensured that African dealers were not without power in coastal bargaining. Even so, Liverpool traders' dominance of slave exports from Bonny and other venues in the Bight of Biafra seemingly brought them rich dividends in enabling them to procure slaves more cheaply, quickly, and securely than other traders. The sources of those advantages lay within Biafran ports and their hinterlands, but Liverpool traders' ability to access them reflected their own enterprise in building favor and trust with the region's coastal merchants. As they did so, they became part of a series of multigenerational, cross-cultural partnerships built on mutually beneficial networking and institutional arrangements that African agency played a central part in constructing. With varying degrees of aplomb and success, that formula was replicated in the other parts of Atlantic Africa that British slave traders frequented before 1807. Without African agency and support, British slaving could not have reached the scale it did. What was true for British carriers was true in varying degrees for others, too.

A very different form of African agency was involved in shaping British abolitionism and its success in 1807. It centered not on African slave dealers but on their victims and, more specifically, on their victims' persistent resistance to their condition. Among the reasons for British traders' enthusiasm for the Biafran trade may have been the apparently relative outward docility of Igbo slaves, who constituted the majority of captives shipped from the region. As measured by the comparative incidence of slave revolts on British ships by place of embarkation, slaves boarding in the Bight of Biafra evinced a lower propensity to rebel than some others.[8] Still, rebellions tended to occur on ships leaving all African ports frequented by British vessels, and reports of them, of their violence, and of their usually brutal outcomes, including severe repression by British sailors, regularly and often appeared in British newspapers from the 1750s. Slave resistance in other forms attracted comment, too, in so-called slave narratives published in Britain between 1772 and 1789. Revealing a determination on the part of some Africans to sacrifice their lives in order to assert their autonomy, such evidence of humanity was simultaneously reinforced by several widely reported British court cases in which enslaved Africans brought to Britain by their West Indian owners sought successfully to resist deportation to the Caribbean against their will. In doing so, they redefined slaves' rights in England while in Scotland they helped to determine that slavery became illegal in 1778. Such heroism, usually against daunting odds, was more than a response to profound personal misery or pain; it was rooted in a principle of self-determination that some liberated Africans felt the enslaved had a duty to assert. Some Britons supported their stand through the courts; a small but celebrated vocal minority even argued in favor of Africans' right violently to resist their captivity. But the reports of the brutality and at times sadism adopted against rebels on British ships also provided for some Britons evidence of the corrupting power of slavery for a society widely considered as civilized. Participation in the slave trade thus provoked debates about British identity at the very moment when, according to Steven Pinker, the nation was embracing a humanitarian revolution, itself prompted in part by a wider revulsion against state-sponsored violence, of which that displayed on board legally sanctioned slave ships could ultimately be portrayed as a prime example. Accordingly, indications of, and reflections on, African humanity prompted by slave resistance helped to redraw the ideological framework within which Britons viewed participation in the Atlantic slave trade from at least the 1780s onward, if not, in some individual cases, much earlier.

If shipboard slave resistance was instrumental in informing abolitionists' narratives concerning the politics of British identity, another form of African agency—slave rebellion in the Americas—helped to determine their legislative triumph in 1807. Some, like Samuel Johnson, anticipated that such rebellions would undermine British American slavery and the traffic in Africans on which it rested. British planters feared that campaigning to end that trade would by itself provoke resistance to plantation slavery and even prompt the slaves to use the latent power they possessed to overthrow their masters. Such existential fears proved largely unfounded until 1791, but that year's massive and bloody slave uprising in Saint-Domingue, seen by some contemporaries and historians as inspired by the French Revolution, reignited them in an unprecedented fashion as a wave of destruction and death swept through the principal French sugar colony, defying efforts from outside to stem it. In the short term the uprising proved damaging to British abolitionism, suggesting that challenging the status quo where slavery and the slave trade were concerned would undermine security in the British sugar islands. But artful reminders, in the wake of Saint-Domingue's formal independence as Haiti in 1804, that the 1791 rebellion from which it originated was preceded by exceptional rates of new slave imports from Africa offered British abolitionists opportunities to argue that continuance of the British slave trade posed a direct threat to the future safety of the nation's West Indian colonies and should therefore be abolished. In tandem with other events, it proved to be an ingenious stratagem, turning the most successful slave revolt in history into a critical ingredient in the political machinations surrounding the final moves to outlaw the British slave trade. Victorious African rebels in Saint-Domingue were thus unknowingly instrumental in allowing the parliamentary leaders of the British anti–slave trade campaign to make history in 1806–7.

The arguments advanced in 1804–7 to achieve that end centered on sound policy rather than morality. Superficially, that finding appears consistent with some historians' claims that national self-interest, not ethics, determined British slave trade abolition. Amongst the first to make such a claim were the German historian Franz Hochstetter in 1905 and the West Indian–born scholar Eric Williams in 1944. Though neither was wholly dismissive of moral arguments against slaving, Williams in particular identified the ideological roots of British antislavery with the rise of industrial capitalism; the particular timing of slave trade abolition with a crisis of overproduction in the British Caribbean (a view Hochstetter previously espoused); and the passing of the act of 1807 as a key moment in the transition from mercantilism to laissez-faire in British economic life and national policy. Others have echoed some of Williams's claims, and in this book I have argued that rapid urbanization associated with industrialization played an important part in facilitating the transformation of the anti–slave trade campaign into a mass movement and giving it political legitimacy. Furthermore, the leadership and supporters of the campaign included individuals and groups with commercial and industrial interests and skills. But neither of these findings confirms the validity of Williams's specific arguments or, more importantly, his tendency to denigrate the ethical component of abolitionism. It is evident that by the 1780s, if not earlier, there was in Britain a convergence of philosophical and religious objections to the slave trade that transcended social and economic interests. Moreover, as historian David Brion Davis argued some forty years ago, there was an intertwining of theories of political economy and humanitarianism in reshaping social values and political action at that time. In short, Williams overdrew distinctions between economics and morality in motivating behavior, political or otherwise. Similarly, whatever fears British planters may have expressed about market conditions for sugar in the years up to 1807, they were insufficient to deter them, if the abolitionist James Stephen and others are to be believed, from opposing curbs on British slaving or from continuing to buy at unprecedented prices newly imported slaves from Africa as long as supplies lasted. The planter community remained largely prosperous, if anxious about abolition, through 1807; the Abolition Act of that year was ultimately conceived and portrayed as a measure intended to protect not undermine that prosperity. Equally, however one regards the relation of that act to long-run shifts in Britain's national economic policy, the mindset dictating the political maneuverings in Parliament relating to the slave trade was essentially a mercantilist one. Framed by concerns over Haitian independence and by economic warfare with Napoleonic France, parliamentary interventions against the slave trade placed imperial and national security above Liverpool's slaving interests. It involved denying the slave merchants an opportunity to supply slaves to foreign colonies or colonies seized by Britain in wartime but that retained strong commercial ties with France and its allies. To conceptualize the timing of such interventions as driven other than by security considerations is to misunderstand the national and international political contexts in which they occurred. At the same time, no specific British economic interests, industrial or otherwise, were immediately and materially advanced as a result of the 1807 Abolition Act.

To offer an alternative and, I believe, more persuasive generic interpretation of the causes and implications of British slave trade abolition, it is useful to explore two sets of issues, the analysis of which helps to uncover the relative importance of principles, human agency, and contingency in shaping the processes involved and, in particular, the "heroism" of principle to which Jane Austen referred in *Mansfield Park*. The first set of issues relates to the relation between shifts in values or beliefs and political action, on the one hand, and, echoing historian C. L. R. James's argument, the historical circumstances that allowed the actual translation of such beliefs, wholly or partly, into public policy, on the other.[9] To pose the issue more specifically, did the use of arguments linked to national and imperial security to motivate parliamentary intervention against the slave trade in 1804–7 diminish moral principle's value to determining the anti–slave trade campaign's ultimate success? A second and related set of issues concerns the historical significance of that intervention, and more specifically its implications for our understanding of later British moves toward international slave trade suppression and the emancipation of British Caribbean slaves. From my perspective, the key questions concern how one should interpret the meaning of the 1807 Abolition Act. Despite the specific circumstances surrounding the act's passing, was it a watershed or defining moment ideologically in Britain's historical relationship with transatlantic slavery? Was it a foundation stone of the nation's slave trade

suppression policy post-1815 as well as a precursor of the contemporane-
ous domestic campaign to liberate the slave population of the British sugar
colonies? And if it was, what insights does the history of the anti–slave trade
movement offer in terms of understanding the weight to be placed on principle, human agency, and contingency in the politics of their development?
I conclude with thoughts on these two wider and related sets of issues.

Historian John Oldfield has posited that in 1804–7 British activists were
able to "turn the international situation to their advantage, in effect aligning national and international interests."[10] In addition to events in Haiti, a
key element in that process was "the seeming spontaneity of America's decision to end the slave trade," which President Thomas Jefferson approved
on 2 March 1807 and which undermined the claim of opponents of British
abolition that others, notably Americans, would fill the void in slave supplies created by such a British move. But the activists' cause was also helped
by events at home, among them Lord Grenville's calling of the 1806 election, which weakened the position of the political faction of Viscount Sidmouth, formerly Henry Addington, a long-standing opponent of abolition,
and in Oldfield's view by Grenville's tactical decision to emphasize the policy rather than the moral aspects of the issue in the parliamentary debates.
Influenced in part by Jefferson's action in early March 1807, Grenville, Oldfield notes, preferred to minimize the risks associated with abolition and
its identification with Britain's national interests rather than the morality
and justice of the case. While acknowledging that "long-term factors [were]
involved," including "religious revivalism and the growth of compassion-
ate humanitarianism," Oldfield argues that victory in 1807 depended on
political contingency and skillful political maneuvering, in which national
interests were privileged over humanitarian and moral ones. It was reflected
in shifting political alliances and in Wilberforce's relinquishing of the lead
in the final debates on slave trade abolition to Lord Grenville and his ministerial allies in the House of Commons. In effect, in an undoubtedly unconscious echo of Oscar Wilde's remark, Oldfield emphasizes politics and
personality rather than principle in determining the passing of the final
Abolition Act.[11]

There is much truth in Oldfield's suggestion that British slave trade abolition is "best understood as a coalescence of different factors, some of them internal and national, others external and international."[12] The timing of the measure was evidently a product of political agency and contingency. But that does not imply, as Oldfield acknowledges, that other factors, among them shifts in moral values, should be overlooked when examining the motivations of activists and their extraparliamentary supporters and the early achievement of political legitimacy for their cause. Religious and other sources of moral scruple about the slave trade were increasingly widely articulated in Britain and elsewhere in the later eighteenth century. They were pivotal in motivating many of the leading figures (and doubtless many outside that group) to commit to the anti–slave trade movement. Lord Grenville was one such figure. What gave the movement political legitimacy, however, was the mass articulation of public hostility to the trade through unprecedented and seemingly mostly spontaneous petitioning of the House of Commons in 1787–92 in favor of abolition. Facilitated by rapid urbanization and networks of religious nonconformists, it provided a barometer of the nation's moral opposition to the trade that some members of the House of Commons from Prime Minister William Pitt down found impossible to ignore. Such weight of public disapproval, and the sense of duty many across numerous walks of life felt politically in opposing the trade, helps explain the perseverance with which William Wilberforce and his allies pursued the cause in Parliament in 1789–99. Moreover, when they elected to resume the campaign after 1803, they dispatched Thomas Clarkson on tour to gauge the public mood. According to Clarkson's *History*, published in 1808, it remained firmly in support of the cause, a view anticipated in some newspaper reports of the 1806 election. In the four years after 1803, abolitionist activism centered on building a parliamentary majority in support of the cause based on "sound policy," but, as Clarkson's consultation of extraparliamentary sympathizers of the cause indicated and the content of the final abolition bill attested, the nation's moral antipathy to the slave trade continued quietly to animate both new and long-standing leaders of the campaign in Parliament even as they resorted to other messages to gain legislative majorities. Agency and contingency may have proved essential to achieving victory in 1807, but it was a victory that had its roots in the heroic decision of a few, subsequently publicly endorsed by many, to challenge on moral grounds a long-established and legitimate business that many informed and influential contemporaries considered fundamental to Britain's historic success as a commercial and colonial power. If agency and contingency expedited abolition's accomplishment, ideological change linked to shifting humanitarian, philosophical, and religious principles was the inspiration and purpose of the anti–slave trade movement that made it possible. In sum, in 1804–7 abolitionist activists and their supporters, including Prime Minister Lord Grenville from January 1806, revealed a remarkable understanding of the political means by which they might finally achieve their humanitarian ends.[13] As the poet Robert Southey reminded the act's deliverer, Lord Grenville, in 1807, "the red-cross flag" was now "redeemed from stain so foul" and "no longer now covereth the abomination" that was the trade.[14] His language captured the sense of moral or righteous indignation that had driven so many in Britain to oppose politically the nation's involvement in the slave trade in the decades before it was outlawed.[15]

The Janus-faced attitude of British industry toward slavery and the slave trade persisted well into the nineteenth century. British manufacturing supply chains that had sustained the nation's slaving activities through 1807 nurtured the activities of other national carriers in later years.[16] In that sense Britons continued to profit from slaving even after Parliament outlawed British slave carrying. Equally, ongoing British industrial growth relied on slave-produced raw materials, thereby fostering expansion of slavery in some of the nation's raw material supply chains in Africa and America, while slave-grown sugar continued to comprise an important element in many Britons' diets through the 1840s. To see, therefore, the demands of industrial capital as being architects of Britain's antislavery movement, of which British slave trade abolition constituted its first telling victory, is to misunderstand the complexities of the interrelationship of British industrial capitalism and transatlantic slavery. If, as Eric Williams controversially and some historians would say misleadingly argued, slavery financed the industrial growth in the eighteenth century, the interconnections between the two persisted, albeit sometimes in new ways, through the mid-nineteenth century at least.

Slavery's continuing part in the nation's economic life galvanized humanitarian inspired abolitionists after 1807 to extend the policy goals of their self-imposed collective remit. In 1808 the crown was persuaded to assume administrative responsibility of the so-called province of freedom in Africa, privately established by abolitionists in 1787 and known from 1792 as the Freetown Colony. Renamed the Crown Colony and Protectorate of Sierra Leone, it became the first British colony in Africa, and with its goal of promoting free-labor values, would play a significant part in remaking abolitionism as a form of colonial expansionism as well as a base for further abolitionist-inspired moves to curb transatlantic slave trafficking.[17] The latter objective began to take shape in 1814–15, when at the Congress of Vienna British foreign secretary Lord Castlereagh, under pressure from abolitionist supporters at home, agreed with seven other European powers to a declaration for the Universal Abolition of the Slave Trade.[18] It represented partial realization of an ambition of which some abolitionists had dreamed almost thirty years earlier.[19] Describing the trade as "repugnant to the principles of humanity and universal morality," the Vienna declaration had few, if any, political teeth and, as with other aspects of humanitarian intervention, produced some unanticipated consequences.[20] But historians have nonetheless seen it as a first purposive step toward framing international action against the slave trade, in the further pursuit of which Britain, under the banner of humanitarianism, would immediately play a leading and pivotal role. Within two years of the declaration, Britain had signed bilateral anti–slave trade treaties with several nations, committing itself to naval suppression of trafficking and to the establishment of courts of mixed commission around the Atlantic charged with passing judgment on ships seized on suspicion of illegal trafficking.[21] The 1815 declaration was thus instrumental in encouraging Britain to extend its policy of humanitarian intervention against their own slave traffickers to transatlantic trafficking by others. The move was not without legal complications and other challenges, and it gave rise at times to international tensions.[22] Nor by itself did it end the Atlantic slave trade, which remained at historically high levels through 1850 and ultimately persisted until 1867. Victims mostly of bilateral slaving voyages outfitted in the Americas, the great majority of the slaves shipped after 1807 landed in Brazil and Cuba.[23] Nonetheless, British commitment to suppression was huge by any standards, helping to ensure that some 167,000 Africans were freed from captivity on board ships brought before mixed commission and other courts during the six decades after 1807.[24] Around three-quarters were freed in Africa, many tasting their newly recovered freedom at Freetown in Sierra Leone. None of these things were conceivable or possible without the resources generated by British industrialization and the shift in political thinking that accompanied the rise of abolitionism.

Ending transatlantic trafficking may have been the primary objective initially of British abolitionists, but bringing an end to slavery itself in British territories was always a goal, too, for many. It represented a challenge in many ways even more daunting than confronting British traffickers. Abolition entailed a threat to planters' historic investment in property rights in enslaved Africans, rights endorsed by Parliament and which, given its constituents, it was unlikely to question under normal conditions. In such circumstances, late eighteenth-century abolitionists confined their ambitions to using the courts to limit or remove owners' rights over slaves in Britain. Largely successful in law by the late 1780s, the process affected the lives of probably at least ten thousand enslaved Africans in Britain.[25] As for the half-million or more enslaved Africans then living in the British West Indies, abolitionist efforts at that time centered on alleviating their suffering rather than on changing their status, a goal to which, it was believed, outlawing the slave trade would make a material contribution by preventing planters from replenishing their labor force through slave imports from Africa. Post-1807 demographic trends among slaves in most of the British Caribbean confounded those expectations.[26] At the same time, slave uprisings in Barbados (1816), Demerara (1823), and Jamaica (1831) confirmed slaves' continuing unhappiness with their lot, indicating that slavery itself rather than the slave trade was the root cause of slave restiveness and thus a threat to the British colonies' security.[27] Moreover, the continuation after 1815 of what Edmund Burke had called in 1792 the "arrant trifling" of colonial legislatures to improve slaves' lives seemed poorly calculated to improve the situation, pointing a finger at colonial intransigence and determining abolitionists increasingly to question the legitimacy of British colonial slavery on both ethical and security grounds in 1816–31.[28] Some proposed gradual abolition, but after the Demerara slave uprising in 1823 and news of its brutal repression reached Britain, cries of immediate abolition grew in intensity and soon became the abolitionists' overriding goal. The Christmas slave rebellion in Jamaica in 1831 gave the issue further urgency. Eighteen months after that rebellion and under the first administration elected after the Reform Act of 1832, the government led by the Whig Earl Grey acceded to public demands for emancipation. It proposed through Colonial Secretary Edward Stanley, later Earl of Derby, to provide for the liberation of all slaves in the British Caribbean beginning in August 1834, to establish through 1838 an apprenticeship system to retrain former slaves, and to compensate all owners for their loss of property rights in the said slaves.[29] The legislation was passed in July 1833, coincidentally just days before William Wilberforce died. The government later borrowed £20 million to pay compensation. Materially, the former slaves received nothing.[30]

In explaining his reasoning behind the emancipation proposals, Stanley acknowledged on 14 May 1833 the "choice of difficulties" that he faced.[31] There were, he argued, "two conflicting parties," one "deeply involved by pecuniary interests," the other moved by "their feelings and opinions," which underlay "a growing determination on the part of the people of this country to put an end to slavery." The latter, he believed, "no one can deny or wisely despise." Consistent with the Overton window theory that informed my discussion in chapter 6, such comments were ones with which later British advocates of social reform such as Robert Tressell would identify. As Tressell saw it, legally driven social reform was pursued by political parties only "when public opinion was so strong in favour of it that they knew there was no getting out of it, and then it was a toss up which side did it."[32] Regardless of whether an alternative government would have done the same in 1833, for Stanley it was a determination "the more absolute, and the less resistible, because founded on sincere religious feelings, and a conviction that things wrong in principle cannot be good in practice." Furthermore, it was more than "a mere ebullition of popular feeling" and "of late or of momentary birth," springing instead "from the deep-settled and long entertained convictions of reflecting men—from that same spirit of lasting humanity, which, fifty years ago, pressed on the Parliament of that day; and which in defiance of the arguments, that we should ruin our trade—in defiance of opposition from many quarters—compelled the Parliament to abolish for ever that iniquitous and disgraceful trade by which supplies of human flesh were obtained from the shores of Africa."

Citing speeches by Burke, Fox, Grenville, and Wilberforce, Stanley reminded his listeners that the supporters of that "politic and humane and just abolition looked forward to the emancipation of the slaves as a consequence of abolishing the Slave Trade" and that "the gradual abolition of slavery remained on their minds" as they assumed, quoting former Tory foreign secretary and prime minister George Canning's words, that attacking the "great outworks of the fortress" of slavery would "cause the fall of the fortress itself." Such arguments, Stanley noted, "prove that the feeling which now pervades the country is not of this day's growth; but that the people of this country have long considered it expedient—have long held it a duty, on the grounds of religion and of justice, to advance any measure which might tend to the early abolition of this disgraceful system." For Stanley, therefore, as for Grenville in 1807, where the slave trade was concerned, though Britain's "maritime commerce" might suffer by emancipation, "higher interests" than economics dictated any decision about the future of British colonial slavery in 1833. That decision, as Stanley made clear, would rest ultimately on a political articulation of fundamental humanitarian principles.[33]

Heroism of principle was not, however, the only factor uniting slave trade abolition in 1807 with British colonial slavery's demise in 1833–38. In both cases, African agency influenced the timing of intervention in the form of slave resistance, in 1807 by Haitian independence three years earlier and in 1833 by rebellion in Jamaica in late December 1831. Fears were raised in London on each occasion about the security of the British West Indies or what, in 1833 Stanley would describe, in a reminder of language used by abolitionist Henry Brougham in his *Concise Statement on the Question of the Abolition of the Slave Trade,* published in 1804, as "the interests, the comforts, the prosperity, perhaps I may say the very existence, of a large population in the West-India colonies depending upon us for support and protection."[34] Compounding those fears before 1807 were claims by abolitionists that British planters were indifferent to the risks posed by continuing dependence on imported slaves from Africa, often perceived as being more rebellious than Creole-born slaves. Reinforcing them in 1833 were concerns about the evident unwillingness of planter-dominated colonial legislatures to introduce measures to ameliorate the conditions under which their enslaved workers lived as proposed by resolutions passed by Parliament at the time of the Demerara uprising in 1823.[35] In both 1807 and 1833, therefore, political intervention by British governments was legitimized by anxiety over colonial security arising from the seeming unpreparedness of Caribbean planters to put the safety of their colonies and thus Britain's national and imperial interests above their own short-term pecuniary gains.

In his propositions on emancipation Stanley also acknowledged that legitimacy for government and parliamentary action against slavery rested on the strength of public sentiment on the issue. "The nation," he noted, "have now loudly, and for a length of time declared that the disgrace of slavery should not be suffered to remain part of our national system." In emphasizing the loudness of the public voice, Stanley echoed the sentiments of Charles James Fox forty-five years earlier, when in supporting Pitt's proposal to launch inquiries into the future of the British slave trade, he drew attention to the weight of petitions on the table of the House of Commons in favor of the trade's abolition. The wave of petitions that began in late 1787 and continued through 1792 also gave the public voice more persistence, strengthening the longer-term political legitimacy of the campaign while reflecting its transformation into a national social cause of exceptional propriety, resolve, purpose, organization, and scale in what the historian Charles Tilly called the age of mass politics. Even as the campaign to end the trade became largely focused on parliamentary maneuvers in 1804–7, abolitionist activists continued to acknowledge the value of public support for the cause. I have argued that activists' imaginative use of opportunities arising from rapid urban growth, religious groups' social networks, and an expanding publishing industry and press, among other things, mobilized that support. Those attributes were recognized in 1792 by Edmund Burke when, in correspondence with Home Secretary Henry Dundas over Dundas's efforts to delay or stall abolition, Burke noted the perseverance and manner with which the "popular spirit" to address the issue "without-doors" had been excited and which had carried it through the Commons in that year.[36] But the speed and scale with which that public expression of sentiment emerged in 1787–92 was indicative, too, of underlying ideological springs of benevolence and shared humanity, as well as feelings of moral outrage at the nation's association with slavery's and slave trading's inherent cruelty and violence, that helped to transform the anti–slave trade campaign into a "precocious pioneer of the modern social movement" that would soon become "a settled and irreversible fixture of national policy."[37] In that process the combination of ideological commitment, of empathy and outrage, and of personal and collective agency that underpinned the anti–slave trade campaign through 1807 was reinforced by continuing expansion of the nation's urban population, by new and even larger petitioning campaigns, by further growth in women's participation, and by ever increasing awareness of contradictions between demands for reform and rights at home and the country's association with colonial slavery. When Stanley noted, therefore, in 1833 the longevity of the nation's antipathy toward slavery, he was surely aware that its roots lay in the large-scale expression of public disquiet at British participation in the slave trade from Africa that first surfaced politically nearly half a century earlier.

It is impossible to explain the rise and successes of British antislavery from 1783 onward without reference to the humanitarian principles it embodied and the sense of duty their advocates assumed to ensure that such principles informed the nation's identity and public policy. That does not mean, however, that we should ignore the contributions of enslaved Africans themselves or of the domestic changes wrought by growth of British industrial capitalism or of international crises to shaping the course and timing of British antislavery's national historic achievements. Like their roots, the consequences of those achievements, it may be argued, ultimately extended beyond Britain's own national and imperial boundaries: indeed, leading British abolitionists such as Thomas Clarkson and Thomas Fowell Buxton, as well as some British government ministers after Colonial Secretary Edward Stanley, anticipated and strove to ensure they did. As they did so they formulated a new British cultural imperialism that would influence the deployment of Britain's growing economic and military power internationally, infuse its relations with other states, and even provide after 1870 a justification for its involvement in the Scramble for Africa. The historian W. E. H. Lecky famously remarked after the American Civil War that Britain's crusade against slavery constituted one of the most virtuous moments in human history. Others have seen in British antislavery the origins of modern human rights agendas. Cynics, including those who place more weight on narrow economic forces in determining historical change, question both. Nonetheless, insofar as both the two former perspectives place humanitarianism at the heart of explanations of why the British embraced and ultimately sought to export their antislavery ideology, they are congruent with this book's argument. In saying that, however, we do well also to recall historian C. L. R. James's remark, cited elsewhere in this work, on how efforts to translate ideas or principles into political practice are shaped by the necessities of the environment in which their architects have to operate. In doing that, it is vital to recognize not only the constraints posed by that environment but also the opportunities that it offered to affect and promote change. As the crucial first victory of British antislavery, the Abolition Act of 1807 was in retrospect, and for some contemporaries in fact, a vital first step in what Edward Stanley would later describe as a "mighty experiment" in the advancement of human freedom. As it evolved, it would redefine the nation's self-image, its international standing, and even its influence over, in Stanley's mind, "the welfare of millions of men in a state of slavery in colonies not belonging to Great Britain." In a wide-ranging critique of Stanley a decade later, the radical *Westminster Review* accused him of not recognizing problems inherent in "the working out of a new and difficult experiment in social sciences," failing indeed to "render British policy an example rather than a warning to all slave-holding communities" and thereby, in "a fit of uncalculating moral enthusiasm," bungling and spoiling "a grand work of national justice and humanity."[38] Be that as it may, it remains the case that the process that culminated in the 1833 Slave Emancipation Act began to take political form in 1787 when a small band of heroic advocates of humanitarian intervention decided to challenge the morality of the slave trade that underpinned growth of British West Indian slavery and, with widespread public support and no little assistance from enslaved Africans themselves, convinced Parliament to outlaw in 1807 what was then the Western world's largest, most vibrant, and most successful national slave-trading business. It is tempting, of course, in hindsight to see the 1807 Abolition Act as an initial step en route toward the abolitionists' ultimate prize, Stanley's mighty experiment. It was, however, in its own right, in its own terms, and in its own time a truly historic and remarkable, even world-changing accomplishment against formidable odds that, in its boldness and execution, rightly continues to fascinate historians over two hundred years later.

Notes

Abbreviations

BNA   The British Newspaper Archive, britishnewspaperarchive.co.uk
BRO   Bristol Record Office
EHR   *Economic History Review*
JEH   *Journal of Economic History*
LRO   Liverpool Record Office
TNA   The National Archives
Voyages   Slave Voyages, www.slavevoyages.org
WMQ   *William and Mary Quarterly*

Introduction

Epigraph: Oscar Wilde, *The Picture of Dorian Gray* (1891; London: Penguin Classics, 2012), 55.

1. David Brion Davis, "Foreword," in David Eltis and David Richardson, *Atlas of the Transatlantic Slave Trade* (New Haven: Yale University Press, 2010), xxii.
2. David Brion Davis, *Inhuman Bondage: The Rise and Fall of Slavery in the New World* (Oxford: Oxford University Press, 2006), 11.
3. Joel Quirk, *The Anti-Slavery Project: From the Slave Trade to Human Trafficking* (Philadelphia: University of Pennsylvania Press, 2011); Seymour Drescher, "Liberty, Equality, Humanity: Antislavery and Civil Society in Britain and France," in *The Rise and Demise of Slavery and the Slave Trade in the Atlantic World,* ed. Philip Misevich and Kristin Mann (Rochester, NY: University of Rochester Press, 2016), 172–95.
4. C. D. Kaufman and R. A. Pape, "Explaining Costly Moral Action: Britain's Sixty-Year Campaign against the Atlantic Slave Trade," *International Organization* 53, no. 4 (1999): 636–37; Eltis and Richardson, *Atlas,* 272; David Eltis, *Economic Growth and the Ending of the Atlantic Slave Trade* (Oxford: Oxford University Press, 1987), 97; Seymour Drescher, *Abolition: A History of Slavery and Antislavery* (Cambridge: Cambridge University Press, 2009).
5. Eric Williams, *Capitalism and Slavery* (Chapel Hill: University of North Carolina Press, 1944), vii. Williams went on famously to claim that the profits

from the triangular (that is, slave) trade provided "one of the main streams of capital accumulation which financed the Industrial Revolution" (52).

6. I examine trends in the scale of British slave trading in chapter 1.

7. Thomas Clarkson, *The History of the Rise, Progress, and Accomplishment of the Abolition of the Slave Trade by the British Parliament,* 2 vols. (London: Longman, Hurst, Rees, and Orme, 1808), 1:257.

8. All figures are from Voyages/estimates/transatlantic/flag = Great Britain (and France)/individual years/embarkations (with disembarkations for 1787).

9. The description is attributed to Lord Grenville, who navigated the abolition bill through the House of Lords in 1807. Clarkson, *History,* 2:579.

10. Particularly valuable for my work have been studies of medieval trade networks and of the Hudson's Bay Company and the Royal African Company in the early modern period. See Avner Greif, "Reputation and Coalitions in Medieval Trade: Evidence on Maghribi Traders," *JEH* 49, no. 4 (1989): 857–82; Ann M. Carlos and Stephen Nicholas, "Agency Problems in Early Chartered Companies: The Case of the Hudson's Bay Company," *JEH* 50, no. 4 (1990): 853–75; Carlos, "Principal-Agent Problems in Early Trading Companies: A Tale of Two Firms," *American Economic Review, Papers and Proceedings* 82, no. 2 (1992): 140–45; Carlos, "Bonding and the Agency Problem: Evidence from the Royal African Company," *Explorations in Economic History* 31, no. 3 (1994): 313–35; and Carlos and Nicholas, "Theory and History: Seventeenth-Century Joint Stock Chartered Trading Companies," *JEH* 56, no. 4 (1996): 916–24.

11. For examples of microhistories that seek to relate individual life stories to wider historical patterns, see Robert Harms, *The "Diligent": A Voyage through the Worlds of the Slave Trade* (New York: Basic Books, 2002); Marcus Rediker, *The Slave Ship: A Human History* (New York: Viking, 2007); Sean M. Kelley, *The Voyage of the Slave Ship "Hare": A Journey into Captivity from Sierra Leone to South Carolina* (Chapel Hill: University of North Carolina Press, 2016); Sowande M. Mustakeem, *Slavery at Sea: Terror, Sex, and Sickness in the Middle Passage* (Champaign: University of Illinois Press, 2016); and Christer Petley, *White Fury: A Jamaican Slaveholder and the Age of Revolution* (Oxford: Oxford University Press, 2018).

12. Wilde, *Dorian Gray,* 9.

13. Cf., e.g., the approach offered by Lynn Hunt, *Inventing Human Rights: A History* (New York: W. W. Norton, 2007), to that of Drescher, "Liberty, Equality, Humanity," where the issue of human rights is concerned.

14. Quote Investigator, 12 November 2017, https://quoteinvestigator.com/2017/11/12/change-world/.

15. Thomas Clarkson, *An Essay on the Slavery and Commerce of the Human Species, Particularly the African* (London: J. Phillips, 1786).

16. Clarkson, *History*, 1:256–57.

17. W. E. H. Lecky, *History of European Morals*, 2 vols. (London: Longman, Green, 1869), 1:160–61.

18. Sir Reginald Coupland, *The British Anti-Slavery Movement* (London: T. Butterworth, 1933), 111 (quotation).

19. Ignoring books published shortly after Wilberforce's death in 1833, the list includes Sir Reginald Coupland, *Wilberforce: A Narrative* (Oxford: Oxford University Press, 1923); William Hague, *William Wilberforce: The Life of the Great Anti-Slave Trade Campaigner* (London: HarperCollins, 2007); and Stephen Tomkins, *William Wilberforce: A Biography* (Grand Rapids, MI: William B. Eerdmans, 2007).

20. Michael Hennell, *John Venn and the Clapham Sect* (Lutterworth, UK: Lutterworth, 1958); David Spring, "The Clapham Sect: Some Social and Political Aspects," *Victorian Studies* 5, no. 1 (1961): 35–48; John Wolffe, "Clapham Sect (act. 1792–1815)," *Oxford Dictionary of National Biography* (Oxford: Oxford University Press, 2004); Milton M. Klein, *Amazing Grace: John Thornton and the Clapham Sect* (New Orleans: University Press of the South, 2004); Stephen Tomkins, *The Clapham Sect: How Wilberforce's Circle Changed Britain* (Oxford: Lion Hudson, 2010).

21. C. L. R. James, *The Black Jacobins: Toussaint L'Ouverture and the San Domingo Revolution* (London: Secker and Warburg, 1938; rev. ed., New York: Random House, 1963). All subsequent references to James's book are to the revised edition.

22. Among many other studies, see David P. Geggus, *The Impact of the Haitian Revolution in the Atlantic World* (Columbia: University of South Carolina Press, 2001); Robin Blackburn, "Haiti, Slavery, and the Age of the Democratic Revolution," *WMQ*, 3rd ser., 63, no. 4 (2006): 633–74; Laurent Dubois, *Avengers of the New World* (Cambridge, MA: Belknap Press of Harvard University Press, 2006); Jeremy D. Popkin, *You Are All Free: The Haitian Revolution and the Abolition of Slavery* (New York: Cambridge University Press, 2010); and Mary Turner, "Slave Worker Rebellions and Revolution in the Americas to 1804," in *The Cambridge World History of Slavery*, vol. 3, *AD 1420–AD 1804*, ed. David Eltis and Stanley L. Engerman (New York: Cambridge University Press, 2011), 677–708.

23. R. J. M. Blackett, *The Captive's Quest for Freedom: Fugitive Slaves, the 1850 Fugitive Slave Law, and the Politics of Slavery* (Cambridge: Cambridge University Press, 2018); Aline Helg, *Slave No More: Self-Liberation before*

Abolitionism in the Americas (Chapel Hill: University of North Carolina Press, 2019).

24. Walter Johnson, "On Agency," *Journal of Social History* 37, no. 1 (2003): 113–24; Marcus Wood, "Significant Silence: Where Was Slave Agency in the Popular Imagery of 2007?," in *Imagining Transatlantic Slavery,* ed. Cora Kaplan and John Oldfield (London: Palgrave Macmillan, 2010), 162–90; Jean M. Hebrard, "Slavery in Brazil: Brazilian Scholars in the Key Interpretive Debates," *Translating the Americas* 1 (2013): 47–95.

25. David Geggus, "Slavery and the Haitian Revolution," in *The Cambridge World History of Slavery,* vol. 4, *AD 1804–AD 2016,* ed. David Eltis, Stanley L. Engerman, Seymour Drescher, and David Richardson (New York: Cambridge University Press, 2017), 321–43. In 1893, 89 years after Haitian independence was declared, the abolitionist and self-liberated former slave Frederick Douglass emphasized the neglect of US opportunities to trade with what he called the first Black republic in the Americas, thereby providing a metaphor for the US failure or unwillingness to engage with issues of domestic race relations in the post–Civil War era. Frederick Douglass, *Lecture on Haiti: The Haitian Pavilion Dedication Ceremonies Delivered at the World's Fair, in Jackson Park, Chicago, 2 January 1893* (Chicago: Violet Agents Supply, 1893).

26. Eric Williams, *Capitalism and Slavery* (Chapel Hill: University of North Carolina Press, 1944). For a commentary on the genesis and significance of Williams's book, albeit from one who would critique its findings, see Seymour Drescher, "Eric Williams: British Capitalism and British Slavery," *History and Theory* 26, no. 2 (1987): 180–96.

27. See, e.g., Robin Blackburn, *The Making of New World Slavery: From the Baroque to the Modern, 1492–1800* (London: Verso, 1998), esp. 509–81.

28. David Eltis, *The Rise of African Slavery in the Americas* (Cambridge: Cambridge University Press, 1999); David Eltis and Stanley L. Engerman, "The Importance of Slavery and the Slave Trade to Industrializing Britain," *JEH* 60, no. 1 (2000): 123–44; Seymour Drescher, "White Atlantic? The Choice for African Slave Labor in the Plantation Americas," in *Slavery in the Development of the Americas,* ed. David Eltis, Frank D. Lewis, and Kenneth L. Sokoloff (Cambridge: Cambridge University Press, 2004), 63.

29. Elizabeth Swanson and James Brewer Stewart, eds., *Human Bondage and Abolition: New Histories of Past and Present Slaveries* (Cambridge: Cambridge University Press, 2018).

30. L. J. Ragatz, *The Decline of the Planter Class in the British Caribbean, 1763–1833: A Study in Social and Economic History* (New York: Century, 1928);

Williams, *Capitalism and Slavery,* 7. In this respect, Williams's argument mirrored what is sometimes seen as "natural limits" claims regarding slavery and was in some respects anticipated by C. L. R. James, who argued that in Saint-Domingue on "new land that was good . . . the slave even though expensive still gave good profits, and was often the only labour available." James, *Black Jacobins,* 136n.

31. Lowell Ragatz stated as "fact" that slavery was "ruinous as a form of labor" and went on to suggest that it "must inevitably have come to an end through the operation of simple economic laws." Ragatz, *Decline,* 238. A later historian, Selwyn H. H. Carrington, cited approvingly an observation by Adam Smith's contemporary Arthur Young that "the culture of sugar by slaves was the dearest species of labour in the world" and went on to assert that by the late eighteenth century slavery as a labor system "undoubtedly had run its course" and that owning slaves was "becoming a losing proposition." Carrington, *The Sugar Industry and the Abolition of the British Slave Trade, 1775–1810* (Gainesville: University of Florida Press, 2002), 98, 218, 221. Yet another historian who postulated connections between economic crisis in the West Indies and slave trade abolition, David Ryden, suggested that in seeking to protect their interests after 1787 planters and their supporters were guilty of defending an "increasingly anachronistic system of labour organization." Ryden, ed., *The British Transatlantic Slave Trade,* vol. 4, *The Abolitionist Struggle: Promoters of the Slave Trade* (London: Pickering and Chatto, 2003), x.

32. David Richardson, "The Ending of the British Slave Trade in 1807: The Economic Context," in *The British Slave Trade: Abolition, Parliament and People,* ed. Stephen Farrell, Melanie Unwin, and James Walvin (Edinburgh: Edinburgh University Press, 2008), 131–33; Christer Petley, ed., *Rethinking the Fall of the Planter Class* (London: Routledge, 2016).

33. Williams, *Capitalism and Slavery,* 120–21.

34. Richard B. Sheridan, "The Wealth of Jamaica in the Eighteenth Century," *EHR* 18, no. 2 (1965): 292–311; Robert Paul Thomas, "The Sugar Colonies of the Old Empire: Profit or Loss for Great Britain?," *EHR* 21, no. 1 (1968): 30–45; Anne O. Krueger, "The Political Economy of the Rent-Seeking Society," *American Economic Review* 64, no. 3 (1974): 291–303; Robert B. Ekelund and Robert D. Tollison, *Mercantilism as a Rent-Seeking Society: Economic Regulation in Historical Perspective* (College Station: Texas A&M University Press, 1982).

35. Christopher Leslie Brown, *Moral Capital: Foundations of British Abolitionism* (Chapel Hill: University of North Carolina Press, 2006).

36. Paul Finkelman, "Regulating the African Slave Trade," *Civil War History* 54, no. 4 (2008): 377–403, esp. 381.

37. According to Adam Smith, "The experience of all ages and nations, I believe, demonstrates that the work done by slaves, though it appears to cost only their maintenance, is in the end the dearest of any. A person who can acquire no property can have no other interest but to eat as much and to labour as little as possible." Smith, *An Inquiry into the Nature and Causes of the Wealth of Nations,* 2 vols. (1776; Indianapolis, IN: Online Library of Liberty, 2013), 1:365.

38. Eric Hobsbawm, *Industry and Empire: From 1750 to the Present Day* (London: Penguin, 1968); John Saville, "Primitive Accumulation and Early Industrialization in Britain," *Socialist Register* 6 (1969): 247–71. Most of Saville's article was concerned with the early development of Britain's rural proletariat, but he also cited approvingly (267) Karl Marx's observations in his discussion of the primitive accumulation of preindustrial wealth that "in systematical combination" its sources included the colonies, the national debt, modes of taxation, and the protectionist system, all of which Marx identified with the brute force of state power, noting that "force is the midwife of every old society pregnant with a new one" and that such force "is an economic power." Marx, *Capital: A Critique of Political Economy,* vol. 1, *The Process of Capitalist Production,* ed. Frederick Engels (1867; Chicago: Charles H. Kerr, 1909), chap. 31, 822. Saville acknowledged the importance of the slave trade, or what Marx himself called "the commercial hunting of black-skins," to that colonial system (822). Others would follow Marx and Indian nationalists in extending Britain's colonial-based process of accumulation to the so-called economic drain of India. Brijesh K. Mistra and Siddhartha Rastogi, "Colonial Deindustrialization of India: A Review of Drain Theory," *South Asian Survey* 24, no. 1 (2018): 37–53.

39. William Darity Jr., "The Williams Abolition Thesis before Williams," *Slavery and Abolition* 9, no. 1 (1988): 29–41; Darity, "British Industry and the West Indies Plantations," *Social Science History* 14, no. 1 (1990): 117–49; Pat Hudson, *The Industrial Revolution* (London: Edward Arnold, 1992), 189–200; Joseph E. Inikori, *Africans and the Industrial Revolution in England* (Cambridge: Cambridge University Press, 2002); Carrington, *Sugar Industry;* David Beck Ryden, *West Indian Slavery and British Abolition, 1783–1807* (Cambridge: Cambridge University Press, 2009).

40. Joseph Miller, *The Problem of Slavery as History: A Global Approach* (New Haven: Yale University Press, 2012), 3–4.

41. Stanley L. Engerman, "Emancipations in Comparative Perspective: A Long and Wide View," in *Fifty Years Later: Antislavery, Capitalism and Moder-*

nity in the Dutch Orbit, ed. Gert Oostindie (Pittsburgh, PA: University of Pittsburgh Press, 1996), 237.

42. Seymour Drescher, *Econocide: British Slavery in the Era of Abolition* (1977; Chapel Hill: University of North Carolina Press, 2010); Drescher, *Capitalism and Antislavery: British Mobilization in Comparative Perspective* (Oxford: Oxford University Press, 1986), 2. Drescher reiterated that remark in print 10 years later in "Epilogue: Reflections," in Oostindie, *Fifty Years Later,* 243.

43. David Brion Davis, *The Problem of Slavery in the Age of Revolution, 1770–1823* (Ithaca, NY: Cornell University Press, 1975), 349–50. Davis subsequently refined his argument to emphasize that he was not advocating "a fixed set of ideas and doctrines used to promote concrete class interests" but rather identifying the linkage as offering a "perceptual lens" on social reality and change. Davis, "Reflections on Abolitionism and Ideological Hegemony," *American Historical Review* 92, no. 4 (1987): 799.

44. Joel Quirk and David Richardson, "Religion, Urbanisation and Anti-Slavery Mobilisation in Britain, 1787–1833," *European Journal of English Studies* 14, no. 3 (2010): 267.

45. David Brion Davis, *The Problem of Slavery in Western Culture* (Ithaca, NY: Cornell University Press, 1966).

46. David Brion Davis, *Slavery and Human Progress* (New York: Oxford University Press, 1984); James Walvin, *England, Slaves and Freedom, 1776–1838* (Jackson: University of Mississippi Press, 1986), 17; David Turley, *The Culture of English Antislavery, 1756–1838* (London: Routledge, 1991), 135; Linda Colley suggests how after 1807 "pulling out of the slave trade" and "actively coercing other powers to do the same . . . crowded out guilt about Britain's earlier, busy slave-trading, and offered proof that empire, modern liberty, and benevolence were fully compatible." Colley, *Captives: Britain, Empire, and the World, 1600–1850* (London: Jonathan Cape, 2002), 367. On humanitarian revolution, see Hunt, *Inventing Human Rights;* and Steven Pinker, *The Better Angels of Our Nature: A History of Violence and Humanity* (London: Penguin, 2012).

47. Marcus Wood, *Blind Memory: Visual Representations of Slavery in England and America, 1780–1865* (Manchester: Manchester University Press, 2000); Brycchan Carey, *British Abolitionism and the Rhetoric of Sensibility: Writing, Sentiment, and Slavery, 1760–1807* (London: Palgrave Macmillan, 2005); Carey, "Slavery and the Novel of Sentiment," in *The Sentimental Novel in the Eighteenth Century,* ed. Albert J. Rivero (Cambridge: Cambridge University Press, 2019), 138–54; Catherine Molineux, *Faces of Perfect Ebony: Encountering*

Atlantic Slavery in Imperial Britain (Cambridge, MA: Harvard University Press, 2012); Hunt, *Inventing Human Rights;* Srividhya Swaminatham and Adam R. Beach, eds., *Invoking Slavery in the Eighteenth-Century British Imagination* (Farnham, UK: Ashgate, 2013); Philip Gould, "Slavery in the Eighteenth-Century Literary Imagination," in *The Cambridge Companion to Slavery in American Literature,* ed. Ezra Tawil (Cambridge: Cambridge University Press, 2016), 16–31.

48. On the explosion, see William St. Clair, *The Reading Nation in the Romantic Period* (Cambridge: Cambridge University Press, 2004), 103–22; on anti-slavery ideas in Europe, see, e.g., Jeremy L. Caradonna, *The Enlightenment in Practice: Academic Prize Contests and Intellectual Culture in France, 1670–1794* (Ithaca, NY: Cornell University Press, 2012), 152–59; and Pauline Kleingeld, *Kant and Cosmopolitanism: The Philosophical Ideal of World Citizenship* (Cambridge: Cambridge University Press, 2012), 92–117.

49. Charles Tilly, *Popular Contention in Great Britain, 1758–1834* (Cambridge, MA: Harvard University Press, 1995).

50. According to C. L. R. James, "The slave-trade and slavery were woven tight into the economics of the eighteenth century" and were also "the economic basis of the French Revolution," having created fortunes in Bordeaux and Nantes and thereby given "the bourgeoisie that pride which needed liberty and contributed to human emancipation." James, *Black Jacobins,* 25–26, 47.

51. The last included Richard Hart, who wrote, among many other works, *Slaves Who Abolished Slavery,* vol. 1, *Blacks in Bondage* (1980), and vol. 2, *Blacks in Rebellion* (1985; Mona, Jamaica: University of the West Indies Press, 2002).

52. James, *Black Jacobins,* x.

53. James, *Black Jacobins,* x–xi.

54. Joseph E. Stiglitz, "Principal and Agent," in *Allocation, Information and Marketing,* ed. John Eatwell, Murray Milgate, and Peter K. Newman (London: Macmillan Palgrave, 1989), 241–53.

55. Another distinction between "principals" and "principles" was sometimes made by eighteenth-century commentators, among them West Indian planters, one of whom saw slaves as "the *principal,* and the *principle,* of a planter's wealth." Cited in Petley, *White Fury,* 47.

56. Friedrich Nietzsche, *Thus Spake Zarathustra* (1883; Ware, UK: Wordsworth Classics, 1997), 55–56, 111–13, 136–40; Nietzsche, *Beyond Good and Evil* (1886; London: Penguin, 1990), 53. Precisely what Nietzsche meant by the concept is not always clear. But in his introduction to the 1990 edition of *Beyond Good and Evil,* Michael Tanner notes how Nietzsche relates the pursuit of knowledge to the defense or support of "a moral order which is a dressed-up ver-

sion of how we want things to be, or how we want them to be forced to be," describing this as "the 'will to power' in action" and identifying it with Nietzsche's own distrust of philosophers who offer prejudice or "a desire of the heart sifted and made abstract" and then defended with reasons "sought after the event" (14–15, 36–37). It is also possible to see British slave trade abolition in 1807 as an early indicator of what David Brion Davis called the willed collective achievement that he identified with the abolition of slavery throughout the Americas some 80 years later. Davis, *Inhuman Bondage,* 11.

Chapter 1. A "Diabolical Traffic"

1. Clements R. Markham, ed., *The Hawkins' Voyages during the Reigns of Henry VIII, Queen Elizabeth, and James I,* rev. ed. (London: Taylor and Francis, 2017).
2. Richard Jobson, *The Golden Trade: or, A Discovery of the River Gambra, and the Golden Trade of the Aethiopians [. . .]* (1623), transcribed by James Eason at http://penelope.uchicago.edu/jobson/, 88–89.
3. Daniel J. Vitkus, ed., *Piracy, Slavery and Redemption: Barbary Captivity Narratives from Early Modern England* (New York: Columbia University Press, 2001); Deborah Baumgold, "Slavery Discourse before the Restoration: The Barbary Coast, Justinian's *Digest,* and Hobbes's Political Theory," *History of European Ideas* 36, no. 4 (2010): 412–18.
4. On English attitudes toward Africans before 1650, see P. E. H. Hair, "Attitudes to Africans in English Primary Sources on Guinea up to 1650," *History in Africa* 26 (1999): 43–68; April Lee Hatfield, "A 'Very Wary People in Their Bargaining' or 'Very Good Merchandise': English Traders' Views of Free and Enslaved Africans, 1550–1650," *Slavery and Abolition* 25, no. 3 (2004): 1–17.
5. Given that enslaved Africans cultivated sugar in the Mediterranean and Atlantic islands before the Americas, the term "sugar revolution" has been contentious when applied to the spread of transatlantic slavery. But there is little doubt that sugar cultivation lay at the heart of what Barry Higman has called "a concatenation of events located in the seventeenth-century Caribbean with far-reaching ramifications for the Atlantic world." B. W. Higman, "The Sugar Revolution," *EHR* 53, no. 2 (2000): 213. See also Russell R. Menard, "The Sugar Industry in the Seventeenth Century: A New Perspective on the Barbadian Sugar Revolution," in *Tropical Babylons: Sugar and the Making of the Atlantic World,* ed. Stuart Schwartz (Chapel Hill: University of North Carolina Press, 2004), 289–330; and Nuala Zahediah, *The Capital and the Colonies:*

London and the Atlantic Economy, 1660–1700 (Cambridge: Cambridge University Press, 2010), 211–14.

6. Voyages/transatlantic/database/flag = Great Britain/by years. Unless otherwise stated, all references to Voyages are to the version launched in 2019 and specifically to the transatlantic slave trade database. All data cited from Voyages in this chapter relate to those available on 30 September 2019. British colonial includes ships leaving British mainland North America for Africa before 1776.

7. On the complex relations among culture, religion, and enslavement in the Americas, see David Eltis, "Europeans and the Rise and Fall of African Slavery in the Americas: An Interpretation," *American Historical Review* 98, no. 5 (1993): 1399–423; and Eltis, *The Rise of African Slavery in the Americas* (Cambridge: Cambridge University Press, 2000).

8. Voyages/estimates/flag = Great Britain/slaves embarked and disembarked. As stated in note 6, above, British colonial here includes slaves embarked and disembarked on ships that had left British mainland North America for Africa before 1776.

9. T. S. Grimshawe, ed., *The Works of William Cowper by William Hayley: His Life and Letters,* 8 vols. (London: Saunders and Otley, 1835), 3:302.

10. Figures on the slave trades other than the British can be found in Voyages/ estimates.

11. It has been pointed out that from 1758 French slavers received a subsidy for each captive delivered to the nation's West Indian colonies, that in 1784 these were increased by a bounty of 40 livres per ton on ships fitting out for Africa and by a raising of the subsidy of slaves delivered to the colonies, and that the bounty on deliveries was yet further raised in 1787 to encourage slave shipments to Saint-Domingue. Prompted by official concerns about the undersupply of slaves to the French colonies, such "government largesse" is said largely to explain "both the sharp rise in the French slave trade after 1783 and the generous returns to some traders." James A. Rawley with Stephen D. Behrendt, *The Transatlantic Slave Trade: A History,* rev. ed. (Lincoln: University of Nebraska Press, 2005), 123.

12. For a brief discussion of the regulations introduced in 1788 under the Dolben Act, which were subsequently revised, see Herbert S. Klein and Stanley L. Engerman, "Slave Mortality on British Ships, 1791–1797," in *Liverpool, the African Slave Trade, and Abolition,* ed. Roger Anstey and P. E. H. Hair, Historic Society of Lancashire and Cheshire, Occasional Series, no. 2 (1976), 119–21.

13. On slave prices, see David Eltis and David Richardson, *Atlas of the Transatlantic Slave Trade* (New Haven: Yale University Press, 2010), 3. On the neat-

ness of European ports, see John Steinbeck, *Cannery Row* (1945; London: Penguin, 2000), 7.

14. For an interpretation of the reforms of the Spanish Bourbon monarchy, see Elena Schneider, "African Slavery and Spanish Empire: Imperial Imaginings and Bourbon Reform in Eighteenth-Century Cuba and Beyond," *Journal of Early American History* 5, no. 1 (2015): 3–29.

15. On early links between Barbados and Surinam (or Dutch Guiana), see Justin Roberts, "Surrendering Surinam: The Barbadian Diaspora and the Expansion of the English Sugar Frontier, 1650–1675," *WMQ*, 3rd ser., 73, no. 2 (2016): 225–56.

16. See Eric Hobsbawm, *Industry and Empire: From 1750 to the Present Day* (1969; London: New Press, 1999), 27, where Hobsbawm argues that Britain's eighteenth-century "war aims were commercial and (what amounts to the same thing) naval" and involved colonial conquest.

17. On trade with Spanish America after 1713, see Colin A. Palmer, *Human Cargoes: The British Slave Trade to Spanish America, 1700–1739* (Champaign: University of Illinois Press, 1981); on the larger and underestimated role of Spanish America as a market for slaves, including that for British traders, see Alex Borucki, David Eltis, and David Wheat, "Atlantic History and the Slave Trade to Spanish America," *American Historical Review,* 120, no. 2 (2015): 433–61.

18. David Eltis, "The Slave Economies of the Caribbean: Structure, Performance, Evolution and Significance," in *UNESCO General History of the Caribbean,* ed. Franklin Knight, 6 vols. to date (New York: Palgrave Macmillan, 1997–), 3:178–202.

19. Of the 2.84 million enslaved Africans entering the Americas in British ships in 1640–1807, more than four-fifths (or 2.32 million) landed in the British Caribbean. Most of the remaining half a million captives disembarked at ports serving the plantation economies of British mainland North America, with the rest entering Spanish America or South Carolina after its independence from Britain. On the intercolonial trade, see Gregory E. O'Malley, *Final Passages: The Intercolonial Slave Trade of British America, 1619–1807* (Chapel Hill: University of North Carolina Press, 2014). More recent estimates suggest that close to a quarter of a million (or about one in nine) of the enslaved Africans entering the British Caribbean were reexported to Spanish America. Borucki, Eltis, and Wheat, "Atlantic History," 444. That excludes some 41,000 slaves entering directly into Cuba in British ships between the Seven Years' War and 1808, most of them, as noted in table 1.2, in the period after 1788. Voyages/database/1760–1808/flag = Great Britain/itinerary = place of landing/total slaves disembarked.

20. The exceptionally high rate of growth of per capita sugar consumption in eighteenth-century Britain is noted in Noel Deerr, *The History of Sugar,* 2 vols. (London: Chapman and Hall, 1949–50); Sidney W. Mintz, *Sweetness and Power: The Place of Sugar in Modern History* (New York: Penguin, 1985); and Jonathan Hersh and Hans-Joachim Voth, "Sweet Diversity: Colonial Goods and the Rise of European Living Standards after 1492" (4 July 2009), 12, available at SSRN: http://dx.doi.org/10.2139/ssrn.1402322. On trends in slave labor productivity, see David Eltis, Frank D. Lewis, and David Richardson, "Slave Prices, the African Slave Trade, and Productivity in the Caribbean, 1674–1807," *EHR* 58, no. 4 (2005): 673–700.

21. As Eric Williams noted, slave-based agriculture "quickly exhausts the soil," making slavery viable only where there were "ever fresh conquests" of new land. Williams, *Capitalism and Slavery* (Chapel Hill: University of North Carolina Press, 1944), 7. Although expansion into new lands allowed slavery to grow, there was also rising productivity in established colonies. Eltis, Lewis, and Richardson, "Slave Prices."

22. Nicholas Barbon, *A Discourse of Trade* (London: Jacob Harry Hollander, 1690), 40–41.

23. Malachy Postlethwayt, *The African Trade, the Great Pillar and Support of the British Plantation Trade in America* (London: J. Robinson, 1745).

24. Thomas Clarkson, *An Essay on the Slavery and Commerce of the Human Species, Particularly the African* (London: J. Phillips, 1786), 105.

25. Thomas Fowell Buxton, *The African Slave Trade and Its Remedy* (London: John Murray, 1840), 199–200.

26. Tho[mas] Southerne, *Oroonoko: A Tragedy, as it is acted at the Theatre Royal* (London: H. Playford, B. Tooke and S Buckley, 1696), 9 (act 1, scene 2); Richard Dunn, *Sugar and Slaves: The Rise of the Planter Class in the English West Indies, 1624–1713* (Chapel Hill: University of North Carolina Press, 1972), 334.

27. Barry W. Higman, "Economic and Social Development of the British West Indies, from Settlement to ca. 1850," in *The Cambridge Economic History of the United States,* vol. 1, *The Colonial Era,* ed. Stanley L. Engerman and Robert E. Gallman (Cambridge: Cambridge University Press, 1996), 297–336, esp. 309, where Higman refers to the demographic "crisis" in the British islands.

28. David Eltis and Paul Lachance, "The Demographic Decline of Caribbean Slave Populations: New Evidence from the Transatlantic and Intra-American Slave Trades," in *Extending the Frontiers: Essays on the New Transatlantic Slave Trade Database,* ed. David Eltis and David Richardson (New Haven: Yale University Press, 2008), 335–63.

29. For the basis of these estimates and calculations, see my "Consuming Goods, Consuming People: Reflections on the Transatlantic Slave Trade," in *The Rise and Demise of Slavery and the Slave Trade in the Atlantic World,* ed. Kristin Mann and Philip Misevich (Rochester, NY: Rochester University Press), 31–63. In 1790 the slave population of the then British Caribbean was around 450,000, which, assuming an annual population reproduction deficit of 2.5 percent, suggests that some 11,000 enslaved Africans had to be imported each year simply to sustain population numbers. With estimated annual slave arrivals from Africa into the British Caribbean averaging 24,600 slaves in 1786–90, that 11,000 figure implies a replacement demand equivalent to 45 percent of newly imported slaves in that period.

30. Richard Rathbone, "Resistance to Enslavement in West Africa," *Slavery and Abolition* 6, no. 3 (1985): 9–23. Africans boarding ship were not the only eighteenth-century people to fear being cannibalized by strangers; so, too, according to Daniel Defoe, was Robinson Crusoe. Defoe, *Robinson Crusoe* (1719; London: Penguin, 2001), 122–36.

31. Foundational to the study of Caribbean slave demography are the works of Barry Higman, notably *Slave Population and Economy in Jamaica, 1807–1834* (Cambridge: Cambridge University Press, 1976); Higman, *Slave Populations of the British Caribbean, 1807–1834* (Baltimore: Johns Hopkins University Press, 1984; repr. Kingston, Jamaica: University of the West Indies Press, 1995); and Higman, *Montpellier, Jamaica: A Plantation Community in Slavery and Freedom, 1739–1912* (Kingston, Jamaica: University of the West Indies Press, 1998).

32. See, e.g., Kenneth F. Kiple, *The Caribbean Slave: A Biological History* (New York: Cambridge University Press, 1984).

33. Kenneth Morgan, "Slave Women and Reproduction in Jamaica, c. 1776–1834," *History* 91, no. 2 (2006): 231–53. Philip Larkin's advice comes from his poem "This Be the Verse": "Man hands on misery to man. / It deepens like a coastal shelf. / Get out as quickly as you can, / And don't have any kids yourself." Larkin, *Collected Poems* (1988; London, Faber and Faber, 2003).

34. Higman, *Slave Population and Economy,* 14–16, 122, 124.

35. For an early example of such a comparison, see Stanley L. Engerman, "Some Economic and Demographic Comparisons of Slavery in the United States and the British West Indies," *EHR* 29, no. 2 (1976): 258–75.

36. Michael Tadman, "The Demographic Cost of Sugar: Debates on Slave Societies and Natural Increase in the Americas," *American Historical Review* 105, no. 5 (2000): 1561. Tadman's conclusion echoed that made by Higman a quarter of a century earlier (see note 31, above) and later reinforced by Higman when he argued that the conditions faced by the enslaved in sugar production,

with its gang labor and manufacturing processes relating to cane, "made demands on human endurance rarely matched on such a scale." Higman, *Slave Populations of the British Caribbean*, 374–75. For a more recent and similar emphasis on the relations among cane holing, high slave mortality and morbidity rates, and demand for jobbing laborers, see Justin Roberts, *Slavery and the Enlightenment in the British Atlantic, 1750–1807* (New York: Cambridge University Press, 2013), 105–10.

37. Alfred Marshall, *Industry and Trade* (London: Macmillan, 1919), 43n. Cf. Herman Melville, who highlighted the human costs of supplying spermaceti oil, arguing, "For God's sake, be economical with your lamps and candles! Not a gallon you burn, but at least one drop of man's blood was spilled for it." Melville, *Moby-Dick* (1851; London: Penguin, 2012), 240.

38. The most detailed study of trends in profits from British sugar plantations remains J. R. Ward, "The Profitability of Sugar Planting in the British West Indies, 1650–1834," *EHR* 36, no. 2 (1978): 197–213. For one contemporary's assessment of the challenges and rewards of sugar cultivation in later eighteenth-century Jamaica, see Petley, *White Fury*, 74–75.

39. Roberts, *Slavery and Enlightenment*, 213.

40. Higman, *Slave Population in Jamaica*, 3, 80, 207.

41. James Currie, preface to William Roscoe, *The Wrongs of Africa, Part the First* (London: R. Faulder, 1787), vi. Currie also noted that it "is the interest of the merchants of England, that the conditions of the negroes in the colonies should not be meliorated, for otherwise, they might multiply in such a manner as to destroy the demand" (vi).

42. Elsa V. Goveia, *Slave Society in the British Leeward Islands at the End of the Eighteenth Century* (New Haven: Yale University Press, 1965), 111.

43. Voyages/database/1640–1808/flag = Great Britain.

44. Voyages/database/1640–1776/flag = United States.

45. Eltis and Richardson, *Atlas*, 32, 39, 49–52.

46. London slave-trading partnerships evidently typically comprised fewer members than those of their Bristol and Liverpool counterparts and included in the 1720s three single-owner or investor firms that, it is claimed, were able to mobilize the capital to engross a sizable proportion, estimated at a quarter in 1726, of the city's slave trading capacity and reflecting a pattern of "individual entrepreneurship" in London's trade that may have been exceptional in the British eighteenth-century trade as a whole. James A. Rawley, *London, Metropolis of the Slave Trade* (Columbia: University of Missouri Press, 2003), 43–45. On agent or ship's husband, see David Richardson, *The Bristol Slave Traders: A Collective Portrait* (Bristol: Bristol Branch of the Historical As-

sociation, 1985); for managing owners, see ship *Bedford* accounts 1803, Chancery Masters Exhibits, C 114/157, TNA, where Thomas Lumley and Co. of London were described as managing owners.

47. The ships of Nantes, which continued with some other French ports to be involved in trafficking after 1815, are estimated to have embarked some 542,000 enslaved Africans, while the ships of La Rochelle, Le Havre, Bordeaux, and Saint-Malo, the next four French slaving ports in importance, are estimated to have embarked, respectively, 166,000, 142,000, 134,000, and 73,000. Eltis and Richardson, *Atlas,* 39.

48. Of the 283,000 enslaved Africans embarking on ships with a British flag in 1641–1700, at least 194,669 (nearly 69 percent) are known to have entered ships that had left from London. Voyages/database/1641–1700/flag = Great Britain/ departure place = London.

49. F. J. Fisher, "London's Export Trade in the Early Seventeenth Century," *EHR* 3, no. 2 (1950): 151–61; Ralph Davis, "English Foreign Trade, 1660–1700," *EHR* 7, no. 2 (1954): 150–66; Nuala Zahediah, *The Capital and the Colonies: London and the Atlantic Economy, 1660–1700* (Cambridge: Cambridge University Press, 2010).

50. George F. Zook, "The Company of Royal Adventurers Trading into Africa," *Journal of Negro History* 4, no. 2 (1919): 134–231; Kenneth G. Davies, *The Royal African Company* (London: Longmans, Green, 1957); P. E. H. Hair and Robin Law, "The English in West Africa to 1700," in *The Oxford History of the British Empire,* vol. 1, *The Origins of Empire: British Overseas Enterprise to the Close of the Seventeenth Century,* ed. Nicholas Canny (Oxford: Oxford University Press, 1998), 242–63.

51. James A. Rawley, "Richard Harris, Slave Trader Spokesman," *Albion* 23, no. 1 (1991): 439–58; William A. Pettigrew, *Freedom's Debt: The Royal African Company and the Politics of the Atlantic Slave Trade, 1672–1752* (Chapel Hill: University of North Carolina Press, 2013).

52. David Richardson, ed., *Bristol, Africa and the Eighteenth-Century Slave Trade to America,* vol. 1, *The Years of Expansion, 1698–1730,* Bristol Record Society's Publications, vol. 38 (1986), xv.

53. Richard Watson, *The Life of the Rev. John Wesley A.M.* (New York: J. Emory and B. Waugh, 1837), 321; William Maginn, *John Manesty, the Liverpool Slave Merchant,* 2 vols. (London: J. Mortimer, 1844), 1:3.

54. Voyages/database/1750–1808/departure places = Liverpool, Bristol, and London.

55. "Account of the Vessels, and the Amount of their Cargoes, now employed by the Merchants of Liverpool in the African Slave Trade—3d March 1790,"

in *House of Commons Sessional Papers of the Eighteenth Century,* ed. Sheila Lambert, 147 vols. (Wilmington, DE: Scholarly Resources, 1975), 72:211–19. At that point the total investment was said to be £1,092,546, of which £361,608 was the value of ships and their outfits, the rest (£730,938) being cargoes of goods exported.

56. David Richardson, ed., *Bristol, Africa and the Eighteenth-Century Slave Trade to America,* vol. 4, *The Final Years, 1770–1807,* Bristol Record Society's Publications, vol. 47 (1996), xviii–xix.

57. Annual Bristol investment in voyages around 1715 was £50,000–£60,000, while in 1713-17 ships leaving Bristol totaled 89 (or 28 percent) of the 316 leaving all British ports for Africa for slaves in those years, suggesting a total annual British investment in the trade around 1715 of perhaps £215,000. Richardson, *Years of Expansion,* xvii; Voyages/database/1713–17/flag = Great Britain/departure place = Bristol. The £3,000 or so investment per voyage implicit in the Bristol data matches that found for a sample of 10 voyages outfitted by a leading London slave merchant in the 1720s. Rawley, *London,* 45.

58. Over the whole period of the Atlantic slave trade, which extended through 1867, ships from Rio de Janeiro and Salvador da Bahia in Brazil carried more slaves from Africa than those from Liverpool, but in 1740–1807 Liverpool outfitted more than twice as many slaving voyages as Bahia, its nearest competitor in the Atlantic world at that time. Voyages/database/1740–1807/departure place = Bahia.

59. Katie McDade, "'A Particular Spirit of Enterprise': Bristol and Liverpool Slave Trade Merchants as Entrepreneurs in the Eighteenth Century" (PhD thesis, University of Nottingham, 2011), esp. chap. 6; McDade, "Liverpool Slave Merchant Entrepreneurial Networks, 1725–1807," *Business History* 53, no. 7 (2011): 1092–109.

60. Mark Granovetter, "Economic Action and Social Structure: The Problem of Embeddedness," *American Journal of Sociology* 91, no. 3 (1985): 481–510.

61. The words are those of Steinbeck, *Cannery Row,* 107.

62. James Wallace, *A General and Descriptive History of the Ancient and Present State of the Town of Liverpool* (Liverpool: J. M'Creevy, 1795), 216–17. John Atkins, writing in 1735, referred to Britain's clandestine trade in slaves to Spanish America, though without attributing particular importance to Liverpool. Atkins, *A Voyage to Guinea, Brasil and the West-Indies* (London: Caesar Ward and Richard Chandler, 1735), 153–54, 157.

63. Elizabeth W. Gilboy, *Wages in Eighteenth Century England* (Cambridge, MA: Harvard University Press, 1934); F. W. Botham and E. H. Hunt, "Wages in Britain during the Industrial Revolution," *EHR* 40, no. 3 (1987): 380–99.

Recent comments on Gilboy's sources and findings have raised questions about the use of her data to project incomes and earnings for eighteenth-century building craftsmen and other groups, but the regional differentials in rates her work explored have been less open to argument. Judy Z. Stephenson, "In Search of the Average Craftsman: Understanding Skilled Work and Wages in the Early Modern Building Industry and Wider Economy," in *Seven Centuries of Unreal Wages,* ed. John Hatcher and Judy Z. Stephenson (London: Palgrave Macmillan, 2018), 117-23.

64. Liverpool ships are thought to have disembarked over 19,000 enslaved Africans in the Americas in 1700–1730, the vast majority in the British Caribbean, with Barbados accounting for almost 47 percent of landings and Jamaica some 13 percent. Voyages/database/1700–1730/departure place = Liverpool/disembarked. In the same period, almost 48,000 slaves are thought to have entered the intra-American trade, with Jamaica accounting for almost 28,000 and Barbados over 6,700, and with Cuba receiving an estimated 5,500, and other parts of Spanish America bordering the Caribbean almost 27,000. Voyages/database/intra-American/1700–1730.

65. Ralph Davis, *The Rise of the English Shipping Industry in the Seventeenth and Eighteenth Centuries* (1962; Newton Abbot, UK: David and Charles, 1972), 296.

66. Richardson, *Years of Expansion,* 177; Tyndall and Assheton to Isaac Hobhouse, 30 January, 3 May 1729, Jamaica, Hobhouse Papers, Jefferies Collection, vol. 13, Bristol Central Library; James Pearce to Thomas Hall, 2 November 1734, Hall Papers, C 103/30, TNA.

67. Daniel Defoe, *A Tour thro' the Whole Island of Great Britain, Divided into Circuits or Journies,* 3 vols. (1724–27), vol. 2, letter 6, part 2, available online at A Vision of Britain through Time, https://www.visionofbritain.org.uk/travellers/Defoe.

68. Defoe, *Tour,* vol. 3, letter 10.

69. The four docks were Saltshouse (1754), George (1771), King's (1788), and Queen's (1796). On Bristol's failure to improve its port facilities and its implications for its Atlantic commerce, including its slave trade, see Alan F. Williams, "Bristol Port Plans and Improvement Schemes in the Eighteenth Century," *Transactions of the Bristol and Gloucestershire Archaeological Society* 81 (1962): 140.

70. For the importance of internal transport links in favoring Liverpool's success, see William Moss, *Georgian Liverpool: A Guide to the City in 1794* (1797; Lancaster: Palatine Books, 2007), 7. For subsequent historical discussions of the wider regional commercial and infrastructural developments of Liverpool,

see T. C. Barker, "Lancashire Coal, Cheshire Salt and the Rise of Liverpool," *Transactions of the Historic Society of Lancashire and Cheshire* 103 (1951): 83–101; Paul G. E. Clemens, "The Rise of Liverpool, 1665–1750," *EHR* 29, no. 2 (1976): 211–25; and Jon Stobart, *The First Industrial Region: North West England, c. 1700–1760* (Manchester: Manchester University Press, 2004).

71. Some of the following factors are noted in Kenneth Morgan, "Liverpool's Dominance in the English Slave Trade, 1740–1807," in *Liverpool and Trans-atlantic Slavery,* ed. David Richardson, Suzanne Schwarz, and Anthony J. Tibbles (Liverpool: Liverpool University Press, 2007), 14–42.

72. On the differences in composition of Liverpool exports to Africa from those of Bristol and London in 1772–87, see Sheila Lambert, ed., *The House of Commons Sessional Papers of the Eighteenth Century,* 145 vols. (Wilmington, DE: Scholarly Resources, 1975), 67:1–52.

73. Henry Thornton, *An Enquiry into the Nature and Effects of the Paper Credit of Great Britain* (1802; New York: Augustus M. Kelley, 1965), 70. That confidence, Thornton argued, "disposes them to lend money to each other," "to bring themselves under various pecuniary engagements by the acceptance and indorsements of bills," and "to sell and deliver goods in consideration of an equivalent promised to be given at a subsequent period" (70). Thornton's words echoed those Thomas Southerne attributed in 1696 to the slave Oroonoko, who, as a former slave supplier tricked into slavery himself, remarked, "Men live and prosper but in Mutual Trust, a Confidence of one another's Truth." Southerne, *Oroonoko,* 15.

74. In addition to the major Bristol merchant James Rogers, details of whose bankruptcy in 1793 are recorded in Chancery Masters' Records, other notable figures involved in the British slave trade experiencing bankruptcy included the Liverpool- and London-based shipmaster, investor, and author Archibald Dalzel, who, according to historian James Rawley, was twice bankrupted, though he "persevered in the trade for nearly half a century" from 1763 onward. Rogers Papers, C 107/6, 107/59, TNA; Rawley, *London,* 98–107 (quotation at 107). Rogers did not recover financially.

75. David Richardson, "Profits in the Liverpool Slave Trade: The Accounts of William Davenport, 1757–1784," in Anstey and Hair, *Liverpool, the African Slave Trade, and Abolition,* 72, 82–77.

76. In merchant Christopher Hasell's slaving voyages, for example, 76.1 percent of trade goods were acquired on credit, compared to just 45.2 percent of the materials to equip the ships for sea (see table 1.3). Accounts of Christopher Hasell, Hasell Family Papers, Private Collection.

77. Credit covered some 72.1 percent of the total outset costs of David Tuohy's voyages before 1772, whereas it covered only about 50 percent of the outfit-

ting costs of 39 voyages before 1772 in which William Davenport invested and for which accounts are available (see table 1.3). Ship papers, 380 TUO 4/1–10, Tuohy Papers, LRO; Richardson, "Davenport," 82–87.

78. Richard Pares, "Merchants and Planters," *EHR,* suppl. no. 4 (1960): 40.

79. At 57.9 percent, the credit-based share of total outset costs on David Tuohy's voyages from 1772 anticipated that on the post-1783 Thomas Leyland voyages (see table 1.3) and was closer to that of all Davenport's voyages in 1757–84. Ship papers, 380 TUO 4/1–10, Tuohy Papers, LRO; Leyland Papers, 387 MD 40–44, LRO; Dumbell Papers, University Library, Liverpool.

80. To paraphrase Henry Thornton, "the level of real activity" among British provincial slave merchants was "substantially altered by the availability of credit." Kenneth J. Weiller and Philip Mirowski, "Rates of Interest in 18th Century England," *Explorations in Economic History* 27, no. 1 (1990): 2.

81. Wallace, *General and Descriptive History,* 224–25.

82. Marshall, *Industry and Trade,* 44. In making his assessment Marshall drew on data on eighteenth-century transatlantic slave prices presented in George L. Craik, *The History of British Commerce,* 3 vols. (London: Charles Knight, 1844), 3:113.

83. Williams, *Capitalism and Slavery,* 36.

84. For expressions of pessimism about the trade's prospects in 1764 and 1766, e.g., see Christopher Hasell to his mother, 16 August 1764, Christopher Hasell Letter Book, 1763–1765, and Hasell to Gale and Hasell, 11 October 1766, Christopher Hasell Letter Book, 1765–1772, Hasell Family Papers, Private Collection, when, in the latter case, he suggested that the Guinea trade was "a very bad one this year & most of the ships have lost money & all that I am concerned in that are arriv'd will loose [*sic*] money."

85. Historians have calculated both voyage and annual rates of profit from slaving ventures, the difference between the two reflecting, among other things, the length of slaving voyages, which commonly exceeded 12 months, and the widespread use of credit in transactions relating, in the contemporary language, to both the "outset" of voyages and returns (or "insets") from them. Many of the latter were made in postdated bills, as noted in chapter 3. Merchants' accounts were typically voyage focused, making no allowance for voyage duration or the mix of cash (or ready money) and credit in outset and inset accounts. Although some historians have preferred to calculate profits in the way that merchants did, such methods make difficult comparisons with returns from other available investment opportunities and therefore an estimation of the net surplus from slaving ventures. Accordingly, estimates of annual rates of return provide a more useful and reliable guide to net profits

from slaving than purely venture ones. They are usually lower than the latter. For annualized profit estimates, see Roger Anstey, *The Atlantic Slave Trade and British Abolition, 1760–1810* (London: Macmillan, 1975), 47; and Richardson, "Davenport," 60–90. For voyage-based estimates, see J. E. Inikori, "Market Structure and the Profits of the British African Trade in the Late Eighteenth Century," *JEH* 41, no. 4 (1981): 745–76, esp. 772; and Nicholas James Radburn, "William Davenport, the Slave Trade, and Merchant Enterprise in Eighteenth-Century Liverpool" (MA thesis, Victoria University of Wellington, 2009), 81. Using a larger sample of voyages than was available to me in 1976, Radburn's estimate of Davenport's voyage profits was, at 10.9 percent, only marginally higher than the voyage as opposed to annual profit I also calculated. Radburn, *Davenport*, 83–84; Richardson, "Davenport," 76. On methodological issues surrounding estimates of slave trading profits, see my "Accounting for Profits in the British Trade in Slaves: Reply to William Darity," *Explorations in Economic History* 26, no. 4 (1989): 492–99.

86. The merchant William Davenport, for example, ran a bead business to supply slaving voyages and for which his accounts contain a "bead book" for the late 1760s, while his contemporary Christopher Hasell noted in 1765 that he was prepared to "keep my own money in the Guinea trade as it will greatly help the roop [*sic*] walk as well as inable [*sic*] me to sell [gun]powder." A rope business, from which he expected to make £180 a year "clear profitt," and a gunpowder-selling agency were two other activities in which Hasell was involved. Richardson, "Davenport"; Christopher Hasell to his mother, 15 July 1765, Christopher Hasell Letter Book, 1765–1772, Hasell Family Papers, Private Collection.

87. For claims in 1788 by John Tarleton and Robert Norris, both Liverpool-based participants in the trade, regarding profit expectations, see Lambert, *Sessional Papers*, 68:8, 50. For similar calculations regarding rates of return from sugar plantations, in which an annual return of 10 percent was considered "an adequate return" given the risks of sugar production, "since, even paying *6£ per cent per annum* on the whole capital" involved, the planter "still has a reserve of *4£ per cent* for his own use." Edward Long, *The History of Jamaica*, 3 vols. (London: T. Lowndes, 1774), 2:461–62.

88. As Thornton put it in 1802: "In order to ascertain how far the desire of obtaining loans . . . may be expected at any time to be carried, we must enquire into the subject of the quantum of profit likely to be derived from borrowing . . . under the existing circumstances. This is to be judged of by considering two points: the amount, first, of interest to be paid on the sum borrowed;

and, secondly, of the mercantile or other gain to be obtain'd by the employment of the borrowed capital. The gain which can be acquired by the means of commerce is commonly the highest which can be had; and it also regulates, in a good measure, the rate in all other cases. We may, therefore, consider this question as turning principally on a comparison of the rate of interest taken at the bank with the current rate of mercantile profit." Thornton, *Paper Credit,* 286–87. Thornton's argument was anticipated by Long, *History of Jamaica,* and by Adam Smith, *An Inquiry into the Nature and Causes of the Wealth of Nations,* 2 vols. (1776; Indianapolis, IN: Online Library of Liberty, 2013), 1:99–100.

89. For Bristol, see Richardson, *Final Years,* xxix, which suggests that mean profit per voyage (as opposed to per annum) was 7.6 percent in 1770–92; for the Dutch Middelburg Commercial Company's profits in 1740–95, see Johannes Postma, *The Dutch in the Atlantic Slave Trade, 1600–1815* (Cambridge: Cambridge University Press, 1990), 280; for the rate of return on investment in French voyages, particularly in 1756–92, see Guillaume Daudin, "Profitability of Slave and Long-Distance Trading in Context: The Case of Eighteenth-Century France," *JEH* 64, no. 1 (2004): 144–71.

Chapter 2. Managing the "Train of Uncertainty"

1. James Wallace, *A General and Descriptive History of the Ancient and Present State of the Town of Liverpool* (Liverpool: J. M'Creevy, 1795), 224–25.

2. Joseph C. Miller, *Way of Death: Merchant Capitalism and the Angolan Slave Trade, 1730–1830* (Madison: University of Wisconsin Press, 1988).

3. In the Liverpool trade mean numbers of slaves per ship rose from 249 in 1726–50 (517 voyages) to 264 (1,726) in 1751–76, and to 351 (537) in 1777–88 before falling back to 298 (1,840) in 1789–1808 following measures in 1788 and 1799 by Parliament to regulate ships' slave carrying capacities, as discussed in chapter 9. Over the same time periods losses of slaves in transit on Liverpool ships from Africa to a port of disembarkation in the Americas declined from 41.0 percent (5 voyages), to 17.8 percent (191), to 11.0 percent (83), and to 6.6 percent (302). Voyages/transatlantic/database/year range as indicated/ itinerary/departure place = Liverpool/summary statistics. References to Voyages in this chapter refer to the transatlantic unless otherwise stated. One other consequence of parliamentary regulation was perhaps to place a premium on loading adult slaves on British ships; the proportion of those categorized as children on Liverpool voyages tended to fall from over 30 percent through 1788 to around half that in 1789–1808.

4. Varying between 323 and 336, mean loadings of slaves on French ships barely changed between 1726–50 and 1783–93, after which the French trade collapsed until 1815, while mean losses in transit remained around 13 percent throughout the period. Voyages/database/1726–50, 1751–76, and 1783–93/flag = France/summary statistics. The exact figures per time range were loadings 323 (761 voyages) and mortality 13.3 percent (228); 323 (1,018) and 11.5 percent (452); and 336 (890) and 13.4 percent.

5. Peter Solar and Klas Ronnback, "Copper Sheathing and the British Slave Trade," *EHR* 68, no. 3 (2015): 806–29.

6. Philip D. Curtin, *The Atlantic Slave Trade: A Census* (Madison: University of Wisconsin Press, 1969). Curtin's census triggered a debate over the scale and distribution of the slave trade that continues to this day. One outcome of that debate was the publication of slavevoyages.org (Voyages) and the *Atlas of the Transatlantic Slave Trade,* by David Eltis and David Richardson (New Haven: Yale University Press, 2010), on which it was based. Like Voyages, the *Atlas* offered port-by-port evidence of slaving activities unavailable when Curtin published his census.

7. Unless otherwise noted, the following discussion is based on evidence provided by Voyages/database.

8. Liverpool was also the leading carrier of slaves from some places just outside the ten principal African "ports" listed in table 2.1. They included Isle de Los, north of Sierra Leone estuary, from which there was a relatively short-lived surge in slave shipments from the 1760s as part of a larger growth of Liverpool trade with the Sierra Leone and Windward Coast regions during the third quarter of the century. Eltis and Richardson, *Atlas,* 108.

9. On the fort-based trade of the Gold Coast, see Randy Sparks, *"Where the Negroes Are Masters": An African Port in the Era of the Slave Trade* (Cambridge, MA: Harvard University Press, 2014); on trade at the Cross River port of Calabar, see David Northrup, *Trade without Rulers: Pre-Colonial Economic Development in South-East Nigeria* (Oxford: Clarendon Press, 1978); G. Ugo Nwokeji, *The Slave Trade and Culture in the Bight of Biafra: An African Society in the Atlantic World* (New York: Cambridge University Press, 2010); and Stephen D. Behrendt, A. J. H. Latham, and David Northrup, eds., *The Diary of Antera Duke, an Eighteenth-Century African Slave Trader* (New York: Oxford University Press, 2010); on the Niger Delta port of Bonny, see Paul E. Lovejoy and David Richardson, "'This Horrid Hole': Royal Authority, Credit and Commerce at Bonny, 1690–1840," *Journal of African History* 45, no. 3 (2004): 363–92.

10. Ships from Nantes before 1808, for example, largely traded in the Bight of Benin and the Loango Coast, with Whydah in the Bight of Benin alone ac-

counting for almost a quarter of the slaves carried in Nantes's ships, where the specific port of loading is known or estimated. Eltis and Richardson, *Atlas,* 39, 59, 122; Voyages/database/1500–1808/departure place = Nantes/principal port of embarkation.

11. According to estimates in Voyages, in 1725–1808 over 960,000 slaves were taken from the Bight of Biafra, of which more than 850,000 left in British ships, with, according to Eltis and Richardson, some 580,000 (or 6 in 10 of the total) embarking on Liverpool ships. Eltis and Richardson, *Atlas,* 52.

12. Voyages/estimates/1641–1700/flag = Great Britain/regions of embarkation; Voyages/estimates/1641–1700/all flags/regions of embarkation; Voyages/database/1641–1700/departure place = London. References to British data cited here exclude slaves carried on ships dispatched to Africa from ports in British America.

13. London ships accounted for almost 85 percent of British slave embarkations in Africa in 1641–1700. Voyages/database/1641–1700/flag = Great Britain/statistics/place where voyage began. For those British ships with a record of the specific port of loading of slaves in the Bight of Biafra in 1641–1700 (number of slaves embarked = 42,140), 25,400 slaves embarked at Calabar, 13,309 at New Calabar, and under 2,000 at Bonny. Voyages/database/1641–1700/flag = Great Britain/statistics/principal port of slave purchase.

14. In addition to Voyages/estimates/1701–1810/flag = Great Britain/major regions of slave embarkation, see, for background to the following discussion, David Richardson, ed., *Bristol, Africa and the Slave Trade to America,* vol. 2, *The Years of Ascendancy, 1730–1745,* Bristol Records Society's Publications, vol. 42 (1987), xii–xxxiv; Paul E. Lovejoy and David Richardson, "Trust, Pawnship and Atlantic History: The Institutional Foundations of the Old Calabar Slave Trade," *American Historical Review* 104, no. 2 (1999): 333–55; and Lovejoy and Richardson, "'Horrid Hole.'"

15. By 1780–1807, two-thirds of the Bight of Biafra's slave exports were supplied through Bonny (rising to over three-quarters if one includes its near neighbor New Calabar or Elem Kalabari), compared to one fifth through Calabar. Lovejoy and Richardson, "'Horrid Hole,'" 369.

16. Noting the lack of naval protection for the port's ships in Africa, one leading Bristol slave merchant in 1744 argued that the resulting rise in insurance costs meant "that the Trade could not support it." Walter Lougher to Edward Southwell MP, 7 March 1744, Bristol, Southwell Papers, B 11160, Bristol Central Library.

17. David Richardson, "Profits in the Liverpool Slave Trade: The Accounts of William Davenport, 1757–1784," in *Liverpool, the African Slave Trade, and Abolition,* ed. Roger Anstey and P. E. H. Hair, Historic Society of Lancashire

and Cheshire, Occasional Series, no. 2 (1976), 60–90; Nicholas James Radburn, "William Davenport, the Slave Trade, and Merchant Enterprise in Eighteenth-Century Liverpool" (MA thesis, Victoria University of Wellington, 2009), 46–50, 86–87.

18. On interregional and interport variations in African demands for imported trade goods, see David Richardson, "West African Consumption Patterns and Their Influence on the Eighteenth-Century English Slave Trade," in *The Uncommon Market: Essays in the Economic History of the Atlantic Slave Trade*, ed. H. A. Gemery and J. S. Hogendorn (New York: Academic Press, 1979), 303–30.

19. Stephen D. Behrendt, David Eltis, and David Richardson, "The Cost of Coercion: African Agency in the Pre-Modern Atlantic World," *EHR* 54, no. 3 (2001): 454–76.

20. Beginning with the Portuguese and Spanish, slaves were valued by their perceived immediate labor potential, the most highly regarded being healthy adult males aged 15–30 and known by the Portuguese as "peca" and the Spanish as "pieza de India." Other categories of slaves were commonly measured as fractions of the peca or pieza. Curtin, *Census,* 22; Luiz Felipe de Alencastro, *The Trade in the Living: The Formation of Brazil in the South Atlantic, Sixteenth to Seventeenth Centuries* (New York: State University of New York Press, 2018), 383n. Slave prices in British America typically reflected such preferences, which encouraged British traders to maximize loadings of males, preferably adults, wherever and whenever possible; one set of voyage shareholders advised their shipmaster destined in 1752 for Angola that it was their "desire" that "you purchase at Least 2/3ds of the Male Kind." Richard Meyler and Co. to John Fowler, 20 August 1752, Account Book of Snow *Molly,* Bright Family Papers, BRO. See also David W. Galenson, *Traders, Planters, and Slaves: Market Behavior in Early English America* (Cambridge: Cambridge University Press, 1986). Voyages shows that when all carriers are included, in 1640–1808 males constituted some 64 percent and children around 18 percent of all slaves carried, yet from the Bight of Biafra the proportions were, respectively, 59.5 percent and almost 23 percent. Voyages/database/1640–1808/all carriers/summary statistics/percentages male and children/all regions of embarkation. Only at Sierra Leone and the Windward Coast were the proportions of children consistently higher than at Biafra, but there, too, the proportion of males was also relatively high. For some discussion of the peculiarities of the Biafran trade, see Nwokeji, *Slave Trade and Culture.* Nwokeji attributes the low proportion of adult males among slave exports from the Bight to Biafra in part to a preference for retaining such slaves within the interior of the region.

21. Darold D. Wax, "Preferences for Slaves in Colonial America," *Journal of Negro History* 58 (1973): 371–401; and see Bryan Edwards, *The History, Civil and Commercial, of the British Colonies in the West Indies*, 3 vols. (1793; London: John Stockdale, 1801), 2:70–102, wherein Edwards, who favored slavery, attributed various characteristics to different African ethnic groups, claiming that the greatest objection to Igbos (or "Eboes") as slaves was "their constitutional timidity, and despondency of mind" (2:89). This did not mean that markets for such slaves, particularly if cargoes comprised exceptionally high proportions of males, were lacking in British America and beyond, but it could have price implications for them relative to some others. George Hamilton to Thomas Hall, 6 May 1744, Barbados, Thomas Hall Papers, C 103/30, TNA; Thomas Leyland and Co. to Captain Caesar Lawson, 18 July 1803, Liverpool, Account Book of Ship *Enterprize*, 1803–1804, Leyland Papers, 387 MD 43, LRO.

22. Based on Voyages/database/1751–1808/flag = Great Britain/summary statistics plus same/place of purchase = Bight of Biafra.

23. Some later eighteenth-century British participants observed that ships trading to Old Calabar were particularly susceptible to high slave mortality in the Atlantic crossing. The Liverpool firm Crosbies and Trafford noted in 1762 that "Callebar is Remarkable for great Mortality in Slaves." A quarter of a century later the Bristol merchant James Jones, who traded heavily to the Bight of Biafra, principally Bonny, claimed that he "allways declined sending" ships to Old Calabar and the Cameroons "as they are Sickly, and the Slaves inferior to any other, very Weakly and liable to great Mortality." Crosbies and Trafford to Capt[ain] Ambrose Lace, 14 April 1762, Liverpool, in Gomer Williams, *History of the Liverpool Privateers and Letters of Marque; with an Account of the Liverpool Slave Trade, 1744–1812*, with introduction by David Eltis (1897; Liverpool: Liverpool University Press, 2004), 486; Behrendt, Latham, and Northrup, *Diary of Antera Duke*, 99, 268n; James Jones to Lord Hawkesbury, 26 July 1788, Bristol, Liverpool Papers, Add. Mss. 38416, f. 154, British Library. There may have been some truth in such suggestions: in 1751–1808, British ships leaving Bonny lost on average 15.7 percent of their slaves in the Atlantic crossing, while those leaving Calabar (Old Calabar) lost 22.0 percent. Voyages/database/1751–1808/flag = Great Britain/place of purchase = Bonny/Calabar. Losses on ships leaving Bonny were still high by comparison with the mean for all British ships at that time. One observer in Dominica in 1788 noted that slaves from Bonny and New Calabar were more highly thought of than those from Calabar and offered price evidence to support his claim. Francis and Robert Smyth to James Rogers, 22 February 1788,

Dominica, Rogers Papers, Chancery Masters Exhibits, C 107/8, 107/10, TNA. There were also indications that slaves from Bonny and Old Calabar might sometimes be sold in different markets at the same island, the preference being given to those from Bonny. John Fletcher to Peleg Clarke, 30 July 1774, London, in *Documents Illustrative of the History of the Slave Trade to America,* ed. Elizabeth Donnan, 4 vols. (Washington, DC: Carnegie Institution, 1930–35), 3:292.

24. On prices, see David Eltis and David Richardson, "Prices of African Slaves Newly Arrived in the Americas, 1673–1865: New Evidence on Long-Run Trends and Regional Differentials," in *Slavery in the Development of the Americas,* ed. David Eltis, Frank Lewis, and Kenneth Sokoloff (Cambridge: Cambridge University Press, 2004), 181–218; on regionally related incidences of revolts and shore-based attacks on ships, see David Richardson, "Shipboard Revolts, African Authority, and the Atlantic Slave Trade," *WMQ,* 3rd ser., 58 (2001): 69–92.

25. Thomas Leyland to Captain John Whittle, 2 July 1798, Liverpool, Account Book of *Lottery,* Leyland Papers, 387 MD 41, LRO. Other masters of slave ships were reminded of the importance of "dispatch" in slaving voyages, not least in Africa. In 1765, William Kendall, master of the Liverpool ship *Cerberus,* was told when trading at Anomabu on the Gold Coast "to gett all the white men's trade you can [that is, trade of the fort occupants], tho it is a little dearer the[n] the Natives, yet dispatch makes up for it." William Gregson and Co. to Captain [William] Kendall, 21 April 1765, Liverpool, Accounts of *Cerberus,* Hasell Family Papers, Private Collection. The urgency of dispatch was noted more directly in other instructions. In 1774 Captain Luke Mann of Liverpool was told simply that "dispatch is the life of the African Trade," a refrain earlier mentioned in the instructions to another master with whom David Tuohy was involved. Spears, Tuohy and Co. to Captain Luke Mann, 5 April 1774, Tuohy Papers, 380 TUO 4/7, LRO, and Henry Trafford and Co. to Alexander Speers, 28 September 1772, Tuohy Papers, 380 TUO 4/6, LRO. It found echoes in 1770 and 1776 in instructions to Bristol shipmasters, one of whom was told in 1776 to "make all possible dispatch at every place you touch at, as dispatch is the life of a Guinea Voyage." John Chilcott and Co. to Thomas Baker, 2 August 1776, Accounts of *Snow Africa,* BRO; see also John Chilcott and Co. to William Llewellin, 2 September 1770, Bristol, Log of the *Hector,* Ms. 92/011, National Maritime Museum, Greenwich.

26. On trends in mean turnaround times of ships in Africa, see David Eltis and David Richardson, "Productivity in the Transatlantic Slave Trade," *Explorations in Economic History* 32 (1995): 477–78.

27. In 1804, one Liverpool merchant, Benjamin Devaynes, specifically attributed his failure to pay a debt on time to a London supplier of trade goods to "the long detention" of his ship, *Lord Saint Vincent,* "on the Coast and which has prevented my being as punctual in remitting you as I could wish." In the event, the ship was lost, and Devaynes and his supplier had to await an insurance settlement before the debt was cleared. Benjamin Devaynes to Thomas Lumley and Co., 14 January, 4 April 1804, Liverpool, Lumley Papers, C 114/2, TNA.

28. British abolitionist Thomas Clarkson claimed in 1786 that "the regularity of the trade, and the small space of time in which a cargo may be compleated are considerations, which have made [New Calabar and Bonny] more resorted to than any other on the coast." Clarkson, *An Essay on the Slavery and Commerce of the Human Species, Particularly the African* (London: J. Phillips, 1786), 31. Two years later in 1788, the major Bristol slave merchant James Jones suggested that ships trading at Bonny and New Calabar purchased slaves "much quicker than at any other place." Add. Mss. 38416, ff. 154–55, British Library. Some historians have noted the same. Gwilym Iwan Jones, *The Trading States of the Oil Rivers* (London: International African Institute, 1963), 46.

29. Paul E. Lovejoy and David Richardson, "Letters of the Old Calabar Slave Trade, 1760–1789," in *Genius in Bondage: Literature of the Early Black Atlantic,* ed. Vincent Carretta and Philip Gould (Lexington: University of Kentucky Press, 2001), 109.

30. Voyages/database/1741–1808/flag = Great Britain/place of purchase = Bonny or Bight of Biafra/summary statistics.

31. Clarkson, *Essay,* 31.

32. Penny's evidence is contained in the "Report on the African Trade" in Sheila Lambert, ed., *House of Commons Sessional Papers of the Eighteenth Century,* 147 vols. (Wilmington, DE: Scholarly Resources, 1975), 69: 47.

33. Alexander Falconbridge, *An Account of the Slave Trade on the Coast of Africa* (London: J. Phillips, 1788), 12. Falconbridge went on to suggest that expeditions upriver commonly involved 20–30 canoes, each capable of carrying 30–40 captives (16).

34. Robin Hallett, ed., *Records of the African Association, 1788–1831* (London: Nelson, 1964), 193–95.

35. Douglass C. North, John Joseph Wallis, and Barry R. Weingast, *Violence and Social Orders: A Conceptual Framework for Interpreting Recorded Human History* (Cambridge: Cambridge University Press, 2009), 42–43.

36. On the Aro network, see Kenneth O. Dike and Felicia Ekejiuba, *The Aro of South-Eastern Nigeria, 1650–1980* (Ibadan: Ibadan University Press, 1990),

96, 102, 176–78, 198–202; Northrup, *Trade without Rulers*, 104–7, 114–45; and Nwokeji, *Slave Trade and Culture*.

37. Voyages data suggest that in 1741–1808, 23 percent of the slaves leaving the Bight of Biafra as a whole were children (290 voyages out of a total sample of 2,320) but that among those leaving Bonny children comprised fewer than 15 percent of slave exports (79 voyages of a sample of 987). The proportion of males among both Bonny and Bight of Biafra slave exports in the same period was more or less the same at about 57 percent–58 percent (397 of 2,320 and 133 of 987 voyages), but the lower proportion of children among Bonny exports suggests that Bonny shipped more adult males than other ports in the region, thereby more closely matching supply with American demand for slaves than its immediate rivals. Voyages/database/1741–1808/itinerary = Bight of Biafra and Bonny/summary statistics.

38. Lovejoy and Richardson, "'Horrid Hole.'"

39. Ray A. Kea, *Settlements, Trade, and Politics in the Seventeenth-Century Gold Coast* (Baltimore: Johns Hopkins University Press, 1984); Robin Law, ed., *The Royal African Company of England in West Africa, 1681–1699*, 3 vols. (Oxford: Oxford University Press, 1998–2007).

40. Lovejoy and Richardson, "Trust"; Paul E. Lovejoy and David Richardson, "The Business of Slaving: Pawnship in Western Africa, c. 1600–1810," *Journal of African History* 42, no. 1 (1999): 25–50.

41. Henry Thornton, *An Enquiry into the Nature and Effects of the Paper Credit of Great Britain,* ed. F. A. von Hayek (1802; New York: Augustus M. Kelley, 1965), 70.

42. In 1790 William Cleveland, who was a slave dealer trading out of Bananas [Banana Islands] in Upper Guinea, owed Robert Bostock of Liverpool at least 92 slaves from two earlier voyages. Robert Bostock to Captain James Fryer, 6 May 1790, 387 MD 55, LRO. He was also heavily indebted to James Rogers of Bristol, another British slave merchant with whom he reportedly dealt. Robert Bostock to [James Cleveland], 13 November 1789, 387 MD 55, LRO. Cleveland died in early 1791, prompting fears that it would "make some detention of the Payments" of slaves owing to two of Rogers's ships. William Roper to James Rogers, 13 April 1791, Isles de Loss [*sic*], C 107/5, TNA. The writer of that advice to Rogers, William Roper, later informed Rogers that he had bartered with another local dealer, John Ormond, for 90 slaves, payable in mid-September 1791 but that Ormand, too, had died, with the payment in slaves not then expected until late January 1792. William Roper to James Rogers, 22 September 1791, Isles de Loss, C 107/5, TNA.

43. On the impact of the racial identity of borrowers in determining credit policy on the part of Liverpool slave merchants in Africa, see Paul E. Lovejoy

and David Richardson, "African Agency and the Liverpool Slave Trade," in *Liverpool and Transatlantic Slavery,* ed. David Richardson, Suzanne Schwarz, and Anthony J. Tibbles (Liverpool: Liverpool University Press, 2007), 43–65.

44. Lovejoy and Richardson, "Trust"; Lovejoy and Richardson, "Business of Slaving." In 1781 Peter Comberbach, master of the Liverpool ship *William,* was advised to "endeavour by all means to get the traders to go into the Country [at Old Calabar] for you and particularly to the Country of Orrop, were you to send 6 or 8000 Coppers [of trade goods] divided amongst the different Traders minding to procure the best pawns that have to be had, by which means you will Insure your Debts, especially if any Ships in the River when you have finished your purchase." W. D. Horsall and Co. to Captain Peter Comberbach, Liverpool, 27 December 1781, Davenport papers, National Museums Liverpool. Comberbach was expected to trade for ivory and palm oil, not slaves, but his orders shed light on general trading practices at Calabar, including credit and its protection. The sum of 6,000–8,000 coppers [the local unit of account] was equivalent to £150 to £200 sterling, according to Comberbach's owners' calculations. The owners' concluding remark to Comberbach reflected the fact that a market in debts (or pawns) existed at Calabar, in which shipmasters exchanged pawns among themselves, allowing one master to complete his purchase by bartering his pawns for slaves or produce on another ship, thereby allowing the former to leave the coast and the other ship perhaps to accelerate completion of its purchase.

45. On dispute resolution, see Lovejoy and Richardson, "Trust." On violence, see Randy J. Sparks, *Two Princes of Calabar: An Eighteenth-Century Atlantic Odyssey* (Cambridge, MA: Harvard University Press, 2004), which examines an infamous massacre at Calabar in 1767 involving Liverpool shipmasters and two local townships and resulting in the seizure and exile of two Calabar merchants.

46. The rest of this paragraph draws on Lovejoy and Richardson, "'Horrid Hole.'"

47. See, e.g., Paul E. Lovejoy and Toyin Falola, eds., *Pawnship in Africa: Debt Bondage in Historical Perspective* (Boulder, CO: Westview, 1994); and Judith Spicksley, "Pawns in the Gold Coast: The Rise of Asante and Shifts in the Security of Debt, 1680–1750," *Journal of African History* 54, no. 2 (2013): 147–75.

48. Panyarring involved the forced seizure of individuals when a debt was unpaid. Olatunji Ojo, "Emu (Amuya): The Yoruba Institution of Panyarring or Seizure for Debt," *African Economic History* 35 (2007): 31–58. Ojo uses nineteenth-century evidence to illustrate the practice, which also had earlier

application in the context of the export slave trade. Sparks, *Negroes Are Masters,* 138; Lovejoy and Richardson, "Business of Slaving," 75.

49. Some contemporaries identified principal-agent conflicts in the context of slaving. John Atkins, *A Voyage to Guinea, Brasil, and the West Indies* (London: Ward and Chandler, 1735), 155. On the historical literature, see Ann M. Carlos, "Principal-Agent Problems in Early Trading Companies: A Tale of Two Firms," *American Economic Review* 82, no. 1 (1992): 140–45; Carlos, "Bonding and the Agency Problem: Evidence from the Royal African Company, 1672–1691," *Explorations in Economic History* 31, no. 3 (1994): 313–35; and Carlos and Jamie Brown Kruse, "The Decline of the Royal African Company: Fringe Firms and the Role of the Charter," *EHR* 49, no. 2 (1996): 291–313.

Chapter 3. The "Wheel of Unfathomable Commerce"

1. Henry Laurens to John Knight, 12 June 1764, Charles Town, in *The Papers of Henry Laurens,* ed. C. James Taylor et al., 16 vols. (Columbia: University of South Carolina Press, 1968–2003), 4:311.

2. Knowledgeable Liverpool observers in 1788 claimed that one reason for British success in the slave trade was the length of credit from domestic suppliers, with one of them noting that "our manufacturers give eighteen months credit, and the French only six." Joseph E. Inikori, *Africans and the Industrial Revolution in England* (Cambridge, Cambridge University Press, 2002), 333. Merchant records support the former claim. A Liverpool supplier of gunpowder reported in 1771 that not one in ten of purchasers of the product for Africa was willing to pay in less than 18 months and that one slave merchant whom he had refused to supply on such terms because of non-payment for a previous consignment had got what he wanted from another supplier. Christopher Hasell to Mark Nesfield, 8 March 1771, Christopher Hasell Letter Book, 1765–1772, Hasell Family Papers, Private Collection. In 1774, "Guinea goods" were reportedly on offer in London at twelve months' credit "and some longer," a pattern that persisted through 1807. Elizabeth Donnan, ed., *Documents Illustrative of the History of the Slave Trade to America,* 4 vols. (Washington, DC: Carnegie Institution, 1930–35), 3:297; Ludlam, Parry and Son to James Rogers, 16 August 1786, London, Rogers Papers, C 107/8, TNA; Journal of sales, London, 1801–1810, Lumley Papers, C 114/154, part 2, TNA. In the meantime, credit provision at Manchester might extend by the 1780s at least to 18 months, with indications that credit terms available to Liverpool merchants were often, though not invariably, more generous than to their Bristol counterparts. Samuel and Thomas Taylor to James Rogers, 15

December 1786, Manchester, C 107/8, TNA; William Woodville Jr. to James Rogers, 25 November 1789, Liverpool, C 107/13, TNA, in which Woodville advised the Bristol-based Rogers that at Liverpool "we suppose you may have everything necessary [for a slaving voyage] on easier terms than with you." Such advantages were consistent with Liverpool's proximity to historically revolutionary changes in Britain's industrial landscape.

3. An analysis of 18 cargoes of trade goods, totaling £83,174 in 1787–93 and assembled by James Rogers, a leading Bristol merchant, reveals that 40 percent came from Bristol, almost 38 percent from London, and around 10 percent each from Birmingham and Manchester. Rogers Papers, C 107/1, 3, 5, 6, 12–15, TNA. Though more impressionistic, several sets of surviving Liverpool merchant papers between the 1760s and 1807 underscore the importance of local suppliers of trade goods to the city's slave merchants while also endorsing the roles of London, Manchester, and Birmingham suppliers. Further evidence of London's importance as a supplier of goods to Liverpool merchants, particularly in the form of East Indian textiles, is to be found in the accounts of Thomas Lumley and Co., whose journal records sales of some £235,410 of such goods in 1801–7, the vast majority of them to Liverpool correspondents. Journal of Sales, 10 February 1801 to 1 October 1810, C 114/154, part 2, TNA.

4. For discussion of similar issues in another eighteenth-century British context, see Robin Pearson, "Moral Hazard and the Assessment of Insurance Risk in Eighteenth- and Early-Nineteenth-Century Britain," *Business History Review* 76, no. 1 (2002): 1–35.

5. Richard B. Sheridan, "The British Credit Crisis of 1772 and the American Colonies," *JEH* 20, no. 2 (1960): 161–86; Francis E. Hyde, Bradbury B. Parkinson, and Sheila Marriner, "The Port of Liverpool and the Crisis of 1793," *Economica,* n.s., 18, no. 72 (1951): 363–78; Peter Marshall, "The Anti-Slave Trade Movement in Bristol," in *Bristol in the Eighteenth Century,* ed. P. V. McGrath (Newton Abbot, UK: David and Charles, 1972), 212–14.

6. One prospective master included a ship surgeon—seen as "assuredly a most desirable acquisition"—among the "principal officers" on whom the conduct of an African voyage depended. William Woodville Jr. to James Rogers, 21 November 1789, Liverpool, C 107/13, TNA. The master's role was paramount, however, as the London merchant Humphry Morice noted in 1723 when he reminded one of his captains that he had "now an opportunity put into your hands to convince me that you are deserving of the favour I have bestowed upon you, and are equall to, and worthy of, the great trust & Confidence I have reposed in you." Humphry Morice to Capt. Edmund Weedon, 23

March 1723, London, Journal of the *Anne* Gally, Morice Papers, Bank of England Archives.

7. See, e.g., the instructions to Captain Earle in 1751, who was acknowledged by his shipowners to be "experienced in the customs" of trade at Old Calabar, to which he was bound, but was still reminded that they depended on "your prudent management with the natives and ships in the river in your trade for our best interest." W[illia]m Whalley and Co. to Captain Earle, 22 May 1751, Liverpool, Davenport papers, National Museums Liverpool.

8. In 1731 Humphry Morice advised the master of one of his ships that "as it is impossible for mee [*sic*] to foresee and provide against innumerable accidents that may happen to you in this Voyage; Therefore I refer to your Prudence, care and good management the Conduct of this ships Cargoe and Investment which I leave intirely to you to dispose of as you find most for my Benefitt and advantage; depending on your Integrity and Experience to do your best for mee in every particular." Humphry Morice to Capt. Jeremiah Pearce, 31 March 1731, London, *Judith Snow* accounts, Morice Papers, Bank of England Archives. Half a century later, in 1782, the Liverpool firm of Francis Ingram and Co. urged Henry Moore, master of their ship *Blaydes,* that "as you are an entire Stran[ger to] the Place or Places you are going to, & have a large Capital [u]nder you, it behoves you to be very circumspect in all yr pro[ce]edings, & very attentive to the minutest part of yr. Conduct, for be assur'd the whole of the Purchase greatly depends on the prudent Behaviour of the Person to whom the Care of the whole is entrus[ted]." Francis Ingram and Co. to Captain Henry Moore, 28 July 1782, Liverpool, Tuohy Papers, 380 TUO 4/9, LRO. And in 1802, another Liverpool firm, Thomas Leyland and Co., simply noted to Charles Kneal, master of the *Lottery,* to "study the Interest of [his] Owners" when acting abroad and in particular that when trading at Bonny to unite with competitors "in every effort to keep down the prices" payable for slaves. Accounts of Ship *Lottery,* 1802–1811, Leyland Papers, 387 MD 42, LRO.

9. As encapsulated in the Nantucket whaling industry, in which Herman Melville noted the concerns and emotional attachments of investors said to be "loathe to say good-bye to a thing [that is, a voyage] so every way brimful of every interest" to them. Melville, *Moby-Dick* (1851; London: Penguin, 2012), 123.

10. For the massacre at Calabar, see Gomer Williams, *History of the Liverpool Privateers and Letters of Marque; with an Account of the Liverpool Slave Trade, 1744–1812,* with introduction by David Eltis (1897; Liverpool, Liverpool University Press, 2004), 529–66; for its commercial fallout, see Paul E.

Lovejoy and David Richardson, "Letters of the Old Calabar Slave Trade, 1760–1789," in *Genius in Bondage: Literature of the Early Black Atlantic,* ed. Vincent Carretta and Philip Gould (Lexington: University Press of Kentucky, 2001), 89–115.

11. Robert Bostock to James Cleveland, 14 September 1790, Liverpool, Bostock Letter Book, 387 MD 55, LRO. As Bostock explained elsewhere he felt particularly vulnerable because he was a "Single Person" or sole investor in the voyages he dispatched, noting that "the tradesmen in this port will either have Money or body, and not be put off." Bostock to [Cleveland], 6 September 1790. He even chose on one occasion to personalize the pressure he felt by observing "we have an Increase in our family Mrs. Bostock has presented me this week with a fine girl, I had rather been presented with Mr. Wilkinsons Debt," Charles Wilkinson being an African dealer who owed Bostock slaves. Bostock to Captain James Fryer, 25 July 1790.

12. William Roper to James Rogers, 14 March 1790, Bananoes, and Roper to Rogers, 21 May 1791, River Sierra Leon[e], Rogers Papers, C 107/5, TNA.

13. In 1790 one shipmaster writing from Bassa south of Sierra Leone observed of James Cleveland, a slave dealer in the area, "I realy think it a grait risk to trus much Property as there is neighther law, nor Principall to bind them to thei[r arran]gements or to compel them to perform, & their lives are very precarious which if anything ware to happen all's lost." Richd. Martin to James Rogers and Co., 10 April 1790, Rogers Papers, C 107/12, TNA.

14. One perennial risk in slave voyages was crew mortality, specifically that of the master, which opened up possibilities for other officers to embezzle cargo or falsify accounts to their own advantage. Thought by one firm to "hath been frequently done," the firm sought to counter that risk by instructing the master to require one of the mates and the surgeon to sign every night the "Day Book" of business the master was expected to keep. Mich[ae]l Becher and Co. to John Bartlett, August 1743, Bristol, Account Book of the *Jason* Gally, 45167, BRO.

15. Henry Bright and Co. to James McTaggart, 5 March 1759, Bristol, Papers of Snow *Swift,* 39659 (2), BRO.

16. John C. Appleby, "'A Business of Much Difficulty': A London Slaving Venture, 1651–1654," *Mariner's Mirror* 81, no. 1 (1995): 6.

17. See Humphry Morice to Capt. Thomas Hill, 30 September 1730, London, Accounts of *Anne* Gally, Morice Papers, Bank of England Archives, in which Hill was allowed "an Adventure" of £600 and four "Negroes freight free," with his fellow officers receiving similar if much smaller allowances. That

practice can still be found in the 1780s though on a smaller scale, when in
accounts of one Bristol slave voyage in 1784 an "Adventure allowed by the
Owners to the Officers" of the ship was revealed, amounting to "5 Negroes"
sold at the average price of all slaves delivered. Sheila Lambert, ed., *House of
Commons Sessional Papers of the Eighteenth Century,* 147 vols. (Wilmington,
DE: Scholarly Resources, 1975), 72:350. Similar "adventures" were evident
in other British long-distance trades such as the East Indian. See Stephen
Taylor, *Caliban's Shore: The Wreck of the Grosvenor and the Strange Fate of
Her Survivors* (New York: W. W. Norton, 2004), 9, 21, where the captain's
"privilege," or allowance for private trade, was said to be 38 tons of goods
on the fateful homeward voyage.

18. Richd. Meyler and Co. to John Fowler, 20 August 1752, Logbook of the Snow
    Molly, BRO; Account *Fanny* sales, 346, 14 December 1756, Case and South-
    worth Papers, 380 MD 33, LRO.

19. For examples of percentages, see accounts of the voyages of the *Cerberus* 1765,
    Dobson 1770–71, and *True Blue* 1772, Hasell Family Papers, Private Collec-
    tion; account of sales from *Barbados Packet,* Tobago, 30 October 1772, *Mer-
    edith,* St. Kitts, 25 November 1772, and *Cavendish,* St. Vincent, 31 July 1772,
    Samuel Sandys Papers, C 109/401, TNA; *Golden Age* sales, Kingston, Jamaica,
    1784, Ms 10.48 Dumbell Papers, Liverpool University Library; and Log of
    the *Hector* of Bristol, 1770, Ms 92/011, National Maritime Museum, Greenwich,
    where the master's privilege was included as a percentage of total sales with
    another form of remuneration, discussed below, and other officers' individ-
    ual privileges were to be calculated on the basis of average prices for the
    whole shipload (in this case less their prime cost of purchase and insurance).

20. For the rationale of paying commissions to shipmasters, see John Leigh and
    Co. to Messrs Sayers, Gordon and Co. (Dublin), 2 October 1805, C 108/212,
    TNA, where they also reminded their correspondent that "the Cargo for an
    African ship are [*sic*] assorted Cloths of Different Discription India and Man-
    chester goods" and that "the Cargo is at all times Intrusted unto the Cap-
    tains Care to barter for Slaves under instruction" and for which the captain
    was paid commission. If the master died after trade began in Africa, at least
    one merchant stipulated that the deceased's heirs should receive half com-
    mission "on what shall be purchased & the succeeding Commanders [should
    be entitled] to their proportionable [*sic*] share." Coast commission, loose pa-
    pers, *African Queen* accounts, Rogers Papers, C 107/59, TNA. Though
    4 percent (or, more exactly, £4 in every £104) of the gross proceeds was more
    or less consistently the commission masters earned from slave sales, commis-
    sion on sales of African products such as ivory or camwood (a dyewood) was

sometimes lower at 3 percent. Accounts of sales of camwood and ivory, 1772 and 1773, *Cavendish* and *Meredith*, Voyage Book, Sandys Papers, C 109/401, TNA.

21. The mean number of slaves per ship disembarked from British ships in 1786–90 was 265. Voyages/transatlantic/database/1786–90/flag = Great Britain/summary statistics.

22. Sandys Papers, C 109/401, TNA.

23. Leyland Accounts, 387 MD 42, LRO. According to one observer in 1788, "the gains of the Masters of the vessels employed in the Trade have been very great," amounting "at £6 per £106, the customary allowance for privilege & coast commission" and exclusive of wages to be "reasonably stated at £60,000 Sterlg." from voyages outfitted in 1787 at Liverpool. W. J. [Edgar Corrie] to Lord Hawkesbury, 27 February 1788, Liverpool Papers, Add. Mss. 38416, ff. 40–41, British Library.

24. For a review and an assessment of Colquhoun's figures, which were published in 1806, see Peter H. Lindert and Jeffrey G. Williamson, "Revising England's Social Tables, 1688–1812," *Explorations in Economic History* 19, no. 4 (1982): 401.

25. See Christopher Hasell to his mother, 20 September 1764, Liverpool, Christopher Hasell Letter Book, 1763–1765, Hasell Family Papers, Private Collection, when Hasell wrote that "the chefe of the Merchts of this town have been Capts of Ships & so made their fortunes & then turn Merchts." In David Tuohy to Stephen Fagan, 28 August 1771, 380 TUO 2/1, LRO, Tuohy notes that "I have been in the Affrican Trade for many years in wch. I have made A pretty Fortune, I am now Inclined to go no more to Affrica but follow the business of merchant in this Town [Liverpool]"; on 7 April 1772, to Christopher Fagan, Tuohy reports having sailed for 14 years to Africa; and on 4 November 1773, to Richard Annesly, he notes that "I made out pretty handsome" from several voyages to Africa. Tuohy was master on four slaving voyages in 1765–71, the last ending in April 1771. Voyages/transatlantic/database/captain's name = Tuohy, David. If what he wrote in April 1772 was correct, Tuohy presumably sailed to Africa before 1765 as a seaman or other officer.

26. Interestingly the Dolben Act, passed in 1788, and intended to improve on humanitarian grounds survival rates of slaves on British ships, introduced a scaled system of premium payments to shipmasters as an inducement to improve such rates.

27. K. G. Davies, "The Origins of the Commission System in the West India Trade," *Transactions of the Royal Historical Society*, 5th ser., 2 (1952): 89–107; David Hancock, ed., *The Letters of William Freeman, London Merchant,*

1678-1685, London Record Society Publications, vol. 36 (2002), introduction; Kenneth Morgan, "Remittance Procedures in the Eighteenth-Century British Slave Trade," *Business History Review* 79, no. 4 (2005): 715-49; Nicholas Radburn, "Guinea Factors, Slave Sales, and Profits in the Transatlantic Slave Trade in Late Eighteenth-Century Jamaica: The Case of John Tailyour," *WMQ,* 3rd ser., 72, no. 2 (2015): 243-86.

28. The calculation assumes mean numbers of slaves per ship of around 265 and a mean nominal price per slave sold of £30. Voyages/database/1786-90/flag = Great Britain/summary statistics; David Eltis and David Richardson, "Prices of African Slaves Newly Arrived in the Americas, 1673-1865: New Evidence on Long-Run Trends and Regional Differentials," in *Slavery in the Development of the Americas: Essays in Honor of Stanley L. Engerman,* ed. David Eltis, Frank Lewis, and Kenneth Sokoloff (New York: Cambridge University Press, 2004), 181-218. For the firm of Watson and Appleton that sold the *Lottery*'s 305 slaves at Montego Bay in 1802 at an average price per slave of just over £70 sterling, commission receipts totaled around £1,930. Leyland Papers, 387 MD 42, LRO.

29. Edward Long, *The History of Jamaica,* 3 vols. (London: T. Lowndes, 1774), 2:459-63; Christer Petley, *White Fury: A Jamaican Slaveholder and the Age of Revolution* (Oxford: Oxford University Press, 2018), 47.

30. Adam Smith, *An Inquiry into the Nature and Causes of the Wealth of Nations,* 2 vols. (1776; Indianapolis, IN: Online Library of Liberty, 2013), 1:359, 2:89. Smith did not quantify the capital flow, but based on the evidence of voyage data, of slave prices, and of ratios of slave bills to total remittances, it was clearly very substantial. The issue merits further attention.

31. William Woodville Sr. to James Rogers, 29 January 1790, Liverpool, C 107/13, TNA. Woodville acknowledged that "the planter will most [lik]ley take three Months more" to clear his debts "for which he pays Interest @ 5 pCt. p An[num]."

32. [9 June 1788], *Prospectus d'une petite expédition pour la traite des Noirs,* Add. Mss. 38416, f. 112, British Library; Robert Stein, "The Profitability of the Nantes Slave Trade, 1783-1792," *JEH* 35, no. 2 (1982): 779-93. As noted in chapter 1, state subsidies helped to underwrite French slaving in 1783-93.

33. Davies, *Royal African Company.*

34. Tyndall and Assheton to Isaac Hobhouse, 15 October 1729, Kingston, Jamaica, Hobhouse Papers, Jefferies Collection, vol. 13, Bristol Central Library.

35. Memorial from Stephen Fuller, agent for Jamaica, to the Board of Trade 1788, containing an appendix of Annual Slave Imports and Re-Exports, CO 137/38, Hh 3, 4, TNA; Lambert, *Sessional Papers,* 69:262-63.

36. Account Book of James Day, 1729–1753, f. 5, 40044 (2), BRO. In merchants' accounts, such remittances were usually identified in a sequence of "inset" statements per voyage.

37. Bristol investment in slaving voyages around 1730 was about £200,000 sterling annually, so failure to receive immediately a quarter of all remittances implied that perhaps as much as £50,000 sterling a year was being advanced by Bristol merchants to underwrite planter slave purchases, a sum that might cause liquidity problems for some were repayment to be delayed or defaulted on. For annual investment estimates, see David Richardson, *Bristol, Africa and the Slave Trade to America,* vol. 2, *The Years of Ascendancy, 1730–1745,* Bristol Record Society Publications, vol. 39 (1987), xv.

38. Jacob M. Price, "Credit in the Slave Trade and the Slave Plantation Economies," in *Slavery and the Rise of the Atlantic System,* ed. Barbara L. Solow (Cambridge: Cambridge University Press, 1991), 293–340.

39. As one commentator remarked in 1745, "The Private Traders are better able to supply our Plantations with Negroes [than the Royal African Company]; because they carry on a constant Intercourse of General Trade with the British Plantations, and have settled Correspondence there with Relations, Friends, and Partners, who will be more careful to do Them Justice, as well as more punctual in making Returns than any Agents appointed by the Company have been for their Account." Charles Hayes, *The Importance of Effectually Supporting the Royal African Company of England Impartially Considered* (1744; London: E. Say, 1745), 46. For one example of Bristol family commercial connections with the West Indies, see Kenneth Morgan, ed., *The Bright-Meyler Papers: A Bristol-West India Connection, 1732–1837* (Oxford: Oxford University Press, 2007). For an emphasis on the role of personal reputation in underpinning transatlantic commerce and drawing heavily on Liverpool evidence, see Sheryllynne Haggerty, *"Merely for Money"? Business Culture in the British Atlantic, 1750–1815* (Liverpool: Liverpool University Press, 2012).

40. Richard Meyler to Whatley, Meyler and Co., 22 November 1754, Richard Meyler Letter Book, 1751–1764, Bright Family Papers, University of Melbourne Archives. On the state of Day's affairs at the time of his death, see Account Book of James Day, 1729–1753, ff. 13–18, 40044 (2), BRO. Peter Day invested in at least 26 slave voyages in 1711–34, 24 of which disembarked their slaves at Jamaica, with the 26 in total shipping an estimated 7,688 slaves in Africa and landing 6,273 in the Americas. The other two ships disembarked slaves at Barbados. Voyages/transatlantic/database/owner = Peter Day/itinerary/place of departure = Bristol/summary statistics.

41. Richard B. Sheridan, "The Commercial and Financial Organization of the British Slave Trade, 1750–1807," *EHR* 11, no. 2 (1958): 249–63; Robin Pearson and David Richardson, "Social Capital, Institutional Innovation, and Atlantic Trade before 1800," *Business History* 50, no. 6 (2008): 765–80.

42. The expectations of at least one Bristol firm in 1759 were still that three-quarters of payments for slaves should be made in produce and good bills to be remitted by the ship, with the balance remitted in 12 months in bills. Henry Bright and Co. to James McTaggart, 5 March 1759, Bristol, Snow *Swift* accounts, 39654 (2), BRO.

43. Price, "Credit in Slave Trade," 311; Kenneth Morgan, "Remittance Procedures in the Eighteenth-Century British Slave Trade," *Business History Review* 79, no. 4 (2005): 715–49.

44. For the increasing reach of the new system from the 1750s onward, see David Richardson, "The British Slave Trade to Colonial South Carolina," *Slavery and Abolition* 12, no. 3 (1991): 125–72.

45. David Richardson, "Profits in the Liverpool Slave Trade: The Accounts of William Davenport, 1757–1784," in *Liverpool, the African Trade, and Abolition,* ed. Roger Anstey and P. E. H. Hair, Historic Society of Lancashire and Cheshire, Occasional Series, no. 2 (1976), 82–87, which shows that up to 95 percent of slave payments to the 74 voyages covered were made in postdated bills.

46. William Grumly to James Rogers, 17 April 1789, Tortola, C 107/5, TNA; Edmund Burke to Rogers, 15 June 1789, Tortola, C 107/8, TNA; in John Sharp to Rogers and Co., 5 March 1791, Jamaica, C 107/10, TNA, Sharp suggests that he "had given over selling of Cargoes, for at the moment I have money out for several ships sold from 1780 to 86"; loose papers, West India Letters and Accounts, Estate of James Rogers, C 107/59, TNA, reveal outstanding debts and interest (at 10 percent per annum) owed to Rogers about 1790 on slave sales in various islands. See also Nicholas Radburn, "Keeping 'the Wheel in Motion': Trans-Atlantic Credit Terms, Slave Prices, and the Geography of Slavery in the British Americas, 1755–1807," *JEH* 75, no. 3 (2015): 660–89. The continuation of older practices alongside the new occasionally prompted comparisons between them. See Francis Grant to Rogers, 30 December 1788, Jamaica, C 107/7, part 2, TNA, who noted that on the few shiploads of slaves he had sold, he had given no guarantees, making remittances "by my own Notes of hand which however have generally been taken up before they become due," and where produce was sent by the ship to discharge part payments, for "the balance I have had one to two years."

47. For one of the earliest and most succinct contemporary accounts of the reformed sale and remittance processes, see John Fletcher to Captain Peleg Clarke, 24 December 1774, London, in Donnan, *Documents,* 3:298–99.

48. There are signs that guarantees on minimum mean prices per slave on whole shiploads were being requested by at least the early 1740s, with payments in bills where possible. George Hamilton to Thos. Hall, 16 August 1740, 26 February, 8 August 1742, all written from Anamaboe (or Anomabu), Thomas Hall Papers, C 103/130, TNA.

49. In February 1784 the Kingston slave factors Allans and Campbell specifically identified the firm of Dyer, Fish and Co. of London as "our Guarantees" for bills they drew to settle their accounts with the merchants involved in one Bristol voyage. Lambert, *Sessional Papers,* 72:351.

50. Taylor et al., *Henry Laurens,* 1:44.

51. Henry Laurens to John Knight, 12 June 1764, in Donnan, *Documents,* 4:391–94, quotations at 394. Laurens observed that interest on planters' bonds could be up to 8 percent a year.

52. For background to this argument, see Pearson and Richardson, "Social Capital."

53. S. G. Checkland, "Finance for the West Indies, 1780–1815," *EHR* 10, no. 3 (1957–58): 461–69.

54. Henry Laurens to John Knight, 18 December 1755, in Taylor et al., *Henry Laurens,* 1:42–45.

55. Grove, Harris, and Papp to James Rogers, 10 March 1793, Kingston, Jamaica, Rogers Papers, C 107/59, TNA.

56. The projection is based on slave arrivals of almost 29,000 slaves in Liverpool ships at American ports in 1793. Voyages/transatlantic/database/1793/place of departure = Liverpool/summary statistics.

57. On the scale of the bill market in general as a measure of London's and of Britain's wealth, see Henry Thornton, *Inquiry into the Nature and Effects of the Paper Credit of Great Britain,* ed. F. A. von Hayek (1802; New York: Augustus M. Kelley, 1965), 78.

58. Robert Bostock to James Cleveland, 9 June 1790, Liverpool, 387 MD/54, LRO.

59. Francis Horner, "Review of Henry Thornton's Paper Credit," *Edinburgh Review* 1, no. 1 (1802): 176.

60. Thornton, *Paper Credit,* 76, 78. Cf. Joseph E. Inikori, "The Credit Needs of the African Trade and the Development of the Credit Economy in England," *Explorations in Economic History* 27 (1990): 197–231, who ascribes exceptional importance to slave bills in the development of the British credit market.

61. Horner, "Review," 175.

62. Joseph Daltera to James Rogers, 16 July 1789, Liverpool, C 107/10, TNA, who noted that "bills on the out ports [or those outside London] are not so easily

discounted as bills on London." The reputation or knowledge of those acting as London guarantors of factors' bills and thus preferences for them still
mattered in the minds of those receiving them, as one leading Liverpool
slave merchant after 1783 reminded a correspondent. Thomas Leyland to
Mitchell and Dagger, 9 December 1786, Liverpool, Letter Book of Thomas
Leyland, 387 MD 59, LRO. On London discounting of bills held by Liverpool merchants, see James Aspinall to Thomas Lumley, 28 July 1801,
Liverpool, Lumley Papers, C 114/2, TNA, who flatters Lumley with being
"a skil[l]ful negotiator" where discounting bills was concerned; and
A. Heywood and Co. to Lumley, 23 August 1806, Liverpool, Lumley Papers,
C 114/158, TNA.

63. John Fletcher to Peleg Clarke, 30 July 1774, London, in Donnan, *Documents*,
3:291–92. Fletcher later further underlined the importance of Hibberts's bills
and their guaranteed status by emphasizing to Clarke that a great deal depended on "a Certainty of the Bills Being paid whin [*sic*] they come home as
both you And my self had strained a point to Carry" the business through.
Fletcher to Clarke, [22 December 1774], London, in Donnan, 3:298.

64. Robert Bostock to Francis Levett, 21 May 1789, Liverpool, 387 MD 55, LRO.

65. The Liverpool merchant Thomas Leyland in 1788 rejected a proposal for a
French-related slaving venture, with payments in Paris "at stated periods,"
noting that those making the proposal had left "without doing any business
for want of securities in London." Leyland to Corn[eliu]s Donovan @ Thomas
Gorman's London, 8 August 1788, Liverpool, Leyland Letter Book, 387 MD
59, LRO. See also George Case to Thomas Lumley, 2 May, 27 June, 23
July 1801, Liverpool, and John and James Parr to Lumley, Liverpool, 12 January 1804, all in Lumley Papers, C 114/2, TNA.

66. Robinson and Heywood to James Rogers and Co., 13 July 1792, Manchester,
C 107/10, TNA.

67. Joseph Caton to James Rogers, 11 January 1790, Liverpool, C 107/13, TNA.

68. William Woodville Jr. to James Rogers, 25 November 1789, Liverpool, C
107/13, TNA.

69. Thornton, *Paper Credit*, 254, 286–87. Adam Smith anticipated Thornton
when he observed, "Double interest is in Great Britain reckoned what the
merchants call a good, moderate, reasonable profit; terms which, I appre-
hend, mean no more than a common and usual profit. In a country where
the ordinary rate of clear profit is eight to ten per cent, it may be reasonable
that one half of it should go to interest, whenever business is carried on with
borrowed money." Smith, *Wealth of Nations*, 1:99–100.

70. For the phrase, see Henry Laurens to John Knight, 12 June 1764, in Taylor
et al., *Laurens Papers*, 4:311. Cf. David Hancock, *Citizens of the World: London*

Merchants and the Integration of the British Atlantic Community, 1735-1785 (Cambridge: Cambridge University Press, 1995), 275; Morgan, "Remittance Procedures"; and Radburn, "Keeping 'the Wheel.'"

71. Thomas Leyland to Justin Brennan (Cadiz), 24 June 1786, Liverpool, Leyland Letter Book, 387 MD 59, LRO.

72. Cf. Ernest Hemingway, *For Whom the Bell Tolls* (1941; London: Arrow Books, London, 2004), where Hemingway depicted contemporary debates about republican strategy in the Spanish Civil War as "a vast wheel, set at an angle, and each time it goes round and then is back to where it starts" (233), but, seen as one that "must be revolving by itself," it was, he argued, a wheel that you cannot ride too long, for it was "probably quite a deadly wheel" (235).

73. Adam Anderson, *An Historical and Chronological Deduction of the Origins of Commerce: From the Earliest Accounts,* 4 vols. (1764; London: Logographic Press, 1789), 4:677. I am grateful to my late former colleague Donald Woodward for this reference.

74. Joseph Caton to James Rogers, 2 December 1790, Liverpool, C 107/13, TNA.

75. Details of Caton's roles as shipmaster and owner in the slave trade are to be found in Voyages/transatlantic/database/master or owner = Caton, Joseph.

Chapter 4. "Vulgar Error"

Title: For the phrase "vulgar error" in the chapter title, see Sir Thomas Browne, *Pseudodoxia Epidemica* (London: Edward Dod, 1658), 405-9, to which I refer later.

1. Ship Wage Book, Ship *Essex* accounts, 1783-1784, Davenport Papers, National Museums Liverpool.

2. Herbert S. Klein, *The Middle Passage: Comparative Studies of the Atlantic Slave Trade* (Princeton, NJ: Princeton University Press, 1978), 86, shows that around two-fifths of slave ships entering Rio de Janeiro in 1795-1811 had enslaved crew, representing about a third to a half of their complement. Cf. Mariana P. Candido, "Different Slave Journeys: Enslaved African Seamen on Board of Portuguese Ships, c. 1760-1820s," *Slavery and Abolition* 31, no. 3 (2010): 399, who shows that enslaved Africans comprised some 3 percent of a sample of some 8,440 crew members of Portuguese slave ships in 1767-1832.

3. David Brion Davis, foreword to David Eltis and David Richardson, *Atlas of the Transatlantic Slave Trade* (New Haven: Yale University Press, 2010), xvii. The impact of global exchange on human history is a core theme of Marcus Rediker, *The Slave Ship: A Human History* (New York: Viking, 2007).

4. David Eltis, preface to James A. Rawley, *London: Metropolis of the Slave Trade* (Columbia: University of Missouri Press, 2003), xiii.

5. John Mair, *Book-keeping Methodiz'd: Or a Methodical Treatise of Merchant-Accompts, According to the Italian Form* (Edinburgh: T. and W. Ruddimane, 1736). A ninth edition appeared in 1773 after Mair's death, using the accounts of Captain Bell of the Liverpool slaver *Rose* as a specimen record to illustrate appropriate bookkeeping procedures in West Indian "sugar colonies" at that time (268ff.). Other manuals had sections relating to the slave trade. See Benjamin Donn, *The Young Shopkeeper's, Steward's, and Factor's Companion* (1768; 2nd ed., London: J. Johnson, 1773), 41–65; and *The Ship Master's Assistant and Owner's Manual* (London: D[avid] Steel, 1788), 233–36.

6. Robin Pearson and David Richardson, "Insuring the Transatlantic Slave Trade," *JEH* 79, no. 2 (2019): 417–46; Jeremy Krikler, "The *Zong* and the Lord Chief Justice," *History Workshop Journal* 64, no. 1 (2007): 36; James Walvin, *The "Zong": A Massacre, the Law, and the End of Slavery* (New Haven: Yale University Press, 2011), 153.

7. Suzanne Schwarz, ed. and intro., *Slave Captain: The Career of James Irving in the Liverpool Slave Trade*, rev. 2nd ed. (Liverpool: Liverpool University Press, 2008), 86–87.

8. James Wallace, *A General and Descriptive History of the Ancient and Present State of the Town of Liverpool* (Liverpool: J. M'Creevy, 1795), 224–25. As an example of such calculation, see Christopher Hasell to Charles Ford, 29 April 1770, Liverpool, Christopher Hasell Letter Book, 1765–1773, Hasell Family Papers, Private Collection, who in referring to the arrival in Barbados of Captain Peter Potter on 16 March with 290 slaves and about two tons of ivory, notes that Potter had lost some 97 slaves after leaving Africa, which, Hasell observed, "was unlucky[,] however he [Potter] has made a great purchase & after all I hope if he makes but a moderate sale he will clere us £3000—wch is very well for so short a voyage."

9. The theme of commodification is central to Stephanie Smallwood's *Saltwater Slavery: A Middle Passage from Africa to American Diaspora* (Cambridge, MA: Harvard University Press, 2007).

10. *Somerset v Stewart* (1772), 98 ER 499. Details of the judgment are usually based on newspaper reports, specifically that in the *General Evening Post* of June 1772. A favorable view of the reliability of such reporting, including cases of Lord Justice Mansfield, who presided in the *Somerset* case, is provided by James Oldham, "Law Reporting in the London Newspapers, 1756–1786," *American Journal of Legal History* 31, no. 3 (1987): 206.

11. The *Somerset* case was reported in at least 13 British newspapers and in 22 out of 24 colonial newspapers. George Van Cleve, "*Somerset's Case* and Its Antecedents in Imperial Perspective," *Law and History Review* 24, no. 2 (2006): 602.

12. Van Cleve, *"Somerset's Case,"* 605. The philosopher William Paley, who, like Lord Mansfield, saw slavery as "odious," seems to have taken up this invitation, if such it was, in 1785, when he remarked that the "great revolution that has taken place in the Western World may probably conduce (and who knows but that it was designed) to accelerate the fall of this abominable tyranny; and now that this contest, and the passions which attend it are now no more, there may succeed perhaps a season for reflecting, whether a legislature which had so long lent its assistance to the support of an institution replete with human misery was fit to be trusted with an empire the most extensive that ever obtained in any age or quarter of the world." An advocate of gradual emancipation, Paley saw Christianity as providing a guide, arguing that by "the mild diffusion of its light and influence, the minds of men are insensibly prepared to perceive and correct the enormities, which folly, or wickedness, or accident have introduced into their public establishments." William Paley, *The Principles of Moral and Political Philosophy*, 2 vols. (London: R. Faulkner, 1785), 2:195–96.

13. Iain Whyte, *Scotland and the Abolition of Black Slavery, 1756–1838* (Edinburgh: Edinburgh University Press, 2006), 18; John Millar, *The Origin of the Distinction of Ranks*, ed. Aaron Garrett (1803; Indianapolis, IN: Liberty Fund, 2012), 280. Millar's *Origins* first appeared in 1771, with revised and extended versions in 1773 and 1781 and a posthumous edition in 1803. The last forms the basis of the Liberty Fund edition, which also includes the reference to the 1778 court decision. Consultation of the original 1781 edition reveals that the comment on the 1778 court decision first appeared in that year. John Millar, *The Origin of the Distinction of Ranks*, 3rd ed. (London: J. Murray, 1781), 362.

14. Van Cleve, *"Somerset's Case,"* 606.

15. Thomas Clarkson, *The History of the Rise, Progress, and Accomplishment of the Abolition of the Slave-Trade*, 2 vols. (London: Longman, Hurst, Rees, and Orme, 1808), 1:84. Clarkson noted that in order to interest the House in the motion, Hartley laid on the House's table some of the chains used in "this cruel traffic," an early example of abolitionists' use of iconography to support their argument.

16. See William Robertson, *The History of America*, vol. 1 (Dublin: Messrs Whitestone et al., 1777), preface, where the author also refers to the war as "this unhappy contest." For the benevolence of Hartley and Savile, consult the History of Parliament website for members David Hartley, https://www.historyofparliamentonline.org/volume/1754-1790/member/hartley-david-1730-1813, and Sir George Savile, https://www.historyofparliamentonline.org/volume/1754-1790/member/savile-sir-george-1726-84. The entries were written

by John Brooke and first published in 1964. Both entries highlight the two MPs' attitudes to the American crisis; interestingly, neither entry refers to the slave trade, which in 1964 assumed a lower profile in historical research than later.

17. See, e.g., Benjamin Franklin, *The Autobiography of Benjamin Franklin,* ed. Leonard W. Labaree, Ralph L. Ketcham, Helen C. Boatfield, and Helene H. Fineman (New Haven: Yale University Press, 1964), 17. It is perhaps no accident that David Hartley was a correspondent with Franklin, whose autobiography is described as a "lay sermon" by its editors, before (and after) the 1776 motion was tabled.

18. Though this is not the place to do so, the circumstances under which Adam Jema was enrolled on the ship *Essex* and their compatibility with Lord Mansfield's judgment in 1772 would repay attention in the context of considering its efficacy in practice.

19. The petition and its signatories were entered in the London Yearly Meeting minutes of the Society of Friends, 17:298–307, and the Meeting for Sufferings minutes, 36:408–13, held at the Society of Friends Library, London; a transcript of Yearly Meeting minutes is available online at the Abolition Project, www.abolition.e2bn.org.

20. James Ramsay, *An Inquiry into the Effects of Putting a Stop to the African Slave Trade, and of Granting Liberty to the Slaves in the British Sugar Colonies* (London: James Phillips, 1784).

21. Ramsay, *Inquiry,* 5, 8.

22. Ramsay, *Inquiry,* 12.

23. As one Jamaican planter wrote in 1784, unless the abolitionists "can substitute some better plan for carrying on the cultivation of the sugar colonies which produce such an immense revenue to this country their request cannot be seriously thought on by the ministry [that is, the British government]." Cited in Karl B. Koth and John E. Serieux, "Sugar, Slavery and Wealth: Jamaica Planter Nathaniel Phillips and the Williams Hypothesis (1761–1813)," *Capitalism: A Journal of History and Economics* 1, no. 1 (2019): 60.

24. Christer Petley, *White Fury: A Jamaican Slaveholder and the Age of Revolution* (Oxford: Oxford University Press, 2018), 141; and see Upper Harley Street [London], Stephen Fuller to Lord Hawkesbury, 29 January 1788, Liverpool Papers, Add. Mss. 38416, f. 6, British Library, in which Fuller, colonial agent for Jamaica, urged Hawkesbury to look "to prevent this matter [of slave trade abolition] being agitated at all in Parliament," thereby tending "to quiet the minds of a great number of his Majesty's subjects, who have purchased Negro Slaves under the Sanction of the Laws of this Country, and

who have just as good a right to the possession of them as they have to any other part of their property in the West Indies."

25. Cf. the title to chapter 10 of John Steinbeck's *Sweet Thursday* (1954; London, Penguin, 2000), 40, where Steinbeck writes of creating a hole in reality, with the rider "through which we can look if we wish."

26. Robertson, *History of America,* 226.

27. Steven Pinker, *The Better Angels of Our Nature: A History of Violence and Humanity* (New York: Penguin, 2012), 210.

28. Seymour Drescher, *The Mighty Experiment: Free Labor versus Slavery in British Emancipation* (Oxford: Oxford University Press, 2004).

29. Claudine Hunting, "The Philosophes and Black Slavery, 1748–1765," *Journal of the History of Ideas* 39, no. 3 (1978): 405–18; Jeremy L. Caradonna, *The Enlightenment in Practice: Academic Prize Contests and Intellectual Culture in France, 1670–1794* (Ithaca, NY: Cornell University Press, 2012), 152–59.

30. See [Charles de Secondat, Baron de Montesquieu], *De L'Esprit des lois* (Geneva: Barrillo et fils, 1748), 383–431, where slavery is discussed. For Montesquieu's influence on British antislavery proponents, including in the 1760s the jurists George Wallace and William Blackstone and the Scottish moral philosopher Adam Ferguson, see F. T. H. Fletcher, "Montesquieu's Influence on Anti-Slavery Opinion in England," *Journal of Negro History* 18, no. 4 (1933): 414–25; and Michael Guenther, "A Peculiar Silence: The Scottish Enlightenment, Political Economy, and the Early American Debates over Slavery," *Atlantic Studies* 8, no. 4 (2011): 453, where Montesquieu's work on laws is described as "a hallmark of the Scottish Enlightenment." Other research has also identified influences on British thinking from the 1760s of Spanish policies toward slaves in the Americas. Emily Berquist, "Early Anti-Slavery Sentiment in the Spanish Atlantic World, 1765–1817," *Slavery and Abolition* 31, no. 2 (2010): 184.

31. Lynn Hunt, *Inventing Human Rights* (New York: W. W. Norton, 2008); Pauline Kleingeld, *Kant and Cosmopolitanism: The Philosophical Ideal of World Citizenship* (Cambridge: Cambridge University Press, 2012), 92–117.

32. Paley, *Principles,* 2:16.

33. Christopher Leslie Brown, *Moral Capital: Foundations of British Abolitionism* (Chapel Hill: University of North Carolina Press, 2006), 27.

34. See, e.g., Quentin Skinner, *Liberty before Liberalism* (Cambridge: Cambridge University Press, 1998), where Skinner identifies "negative" liberty's association with "neo-Roman" ideas of juxtaposing freedom and slavery; and Skinner, "Isaiah Berlin Lecture: A Third Concept of Liberty," *Proceedings of the British Academy* 117 (2002): 237–68, esp. 247–48.

35. John Trenchard and Thomas Gordon, *Cato's Letters* (1720–23), Letter No. 62, "An Enquiry into the Nature and Extent of Liberty; with its Loveliness and Advantages, and the Vile Effects of Slavery" (signed G), available online at https://en.wikisource.org/wiki/Cato%27s_Letters/Letter_62.

36. See *A Dictionary of the English Language: A Digital Edition of the 1755 Classic by Samuel Johnson,* ed. Brandi Besalke, https://johnsonsdictionaryonline.com.

37. See Quentin Skinner, "John Milton and the Politics of Slavery," *Prose Studies: History, Theory, Criticism* 23, no. 1 (2000): 1–22, on domestic politics; and Linda Colley, *Captives: Britain, Empire, and the World, 1600–1830* (New York: Anchor Books, 2002), 63, on enslavement by Barbary corsairs and the extent of knowledge of it in British print culture through 1730.

38. Jonathan Swift, *Gulliver's Travels* (1726; Oxford: Oxford World Classics, 1998), 90.

39. Daniel Defoe, *Robinson Crusoe* (1719; London: Penguin, 2001), 29.

40. The Liverpool trader James Irving saw his own (temporary) captivity in Morocco in 1789 after his African-bound slave ship ran ashore as "the most intollerable Slavery" and "a Slavery more detestable than Death," attributing his status variously to "Misfortune" and an "Unfortunate Accident." Schwarz, *Slave Captain,* 76–77, 98–99.

41. David Richardson, "Introduction," in *The Mediterranean Passes* (Wakefield, UK: Micromethods, 1981).

42. Lewes Roberts, *The Treasure of Traffick, or a Discoourse [sic] of Forraign Trade* [1641], in John Ramsay McCulloch, *A Select Collection of Early English Tracts on Commerce, from the Originals of Mun, Roberts, North, and Others* (1856; Indianapolis, IN: Liberty Fund, 2004), 69–70.

43. Max Beer, *Early British Economics from the XIIIth to the Middle of the XVIIIth Century* (London: George Allen and Unwin, 1938), 188–89.

44. William Deringer, "'It Was Their Business to Know': British Merchants and Mercantile Epistemology in the Eighteenth Century," *History of Political Economy* 49, no. 2 (2017): 177–206.

45. For Sir Josiah Child and Charles Davenant, see David Brion Davis, *The Problem of Slavery in Western Culture* (Ithaca, NY: Cornell University Press, 1966), 151. For Postlethwayt, see Malachy Postlethwayt, *The African Trade, the Great Pillar and Support of the British Plantation Trade in America* (London: J. Robinson, 1745); Postlethwayt, *The National and Private Advantages of the African Trade Considered* (London: John and Paul Knapton, 1746); Robert J. Bennett, "Malachy Postlethwayt, 1707–1767: Genealogy and Influence of an Early Economist and 'Spin-Doctor,'" *Genealogists' Magazine* 31 (2011): 1–7; and Dean Lymath, "'Render Them Absolutely Subservient': The

Political Economy of Malachy Postlethwayt's Metropolism" (MA thesis, University of Nottingham, 2013). Davis, 152, points out that some French economists shared similar views at the same time.

46. Postlethwayt, *African Trade,* 40–41; Christopher Leslie Brown, "The Origins of 'Legitimate Commerce,'" in *Commercial Agriculture, the Slave Trade, and Slaving in Atlantic Africa,* ed. Robin Law, Suzanne Schwarz, and Silke Stricktrodt (Woodbridge, UK: Boydell and Brewer, 2013), 145–46; Brown, *Moral Capital,* 272–74. Both quotations, cited in the two sources, are from Postlethwayt's *Universal Directory of Trade and Commerce,* 3rd ed., 2 vols. (London: H. Woodfall et al., 1766), 1:vii, but anticipated in part in other works published after 1749.

47. William Snelgrave, *A New Account of Some Parts of Guinea, and the Slave Trade* (London: P. Knapton, 1734), 159–60. Snelgrave's account has also proved valuable to historians of West Africa. Robin Law, "The Original Manuscript Version of William Snelgrave's *New Account of Some Parts of Guinea,*" *History in Africa* 17 (1990): 367–72.

48. William Pettigrew, *Freedom's Debt: The Royal African Company and the Politics of the Atlantic Slave Trade, 1672–1752* (Chapel Hill: University of North Carolina Press, 2013), 111.

49. Samuel Fortrey, *England's Interest and Improvement* (London: Nathanael Brook, 1673), in McCulloch, *Select Collection,* 335.

50. Domenico Losurdo, *Liberalism: A Counter-History,* trans. Gregory Elliott (London: Verso, 2011), 35–67. Arguments in eighteenth-century works revealing Britons' own sense of their singular devotion to freedom relative to other nations and peoples are discussed in Seymour Drescher, *Capitalism and Antislavery: British Mobilization in Comparative Perspective* (London: Palgrave Macmillan, 1986), 1–24.

51. Thomas Phillips, "A journal of a voyage in the Hannibal from London, Ann. 1693, 1694," in *Collection of Voyages and Travels,* ed. Awnsham Churchill, 3rd ed., 6 vols. (London: H. Lintot, 1746), 6:219.

52. Snelgrave, *New Account,* preface.

53. John Richardson, *Slavery and Augustan Literature: Swift, Pope, Gay* (London: Routledge, 2004), 4; Paul Cavill, *The Christian Tradition in English Literature* (New York: Zondervan Academic, 2009), 225–26.

54. Franklin, *Autobiography,* 65, 88 (emphasis in original).

55. Steven Jablonski, "Ham's Vicious Race: Slavery and John Milton," *Studies in English Literature, 1500–1900* 37, no. 1 (1997): 185.

56. See David M. Whitford, *The Curse of Ham in the Early Modern Era: The Bible and the Justifications for Slavery* (2009; New York: Routledge, 2016),

121, where Whitford argues that in his editing of George Best's *True Discourse of the Late Voyages of Discovery*, written in 1578, the chronicler Richard Hakluyt made blackness and the curse "inseparable," facilitating the exploitation of "Blackamoors," as Best labeled Africans, as part of British imperial expansion. But a popular scientific work published in 1646 and reprinted six times claimed the curse to be wrong, and by the 1680s some English clerics were openly damning of what was called by one "Cain's Mark." Browne, *Pseudodoxia Epidemica,* 405–9; Morgan Godwyn, *The Negro's & Indians Advocate, Suing for their Admission into the Church* (London: Printed by himself, 1680), 14–19, 43–61. It continued, however, to surface in other English literature in the seventeenth and eighteenth centuries, sometimes being depicted, as in 1678, as offering through its endorsement of African slavery a "new Blessing" for West India planters and London grocers, and prompting the poet Robert Merry in 1788 to denounce the curse that had "form'd the negroes for disgrace," with the "doom of slav'ry stampt upon their face." Jablonski, "Ham's Vicious Race"; James G. Basker, *Amazing Grace: An Anthology of Poems about Slavery, 1660–1810* (New Haven: Yale University Press, 2005), 16, 367. For the earliest roots of the curse and its identification with blackness and race, see David M. Goldenberg, *The Curse of Ham: Race and Slavery in Early Judaism, Christianity, and Islam* (Princeton, NJ: Princeton University Press, 2005).

57. In a remarkable rejection of the social construction of race to justify enslaving Africans, the London trader Thomas Phillips privately noted in his journal in 1693–94 that he could "not imagine why they should be despis'd for their colour, being what they cannot help, and the effect of the climate it has pleas'd God to appoint them." He went on to add that "I can't think there is any intrinsick value in one colour more than another, nor that white is better than black, only we think it so because we are so." Phillips, "Journal of a voyage," 219. His remarks were not publicized until 1746.

58. Snelgrave, *New Account,* 160–61.

59. See P. E. H. Hair, Adam Jones, and Robin Law, eds., *Barbot on Guinea: The Writings of Jean Barbot on West Africa, 1678–1712,* 2 vols. (London: Hakluyt Society, 1992), 1:550, where Barbot argues that, because of "barbarous usage" within Africa, the fate of slaves sold to Europeans was "less deplorable than that of those who end their days in their native country"; and Robert Norris, *Memoirs of the Reign of Bossa Ahadee, King of Dahomy, an Inland Country of Guiney, to which are Added, the Author's Journey to Abomey, the Capital; and a Short Account of the African Slave Trade* (London: W. Lowndes, 1789), 156–57, where in analyzing the demographic and social history of Africa, Norris

depicted the export slave trade as rescuing a "surplus" of inhabitants "from that certain death [from slaughter and sacrifice], which awaited them in their own country." Norris's argument was anticipated by Edward Long, who in 1774 saw Britain's taking slaves from Africa as "a meritorious act," rescuing "human victims from suffering death and torture" under regimes that practiced "idolatrous and savage customs." Long, *The History of Jamaica,* 3 vols. (London: T. Lowndes, 1774), 1:387. Like Snelgrave, Barbot, Long, and Norris were invested in the trade.

60. Howard Erskine-Hill, "World and Word—Pope and Slavery," *Proceedings of the British Academy* 91 (1997): 27–53, esp. 35–39; John Richardson, "Alexander Pope's *Windsor Forest:* Its Context and Attitudes towards Slavery," *Eighteenth-Century Studies* 35, no. 1 (2001): 1–17. Pope's most celebrated reference to slavery in *An Essay on Man* (1733–34) is to be found in epistle 1, lines 110–13.

61. John Atkins, *A Voyage to Guinea, Brasil and the West Indies; in His Majesty's Ships the Swallow and Weymouth* (London: Caesar Ward and Richard Chandler, 1735), 61–62, 176–78.

62. Snelgrave, *New Account,* 160.

63. See Atkins, *Voyage to Guinea,* 41–42, 119–26, where he instances without criticism an example of an African village leader who killed some resident white or mulatto dealers in the course of resisting British traders and was subsequently captured and made another dealer's property.

64. David Eltis, *The Rise of African Slavery in the Americas* (Cambridge: Cambridge University Press, 1999), 1–28.

65. Browne, *Pseudodoxia Epidemica,* 405–9.

66. George Fox, *The Works of George Fox, 1624–1691,* 8 vols. (Philadelphia: Marcus T. Gould, 1831), 7:144–45.

67. One was the English-born, Harvard-trained Michael Wigglesworth, who in 1667 urged that "Although Affliction tannes the Skin / Such Saintes are Beautiful within," and that "As God is dear to them, / So they to Him are dear." Quoted in Basker, *Amazing Grace,* 11.

68. Richard Baxter, *A Christian Directory, or a Summ of Practical Theology and Cases of Conscience* (London: Nevill Simmons, 1673), 557–78.

69. Nathan Kite, "First Germantown Friends," *Friend* 17, no. 16 (1844): 125.

70. Godwyn, *Negro's & Indians Advocate;* Morgan Godwyn, *A Supplement to the Negro's and Indian's Advocate* (London: J. D., 1681); Godwyn, *Trade preferr'd before religion AND Christ made to give place to Mammon* (London: B. Tooke, 1685); Thomas Tyron, *Friendly Advice to the Gentleman Planters of the East and West Indies* (London: Andrew Sowle, 1684); Tyron, *Some Memoirs of the Life of Mr. Tho. Tyron* (London: T. Sowle, 1705), 76.

71. See Godwyn, *Negro's & Indians Advocate,* 4–5, for Godwyn's recognition of the influence of Quakers on his thinking. In the unpaginated preface to the same work, he insists on "the *Negro's Humanity*" and that "neither their *Complexion* nor Bondage, Descent nor Country, can be any impediment thereto," and reiterates the same elsewhere. *Negro's & Indians Advocate,* 36; Godwyn, *Trade,* 17, 22, 27–28.

72. Tyron, *Friendly Advice,* 77.

73. Kite, "Germantown Friends," 125 (emphasis added).

74. As noted in Jablonski, "Ham's Vicious Race," 185.

75. Cf. J. R. R. Tolkien, *The Lord of the Rings,* book 1, *The Fellowship of the Ring* (1954; London: HarperCollins, 2002), 111. Godwyn first delivered his tract as a sermon in London. When he published it in 1685, Godwyn sensed being "under no small danger of Censure" from "divers here at home" as well as "incensed MAMMONISTS from abroad." Godwyn, *Trade,* preface, 1.

76. For context and background of the debates, see Pettigrew, *Freedom's Debt;* and Holly Brewer, "Slavery, Sovereignty and 'Inheritable Blood': Reconsidering John Locke and the Origins of American Slavery," *American Historical Review* 122, no. 4 (2017): 1038–78.

77. I do not look here at the religious underpinnings of Locke's political philosophy, which has attracted some recent attention. Nathan Guy, *Finding Locke's God: The Theological Basis of John Locke's Political Thought* (London: Bloomsbury Academic, 2020). But even though it is unlikely that Locke shared the "enthusiasms" of Baxter or Godwyn, others have seen a liberal Anglican input into his vision of North American development that is not incompatible with Baxter's and Godwyn's views of how Africans should be treated. Jack Turner, "John Locke, Christian Mission, and Colonial America," *Modern Intellectual History* 8, no. 2 (2011): 267–99.

78. Mark Goldie, ed., *The Enhanced Edition of John Locke's Two Treatises of Civil Government* (1690, 1764; Indianapolis, IN: Liberty Fund, 2010); John Locke, *An Essay Concerning Human Understanding* (London: Thomas Basset, 1690). Though published first in 1690, much of the writing of the two treatises is now believed to date from before 1683. David Armitage, "John Locke, Carolina, and the *Two Treatises of Government,*" *Political Theory* 32, no. 5 (2004): 605–6.

79. Goldie, *Locke's Two Treatises,* book 1, chapter 1, section 1.

80. Algernon Sidney, *Discourses concerning Government by Algernon Sidney [. . .]; published from an original manuscript by the author* (London: n.p., 1698), chapter 1, sections 2, 5, 11, chapter 2, section 11.

81. For a review of interpretations, see Wayne Glausser, "Three Approaches to Locke and the Slave Trade," *Journal of the History of Ideas* 51, no. 2 (1990): 199–216.

82. Jennifer Welchman, "Locke on Slavery and Inalienable Rights," *Canadian Journal of Philosophy* 25, no. 1 (1995): 67–81. Locke favored freedom of religion in the Carolinas, extendable to slaves (though subject to their owners' approval), but saw no basis for the removal or ill treatment of Native Americans in what he saw as their idolatry or lack of Christianity. Armitage, "John Locke," 609. In 1698, he still considered those issues a matter "of such importance and difficulty" as to require "a Treatise of it Self." Brewer, "Slavery, Sovereignty and Inheritable Blood," 1063.

83. Vicki Hsueh, "Theory and Practice in the Fundamental Constitutions of Carolina," *Journal of the History of Ideas* 63, no. 2 (2002): 425–46; Armitage, "John Locke," 602–27 (quotation at 602); James Farr, "Locke, Natural Law, and New World Slavery," *Political Theory* 36, no. 4 (2008): 495–522; Brad Hinshelwood, "The Carolinian Context of John Locke's Theory of Slavery," *Political Theory* 41, no. 4 (2013): 562–90; Brewer, "Slavery, Sovereignty and Inheritable Blood"; Holly Brewer, "Slavery-Entangled Philosophy: Does Locke's Entanglement with Slavery Undermine His Philosophy?," https://aeon.co/essays/does-lockes-entanglement-with-slavery-undermine-his-philosophy, 12 September 2018; John Quiggin, "Leave John Locke in the Dustbin of History," Jacobin, 6 March 2019, https://www.jacobinmag.com/2019/03/john-locke-freedom-slavery-united-states/.

84. On Jean Bodin's views and their context, see Henry Heller, "Bodin on Slavery and Primitive Accumulation," *Sixteenth Century Journal* 25, no. 1 (1994): 53–65.

85. William Uzgalis, "John Locke, Racism, Slavery, and Indian Lands," in *The Oxford Handbook of Philosophy and Race,* ed. Naomi Zack (Oxford: Oxford University Press, 2017), 18–30.

86. Davis, *Problem of Slavery,* 119–20.

87. See Mary Nyquist, *Arbitrary Rule: Slavery, Tyranny, and the Power of Life and Death* (Chicago: University of Chicago Press, 2013), 218–26, which discusses Bodin and Grotius on war slavery.

88. Goldie, *Locke's Two Treatises,* 213–215 (book 2, chapter 4, section 23). All quotations from Locke in this paragraph are from book 2, chapter 4, sections 23–24.

89. Cf. J. R. R. Tolkien, *The Lord of the Rings,* book 3, *The Return of the King* (1955; London: HarperCollins, 1999), 362.

90. Hinshelwood, "Carolinian Context," 565–67.

91. Pettigrew, *Freedom's Debt*, 184–88.

92. See Nicholas Barbon, *A Discourse of Trade*, ed. Jacob H. Hollander (1690; Baltimore: Johns Hopkins University Press, 1903), which emphasizes the virtues of maritime empire.

93. Steven Pincus, "Empire and the Treaty of Utrecht (1713)," in *New Worlds? Transformations in the Culture of International Relations*, ed. Inken Schmidt-Voges and Ana Crespo Solana (London: Routledge, 2017), 163–85.

94. Aphra Behn, *Oroonoko, or the Royal Slave: A True History* (1688), was subsequently adapted for the stage by Thomas Southerne as *Oroonoko: A Tragedy* (1696); Jeffrey Galbraith, "Slavery and Obedience in Restoration and Early Eighteenth-Century Drama," in *Invoking Slavery in the Eighteenth-Century British Imagination*, ed. Srividhya Swaminathan and Adam R. Beach (Burlington, VT: Ashgate, 2013), 77–92.

95. Karen O'Brien, "Poetry against Empire: Milton to Shelley," *Proceedings of the British Academy* 117 (2001): 269–96.

96. Richardson, *Slavery and Literature*.

97. Brewer, "Slavery, Sovereignty, and Inheritable Blood."

98. Nyquist, *Arbitrary Rule*, 221.

99. Ralph Davis, "English Foreign Trade, 1660–1700," *EHR* 7, no. 2 (1954): 150–66; Richard B. Sheridan, "The Molasses Act and the Market Strategy of the British Sugar Planters," *JEH* 17, no. 1 (1957): 62–83.

100. Ronald Hamowy, "Cato's Letters, John Locke and the Republican Paradigm," *History of Political Thought* 11, no. 2 (1990): 273–94.

Chapter 5. Contrary to "the Laws of God, and the Rights of Man"

1. William Snelgrave, *A New Account of Some Parts of Guinea, and the Slave Trade* (London: P. Knapton, 1734).

2. John Atkins, *A Voyage to Guinea, Brasil and the West Indies; in his Majesty's Ships Swallow and Weymouth* (London: Caesar Ward and Richard Chandler, 1735), 61.

3. The phrasing of Hartley's resolution is from Thomas Clarkson, *The History of the Rise, Progress, and Accomplishment of the Abolition of the Slave-Trade*, 2 vols. (London: Longman, Hurst, Rees, and Orme, 1808), 1:84.

4. T. E. Drake, *Quakers and Slavery in America* (New Haven: Yale University Press, 1950), 51. See also Thomas P. Slaughter, *The Beautiful Soul of John Woolman, Apostle of Abolition* (New York: Pendle Hill, 2008).

5. John Woolman, *A Journal of the Life and Travels of John Woolman, in the Service of the Gospel* (1774; London: James Phillips, 1775), 26–27.

6. John Woolman, *Some Considerations on the Keeping of Negroes* (Philadelphia: James Chattin, 1754), 3, 6, 11, 15–16, 21. Woolman's writings had resonances of John Locke, particularly when commenting on purchasing "a Man who hath never forfeited his Liberty" and keeping "him *and his Posterity* in Servitude and Ignorance" (11, emphasis added).

7. Phillips Moulton, "John Woolman's Approach to Social Action—as Exemplified in the Relation to Slavery," *Church History* 35, no. 4 (1966): 399–410.

8. On the purpose of his trip, see Woolman, *Journal*, "The Testimony of Friends in Yorkshire," 5–8.

9. For Anthony Benezet's early life and its influence on his later work, see Maurice Jackson, "The Social and Intellectual Origins of Anthony Benezet's Antislavery Radicalism," *Pennsylvania History* 66 (1999): 86–112.

10. Anthony Benezet, *Observations on the inflowing, importing, and purchasing of Negroes* (Germantown, PA: Christopher Sower, 1760), 9.

11. Anthony Benezet, *A short account of that part of Africa inhabited by the negroes* (Philadelphia: W. Dunlap, 1762); Benezet, "A caution and warning to Great Britain and her colonies," in *A short representation of the calamitous state of the enslaved Negroes in the British dominions* (Philadelphia: Henry Miller, 1766); Benezet, *Some Historical Account of Guinea* (Philadelphia: Joseph Crukshank, 1771); Roberts Vaux, *Memoirs of the Life of Anthony Benezet* (Philadelphia: W. Alexander, 1817), 30 (quotations).

12. See, e.g., Sharp to Benezet, 22 September 1772, Documents relating to 1765–1774, reference GLCO7483.03, American History, 1493–1945 collection, Gilder Lehrman Institute of American History, New York, where Sharp exchanges thoughts with Benezet comparing conditions of servitude among Scots Highlanders at that time with slavery.

13. Anthony Benezet to Benjamin Franklin, 27 April 1772, in *The Papers of Benjamin Franklin*, vol. 19, *January 1, 1772, through December 31, 1772*, online edition, franklinpapers.org.

14. Franklin to Benezet, 22 August 1772, in *Papers*, vol. 19.

15. Thomas Clarkson, *An Essay on the Slavery and Commerce of the Human Species, Particularly the African* (London: J. Phillips, 1786), xxv.

16. Benezet's antislavery ideas reached his French homeland, too. Marie-Jeanne Rossignol, "Anthony Benezet's Antislavery Reputation in France: An Investigation," in *The Atlantic World of Anthony Benezet (1713–1784)*, ed. Marie-Jeanne Rossignol and Bertrand van Ruymbeke (Leiden: Brill, 2016), 164–84.

17. John Coffey reminds us that some early evangelicals evinced support for (or at best indifference to) slavery and the slave trade. See John Coffey, "Evan-

gelicals, Slavery, and the Slave Trade: From Whitefield to Wilberforce," *AN-VIL* 24, no. 2 (2007): 97–119.

18. S. T. Kimbrough Jr., "Charles Wesley and Slavery," in *Proceedings of the Charles Wesley Society*, vol. 13, ed. S. T. Kimbrough Jr. (Madison, NJ: Charles Wesley Society, 2010), 35–53.

19. Brycchan Carey, "John Wesley's *Thoughts upon Slavery* and the Language of the Heart," *Bulletin of the John Rylands University Library of Manchester* 85, nos. 2–3 (2003): 273, 281.

20. John Wesley, *Thoughts upon Slavery* (1774; Philadelphia: Joseph Crukshank, 1778).

21. Kimbrough, "Charles Wesley," 39.

22. Cf. James E. Bradley, *Religion, Revolution and English Radicalism: Non-Conformity in Eighteenth-Century Politics and Society* (Cambridge: Cambridge University Press, 1992), 410, where he argues that "the ideology of resistance to oppression was wonderfully well suited to their own needs" among dissenting communities in pursuing their own freedoms and independence in Britain in the age of the American Revolution.

23. Cf. Karen O'Brien, "Poetry against Empire: Milton to Shelley," *Proceedings of the British Academy* 117 (2001): 280, who argues that inwardness would ultimately be "the true route to anti-empire; anti-colonial political struggle would not be enough." On Wesley's sentimentalism, see Carey, "John Wesley," 283–84.

24. On Benezet's use of philosophical texts, traders' journals, and travel accounts to construct his antislavery case, see Jackson, "Social and Intellectual Origins," 93.

25. For the concept of "public theologian," see David N. Field, "John Wesley as a Public Theologian: The Case of Thoughts upon Slavery," *Scriptura* 114 (2015): 1–13.

26. Wesley, *Thoughts on Slavery*, 6–49 (quotations at 6, 25).

27. In 1766, Benezet contextualized his assault on slavery by referencing "the general rights and liberties of mankind, and the preservation of those valuable privileges transmitted to us from our ancestors, [which] are become so much the subjects of universal consideration." Benezet, *Caution*, 3.

28. Wesley, *Thoughts on Slavery*, 39; John Millar, *The Origin of the Distinction of Ranks*, ed. Aaron Garrett (1803; Indianapolis, IN: Liberty Fund, 2012), 279 (original quotation). Millar's *Origin* first appeared in 1771, with revised and extended versions in 1773 and 1781 and a posthumous edition in 1803. The last forms the basis of the Liberty Fund edition, though the material from Millar cited here and elsewhere in this chapter first appeared, unless otherwise stated, in the 1770s editions.

29. Some of the earliest linkages between religion and economics arose in the writings of the English clerics and philosophers Josiah Tucker and his mentor, Joseph Butler. Their work, particularly Butler's concept of impartial spectator, is thought to have influenced the Scottish philosopher Adam Smith. Peter Xavier Price, "Liberty, Poverty and Charity in the Political Economy of Josiah Tucker and Joseph Butler," *Modern Intellectual History* 16, no. 3 (2019): 741–70.

30. David Spadafora, *The Idea of Progress in Eighteenth-Century Britain* (New Haven: Yale University Press, 1990), 261.

31. Clarkson, *History*, 1:87.

32. Colin Heydt, "Hutcheson's *Short Introduction* and the Purposes of Moral Philosophy," *History of Philosophy Quarterly* 26, no. 3 (2009): 293–305.

33. Francis Hutcheson, *A System of Moral Philosophy* (Glasgow: Robert Foulis, 1755), 299–302. In 1742 David Hume described the ancients' descriptions of slaves as foreigners and speakers of barbarous languages as "an imitation of nature." Hume, *Essays Moral, Political, and Literary,* ed. Eugene F. Miller (1777; Indianapolis, IN: Liberty Fund, 1987), part 2, essay 11, 224.

34. Francis Hutcheson, *A Short Introduction to Moral Philosophy* (Glasgow: Robert Foulis, 1747; originally published in Latin in 1742), 274.

35. Hutcheson, *Short Introduction*, 277. In the same section Hutcheson also proposed that "children of slaves of any sort are all born free."

36. Gershom Carmichael, *Supplements and Observations upon Samuel Pufendorf's On the Duty of Man and Citizen according to the Law of Nature* [1724], in *Natural Rights on the Threshold of the Scottish Enlightenment: The Writings of Gershom Carmichael,* ed. James Moore and Michael Silverthorne (Indianapolis, IN: Liberty Fund, 2002), 140–41.

37. Terence W. Hutchison, *Before Adam Smith: The Emergence of Political Economy, 1662–1776* (New York: Basil Blackwell, 1988), 192.

38. A synopsis of these elements of Hutcheson's moral theory is provided by Jack P. Greene, *The Intellectual Heritage of the Constitutional Era: The Delegates' Library* (Philadelphia: Library Company of Philadelphia, 1986), 45–47.

39. Adam Smith, *The Theory of Moral Sentiments* (London: A. Millar, 1759). Cf. Leo Tolstoy, *Anna Karenina* (1877; London: Penguin, 2006), 247: "The chief task of philosophy" is finding "the connection that necessarily exists between personal and common interests."

40. The charge of racism leveled at Hume largely arises from a reference in the 1753 version of his essay "Of National Characters," first published in 1748, on white superiority over other "species of men," including specifically

"negroes," and which appeared in some other subsequent versions. For discussion of the context and contemporary reaction to Hume's remarks, see Aaron Garrett and Silvia Sebastiani, "David Hume on Race," in *Oxford Handbook of Philosophy and Race,* ed. Naomi Zack (Oxford: Oxford University Press, 2017), 31–43. Clarkson in 1808 referred to another Scot, James Beattie, in his work *An Essay on the Nature and Immutability of Truth* (1770), "vindicating the intellectual powers of the Africans from the aspersions of Hume." Clarkson, *History,* 1:83. Hume's racist remarks echoed those of such earlier philosophers as Gottfried Wilhelm Leibniz; they illustrate the point that although racism was used historically to justify enslavement of some people, it was not synonymous with slavery, as Hume's general opposition to the institution suggests.

41. Hume, *Essays Moral, Political, and Literary,* part 2, essay 11, 219–52.

42. Adam Smith, *Lectures on Justice, Police, Revenue and Arms delivered at the University of Glasgow,* ed. Edwin Cannan (Oxford: Clarendon Press, 1896), 96; Adam Smith, *Lectures on Jurisprudence,* ed. R. L. Meek, D. D. Raphael, and P. G. Stein (Oxford: Oxford University Press, 1978), 178–93 (quotation at 178); Knud Haakonssen, "Adam Smith's Lectures on Jurisprudence," in *Adam Smith: His Life, Thought, and Legacy,* ed. Ryan Hanley (Princeton, NJ: Princeton University Press, 2016), 48–66.

43. Millar, *Origin,* 257–81 (quotation at 271). For a fuller discussion of Millar's views on slavery, see Fred Ablondi, "Millar on Slavery," *Journal of Scottish Philosophy* 7, no. 2 (2009): 163–75, which highlights some normative differences between Millar's and Smith's views on the subject.

44. Garrett, "Introduction" to Millar, *Origin,* section "The Argument of Ranks." In the same essay Garrett also observes that Millar viewed rights in evolutionary terms through the prism of his "stadial theory," with changes in the scope of rights arising from changing needs.

45. Smith, *Moral Sentiments;* Smith, *Jurisprudence,* 185.

46. Millar, *Origin,* 274. On Montesquieu's influence on Smith's thinking about slavery, see John Salter, "Adam Smith on Slavery," *History of Economic Ideas* 4, nos. 1–2 (1996): 237.

47. For the quotation, see Clarkson, *History,* 1:453, citing a speech by Major John Cartwright, MP, in 1789 on the slave trade. Before supporting abolition, Cartwright in 1775 published a tract favoring the colonial cause against Britain and in 1780 joined abolitionist Granville Sharp in forming the Society for Constitutional Reform. Henry Colburn, "Obituary: John Cartwright Esq," *New Monthly Magazine,* November 1824, 522. Millar's and Smith's views on the incompatibility of slavery with British civilized values can also be seen

to contain the thread of a discourse that would, according to some scholars, shape the nation's "racialised" vision of its relationship with much of the rest of the world in the era of modern imperialism. Edward Said, *Orientalism* (London: Pantheon Books, 1979).

48. Millar, *Origins,* 272.

49. Smith, *Lectures,* 185–86; Adam Smith, *An Inquiry into the Nature and Causes of the Wealth of Nations,* 2 vols. (1776; Indianapolis, IN: Online Library of Liberty, 2013), 1:365. As Smith explained it, "A person who can acquire no property can have no other interest but to eat as much and to labour as little as possible. Whatever work he does beyond what is sufficient to purchase his own maintenance, can be squeezed out of him by violence only, and not by any interest of his own."

50. Simona Pisanelli, "James Steuart: Slavery and Commercial Society in His Principles of Political Economy," in *The Economic Thought of Sir James Steuart: First Economist of the Scottish Enlightenment,* ed. Jose M. Menudo (London: Routledge, 2019), 32–45; Salim Rashid, "Adam Smith's Rise to Fame: A Re-Examination of the Evidence," *Eighteenth Century* 23, no. 1 (1982): 68–69.

51. It was, of course, one that David Brion Davis acknowledged. Davis, *Slavery and Human Progress* (New York: Oxford University Press, 1984).

52. Smith, *Jurisprudence,* 181, 187.

53. Spencer J. Pack, "Slavery, Adam Smith's Economic Vision and the Invisible Hand," *History of Economic Ideas* 4, no. 2 (1996): 255–56; cf. Moses I. Finley, *Ancient Slavery and Modern ideology,* ed. B. D. Shaw (Princeton, NJ: Princeton University Press, 1998), 308, where Finley posits the importance of the psychological and ideological aspects over the economic in reflecting on slavery.

54. Salter, "Adam Smith on Slavery," 240–41. Smith's pessimism perhaps deepened further in his last years given the mixed reviews his magnum opus received as well as its apparently limited impact on commercial policy before his death in 1790. Richard F. Teichgraeber III, "'Less Abused Than I Had Reason to Expect': The Reception of *The Wealth of Nations* in Britain, 1776–1790," *Historical Journal* 30, no. 2 (1987): 337–66.

55. James Ramsay, *An Inquiry into the Effects of Putting a Stop to the African Slave Trade, and of Granting Liberty to the Slaves in the British Sugar Colonies* (London: James Phillips, 1784), 32.

56. Clarkson, *History,* 1:86.

57. Eric Williams, *Capitalism and Slavery* (Chapel Hill: University of North Carolina Press, 1944).

58. Richard Lamb, "Adam Smith's Concept of Alienation," *Oxford Economic Papers,* n.s., 25, no. 2 (1973): 275–85. On unsociable sociability, see Allen W. Woods, "Unsociable Sociability: The Anthropological Basis of Kantian Ethics," *Philosophical Topics* 19, no. 1 (1991): 325–51; and Iain McDaniel, "Unsocial Sociability in the Scottish Enlightenment: Ferguson and Kames on War, Sociability and the Foundations of Patriotism," *History of European Ideas* 41, no. 5 (2015): 662–82. I turn briefly to this issue in chapter 8.

59. David Brion Davis, *The Problem of Slavery in the Age of Revolution, 1770–1823* (Ithaca, NY: Cornell University Press, 1975), 349–50.

60. William Cowper, *Poems* (1782; Ann Arbor, MI: Text Creation Partnership, 2011), 187.

61. See, e.g., Anne Stott, *Wilberforce: Family and Friends* (Oxford: Oxford University Press, 2012), 36, where Wilberforce is described as using the concept of the impartial spectator from Smith's *Theory of Moral Sentiments* in his first major speech to Parliament in 1789 on the slave trade; and Robert and Samuel Wilberforce, eds., *The Correspondence of William Wilberforce,* vol. 1 (London: John Murray, 1840), 387, where in 1810 Wilberforce refers to *Dialogues on Political Economy* as a work of "uncommon excellence" and containing major works of Dr. Adam Smith.

62. Christopher Leslie Brown, *Moral Capital: Foundations of British Abolitionism* (Chapel Hill: University of North Carolina Press, 2006).

63. John Oldfield, *Popular Politics and British Anti-Slavery: The Mobilisation of Public Opinion against the Slave Trade, 1787–1807* (Manchester: Manchester University Press, 1995); Seymour Drescher, "History's Engines: British Mobilization in the Age of Revolution," *WMQ,* 3rd ser., 66, no. 4 (2009): 737–56. As I note elsewhere, estimates suggest that up to one-sixth of British adult males may have signed anti–slave trade petitions in 1788–92.

Chapter 6. "Tumults of Imagination"

1. See Christopher Leslie Brown, *Moral Capital: Foundations of British Abolitionism* (Chapel Hill: University of North Carolina Press, 2006), 40–41 and n., where Brown refers to the antislavery "interpretative tradition," identified among others with David Brion Davis, *The Problem of Slavery in the Age of Revolution, 1770–1823* (Ithaca, NY: Cornell University Press, 1976), 39–49, and which, Brown proposes, "overemphasizes the reach of ideas and wrongly minimizes the social and political context that allowed ideas to matter."

2. Adam Smith, "History of Astronomy," in Dugald Stewart, *Essays on Philosophical Subjects by the Late Adam Smith* (London: T. Cadell Jr. and W. Davies, 1795), 20 (quotations).

3. See Daniel Defoe, *Robinson Crusoe* (1729; London: Penguin, 2001), preface, where Defoe refers to the book as offering "instruction of others by this example."

4. E. P. Thompson, *The Making of the English Working Class* (London: Victor Gollancz, 1963), 11 (quotation); Thompson, "Eighteenth-Century English Society: Class Struggle without Class?" *Social History* 3, no. 2 (1978): 133–65.

5. Lynn Hunt, *Inventing Human Rights: A History* (New York: W. W. Norton, 2007), 34.

6. The full quotation is: "There are some secret moving springs in the affection which when they are set a going by some object in view, or be it some object, though not in view, yet render'd present to the mind by the power of imagination, that motion carries out the soul by its impetuosity to such violent eager embracings of the object, that the absence of it is insupportable." Defoe, *Robinson Crusoe*, 148–49.

7. Seymour Drescher, "Liberty, Equality, Humanity: Antislavery and Civil Society in Britain and France," in *The Rise and Demise of Slavery and the Slave Trade in the Atlantic World,* ed. Philip Misevich and Kristin Mann (Rochester, NY: University of Rochester Press, 2016), 171–95.

8. Brian Michael Norton, *Fiction and the Philosophy of Happiness: Ethical Enquiries in the Age of Enlightenment* (Lewisburg, PA: Bucknell University Press, 2012), 1–23 (quotations at 11).

9. Ian Watt, *The Rise of the Novel: Studies in Defoe, Richardson, and Fielding* (Berkeley: University of California Press, 1957); John Brewer, *The Pleasures of the Imagination: English Culture in the Eighteenth Century* (London: Taylor and Francis, 2013).

10. Steven Pinker, *The Better Angels of Our Nature: A History of Violence and Humanity* (New York: Penguin, 2010), 210.

11. See J. R. R. Tolkien, *The Lord of the Rings,* book 1, *The Fellowship of the Ring* (1954; London: HarperCollins, 2002), 354–55, where Tolkien reinforces his point by noting how only "a small part is played in great deeds by any hero."

12. Pitt moved in May 1788 for Parliament in the next session to proceed "to take account of the circumstances complained of in the said petitions, and what may be fit to be done thereupon," while, responding, Fox observed how the table of the Commons "had been loaded with petitions from various parts of the kingdom" and that only a parliamentary inquiry "would have the benefit of every circumstance of publicity; which was a most material benefit indeed, and that which of all others made the manner of conducting the parliamentary proceedings of Great Britain the envy and the admiration of the world." Thomas Clarkson, *The History of the Rise, Progress, and Accomplishment of the Abolition of the African Slave-Trade by the British Parliament,* 2 vols. (London: Longman, Hurst, Rees, and Orme, 1808), 1:509.

13. Clarkson, *History,* 1:470.

14. Cited in Allen C. Guelzo, "Public Sentiment Is Everything: Abraham Lincoln and the Power of Public Opinion," in *Lincoln and Liberty: Wisdom for the Ages,* ed. Lucas E. Morel (Lexington: University of Kentucky Press, 2014), 171. Guelzo also notes that in 1860 Lincoln observed that for "any policy to be permanent" it "must have public opinion at the bottom."

15. The Overton window is identified with the Mackinac Center for Public Policy. For usages of the theory, see Glenn Beck, *The Overton Window* (New York: Threshold Editions, 2010), a fictional political thriller that links the theory to a conspiracy; and Owen Jones, *The Establishment and How They Get Away with It* (London: Penguin, 2015), in which Jones examines how "neo-liberal ideologues" achieved "stunning political victories" that enabled the implementation of schemes "once seen as extreme and unworkable" (xv). For commentaries on the theory, focusing primarily on recent politics in Britain and the United States, see Laura Marsh, "The Flaws of the Overton Window Theory," *New Republic,* 27 October 2016; and Patricia Lustig and Gill Ringland, "Shifting the Overton Window," Long Finance, 10 September 2019, longfinance.net/news/pamphleteers/shifting-overton-window/.

16. William Alexander Mackinnon, *On the Rise, Progress and Present State of Public Opinion in Great Britain, and in Other Parts of the World* (London: Saunders and Otley, 1828).

17. The numbers are discussed in John Oldfield, *Popular Politics and British Anti-Slavery: The Mobilisation of Public Opinion against the Slave Trade, 1787–1807* (Manchester: Manchester University Press, 1995); and Seymour Drescher, "History's Engines: British Mobilization in the Age of Revolution," *WMQ,* 3rd ser., 66, no. 4 (2009): 737–56.

18. *Belfast Commercial Chronicle,* 24 November 1806, 4.

19. [William Bell Crafton], *A Short Sketch of the Evidence Delivered before a Committee of the House of Commons for the Abolition of the Slave Trade* (Tewkesbury, UK: Dyde and Son, 1792), 25. For identification of Crafton, a Quaker, as the author, see Judith Jennings, *The Business of Abolishing the British Slave Trade, 1783–1807* (London: Frank Cass, 1997), 68.

20. Remarking on the volume of petitions in 1788, Fox emphasized how they were "signed by such numbers of persons of respectable character." Clarkson, *History,* 1:509.

21. [Crafton], *Short Sketch,* [3].

22. Cf. the proslavery writer Bryan Edwards, who identified slavery as making people "distrustful and cowardly" since "so degrading is the nature of slavery, that fortitude of mind is lost as free agency is restrained." Edwards, *The His-*

tory, Civil and Commercial, of the British Colonies in the West Indies, 3 vols, (1793; London: John Stockdale, 1801), 2:93. Edwards likely confused distrustfulness with resistance among enslaved Africans to their condition.

23. Cited in Hunt, *Inventing Human Rights,* 27–28.

24. Perry Gauci, *William Beckford: The First Prime Minister of the London Empire* (New Haven: Yale University Press, 2013), 107; Christer Petley, *White Fury: A Jamaican Slaveholder and the Age of Revolution* (Oxford: Oxford University Press, 2018), 20.

25. Oliver Goldsmith, *The Vicar of Wakefield* (1766; Oxford: Oxford World's Classics, 2006), 87–88.

26. Mackinnon, *Rise,* 15–21 (quotation at 15). Mackinnon distinguished between public opinion and public clamor, the former being based on information, the latter on ignorance and prejudice. Interestingly, proslavery interests frequently urged Parliament not to give way to outside clamor when considering the future of the slave trade, as I note elsewhere, thereby insinuating the campaign to abolish it to be disreputable or illegitimate. David Richardson, "The Ending of the British Slave Trade in 1807: The Economic Context," in *The British Slave Trade: Abolition, Parliament and People,* ed. Stephen Farrell, Melanie Unwin, and James Walvin (Edinburgh: Edinburgh University Press, 2007), 127–40.

27. Parliamentary Archives, Parliament and the British Slave Trade, https://www.parliament.uk/about/living-heritage/transformingsociety/tradeindustry/slavetrade/; "The humble Petition of the undersigned Manufacturers and Merchants on behalf of themselves and others of the town and Neighbourhood of Manchester," Parliamentary Archives HL/PO/JO/10/8/106.

28. Sami Pinabarsi, "Manchester Antislavery, 1792–1807," *Slavery and Abolition* 41, no. 2 (2020): 349–76.

29. Charles James Fox to Thomas Walker, date unknown but possibly as early as 1788, as reported in Bonhams catalog, "Letters to Thomas Walker, c. 1790–1805," lot 98, 10 November 2009, Bonhams.com. Walker corresponded with other leading abolitionist figures, including Thomas Clarkson. I attribute the dating of the remarks by Fox cited here to his comment to Walker that "my sentiments on the African Trade are just what you suppose them, and I had some thoughts of having attacked it myself in Parliament if Mr. Wilberforce had not been beforehand with me." Wilberforce first addressed the Commons on the issue in May 1789, illness having prevented him from doing so earlier.

30. Kazuo Ishiguro, *The Remains of the Day* (1989; London: Faber and Faber, 2005), 120.

31. David Killingray, "Kent and the Abolition of the Slave Trade: A County Study, 1760s–1807, *Archaeologia Cantiana* 118 (2007): 107–25 (quotation at 117).

32. Claire Midgley sees middle-class and aristocratic women as "shadowy private figures" who deployed their influence as "guardians of religion and morality," as marriage partners, and as hostesses of social gatherings to cement "the close evangelical Anglican social and family network" that underpinned "the public work of the male leadership of the movement." Midgley, *Women against Slavery: The British Campaigns, 1780–1870* (London: Routledge, 1992), 16.

33. Olaudah Equiano, *The Interesting Narrative of the Life of Olaudah Equiano, or Gustavus Vassa, the African, Written by Himself* (London: Printed for the author, 1789), subscription list.

34. Paul E. Lovejoy and Suzanne Schwarz, "Sierra Leone in the Eighteenth and Nineteenth Centuries," in *Slavery, Abolition, and the Transition to Colonialism in Sierra Leone,* ed. Paul E. Lovejoy and Suzanne Schwarz (Trenton, NJ: Africa World Press, 2014), 2.

35. Based on the estimates of English per capita income figures for 1801–3 produced by the contemporary political economist Patrick Colquhoun and evaluated in Peter H. Lindert and Jeffrey G. Williamson, "Revising England's Social Tables, 1688–1812," *Explorations in Economic History* 19, no. 4 (1982): 385–408, at 401.

36. I am grateful to Nicholas Evans and Suzanne Schwarz for access to the subscription list of sponsors to the Sierra Leone project on which they are working.

37. Benjamin Franklin, *The Autobiography of Benjamin Franklin,* ed. Leonard W. Labaree, Ralph L. Ketcham, Helen C. Boatfield, and Helene H. Fineman (New Haven: Yale University Press, 1964), 257. Franklin coined the phrase about 1782.

38. Of the 309 who subscribed to Equiano's *Interesting Narrative* in 1789, 37 were female.

39. Oldfield, *Popular Politics.*

40. Nicholas Rogers, *Crowds, Culture, and Politics in Georgian Britain* (Oxford: Clarendon Press, 1998), 171.

41. Mark Jones, "The Mobilisation of Public Opinion against the Slave Trade and Slavery: Popular Abolitionism in National and Regional Politics, 1787–1838" (DPhil thesis, University of York, 1998), 40–41.

42. *Sheffield Register,* February 1788, Sheffield Local Studies Library.

43. Jones, "Mobilisation," 41. Jones points out that other "pockets" of abolitionism were clustered around Bristol, Norwich, Plymouth, and Exeter in 1788,

but that only 11 petitions were organized at the English county level, their organization proving more complex than in towns.

44. Adam Hochschild, *Bury the Chains: Prophets and Rebels in the Fight to Free an Empire's Slaves* (New York: Houghton Mifflin Harcourt, 2005), 5, 138.

45. Oldfield, *Popular Politics,* 114.

46. [Crafton], *Short Sketch,* 23.

47. Charles Tilly, *Popular Contention in Great Britain, 1758–1834* (Cambridge, MA: Harvard University Press, 1995), 144.

48. John Brewer, *Party Ideology and Popular Politics at the Accession of George III* (Cambridge: Cambridge University Press, 1976), 139–60 (quotations at 139, 148, 158, 160).

49. *The Idler,* 27 May 1758, cited in C. A. Cranfield, *The Development of the Provincial Newspaper, 1700–1760* (Oxford: Clarendon Press, 1962), 271.

50. Dugald Stewart, "An Account of the Life and Writings of the Author," in *Essays on Philosophical Subjects by the Late Adam Smith* (London: T. Cadell Jr. and W. Davies, 1795), lxxxix.

51. Joseph Gales editorial, 9 June 1787, *Sheffield Register,* cited in Julie Macdonald, "'The Freedom of Election': The Company of Cutlers in Hallamshire and the Growth of Radicalism in Sheffield, 1784–1792" (PhD thesis, University of Sheffield, 2005), 141.

52. Francis Hutcheson, *An Enquiry into the Original of Our Ideas of Beauty and Virtue,* ed. Wolfgang Leidhold (1725; Indianapolis, IN: Liberty Fund, 2004), 173.

53. Andrew Dickson, "An Introduction to 18th-Century British Theatre," 21 June 2018, British Library, https://www.bl.uk/restoration-18th-century -literature/articles/18th-century-british-theatre#. Whether those figures include "illegitimate" or, after 1737, unlicensed theaters is unclear, but according to Jane Moody there was a theatrical revolution or growth of illegitimate theater as part of a cultural transformation in British theater during and after the last quarter of the eighteenth century. Moody, "The Theatrical Revolution, 1776–1843," in *The Cambridge History of British Theatre,* 3 vols., ed. Joseph Donohue et al. (Cambridge: Cambridge University Press, 2004), 2:199–215.

54. Gillian Russell, "Theatrical Culture," in *The Cambridge Companion to English Literature, 1740–1830,* ed. Thomas Keymer and John Mee (Cambridge: Cambridge University Press, 2004), 100–119.

55. Peter Holland and Michael Patterson, "Eighteenth-Century Theatre," in *The Oxford Illustrated History of the Theatre,* ed. John Russell-Brown (Oxford: Oxford University Press, 2001), 270.

56. David Vincent, *The Rise of Mass Literacy: Reading and Writing in Modern Europe* (Cambridge: Polity, 2000), 8.

57. On the concept of the knowledge economy and its early British manifestation, see Joel Mokyr, *The Gifts of Athena: Historical Origins of the Knowledge Economy* (Princeton, NJ: Princeton University Press, 2002); and Mokyr, *The Enlightened Economy: An Economic History of Britain, 1700-1850* (New Haven: Yale University Press, 2012).

58. Brewer, *Party Ideology,* 156.

59. The circulation through the press of antislavery ideas was not confined to white Britons but by the late 1780s was apparently evident among the enslaved population of the West Indies. Fearing slave unrest, Stephen Fuller, colonial agent for Jamaica, noted in 1788 that "during the time this business [of slave trade abolition] is agitated in Parliament, the slaves will be minutely acquainted with all the proceedings; many of the domestic slaves, born in the islands, & brought up in the dwelling houses, read all the public prints, and instantly communicate any intelligence respecting themselves to their fellow slaves employed in the field." Stephen Fuller to Lord Hawkesbury, [London], 29 January 1788, Liverpool Papers, Add. Mss. 38416, British Library.

60. William St. Clair, *The Reading Nation in the Romantic Period* (Cambridge: Cambridge University Press, 2004), 562.

61. Clarkson, *History,* 1:365-71.

62. As Jones notes, Clarkson's efforts to elicit support from newspaper editors followed signs of Manchester newspaper editors' and proprietors' assistance in mobilizing support for petitioning in 1787. Jones, "Mobilisation," 31-39.

63. Cf. Hilary Mantel, *The Mirror and the Light* (London, Fourth Estate, 2020), 867.

64. John Feather, "The Book Trade, 1770-1823," in *The Oxford Handbook of the Eighteenth-Century Novel,* ed. J. A. J. Downie (Oxford: Oxford University Press, 2016), 292. For background to the growth of the English book trade, see James Raven, *The Business of Books: Booksellers and the English Book Trade, 1450-1850* (New Haven: Yale University Press, 2007); and Raven, "The Book as a Commodity," in *The Cambridge History of the Book in Britain,* ed. Michael F. Suarez and Michael L. Turner (Cambridge: Cambridge University Press, 2009), 83-117.

65. St. Clair, *Reading Nation,* 242-45. John Brewer notes that lending libraries, which expanded from the 1740s and totaled perhaps 380 in England by 1800, also stocked copies of London and provincial newspapers, increasing their potential readership. Brewer, *Party Ideology,* 151.

66. For various estimates, see Jeremy Black, *The English Press in the Eighteenth Century* (1987; London Routledge, 2010), 71-72; Hannah Barker, *Newspapers,*

Politics and English Society, 1695-1855 (London: Routledge, 1999), 256; and Brewer, *Party Ideology,* 142.

67. St. Clair, *Reading Nation,* 576.

68. Cranfield, *Provincial Newspaper,* v. It is worth noting that London newspapers circulated widely outside the capital, with some 1 million copies of London papers being sent out to the country through the post office in 1764 and 4.5 million in 1790. Jeremy Black, "The Development of the Provincial Newspaper Press in the Eighteenth Century," *Journal for Eighteenth-Century Studies* 31, no. 1 (2008): 169.

69. James E. Bradley, *Religion, Revolution and English Radicalism: Non-Conformity in Eighteenth-Century Politics and Society* (Cambridge: Cambridge University Press, 1990), 16.

70. Penelope J. Corfield, "Walking the City Streets: The Urban Odyssey in Eighteenth Century England," *Journal of Urban History* 16, no. 2 (1990): 132-74 (quotation at 141).

71. In locating newspapers at the heart of her study of British provincial urban political culture, Kathleen Wilson observes that it was a politics notable for "the degree to which cultural forms were circulated among and shared by different social groups." Wilson, *The Sense of the People: Politics, Culture and Imperialism in England, 1715-1785* (Cambridge: Cambridge University Press, 1994), 13.

72. Indicators of the commercialization of the press were the large amount of space given to advertising and the recruitment of agents to solicit advertisements. Black, "Provincial Newspaper," 166.

73. Cranfield, *Provincial Newspaper,* 93-116.

74. John Mullan, *Sentiment and Sociability: The Language of Feeling in the 18th Century* (Oxford: Clarendon Press, 1988), 63-64, 98.

75. James Boswell, *Life of Samuel Johnson,* 2 vols. (London: Charles Dilly, 1791), 1:109.

76. Jayoung Min, "Novel Addiction: Consuming Popular Novels in Eighteenth-Century Britain" (PhD diss., Duke University, 2011).

77. Mullan, *Sentiment,* 67, 81; Robert D. Spector, *Smollett's Women: A Study in an Eighteenth-Century Masculine Sensibility* (Westport, CT: Praeger, 1994).

78. Defoe, *Robinson Crusoe,* 154, 161. In *Pamela,* the heroine is described as refusing to be a "a kept mistress, or rather a kept slave" to her male employer, while Richardson later insists that slaves and others are equal in "nature's chain" and leveled "in the silent grave." Samuel Richardson, *Pamela; or, Virtue Rewarded* (1740; London: Everyman, 1962), 118, 230; see also James G. Basker, ed., *Amazing Grace: An Anthology of Poems about Slavery, 1660-1810* (New Haven: Yale University Press, 2002), 82. In *Clarissa,* reference is made

on more than one occasion to the female victim being treated like a slave; on another she expresses a preference for being sent as a "slave to the Indies" rather than accepting "a man I cannot endure"; and on yet another Clarissa identifies her situation with the violence practiced on slaves, considering herself "a slave, such a poor slave, as to be brought to change my mind by the violent usage I have met with." Samuel Richardson, *Clarissa; or, the History of a Young Lady* (1748; London: Harrison, 1784), 53, 66, 144, 233.

79. James Grainger, *The Sugar-Cane! A Poem* (London: R. and J. Dodsley, 1764), in John T. Gilmore, *The Poetics of Empire: A Study of James Grainger's "The Sugar Cane"* (London: Athlone, 2000); John Singleton, *A Description of the West-Indies: A Poem* (1767; 2nd ed., London: Gale Ecco, 2010).

80. Aphra Behn, *Oroonoko; or, The Royal Slave* (London: Will. Canning, 1688); John Skinner, *An Introduction to Eighteenth-Century Fiction: Raising the Novel* (London: Palgrave, 2001), 131–57.

81. On the noble savage, see Wylie Sypher, *Guinea's Captive Kings: British Anti-Slavery Literature of the XVIIIth Century* (Chapel Hill: University of North Carolina Press, 1942); on women and antislavery, see Moira Ferguson, *Subject to Others: British Women and Colonial Slavery, 1670–1834* (London: Routledge, 1992), 27–50; on Southerne's play, see Thomas Southerne, *Oroonoko,* ed. Maximillian E. Novak and David Stuart Rodes (Lincoln: University of Nebraska Press, 2003).

82. Basker, *Anthology,* 29. There were also rewrites of Southerne's version of the play, with no fewer than three in 1759–60. Nicholas Hudson, "'Britons Never Will Be Slaves': National Myth, Conservatism and the Beginnings of British Antislavery," *Eighteenth-Century Studies* 34, no. 4 (2001): 564.

83. Diana Jaher, "The Paradoxes of Slavery in Thomas Southerne's *Oroonoko,*" *Comparative Drama* 42, no. 1 (2008): 51–71; Basker, *Anthology,* 29.

84. Basker, *Anthology,* 52–56, 329–32.

85. Defoe, *Robinson Crusoe,* 165.

86. Samuel Johnson, *The Vanity of Human Wishes* (1749; Oxford: Clarendon Press, 1927), 26.

87. Among the Bristol-born poets were Thomas Chatterton and Hannah More, while Liverpool-connected advocates included former slave shipmaster turned cleric John Newton, William Roscoe, who began to condemn slavery in the late 1760s by noting the human cost of sugar cultivation, and Edward Rushden, who like Newton had experienced life on a slave ship.

88. Based on dates of publication in Basker, *Anthology,* list of contents.

89. Isaac John Bickerstaffe and Charles Dibdin, *The Padlock* (London: W. Griffin, 1768); Richard Cumberland, *The West Indian* (London: W. Griffin, 1771); Felicity Nussbaum, "'Mungo Here, Mungo There': Charles Dibdin and Ra-

cial Performance," in *Charles Dibdin and Late Georgian Culture,* ed. Oskar Cox Jensen, David Kennerley, and Ian Newman (Oxford: Oxford University Press, 2018), 23–43. Cumberland's comedy on West Indian manners has been called "the most discussed eighteenth-century comedy of the sentimental school" and, with numerous documented performances in London in the later eighteenth century, is said to have enjoyed "unceasing popularity." Stanley T. Williams, "Richard Cumberland's *West Indian," Modern Language Notes* 35, no. 7 (1920): 413–17 (quotations at 413, 417). *The Padlock* had an initial run of 54 performances and a further 200 or more in London through 1776. Nussbaum, "'Mungo Here,'" 24. For a more general review of theater and the issue of slavery in Britain from around 1760, see Franca Dellarosa, *Slavery on Stage: Representations of Slavery in British Theatre, 1760s–1830s; with an Anthology of Texts* (Bari: Edizioni Dal Sud, 2009).

90. Sarah Scott, *The History of Sir George Ellison,* 2 vols., ed. Betty Rizo (1766; Lexington: University of Kentucky Press, 1996); Laurence Sterne, *The Life and Opinions of Tristram Shandy, Gentleman,* 9 vols., ed. Günter Jürgens-meier (1759–67; Munich: n.p., 2005).

91. Manuscript copies of this and other of Dibdin's works are to be found in the Freemantle Collection, Brotherton Library, University of Leeds.

92. Sterne, *Tristram Shandy,* 9:552. The context of Sterne's observations was an encounter with "a poor negro girl," who was seen to be flapping away, rather than killing, flies in a sausage shop, her apparent "mercy" being attributed to her "nature as well as the hardships" she had endured.

93. Laurence Sterne, *Sentimental Journey through France and Italy* (1768; London: P. Miller and J. White, 1774), 91–92. The words used by Sterne in 1768 echoed those he wrote in 1766 when, in a sermon based on Job 14:1, 2 ("Man that is born of a woman, is of few days, and full of trouble"), he noted slavery's bitter draught and went on to observe how "it can poison all earthly happiness when examined barely upon our bodies, what must it be, when it comprehends both the slavery of body and mind?" Laurence Sterne, *The Sermons of Mr. Yorick,* vol. 2 (1766; London: J. Dodsley, 1767), 78.

94. Scott, *Sir George Ellison,* 1:10–13. The ownership of slaves was said to have "embittered" Sir George's "possession" of the plantation, few lamenting more than he did to be "enslaved by marriage" and thereby becoming "the enslaver of others" (10).

95. Sypher, *Guinea's Captive Kings,* 232; Felicity A. Nussbaum, "The Theatre of Empire: Racial Counterfeit, Racial Realism," in *A New Imperial History: Culture, Identity, and Modernity in Britain and the Empire, 1660–1840,* ed. Kathleen Wilson (Cambridge: Cambridge University Press, 2004), 73–74n.

96. Brycchan Carey, "Slavery and the Novel of Sentiment," in *The Sentimental Novel in the Eighteenth Century,* ed. Albert J. Rivero (Cambridge: Cambridge University Press, 2019), 138; Ulrich Pallua, "'Slavery Was Agreeable, Its Fortune Desirable': The Acceptance of the Evils of Slavery as a Social Phenomenon: An Indicator of a Pro-Slavery Approach," *AAA* 32, no. 2 (2007): 197–220.

97. Ramesh Mallipeddi, *Spectacular Suffering: Witnessing Slavery in the Eighteenth-Century British Atlantic* (Charlottesville: University of Virginia Press, 2016), chap. 3.

98. J. R. Oldfield, "The 'Ties of Soft Humanity': Slavery and Race in British Drama, 1760–1800," *Huntington Library Quarterly* 56, no. 1 (1993): 1–14.

99. Nussbaum, "'Mungo Here,'" 30.

100. "Epilogue to *The Padlock,*" *Gentleman's Magazine,* October 1787, 913–14.

101. The phrase "political tool" comes from Carey, "Novel of Sentiment," 138, 146.

102. On the publication of the correspondence, see Laurence Sterne, *The Letters of the late Rev. Mr. Laurence Sterne, to his most intimate friends,* 3 vols., ed. Lydia Sterne de Medalle (London: T. Becket, 1775), 3:22–30; and Ignatius Sancho, *The Letters of the Late Ignatius Sancho, an African,* ed. Vincent Carretta (Peterborough, ON: Broadview, 2015).

103. Brett D. Wilson, "Hannah More's *Slavery* and James Thomson's *Liberty:* Fond Links, Mad Liberty, and Unfeeling Bondage," in *Invoking Slavery in the Eighteenth-Century British Imagination,* ed. Srividhya Swaminathan and Adam R. Beach (2013; London: Routledge, 2016), 93–112.

104. J. Philmore, *Two Dialogues on the Man-Trade* (London: J. Waugh, W. Fenner et al., 1760), 57; Nicholas Hudson, "'Britons Never Will Be Slaves': National Myth, Conservatism, and the Beginnings of British Antislavery," *Eighteenth-Century Studies* 34, no. 4 (2001): 559–76.

105. Esther Chadwick, Meredith Garner, and Cyra Levenson, *Figures of Empire: Slavery and Portraiture in the Eighteenth-Century Atlantic Britain* (New Haven: Yale Center for British Art, 2014).

106. Hudson, "National Myth."

107. Philmore, *Man-Trade,* 57.

108. On the costs of books and their circulation, ca. 1800–1820, see St. Clair, *Reading Nation,* 245, 512.

109. Benjamin Franklin, *The Autobiography of Benjamin Franklin,* ed. Leonard W. Labaree, Ralph L. Ketcham, Helen C. Boatfield, and Helene H. Fineman (New Haven: Yale University Press, 1964), 163–64.

110. I return to Franklin's interventions on this issue in chapter 7.

111. Basker, *Anthology,* 220.

112. For the *Chester Chronicle,* see BNA.

Chapter 7. Reaching "the Common People"

1. Laurence Sterne, *The Letters of the late Rev. Mr. Laurence Sterne, to his most intimate friends*, 3 vols., ed. Lydia Sterne de Medalle (London: T. Becket, 1775), 3:22–30.

2. *The Diary; or, Woodfall's Register*, 25 April 1789, BNA (emphasis added).

3. See Hannah Barker, *Newspapers and English Society, 1695–1855* (London: Routledge, 2014), 5, where Barker also suggests that newspapers were important in "putting 'the people' into English politics" and in "uniting sections within the increasingly powerful body of 'the public.'" For Stewart, see chap. 6, n. 50, above.

4. C. A. Cranfield, *The Development of the Provincial Newspaper, 1700–1760* (Oxford: Clarendon Press, 1962), vi, 92.

5. Based in London, the BNA includes the newspaper material assembled by the Rev. Charles Burney (1757–1817) and held at the British Library that Gage digitized in 2007. The original Burney Collection contained copies of almost 1 million pages from 1,300 newspapers, periodicals, pamphlets, and broadsides and thus embraced more than newspapers. It contained relatively few provincial newspapers, a deficiency that the electronically searchable BNA has begun to rectify, thus explaining its use here. Maria Goff, ed., "Introduction," in *The Burney Newspapers and the British Library* (Detroit, MI: Gale, 2007).

6. There were 1,185 references to "slave" in 1700–1749, rising to 18,681 in the following sixty years; with "Africa," citations rose from 1,160 to 30,457 in the same period (search date 18 August 2018). With the exception of "Africa," for which citations fell in BNA sources in the 1790s compared to the 1780s, references to the two key words singly rose in each successive decade from 1750–59 onward, with numbers peaking in each case in 1800–1809.

7. To illustrate: in the original Burney Collection, items classified as news and business comprised around 60 percent of citations referring to "Africa" in 1701–50 and around 80 percent in 1751–1800 (search date 18 August 2018).

8. For example, *Drewry's Derby Mercury*, later known as the *Derby Mercury*, which first appeared in 1732, carried a slave-related item in one in 10 of its 2,595 issues published between 1750 and 1799. Later entrants into the industry, such as the *Manchester Mercury*, which first appeared in 1752, and the splendidly named Dublin-based *Hibernian Journal or Chronicle of Liberty*, followed where the Derby paper led.

9. Much of the place-specific data for trade in Africa as reported in chapter 2 came by 1750 from newspapers.

10. BNA, using the key words "slave trade." I used date filters 1700–1749, 1750–99, 1800–1849, and decadal subdivisions for 1750–1849. Citations reached 300 a year on average in 1790–99 and 470 in 1800–1809.

11. David Richardson, "Shipboard Slave Revolts, African Authority, and the Atlantic Slave Trade," *WMQ*, 3rd ser., 58, no. 1 (2001): 69–92.

12. In 1760, one participant in a dialogue on the slave trade is reported to have read in a newspaper an account of "a ship belonging to Liverpool, that had a hundred and ninety slaves on board, eighty of whom died on the voyage, which is more than two-fifths," with the other participant responding that he remembered "the account too, but that it was something extraordinary, and as such it was put into the newspaper." J. Philmore, *Two Dialogues on the Man-Trade* (London: J. Waugh, W. Fenner et al., 1760), 35. The vessel involved in this story has not been identified.

13. *London Magazine: or, Gentleman's Monthly Intelligencer* 22 (1753): 91, 181–82.

14. *Felix Farley's Bristol Journal*, 24–31 March 1753; *London Evening Post*, 5 April 1753. The correspondent was John Harris.

15. *Gentleman's Magazine* 23 (1753): 97.

16. Voyages/transatlantic/database/voyage id 17322.

17. Voyages/transatlantic/database/year range = 1698–1808/nation = Great Britain/outcome = African resistance. Almost a quarter of known revolts on slave ships in the Atlantic slave trade (around 180 of 600) that involved some loss of life occurred on British-flagged ships.

18. David Eltis and Stanley L. Engerman, "Shipboard Slave Revolts and Abolition," in *Who Abolished Slavery? Slave Revolts and Abolitionism,* ed. Seymour Drescher and Pieter C. Emmer (New York: Berghahn, 2010), 149–50.

19. James G. Basker, "'The Next Insurrection': Johnson, Race and Rebellion," *Age of Johnson* 11 (2000): 37–51.

20. Vincent Brown, *Tacky's Revolt: The Story of an Atlantic Slave War* (Cambridge, MA: Belknap Press of Harvard University Press, 2020).

21. Devin Leigh, "The Origin of a Source: Edward Long, Coromantee Slave Revolts and *The History of Jamaica,"* *Slavery and Abolition* 40, no. 2 (2019): 295–320.

22. Balthazard-Marie Émérigon, *Treatise on Insurances by Balthazard-Marie Émérigon,* ed. Samuel Meredith (London: Henry Butterworth, 1850; originally published in French, 1783), 325.

23. The estimate that one in 10 ships experienced revolts derives from French slave-trade data. Stephen D. Behrendt, David Eltis, and David Richardson, "The Costs of Coercion: African Agency in the Pre-Modern Atlantic World,"

EHR 54, no. 3 (2001): 454–76. A revolt is defined as one that occasioned deaths among Africans, Europeans, or both.

24. Ottobah Cugoano, *Thoughts and Sentiments on the Evil and Wicked Traffic of the Slavery: and Commerce of the Human Species* (London: n.p., 1787), 74–75. In 1857 Frederick Douglass asserted that "the limits of tyrants are prescribed by the endurance of those whom they oppress." Find out, he went on, "just what any people will quietly submit to and you have found out the exact measure of what injustice and wrong will be imposed upon them." Those wrongs, he continued, will persist "till they are resisted with either words or blows, or with both." Consistent with the idea of the Overton window, these words were spoken in an address in upstate New York to mark the anniversary of British West Indian slave emancipation in 1834. Douglass described that as a "triumph for a great moral principle" over a system of "devilish brutality" and a reflection of "the sacredness of humanity." For him, however, its lesson was that "progress without struggle" was impossible and that in that context a "general sentiment of mankind" was that "a man who will not fight for himself, when he has the means to do so, is not worth being fought for by others." By such words, Douglass made a plea for enslaved Africans to speak truth to power by whatever means possible, even justifying force if necessary. Douglass, *Two Speeches by Frederick Douglass; One on West India Emancipation, [. . .] and the Other on the Dred Scott Decision [. . .]* (Rochester, NY: C. P. Dewey, 1857). The version cited here is West India Emancipation, speech delivered at Canandaigua, New York, August 3, 1857, University of Rochester Frederick Douglass Project, rbscp.lib.rochester.edu /4398.

25. Nelson Mandela, *Conversations with Myself* (London: Macmillan, 2010), 16.

26. Adam Smith, *The Theory of Moral Sentiments* (1759; London: Prometheus Books, 2000), 298–302. Writing half a century later, the abolitionist Elizabeth Heyrick interpreted the rebelliousness of enslaved Africans as a human being's natural response to his or her status. For Heyrick, "As long as a human being is bought and sold,—regarded as goods and chattels,—compelled to labour without wages,—branded, chained, and flogged at the caprice of his owner; he will, of necessity, as long as the feeling of pain, the sense of degradation and injury remain, he will, unless he have the spirit of a Christian martyr, be vindictive and revengeful." Heyrick, *Immediate, not Gradual, Emancipation, Or, An Inquiry into the Shortest, Safest, and Most Effectual Means of Getting Rid of West Indian Slavery* (London: Hatchard, 1824), 13.

27. James G. Basker, Amazing Grace: An Anthology of Poems about Slavery, 1660–1810 (New Haven: Yale University Press, 2005), 155. Published in 1764,

the full poem is reproduced with commentary in John T. Gilmore, *The Poetics of Empire: A Study of James Grainger's "The Sugar Cane"* (London: Athlone, 2000), the quotations here coming from part 4.

28. The stereotype persisted among West Indian planters through 1807, with Bryan Edwards noting the "ferociousness of disposition" and "contempt of death" of Gold Coast slaves within a character marked by "evident superiority" and "firmness and intrepidity" notable from birth. Edwards, *The History, Civil and Commercial of the British Colonies in the West Indies*, 3 vols. (1793; London, John Stockdale, 1801), 2:73–83, at 74, 82, 83.

29. Smith, *Moral Sentiments*, 300.

30. Grainger, "The Sugar-Cane," in Gilmore, *Poetics*, 148.

31. In an untitled epitaph in 1773 for John Jack, "a Native of Africa," Daniel Bliss noted: "Tho' born in a land of slavery," Jack "was born free." Basker, *Anthology*, 202. Other references in the same anthology to freedom in Africa included the poets Richard Savage, who in 1737 decried the selling of African children into slavery "though formed by Nature free" (78), and Hugh Mulligan, who in 1784, in *The Lovers, An African Eclogue*, saw Africa as a "Once happy land! Where all were free and blest" (314). As Basker's anthology further reveals, echoes of native African freedom were to be found in the poetry of William Roscoe (1787) and William Cowper (1782, 1784). Basker, 196, 294, 300.

32. C. L. R. James, *The Black Jacobins: Toussaint L'Ouverture and the San Domingo Revolution*, rev. ed. (New York: Random House, 1963; originally published in 1938), 46.

33. William Cowper, "Sweet Meat Has a Sour Sauce; or, The Slave Trader in the Dumps," in *The Complete Poetical Works of William Cowper*, ed. H. S. Milford (London: Henry Frowde, 1905), 374–75.

34. James Field Stanfield, *The Guinea Voyage: A Poem* (London: J. Phillips, 1789), 26; William Cobbett, *The Parliamentary History of England: From the Norman Conquest in 1066 through the Year 1803*, 36 vols. (London: T. Curson Hansard, 1806–20), 28:cols. 45–46. On the contemporary reporting of the speech, see Brycchan Carey, "William Wilberforce's Sentimental Rhetoric: Parliamentary Reportage of the Abolition Speech of 1789," *Age of Johnson* 14 (2003): 281–305, which, among other things, references the reporting of the phrase about misery condensed "in so little room" in the London *Morning Star* on 13 May 1789.

35. On oceanic conditions and their effects on the human psyche, see the vivid descriptions in William Golding's *Rites of Passage*, where he refers to "the *strangeness* of this life in this strange part of the world among strange people

and in this strange construction of English oak which both transports and imprisons" those who travel in it. Golding, *Rites of Passage* (London: Faber and Faber, 1980), 194–95, 219–23 (quotation at 223, emphasis in original). Golding was referring, of course, to life on an emigrant ship to Australia, not a slave ship. For a study highlighting the psychological trauma of the Atlantic slave trade, see Stephanie E. Smallwood, *Saltwater Slavery: A Middle Passage from Africa to American Diaspora* (Cambridge, MA: Harvard University Press, 2008).

36. See David Brion Davis, *The Problem of Slavery in the Age of Revolution, 1770–1823* (Ithaca, NY: Cornell University Press, 1976), 366, who cites Edward Thompson's *Making of the English Working Class* (1963) in seeing links between misery and rebelliousness. On famine and monsters, see Hilary Mantel, *Bring Up the Bodies* (London: Fourth Estate, 2013), where she observes that "full bellies breed gentle manners. The pinch of famine makes monsters" (34).

37. Maya Angelou, "Still I Rise," in *And Still I Rise* (London: Virago, 1986); Richard Rathbone, "Resistance to Enslavement in West Africa," *Slavery and Abolition* 6, no. 3 (1985): 9–23.

38. Fyodor Dostoyevsky, *The House of the Dead* (1862; London: Penguin, 1985), 145.

39. For one of the most succinct summaries of slavery in Africa, see Paul E. Lovejoy, *Transformations in Slavery: A History of Slavery in Africa* (Cambridge: Cambridge University Press, 2000).

40. Francis Moore, *Travels into the Inland Parts of Africa: Containing a Description of the Several Nations for the Space of Six Hundred Miles up the River Gambia* (London: E. Cave, 1738), 43.

41. Nathan Nunn, "The Long-Term Effects of Africa's Slave Trades," *Quarterly Journal of Economics* 123 (2008): 139–76; James Fenske and Namrata Kala, "Climate and the Slave Trade," *Journal of Development Economics* 112 (C) (2015): 19–32; Fenske and Kala, "1807: Economic Shocks, Conflict and the Slave Trade," *Journal of Development Economics* 126 (C) (2017): 66–76.

42. See the essays in Sylviane Diouf, ed., *Fighting the Slave Trade: West African Strategies* (Athens: Ohio University Press, 2003).

43. Duke Ephraim to Rogers and L. Roach [Laroche], 16 October, 17 November 1789, Old Callabar [*sic*], Chancery Masters Exhibits, C 107/12, TNA.

44. Paul E. Lovejoy and David Richardson, "Anglo-Efik Relations and Protection against Illegal Enslavement at Old Calabar, 1740–1807," in Diouf, *Fighting the Slave Trade*, 101–21.

45. Brown, *Tacky's Revolt*.

46. *A Narrative of the Most Remarkable Particulars in the Life of James Albert Ukawsaw Gronniosaw, An African Prince. As Related by Himself* (Bath: W. Gye, 1772); Ignatius Sancho, *The Letters of the Late Ignatius Sancho, an African,* ed. Vincent Carretta (1782; Peterborough, ON: Broadview, 2015); Cugoano, *Sentiments;* Olaudah Equiano, *The Interesting Narrative of the Life of Olaudah Equiano, or Gustavus Vassa, the African, Written by Himself* (London: Printed for the author, 1789). The most comprehensive biography of Equiano remains Vincent Carretta, *Equiano, the African: Biography of a Self-Made Man* (Athens: University of Georgia Press, 2005).

47. Henry Louis Gates Jr., *The Signifying Monkey* (New York: Oxford University Press, 1988), 133–40; Ryan Hanley, "Calvinism, Proslavery and James Albert Ukawsaw Gronniosaw," *Slavery and Abolition* 36, no. 2 (2015): 360–81.

48. Philip Gould, "The Rise, Development, and Circulation of the Slave Narrative," in *The Cambridge Companion to the African American Slave Narrative,* ed. Audrey A. Fisch (Cambridge: Cambridge University Press, 2007), 11–27 (quotations at 19). On the power of the print media as used by some Black authors in proselytizing the slave narrative, see Vincent Carretta, "'Property of Author': Olaudah Equiano's Place in the History of the Book," in *"Genius in Bondage": Literature of the Early Black Atlantic,* ed. Vincent Carretta and Philip Gould (Lexington: University of Kentucky Press, 2001), 130–52; Joseph Rezek, "Print, Writing, and the Difference Media Make: Revisiting 'The Signifying Monkey' after Book History," *Early American Literature* 50, no. 3 (2015): 891–900.

49. John Sekora, "Black Message/White Envelope: Genre, Authenticity, and Authority in the Antebellum Slave Narrative," *Callaloo* 32 (1987): 482–515.

50. William Roscoe, *Mount Pleasant: A Descriptive Poem* (Warrington, UK: J. Johnson and S. Crane, 1777), 14, where Roscoe refers to the shame of Britons, "Who all the sweets of Liberty can boast; / Yet, deaf to every human claim, deny / That bliss to others, which they themselves enjoy." In the preface Roscoe noted that he had composed the poem a few years earlier.

51. In [Thomas Kitchin], *The Present State of the West-Indies, Containing an Accurate Description of What Parts are Possessed by the Various Powers in Europe* (London: R. Baldwin, 1778), the author described the slave trade as the "disgrace of the age" and if it has "so deeply taken root, it is because as necessary to the present state of affairs, and our wants have justified it in a manner so absolute, that is now almost a ridiculous common-place to cry out against the barbarity and cruelty of it" (11). Six years earlier, Edward Long, who published a well-known work on Jamaica in 1774, levied the charge against Lord Chief Justice Mansfield of "*washing* the Black-a-moor *white*" and creating "inconveniences" for planters "in respect of Negroes acciden-

tally coming into the kingdom," when he accused him in the celebrated *Somerset* case in 1772 of "such a liberal discussion, not more to the character of his predecessors on the Bench, than to the expectations of the public, who were deeply interested in the event of the cause." [Edward Long], *Candid Reflections upon the Judgement lately awarded by the Court of King's Bench, in Westminster-Hall, On what is commonly called The Negroe-Cause, by a Planter* (London: T. Lowndes, 1772), iii, 2 (emphasis in original).

52. Christer Petley, "'Devoted Islands' and 'That Madman Wilberforce': British Proslavery Patriotism in the Age of Abolition," *Journal of Imperial and Commonwealth History* 39, no. 3 (2011): 393–415.

53. Bernard Bailyn, *The Ideological Origins of the American Revolution: Fiftieth Anniversary Edition* (Cambridge: Harvard University Press, 2017).

54. Kathleen Wilson, *The Sense of the People: Politics, Culture and Imperialism in England, 1715–1785* (Cambridge: Cambridge University Press, 1995), 7.

55. Wilson, *Sense of the People,* 26.

56. Nicholas Hudson, "'Britons Never Will Be Slaves': National Myth, Conservatism and the Beginnings of British Antislavery," *Eighteenth-Century Studies* 34, no. 4 (2001): 559–76. On the role of moral reputation in uniting individuals from different religious denominations against slavery, see Kevin Macdonald, "The Antislavery Movement as an Expression of the Eighteenth-Century Affective Revolution in England," in *Reasoning Beasts: Evolution, Cognition and Culture, 1720–1820,* ed. Michael Austin and Kathryn Stasio (Norwalk, CT: AMS, 2017), 23–60.

57. Elizabeth Baigent and James E. Bradley, "The Social Sources of Late Eighteenth-Century English Radicalism: Bristol in the 1770s and 1780s," *English Historical Review* 124, no. 5 (2009): 1075–108 (quotation at 1081).

58. Wilson, *Sense of the People,* 238.

59. Samuel Johnson, *Taxation No Tyranny: An Answer to the Resolutions and Address of the American Congress* (London: T. Cadell, 1775), 89. Johnson's remark reminds one of the Scottish philosopher John Millar, who, writing of slavery in 1773, suggested that it "affords a curious spectacle to observe, that the same people who talk in a high strain of political liberty, and who consider the privilege of imposing their own taxes as one of the unalienable rights of mankind, should make no scruple of reducing a great proportion of their fellow-creatures into circumstances by which they are not only deprived of property, but almost of every species of right. Fortune perhaps never produced a situation more calculated to ridicule a liberal hypothesis." John Millar, *The Origin of the Distinction of Ranks,* ed. Aaron Garrett (1803; Indianapolis, IN: Liberty Fund, 2012), 278–79.

60. A. B. [Tom Paine], "African Slavery in America," in *The Writings of Thomas Paine,* ed. Moncure Daniel Conway, vol. 1, *1774–1779* (New York: G. P. Putnam and Son, 1894), 4–10.

61. The society was known initially as the Society for the Relief of Free Negroes Unlawfully Held in Bondage before being reconstituted after 1783. Edward Raymond Turner, "The First Abolition Society in the United States," *Pennsylvania Magazine of History and Biography* 36, no. 1 (1912): 94.

62. "Common Sense," in *Writings of Paine,* where Paine accused the British in February 1776 in "declaring war against the natural rights of all mankind" (67). On Lord Dunmore's action and its consequences, see Simon Schama, *Rough Crossings: Britain, the Slaves and the American Revolution* (London: BBC Books, 2005).

63. For Hartley, consult the History of Parliament website for member David Hartley,   https://www.historyofparliamentonline.org/volume/1754-1790 /member/hartley-david-1730-1813.

64. [David Hartley] to Benjamin Franklin, 14 November 1775, in *The Papers of Benjamin Franklin,* vol. 6, *April 1, 1775, through September 24, 1776,* online edition, franklinpapers.org.

65. In his edition of abolitionist Granville Sharp's memoirs published in 1820, Prince Hoare reported Sharp's reflection that by 1787 the "very memory" of Hartley's 1776 motion, which had "failed entirely of support," had "nearly vanished," before Sharp proceeded to note that "trials which had occurred with regard to Negroes in this country, had awakened a very general attention to the subject of African slavery." Sharp, of course, was closely involved in those trials. Prince Hoare, *Memoirs of Granville Sharp, Esq., Composed from His Own Manuscripts* [. . .], 2 vols. (1820; 2nd ed., London: Henry Colburn, 1828), 2:205–6.

66. Cobbett, *Parliamentary History,* 28:col. 48. On the four stages of moral reasoning, which included sensitivity, judgment in determining what is right and wrong, capacity to distinguish personal from moral values, and determination to act, see James R. Rest et al., *Postconventional Moral Thinking: A Neo-Kohlbergian Approach* (Mahweh, NJ: Lawrence Erlbaum, 1999).

67. Hoare, *Memoirs,* 2:205–6.

68. Benjamin Franklin, *The Autobiography of Benjamin Franklin,* ed. Leonard W. Labaree, Ralph L. Ketcham, Helen C. Boatfield, and Helene H. Fineman (New Haven: Yale University Press, 1964), 139.

69. P. J. Marshall and J. A. Woods, eds., *The Correspondence of Edmund Burke,* vol. 7, *January 1792–August 1794* (Cambridge: Cambridge University Press, 1968), 122–23.

70. John Raby, *Doubts on the Abolition of the Slave Trade; by an Old Member of Parliament* (London: John Stockdale, 1790), preface.

71. Edwards, *History*, 2:40, 169. For background to Edwards, see Olwyn M. Blouet, "Bryan Edwards, F.R.S., 1743–1800," *Notes and Records of the Royal Society of London* 54, no. 2 (2000): 215–22.

72. For Savile, consult the History of Parliament website for member Sir George Savile, https://www.historyofparliamentonline.org/volume/1754-1790/member /savile-sir-george-1726-84.

73. Cf. Fyodor Dostoyevsky: "You have the faith, but one wants will." Dostoyevsky, *The Devils* (1871–72; London: Penguin, 2008), 375.

Chapter 8. "To Interest Men of Every Description in the Abolition of the Traffic"

1. I follow John Oldfield in emphasizing the London Society's role as part of a metropolitan influence on British abolitionism. J. R. Oldfield, "The London Committee and the Mobilization of Public Opinion against the Slave Trade," *Historical Journal* 35, no. 2 (1992): 331–43.

2. Cited in Roger Anstey, *The Atlantic Slave Trade and British Abolition, 1760–1810* (Atlantic Highlands, NJ: Humanities Press, 1975), 255.

3. Charles Tilly, *Popular Contention in Great Britain, 1758–1834* (Cambridge, MA: Harvard University Press, 1995), 147.

4. Tilly, *Popular Contention*, 144.

5. In addition to Tilly, particularly valuable for my analysis in this chapter have been: John D. McCarthy and Mayer N. Zald, "Resource Mobilization and Social Movements: A Partial Theory," *American Journal of Sociology* 82, no. 6 (1977): 1212–41; Doug McAdam, John D. McCarthy, and Mayer N. Zald, "Introduction: Opportunities, Mobilizing Structures, and Framing Processes— Towards a Synthetic, Comparative Perspective on Social Movements," in *Comparative Perspectives on Social Movements: Political Opportunities, Mobilizing Structures, and Crucial Framings,* ed. McAdam, McCarthy, and Zald (New York: Cambridge University Press, 1996), 1–20; McCarthy and Zald, "The Enduring Vitality of the Resource Mobilization Theory of Social Movements," in *Handbook of Sociology,* ed. Jonathan H. Turner (Boston: Springer, 2001), 533–65; and Douglas McAdam, Sidney Tarrow, and Charles Tilly, *Dynamics of Contention* (New York: Cambridge University Press, 2001).

6. Tilly, *Popular Contention*, 33.

7. Cf. Aurelian Craiutu, *A Virtue for Courageous Minds: Moderation in French Political Thought, 1748–1830* (Princeton, NJ: Princeton University Press, 2012), 5.

8. James Ramsay, *An Essay on the Treatment and Conversion of African Slaves in the British Sugar Colonies* (Dublin: T. Walker et al., 1784).

9. Cf. James Ramsay, *Objections to the Abolition of the Slave Trade, with Answers* (London: James Phillips, 1788), who considered immediate emancipation an "indiscreet measure," arguing that "our slaves are not yet generally in a state, wherein full liberty would be a blessing," though accepting that "humanity looks forward to full emancipation, whenever they shall be found capable of making a proper use of it" (2).

10. James Walvin, *The "Zong": A Massacre, the Law, and the End of Slavery* (New Haven: Yale University Press, 2011); Thomas Clarkson, *An Essay on the Slavery and Commerce of the Human Species, Particularly the African* (London: J. Phillips, 1786).

11. Thomas Clarkson, *The History of the Rise, Progress and Accomplishment of the Abolition of the African Slave-Trade by the British Parliament,* 2 vols. (London: Longman, Hurst, Rees, and Orme, 1808), 1:282–89 (quotation at 286).

12. See Seymour Drescher, *Capitalism and Antislavery: British Mobilization in Comparative Perspective* (New York: Oxford University Press, 1986), 71, 211, where the Manchester petition is reputed to have triggered "a sea-change in public opinion."

13. James W. LoGerfo, "Sir William Dolben and 'The Cause of Humanity': The Passage of the Slave Trade Regulation Act of 1788," *Eighteenth-Century Studies* 6, no. 4 (1973): 431–51.

14. William Cobbett, *The Parliamentary History of England: From the Norman Conquest in 1066 through the Year 1803,* 36 vols. (London: T. Curson Hansard, 1806–20), 27:col. 644; LoGerfo, "Dolben," 447.

15. Judith Jennings, *The Business of Abolishing the British Slave Trade, 1783–1807* (New York: Routledge, 1997), esp. 1–22.

16. James Walvin, "The Public Campaign in England against Slavery, 1781–1834," in *The Abolition of the Atlantic Slave Trade: Origins and Effects in Europe, Africa, and the Americas,* ed. David Eltis and James Walvin (Madison: University of Wisconsin Press, 1982), 76.

17. Using the same methodology and newspaper sources noted in chapter 7, it appears that newspaper stories about the slave trade averaged around 100 a year (or roughly one every three days) in 1780–87 but then leapt to 768 (or two a day) in 1788, averaged 575 a year in 1788–92, and reached an unprecedented 914 a year (or nine times the 1780–87 mean) in 1792.

18. See Mark Jones, "The Mobilisation of Public Opinion against the Slave Trade and Slavery: Popular Abolitionism in National and Regional Politics, 1787–1838" (PhD thesis, University of York, 1998), 1–39, who emphasizes the early involvement of abolitionists outside London, including Quakers, in such efforts as well as distributing anti–slave trade materials more generally.

19. Cf. Anton Chekhov, "My Life (A Provincial's Story)," in *The Lady with the Little Dog and Other Stories, 1896–1904* (London: Penguin Books, 2002), 201.

20. Richard Huzzey, "A Microhistory of British Anti-Slavery Petitioning," *Social Science History* 43, no. 3 (2019): 599–623.

21. Kinga Makovi, "The Signatures of Social Structure: Petitioning for the Abolition of the Slave Trade in Manchester," *Social Science History* 43, no. 3 (2019): 625–52.

22. Sidney Tarrow, *Power in Movement: Social Movements, Collective Action and Politics* (Cambridge: Cambridge University Press, 1994), 150.

23. As noted, e.g., in Jones, "Mobilisation"; John R. Oldfield, *Popular Politics and British Anti-Slavery: The Mobilisation of Public Opinion against the Slave Trade, 1787–1807* (Manchester: Manchester University Press, 1995); and Iain Whyte, *Scotland and the Abolition of Black Slavery, 1756–1838* (Edinburgh: Edinburgh University Press, 2006), 70–107. Cf. Fyodor Dostoyevsky, who refers to a "knot of networks" linking revolutionary activity in mid-nineteenth-century Russia. Dostoyevsky, *The Devils* (1871–72; London: Penguin, 2008), 566.

24. John Oldfield, ed., *British Transatlantic Slave Trade*, vol. 3, *The Abolitionist Struggle: Opponents of the Slave Trade* (London: Pickering and Chatto, 2003), 321.

25. Mary Wollstonecraft, *A Vindication of the Rights of Women: With Strictures on Political and Moral Subjects*, ed. Miriam Brady (1792; London: Penguin, 2004).

26. See Mary Birkett, *A Poem on the African Slave Trade. Addressed to her own Sex* (1791; Dublin: J. Jones, 1792), where she uses Laurence Sterne's comment on slavery's bitter draught, noted in chapter 7, as context for her work; and William Fox, *An Address to the People of Great Britain, on the Propriety of Refraining from the Use of West India Sugar and Rum* (London: Swinney and Walker, 1791), where, referencing the poet William Cowper's writings against slavery, Fox describes slave-grown sugar as a "loathsome potion."

27. On the circulation of Fox's work, which identified slavery with British luxury, and the role played by the London bookseller and Baptist Martha Gurney in its distribution, see Timothy Whelan, "Martha Gurney and the Anti-Slave Trade Movement, 1788–1794," in *Women, Dissent, and Anti-Slavery in Britain and America, 1790–1865*, ed. Elizabeth J. Clapp and Julie Roy Jeffrey (Oxford: Oxford University Press, 2011), 44–65.

28. Elizabeth Heyrick, *Immediate, not Gradual Abolition* (London: Hatchard, 1824), 23.

29. Patrick O'Brien, "Agriculture and the Home Market for English Industry, 1660–1820," *English Historical Review* 100 (1985): 799–800.

30. Joel Mokyr, *The Gifts of Athena: Historical Origins of the Knowledge Economy* (Princeton, NJ: Princeton University Press, 2002).

31. W. W. Rostow, "The Stages of Economic Growth," *EHR* 12, no. 1 (1959): 1–16.

32. Charles Tilly, *Contentious Performances* (New York: Cambridge University Press, 2008), 126, 133; Joel Quirk and David Richardson, "Religion, Urbanisation and Anti-Slavery Mobilisation in Britain, 1787–1833," *European Journal of English Studies* 14, no. 3 (2010): 263–79.

33. Robin Pearson and David Richardson, "Business Networking in the Industrial Revolution," *EHR* 54, no. 4 (2001): 655–77.

34. Lynn Hunt, *Inventing Human Rights: A History* (New York: W. W. Norton, 2008), 34.

35. Oldfield, *Popular Politics*, 127–29.

36. In his 1791 *Address*, Fox identifies the "slave-dealer, the slave-holder, and the slave-driver" as "virtually the agents of the consumer," and with "every pound of sugar used" being considered "as consuming two ounces of human flesh, besides an alarming number of ounces destroyed by the slave trade" (2–4).

37. Charlotte Sussman, "Women and the Politics of Sugar, 1792," *Representations* 48 (1994): 48–69; Julie L. Holcomb, "Blood-Stained Sugar: Gender, Commerce and the British Slave Trade Debate," *Slavery and Abolition* 35, no. 4 (2014): 611–28.

38. There has been some debate over the interrelationship between transatlantic slavery, which Wollstonecraft evidently saw as inhuman, and her thoughts on domestic female subjugation, which she saw as a form of moral corruption or "slavery" in which its victims were complicit. Moira Ferguson, "Mary Wollstonecraft and the Problematic of Slavery," *Feminist Review* 42 (1992): 82–102; Carol Howard, "Wollstonecraft's Thought on Slavery and Corruption," *Eighteenth Century* 45, no. 1 (2004): 61–86.

39. For women's status in marriage, see [Sarah Chapone], *The Hardships of the English Laws in Relation to Wives* (London: W. Bowyer, 1735), 2–5, which suggested that law put wives in a worse condition than slavery; Amy Louise Erickson, *Women and Property in Early Modern England* (London: Routledge, 1993); and David Lemmings, "Marriage and the Law in the Eighteenth Century: Hardwicke's Marriage Act of 1753," *Historical Journal* 39, no. 2 (1996): 339–60.

40. On the latitude available to women, married or otherwise, in terms of consumer spending and credit, see Joanne Bailey, "Favoured or Oppressed? Married Women, Property and 'Coverture' in England, 1660–1800," *Continuity and Change* 17, no. 3 (2002): 351–72. See also *Madam Johnson's Present: or, Every Young Woman's Companion, in Useful and Universal Knowledge*

(1753; 4th ed., Dublin: James Williams, 1770), esp. part 5, "An Estimate of the Expenses of a Family in the Middling Station of Life." The wives of agricultural laborers were also seen to have designated domestic roles; when "not working in the fields" they were said to be "well occupied at home," and if only seldom "earning money," they were "baking their bread, washing and mending their garments, and rocking the cradle." David Davies, *Cases of Labourers in Husbandry: Stated and Considered in Three Parts* (Bath: R. Cruttwell, 1795), 6. A cleric, Davies spent part of his early life in Barbados, where, among other things, he managed a sugar plantation and formed a lifelong hostility to slavery, testifying against it to Parliament in 1791. Pamela Horn, "David Davies (1742–1819)," in *Oxford Dictionary of National Biography* (Oxford: Oxford University Press, 2004).

41. In his 1791 pamphlet, Fox calculated annual per capita consumption of sugar in terms of its cost to African bodies, encouraging some to see consuming sugar as equivalent to cannibalism. Sussman, "Women and Politics," 52–53.

42. Jones, "Mobilisation," 40.

43. Julie Macdonald, "'The Freedom of Election': The Company of Cutlers in Hallamshire and the Growth of Radicalism in Sheffield, 1784–1792" (PhD thesis, University of Sheffield, 2005), 2–3; Albert Goodwin, *The Friends of Liberty: The English Democratic Movement in the Age of the French Revolution* (London: Hutchinson, 1979), 159.

44. The following draws on Macdonald, "Company of Cutlers," 1–118, which situates radicalism within socioeconomic change in the cutlery trades.

45. Cf. Edward Thompson, *The Making of the English Working Class* (London: Victor Gollancz, 1968), 45–48.

46. Clarkson, *History*, 1:418–22.

47. See Sami Pinarbasi, "Manchester Antislavery, 1792–1807," *Slavery and Abolition* 41, no. 2 (2020): 349–76, for a discussion of the town's two constituencies on the issue.

48. John Aikin, *A Description of the Country from Thirty to Forty Miles Round Manchester* (London: John Stockdale, 1795), 156–81; Jon Stobart, *The First Industrial Region* (Manchester: Manchester University Press, 2004), 212.

49. Jane Humphries, *Childhood and Child Labour in the British Industrial Revolution* (Cambridge: Cambridge University Press, 2010), 44.

50. On the exceptionally high contribution of child labor to family income in industrial districts, see Emma Griffin, "Diets, Hunger, and Living Standards during the British Industrial Revolution," *Past and Present* 239, no. 1 (2018): 85.

51. B. W. Higman, "Economic and Social Development of the British West Indies, from Settlement to ca. 1850," in *Cambridge Economic History of the United States,* vol. 1, *The Colonial Era,* ed. Stanley L. Engerman and Robert E. Gallman (New York: Cambridge University Press, 1996), 323.

52. John Steinbeck, *Tortilla Flat* (1935; London, Penguin, 2000), 112.

53. Sidney Pollard, "Factory Discipline in the Industrial Revolution," *EHR* 16, no. 2 (1963): 254–56.

54. Richard Lamb, "Adam Smith's Concept of Alienation," *Oxford Economic Papers,* n.s., 25, no. 2 (1973): 275–85 (quotation at 279).

55. Dugald Stewart, "An Account of the Life and Writings of the Author," in *Essays on Philosophical Subjects by the Late Adam Smith* (London: T. Cadell Jr. and W. Davies, 1795), lxxxix. It has been observed that, among Smith's contemporaries, Adam Ferguson and John Millar had similar views on the issue of workers' alienation. Lamb, "Smith's Concept."

56. William Morris, "Useful Work versus Useless Toil [1884]," in *The Collected Works of William Morris,* ed. Mary Morris, 24 vols. (1910–15; Cambridge: Cambridge University Press, 2012), 23:98–120.

57. William Blake, *Milton: A Poem in Two Books* (London: William Blake, 1808), preface, 2.

58. R. S. Fitton and A. P. Wadsworth, *The Strutts and the Arkwrights, 1758–1830* (Manchester: Manchester University Press, 1958), 109–10.

59. E. P. Thompson, "Time, Work-Discipline and Industrial Capitalism," *Past and Present* 38 (1967): 83–84; Thompson, *Working Class,* 385–98. Thompson's argument was a subset of a much larger debate dating from the time of Marx, whereby religious revivalism and especially Methodism were seen to have had a more soporific impact on working-class behavior compared to their more reformist influence on antislavery proposed here.

60. Christer Petley, *White Fury: A Jamaican Slaveholder and the Age of Revolution* (Oxford: Oxford University Press, 2018), 139.

61. Edward Rushton, "Eclogue the First," in *West Indian Eclogues* (London: W. Lowndes, J. Phil[l]ips, 1797), 1. For recent appraisals of Rushton's work in the context of antislavery, see Franca Dellarosa, *Talking Revolution: Edward Rushton's Rebellious Poetics, 1782–1814* (Liverpool: Liverpool University Press, 2015), which includes a specific chapter on the Eclogues; and Gregory Pierrot, "*Droit du Seigneur,* Slavery, and Nation in the Poetry of Edward Rushton," *Studies in Romanticism* 56, no. 1 (2017): 15–35. It is worth noting that even as they defended the slave trade, factory masters such as Sir Robert Peel felt impelled by growing public awareness of conditions in cotton mills to promote legislation intended to ameliorate working conditions for ap-

prenticed children in the mills, notably before 1807 in the 1802 Health and Morals of Apprentices Act (42 Geo III, c. 73).

62. Oldfield, *Popular Politics,* 61.

63. Numbers of newspaper "slave trade" citations were 300 a year in 1790–99 and 470 in 1800–1809.

Chapter 9. Finding "a Pathway for the Humanities"

Title: John Steinbeck, *Tortilla Flat* (1935; London: Penguin, 2000), 84.

1. William Fox, *An Address to the People of Great Britain, on the Propriety of Refraining from the Use of West India Sugar and Rum* (London: Swinney and Walker, 1791), 12.

2. Edmund Burke, *An Appeal from the New to the Old Whigs* (London: J. Dodsley, 1791), 19; Burke, *Thoughts on the Prospect of a Regicide Peace; in a Series of Letters* (London: J. Owen, 1796), 70. The anti-abolitionist pamphleteer John Raby, who knew Samuel Johnson's biographer and proslavery sympathizer James Boswell, made a similar point in 1790 when he suggested that MPs pondering abolition should reflect that "as the abolition of the slave trade is avowed to be a measure, not of policy but humanity, not of advantage but justice, not of expedient but experiment, it is the duty of the legislature to be satisfied, that the claim of humanity and justice is well founded; that the experiment promises success, and that the interest and strength of the nation are not hazarded in a vain pursuit of unattainable purity and perfection." Raby, *Doubts on the Abolition of the Slave Trade; by an Old Member of Parliament* (London: John Stockdale, 1790), 123.

3. John Elliott Cairnes, *The Slave Power: Its Character, Career, and Probable Designs* (London: Parker, Son, 1862), 25.

4. Moses I. Finley, *Ancient Slavery and Modern Ideology* (1980; Princeton, NJ: Markus Wiener, 1998), 9. Finley placed ancient Greece and Rome in the same category. His classification has been subject to much debate, most recently in Noel Lenski and Catherine M. Cameron, eds., *What Is a Slave Society? The Practice of Slavery in Global Perspective* (Cambridge: Cambridge University Press, 2018).

5. Cairnes, *Slave Power,* 61.

6. Cairnes, *Slave Power,* 63.

7. Eric Williams, *Capitalism and Slavery* (Chapel Hill: University of North Carolina Press, 1944).

8. Cf. F. Scott Fitzgerald, *The Beautiful and Damned* (1922; London: Penguin, 2004), 17.

9. I review the evidence in "The Ending of the British Slave Trade in 1807: The Economic Context," in *The British Slave Trade: Abolition, Parliament and People,* ed. Stephen Farrell, Melanie Unwin, and James Walvin (Edinburgh: Edinburgh University Press, 2007), 127-40.

10. Fundamental to that strategy was a "blue-water" policy that in shaping imperial expansion had the potential to make admirals into national heroes. Daniel A. Baugh, "Great Britain's 'Blue-Water' Policy, 1689-1815," *International History Review* 10, no. 1 (1988): 33-58; Kathleen Wilson, "Empire, Trade and Popular Politics in Mid-Hanoverian England: The Case of Admiral Vernon," *Past and Present* 121 (1988): 74-109; Gerald Jordan and Nicholas Rogers, "Admirals as Heroes: Patriotism and Liberty in Hanoverian England," *Journal of British Studies* 28, no. 3 (1989): 201-24.

11. See, e.g., Richard Pares, *A West-India Fortune* (London: Longmans, Green, 1950); and Perry Gauci, *William Beckford: First Prime Minister of the London Empire* (New Haven: Yale University Press, 2013).

12. David Hancock, *Citizens of the World: London Merchants and the Integration of the British Atlantic Community, 1735-1785* (New York: Cambridge University Press, 1995); Simon D. Smith, *Slavery, Family, and Gentry Capitalism in the British Atlantic: The World of the Lascelles, 1684-1834* (Cambridge: Cambridge University Press, 2006).

13. Cited in Andrew J. O'Shaughnessy, *An Empire Divided: The American Revolution and the British Caribbean* (Philadelphia: University of Pennsylvania Press, 2000), 11.

14. Nicholas Draper, *The Price of Emancipation: Slave-Ownership, Compensation and British Society at the End of Slavery* (New York: Cambridge University Press, 2010).

15. Madge Dresser, *Slavery Obscured: The Social History of the Slave Trade in an English Provincial Port* (London: Bloomsbury Academic, 2001), 96-128.

16. See, e.g., N. Draper, "The City of London and Slavery: Evidence from the First Dock Companies, 1795-1800," *EHR* 61, no. 2 (2008): 432-66.

17. M. W. McCahill, ed., "The Correspondence of Stephen Fuller, 1788-1795: Jamaica, the West India Interest at Westminster and the Campaign to Preserve the Slave Trade," *Parliamentary History,* Special Issue: Text and Studies Series 9 (2014): 19-20.

18. Seymour Drescher, *Capitalism and Antislavery: British Mobilization in Comparative Perspective* (London: Palgrave Macmillan, 1986), 50.

19. Andrew J. O'Shaughnessy, "The Formation of a Commercial Lobby: The West India Interest, British Colonial Policy and the American Revolution," *Historical Journal* 40, no. 1 (1997): 71-95; David Beck Ryden, *West India*

Slavery and British Abolition, 1783–1807 (Cambridge: Cambridge University Press, 2009); Angelina G. Osborne, "Power and Persuasion: The London West India Committee, 1783–1833" (PhD thesis, University of Hull, 2014).

20. Drescher, *Mobilization,* 50.

21. Anne O. Krueger, "The Political Economy of the Rent-Seeking Society," *American Economic Review* 64, no. 3 (1974): 291–303; Robert B. Ekelund and Robert D. Tollison, *Mercantilism as a Rent-Seeking Society: Economic Regulation in Historical Perspective* (College Station: Texas A&M University Press, 1982); John Brewer, *Sinews of Power: Money and the English State, 1688–1783* (Cambridge, MA: Harvard University Press, 1990), 231–49.

22. Christer Petley, *White Fury: A Jamaican Slaveholder and the Age of Revolution* (Oxford: Oxford University Press, 2018), 41.

23. McCahill, "Stephen Fuller," 4–5. McCahill's introduction to the same offers the fullest available discussion of Fuller's efforts on behalf of Jamaica in 1788–95.

24. O'Shaughnessy, *Empire Divided,* 17; Richard B. Sheridan, *Sugar and Slavery: An Economic History of the British West Indies, 1623–1775* (Baltimore: Johns Hopkins University Press, 1974), 60–65.

25. Trevor Burnard, "Harvest Years? Reconfigurations of Empire in Jamaica, 1756–1807," *Journal of Imperial and Commonwealth History* 40, no. 4 (2012): 548.

26. McCahill, "Stephen Fuller," 229–33.

27. B. W. Higman, "The West India 'Interest' in Parliament, 1807–1833," *Historical Studies* 13, no. 49 (1967): 1–19; see also McCahill, "Stephen Fuller," 25–26, where it is noted that differences arose between island planters and others in Britain over issues of slave trade regulation, which Liverpool merchants opposed, and planters eager to portray themselves as humane, as well as over planter questioning of Parliament's right to interfere in colonial affairs, which raised specters of the colonial crisis of 1763–75 and troubled sections of the West India interest in London and Parliament in 1788–92.

28. Sheridan, *Sugar and Slavery,* 67.

29. Robert Isaac Wilberforce and Samuel Wilberforce, *The Life of William Wilberforce,* 5 vols. (London: J. Murray, 1838), 1:291, 2:48. One argument against the Foreign Trade bill in 1794 was that continuation of that branch was "essential from its magnitude to the existence of the general [British] trade" in slaves (2:49), an issue that would resurface a decade later, as noted below.

30. Contemporary British publications supportive of the anti-abolition case are included in the compilations edited by Lowell Joseph Ragatz, *A Guide for*

the Study of British Caribbean History, 1763–1834, including the Abolition and Emancipation Movements (Washington, DC: Government Printing Office, 1932), 405–74; and Peter Hogg, *The African Slave Trade and Its Suppression: A Classified and Annotated Bibliography of Books, Pamphlets and Periodical Articles* (1973; London: Routledge, 2014), 135–343.

31. Ragatz, *Guide,* 469, which notes that 8,000 copies of "A Plain Man," *The True State of the Question, Addressed to the Petitioners for the Abolition of the Slave Trade* (London: J. Bell, 1792), were circulated by the Society of West Indian Planters and Merchants of London.

32. See, e.g., Gordon Turnbull, *An Apology for the Negro Slavery: or the West India Planters Vindicated from the Charge of Inhumanity,* 2nd ed. (London: J. Strachan, R. Faulder and W. Richardson, 1786), which sought "to dispel the clouds of error, and of prejudice, that have generally obscured the minds of the people of this country" with regard to West Indian slavery (5); to challenge the "ill-founded, partial and unjust" claims of abolitionists regarding African enslavement practices (6); to demonstrate the consistency of British slave trading with sustaining the sugar trade and thus sound policy (9); and to accuse as fanatics masquerading as reformers authors of anti–slave trade works such as James Ramsay, whom he described as a "wild and incoherent speculatist" (18). See also "A West India Planter," *Considerations on the Emancipation of Negroes and on the Abolition of the Slave Trade* (London: J. Johnson and J. Debrett, 1788), which acknowledged slavery as an evil but saw it as financially and politically impracticable to abolish by Britain alone; and Anon., *Considerations upon the Fatal Consequences of Abolishing the Slave Trade in the Present Situation of Great Britain* (London: J. Debrett, 1789), which suggested that abolition would not mitigate the fate of Africans but would allow the French colonies to prosper at Britain's expense.

33. *An Address to the Inhabitants, in general, of Great Britain and Ireland, relating to a few of the Consequences which must naturally result from the Abolition of the Slave Trade* (London: Mrs Egerton Smith, Thomas Evans and John Hamilton Moore, 1788); *A Country Gentleman's Reasons for Voting Again[st] Mr Wilberforce's Motion for a Bill to Prohibit the Importation of African Negroes into the Colonies* (London: J. Debrett, 1792).

34. Raymund [*sic*] Harris, *Scriptural Researches on the Licitness of the Slave Trade* (London: John Stockdale, 1788), vii. See also A Clergyman, *A Proposal for the Consideration of those who interest themselves in the Abolition or Preservation of the Slave Trade* (Wolverhampton: The author, 1788).

35. Paul Ingram and Brian S. Silberman, "The Cultural Contingency of Structure: Evidence from Entry to the Slave Trade in and around the Abolition

Movement," *American Journal of Sociology* 122, no. 3 (2016): 755–97 (quotation at 766).

36. "A Jamaica Planter," *Observations on the African Slave Trade and on the Situation of the Negroes in the West Indies, with some proposed Regulations for a more Mild and Humane Treatment of them* (London: Law, 1788).

37. Drescher, *Mobilization*, 49.

38. *Remarks on the Evidence given by Thomas Irving, Esq. Inspector General of the Exports and Imports of Great Britain, before the Select Committee appointed to take the Examination of Witnesses on the Slave Trade* (London: Unnamed, 1791).

39. F. E. Sanderson, "The Liverpool Delegates and Sir William Dolben's Bill," *Transactions of the Historic Society of Lancashire and Cheshire* 124 (1972): 57–84.

40. William Cobbett, *The Parliamentary History of England: From the Norman Conquest in 1066 through the Year 1803*, 36 vols. (London: T. Curson Hansard, 1806–20), 27:col. 644; Clarkson, *History*, 1:553. Lord Thurlow, then lord chancellor and to whom I refer later, was the less charitable commentator.

41. Thomas Clarkson, *An Essay on the Comparative Efficiency of Regulation or Abolition, as Applied to the Slave Trade: Shewing That the Latter Only Can Remove the Evils to be Found in that Commerce* (London: J. Phillips, 1789).

42. Clarkson, *History*, 2:565.

43. 34 Geo III (1794) c. 80, art. 10; 39 Geo III (1799) c. 80. The 1794 measure arose against a background of litigation in the context of the *Zong* case, examined in James Oldham, "Insurance Litigation Involving the *Zong* and Other British Slave Ships, 1780–1807," *Journal of Legal History* 28, no. 3 (2007): 299–318.

44. A. Aspinall, ed., *The Later Correspondence of George III*, vol. 4, *1802–1807* (Cambridge: Cambridge University Press, 1968), 322. George III's proslavery views were shared by the Duke of Clarence, later William IV (1830–37), but rejected by Prince William Frederick, Duke of Gloucester and Edinburgh. Suzanne Schwarz, "Slave Trade, Slavery and Abolition in the Royal Archives, c. 1785–1810," Georgian Papers Programme (blog), 23 January 2017, https://georgianpapers.com/2017/01/23/georgian-papers-programme-slave-trade-slavery-abolition-royal-archives-c-1785-1810[1].

45. See Ragatz, *Guide*, 438, citing *Memorial of the West India Planters and Merchants, respecting the Revolt in Dominica, to Lord Grenville, March 1791* (London: n.p., 1791); McCahill, "Stephen Fuller," 150, 159, 179, where Fuller reported in March 1791 on slaves refusing in Dominica to work more than three days a

week because "Parliament had made them free; and that they were at liberty to work just as much, or as little as they pleased" (159); and Bernard Marshall, "Slave Resistance and White Reaction in the British Windward Islands, 1763–1833," *Caribbean Quarterly* 28, no. 3 (1982): 41.

46. The terms were attributed to Lord Carlisle and are cited at the History of Parliament website, member Hon. Charles James Fox, https://www.history ofparliamentonline.org/volume/1790-1820/member/fox-hon-charles-james -1749-1806. The entry was written by R. G. Thorne and is cited hereafter as Thorne, "Fox."

47. Edmund Burke, *Observations on the Conduct of the Minority* (1793), in *The Works of the Right Honourable Edmund Burke, Collected in Three Volumes* (London: J. Dodsley, 1802), 1:230.

48. The term is from Thorne, "Fox."

49. David Wilkinson, *The Duke of Portland: Politics and Party in the Age of George III* (London: Palgrave-Macmillan, 2002), 68.

50. Sheryllynne Haggerty and Susanne Seymour, "Imperial Careering and Enslavement in the Long Eighteenth Century: The Bentinck Family, 1710–1830s," *Slavery and Abolition* 39, no. 4 (2018): 642–62.

51. Clarkson, *History,* 1:354.

52. Thorne, "Fox."

53. John Wolffe, "Clapham Sect (act. 1792–1815)," in *Oxford Dictionary of National Biography* (Oxford: Oxford University Press, 2004). The group became known through its residential association with the South London village of Clapham. Their contemporary label was "Saints," the label "sect" by which they later became more popularly known first being used in 1844.

54. Clarkson, *History,* 2:502; Judith Jennings *The Business of Abolishing the British Slave Trade, 1783–1807* (London: Frank Cass, 1997), 104–5.

55. Clarkson, *History,* 2:502.

56. Clarkson, *History,* 2:489–490.

57. Henry Brougham, *A Concise Statement of the Question regarding the Abolition of the Slave Trade* (London: J. Hatchard, 1804), 5.

58. Clarkson, *History,* 2:490.

59. Robert Hume to Thomas Lumley and Co., 2 June 1804, Liverpool, Lumley Papers, Chancery Masters Exhibits, C 114/2, TNA; Roger Anstey, *The Atlantic Slave Trade and British Abolition, 1760–1810* (Atlantic Highlands, NJ: Humanities Press, 1975), 344–45. Some slave merchants in July 1804 believed that "Mr Wilberforce's Bill has been well disposed of in the House of Lords," though it may not have gone to a vote. William and Samuel Hinde to Thomas Lumley and Co., 9 July 1804, Lumley Papers. See also J. R. Oldfield, *Trans-*

atlantic Abolitionism in the Age of Revolution: An International History of Anti-Slavery, c. 1787–1820 (Cambridge: Cambridge University Press, 2013), 172.

60. Clarkson, *History,* 2:499. Clarkson also suggested that some regular supporters failed to turn out to vote in 1805, believing that the bill "was safe," thus claiming that the "causes of the failure" were "found accidental, and capable of remedy," and thereby encouraging its reintroduction in "a new form," or a bill to abolish the "foreign part of the Slave-trade" (500).

61. Mercator [John Gladstone], *Letters Concerning the Abolition of the Slave-Trade, and Other West-India Affairs* (London: C. and W. Galabin, 1807); A Planter, *A Letter Addressed to Mercator in Reply to His Letters on the Abolition of the Slave Trade* (London: n.p., 1807); Mercator [John Gladstone], *Third Letter on the Abolition of the Slave-Trade and Other West-India Affairs* (London: C. and W. Galabin, 1807); Eric Williams, *Capitalism and Slavery* (Chapel Hill: University of North Carolina Press, 1944), 145–50. Forty years before Williams published his seminal work, the idea of an overproduction crisis triggering abolition had been proposed by Franz Hochstetter, *Die Wirthschaftlichen und Politischen Motive für die Abschaffung des britischen Sklavenhandels in Jahre 1806–1807* (Leipzig: Duncker und Humblot, 1905), which was reviewed by Helene Reinherz, *Economic Journal* 16, no. 62 (1906): 267–70, and who noted that, in Hochstetter's view, "moral causes *alone,* without the support afforded by favourable material conditions, would not have sufficed to win the day" (269, emphasis in original).

62. Ryden, *West Indian Slavery,* 254–62.

63. Seymour Drescher, *Econocide: British Slavery in the Era of Abolition* (Pittsburgh: University of Pittsburgh Press, 1977), 15–37, emphasized that the British West Indies' share of British overseas trade peaked at 21 percent in 1803–7.

64. A Planter, *Letter to Mercator.*

65. James Stephen, *The Crisis in the Sugar Colonies; Or, An Enquiry into the Objects and Possible Effects of the French Expedition to the West Indies: And Their Connection with the Colonial Interests of the British Empire* (London: J. Hatchard, 1802), 90.

66. David Eltis and David Richardson, *Atlas of the Transatlantic Slave Trade* (New Haven: Yale University Press, 2010), 3; David Eltis, Frank D. Lewis, and David Richardson, "Slave Prices, the African Slave Trade and Productivity Growth in the Caribbean," *EHR* 58, no. 4 (2005): 673–700.

67. In 1783–1808 no less than 32 percent of the 792,000 arrivals in British ships were sold in markets outside what constituted the British Empire at the start

of that period. Voyages/transatlantic/database/1783-1808/flag = Great Britain/ sum of disembarked slaves/specific regions of slave disembarkations (searched on 28 August 2018). The territories identified as British in 1783 were Tortola, Antigua, St. Kitts, Nevis, Montserrat, Dominica, St. Lucia, Barbados, St. Vincent, Grenada, Jamaica, the Bahamas, British Honduras, and "other British Caribbean." The remaining places in the menu of specific regions were identified as non-British in 1783. The proportion of arrivals sold in markets outside the British Empire in 1783 rose through time, as markets in the United States and in West Indian territories seized in wartime joined Cuba in absorbing increasing numbers of slaves carried in British ships.

68. Stephen, *Crisis,* 101.

69. Stephen, *Crisis,* 109.

70. Stephen, *Crisis,* 158.

71. Stephen, *Crisis,* 158.

72. Brougham, *Concise Statement,* 53.

73. Mercator, *Third Letter,* 15-17.

74. Petley, *White Fury,* 178-90.

75. John Hinde and Co. to Thomas Lumley and Co., 7 September 1806, Kingston, Lumley Papers, C 114/1, TNA.

76. Hinde and Co. to Lumley and Co., 15 March 1807, Kingston, Lumley Papers, C 114/158, TNA.

77. Stephen, *Crisis,* 159.

78. Stephen, *Crisis,* 107n, 121.

79. Oldfield, *Transatlantic Abolitionism,* 166.

80. Henry Brougham, *An Inquiry into the Colonial Policy of the European Powers,* 2 vols. (London: D. Willison, 1803).

81. Brougham, *Concise Statement,* 33-42. To reinforce his arguments in this section, Brougham updated evidence presented by Clarkson some fifteen years earlier to Parliament, which sought to demonstrate that the slave trade was a graveyard rather than a nursery of British seamen, on balance therefore weakening rather than strengthening Britain's naval capabilities in wartime.

82. Brougham, *Concise Statement,* 43.

83. Brougham, *Concise Statement,* 5, 48 (quotation).

84. Brougham, *Concise Statement,* 92.

85. Gelien Matthews, *Caribbean Slave Revolts and the British Abolitionist Movement* (Baton Rouge: Louisiana University Press, 2006), 61-64.

86. Brougham, *Concise Statement,* 78.

87. Marcus Rainsford, *An Historical Account of the Black Empire of Hayti* ([London]: Albion Press, 1805), 364.

88. Zachary Macaulay, *The Horrors of the Negro Slavery Existing in Our West Indian Islands, Irrefragably Demonstrated from Official Documents Recently Presented to the House of Commons* (London: n.p., 1805).

89. Macaulay, *Horrors*, 2.

90. Macaulay, *Horrors*, 16, 25.

91. Macaulay, *Horrors*, 27.

92. Macaulay, *Horrors*, 36.

93. James Stephen, *War in Disguise; or, The Frauds of the Neutral Flags*, 2nd ed. (London: J. Hatchard and J. Butterworth, 1805). On the wider import of Stephen's text, see Stephen C. Neff, "James Stephen's 'War in Disguise': The Story of a Book," *Irish Jurist* 38 (2003): 331–51. For background to Stephen's identification of the war with France as providing a vehicle for achieving abolition, see Ann M. Burton, "British Evangelicals, Economic Warfare, and the Abolition of the Atlantic Slave Trade, 1794–1810," *Anglican and Episcopal History* 65, no. 2 (1996): 197–225.

94. Stephen, *War in Disguise*, 9.

95. Stephen, *War in Disguise*, 9.

96. Stephen, *War in Disguise*, 32.

97. Stephen, *War in Disguise*, 41.

98. Francois Crouzet, "Wars, Blockade, and Economic Change in Europe, 1792–1815," *JEH* 24, no. 4 (1964): 569–70; Douglass C. North, *The Economic Growth of the United States, 1790–1860* (Englewood Cliffs, NJ: Prentice-Hall, 1961), 36–46.

99. Stephen, *War in Disguise*, 115.

100. Roger Anstey, "The Historical Debate on the Abolition of the British Slave," in *Liverpool, the African Slave Trade, and Abolition,* ed. Roger Anstey and P. E. H. Hair, Historic Society of Lancashire and Cheshire, Occasional Series, no. 2 (1976), 164.

101. Cited in Oldfield, *Transatlantic Abolitionism*, 172.

102. William Wilberforce, *A Letter on the Abolition of the Slave Trade; Addressed to the Freeholders and Other Inhabitants of Yorkshire* (London: R. Cadell, W. Davies, and J. Hatchard, 1807), 321–22.

103. On the drafting, see Burton, "British Evangelicals," 212.

104. Anstey, *British Abolition*, 375. It is sometimes assumed that the 1806 act affected up to two-thirds of the British trade, but figures for British slave deliveries in 1805–6 indicate that of the 63,600 slaves landed in that period, fewer than 25,000, or under 40 percent, would have been banned by the 1806 act, thereby elevating the significance of the 1807 act. Voyages/transatlantic/database/1805–6/flag = Great Britain/specific disembarkations.

105. Cf. Roger Anstey, who argued that the passing of the final Abolition Act in 1807 rested "four square on the appeal to humanity." Anstey, "Historical Debate," 165.

106. In Liverpool's case, see David M. Williams, "Abolition and the Re-Deployment of the Slave Fleet, 1807-1811," *Journal of Transport History* 2, no. 2 (1973): 103-15; and Martin Lynn, "Liverpool and Africa in the 19th Century: The Continuing Connection," *Transactions of the Historic Society of Lancashire and Cheshire* 147 (1998): 27-54. Liverpool's longer-term adjustment to slave trade abolition depended heavily on continuing and growing overseas trade connections with regions and goods still associated with slavery, including West African palm oil and southern US cotton. Dale W. Tomich, ed., *New Frontiers of Slavery* (Albany: State University of New York Press, 2017); Tomich, "The Second Slavery and World Capitalism: A Perspective for Historical Inquiry," *International Review of Social History* 63, no. 3 (2018): 477-501.

107. Jennings, *Business*, 105.

108. On Danish abolition, see Erik Gobel, *The Danish Slave Trade and Its Abolition* (Leiden: Brill, 2016); on the wartime collapse of the French and Dutch slave trades from 1793, see Voyages/transatlantic/estimates/national carriers/ decadal totals.

109. Stephen D. Behrendt, David Eltis, and David Richardson, "The Cost of Coercion: African Agency in the Pre-Modern Atlantic World," *EHR* 54, no. 3 (2001): 454-76. The exceptional boom in French slaving 1783-91 observable in Voyages centered on supplying slaves to Saint-Domingue, which effectively disappeared as a slave market following the slave uprising of 1791.

110. Oldfield, *Transatlantic Abolitionism*, 180-88.

Chapter 10. On the "Heroism of Principle"

Title: Jane Austen, *Mansfield Park* (1814; London: Wordsworth Editions, 1992), 213.

1. Jane Austen's sentiment in *Mansfield Park*, in which she looks to link principle, character, and duty, finds powerful echoes in the writings of other leading novelists. Ernest Hemingway, for example, saw people as "instruments" to do their "duty," while William Golding, in his *Rites of Passage*, a story of a British voyager to Australia set in the early nineteenth century, observed that social privilege brought responsibility and that it was a "Good Man" who recognized it in the pursuit of "Justice" to one for whom life had been made "intolerable." Austen, *Mansfield Park*, 213; Hemingway, *For Whom the*

Bell Tolls (1941; London, Arrow Books, 2004), 46; Golding, *Rites of Passage* (London: Faber and Faber, 1980), 129, 136, 139.

2. Peter M. Solar and Klas Ronnback, "Copper Sheathing and the British Slave Trade," *EHR* 68, no. 3 (2014): 806–29.

3. J. R. Oldfield, *Transatlantic Abolitionism in the Age of Revolution* (Cambridge: Cambridge University Press, 2013). Oldfield highlights English-speaking social and other connections, but as noted in this book, there were links between British and continental European, especially French, ideas on the immorality of slavery.

4. Charles Tilly, *Popular Contention in Great Britain, 1758–1834* (Cambridge, MA: Harvard University Press, 1995), 147.

5. See, e.g., Nathan Nunn, "The Long-Term Effects of Africa's Slave Trades," *Quarterly Journal of Economics* 123, no. 1 (2008): 139–76; and Nunn and Leonard Wantchekon, "The Slave Trade and the Origin of Mistrust in Africa," *American Economic Review* 101, no. 7 (2011): 3221–52.

6. Robin Hallett, ed., *Records of the African Association: 1788–1831* (London: Nelson, 1964), 198.

7. Paul E. Lovejoy and David Richardson, "The Initial 'Crisis of Adaptation': The Impact of British Abolition on the Atlantic Slave Trade in West Africa," in *From Slave Trade to "Legitimate" Commerce: the Commercial Transition in Nineteenth-Century West Africa*, ed. Robin Law (Cambridge: Cambridge University Press, 1995), 32–56.

8. David Richardson, "Shipboard Slave Revolts, African Authority and the Atlantic Slave Trade," *WMQ,* 3rd ser. 58, no. 1 (2001): 69–92.

9. Cf. F. Scott Fitzgerald, who proposed that "Intelligence is a mere instrument of circumstances" and "is little more than a short foot-rule by which we measure the infinite achievements of circumstances." Fitzgerald, *The Beautiful and Damned* (1922; London: Penguin, 2004), 212.

10. Oldfield, *Transatlantic Abolitionism,* 173.

11. Oldfield, *Transatlantic Abolitionism,* 184–88.

12. Oldfield, *Transatlantic Abolitionism,* 189.

13. Cf. Charles K. Webster, who in referring to Castlereagh proposed: "There probably never was a statesman whose ideas were so right and whose attitude to public opinion so wrong. Such disparity between the grasp of ends and the understanding of means amounts to a failure of statesmanship." Webster, *The Foreign Policy of Castlereagh, 1812–1815: Britain and the Reconstruction of Europe* (London: G. Bell and Son, 1931), 231.

14. James G. Basker, ed., *Amazing Grace: An Anthology of Poems about Slavery, 1660–1810* (New Haven: Yale University Press, 2002), 435.

15. Michael E. Woods, "A Theory of Moral Outrage: Indignation and Eighteenth-Century British Abolitionism," *Slavery and Abolition* 36, no. 4 (2016): 662–83.

16. David Eltis, "The British Contribution to the Nineteenth-Century Transatlantic Slave Trade," *EHR* 32, no. 2 (1979): 211–27.

17. Padraig X. Scanlan, "The Colonial Rebirth of British Anti-Slavery: The Liberated African Villages of Sierra Leone, 1815–1824," *American Historical Review* 121, no. 4 (2016): 1085–113; Richard Anderson, "Sierra Leone: African Colony, African Diaspora," in *Abolition in Sierra Leone: Re-Building Lives and Identities in Nineteenth-Century West Africa,* ed. Richard Anderson (Cambridge: Cambridge University Press, 2020), 1–29.

18. On the domestic pressure to pursue the anti–slave trade agenda at Vienna, see Seymour Drescher, "History's Engines: British Mobilization in the Age of Revolution," *WMQ,* 3rd ser., 66, no. 4 (2009): 749.

19. On 26 March 1788 the mayor, gentlemen, clergy, and other inhabitants of the city of Exeter, totaling around 1,000 signatories, declared their "extreme abhorrence" of the slave trade, seeing it as "in the highest degree disgraceful to a Christian nation" and dismissing it as a "political necessity," before going on to claim *"good reason to hope that the example of abolition being once given by this enlightened country, will soon be followed by the other nations of Europe."* *Trewman's Exeter Flying Post,* 27 March 1788, emphasis added.

20. Alan Forrest, "The Hundred Days, the Congress of Vienna and the Atlantic Slave Trade," in *Napoleon's Hundred Days and the Politics of Legitimacy,* ed. Katherine Astbury and Mark Philp (London: Palgrave Macmillan, 2018), 163–81. On the wider issue, see Marcel van der Linden, "Unanticipated Consequences of 'Humanitarian Intervention': The British Campaign to Abolish the Slave Trade, 1807–1900," *Theory and Society* 39 (2010): 281–98.

21. Leslie Bethell, "The Mixed Commissions for the Suppression of the Transatlantic Slave Trade in the Nineteenth Century," *Journal of African History* 7, no. 1 (1966): 79–83.

22. David Eltis, *Economic Growth and the Ending of the Atlantic Slave Trade* (New York: Oxford University Press, 1987), 81–124.

23. David Eltis and David Richardson, *Atlas of the Transatlantic Slave Trade* (New Haven: Yale University Press, 2010), 23, 200–203.

24. Eltis, *Economic Growth,* 97; C. D. Kaufman and R. A. Pape, "Explaining Costly Moral Action: Britain's Sixty-Year Campaign against the Atlantic Slave Trade," *International Organization* 53, no. 4 (1999): 636–37; David Blair, "All the Ships That Never Sailed: Lessons for the Modern Antislavery Movement from the British Naval Campaigns against the Atlantic Slave Trade," in

Human Bondage and Abolition: New Histories of Past and Present Slaveries, ed. Elizabeth Swanson and James Brewer Stewart (Cambridge: Cambridge University Press, 2018), 221–61. I thank David Eltis for data on freed slaves.

25. There are higher estimates of the Black population in eighteenth-century Britain, which one scholar cautiously suggested were "rather too high" and in any case may include free as well as enslaved Africans. Folarin O. Shyllon, *Black People in Britain, 1555–1833* (London: Oxford University Press for the Institute of Race Relations, 1977), 102.

26. On population trends, see, e.g., B. W. Higman, *Slave Population and Economy in Jamaica, 1807–1834* (New York: Cambridge University Press, 1977).

27. On the three slave rebellions and how abolitionists adapted their strategy to them, see Gelien Matthews, *Caribbean Slave Revolts and the British Abolitionist Movement* (Baton Rouge: Louisiana State University Press, 2006).

28. On Burke's comment in 1792, see P. J. Marshall and J. A. Woods, eds., *The Correspondence of Edmund Burke,* vol. 7, *January 1792–August 1794* (Cambridge: Cambridge University Press, 1968), 125.

29. The idea of compensating owners for slaves was not new in 1833 but had been raised as early as 1788. A pamphlet by "A West India Planter" suggested that emancipation was financially and politically impracticable, requiring perhaps £60 million in compensation. A West India Planter, *Considerations on the Emancipation of Negroes and on the Abolition of the Slave Trade* (London: J. J. Johnson, 1788), 5–6. The idea of compensating slaveholders (and thus the figure claimed) was challenged at that time. Francis Randolph, *A Letter to the Right Honourable William Pitt on the Proposed Abolition of the African Slave Trade* (London: T. Cadell, 1788), 24–25; James Ramsay, *Objections to the Abolition of the Slave Trade, with Answers* (London: James Phillips, 1788), 3, 54. For a discussion of the early raising of the issue of compensation as part of wider proslavery arguments in Britain, see Paula E. Dumas, *Proslavery Britain: Fighting for Slavery in an Era of Abolition* (Basingstoke, UK: Palgrave Macmillan, 2016).

30. For discussion of the terms offered in 1833, see Nicholas Draper, *The Price of Emancipation: Slave-Ownership, Compensation and British Society at the End of Slavery* (New York: Cambridge University Press, 2010).

31. "Ministerial Proposition for the Emancipation of Slaves," House of Commons, Debates, 14 May 1833, Hansard, 17:cols. 1193–262, available online at https://api.parliament.uk/historic-hansard/commons/1833/may/14/ministerial-proposition-for-the. All the following quotations from Stanley are from this source.

32. Robert Tressell, *The Ragged Trousered Philanthropists* (1914; London, Penguin, 2004), 631.

33. On the ambiguity of "justice" where slave emancipation was concerned, see Jean Rhys, *Wide Sargasso Sea* (1966; London: Penguin, 2000), 121.

34. Cf. Henry Brougham, *A Concise Statement of the Question regarding the Abolition of the Slave Trade* (London: J. Hatchard, 1804), 78, where he wrote of abolition of the slave trade and slavery being necessary to preserve "the existence of white men in the Charaibean [*sic*] sea."

35. As foreign secretary of the Conservative Liverpool administration George Canning noted in May 1824, when commenting on the Commons resolutions of May 1823 on the amelioration of the condition of slaves, that the passing of the resolutions was intended to "look forward to the termination of slavery, as a result of a gradual and general improvement in the condition of the slaves, and not as the consequence of an instantaneous proclamation of general freedom." "Amelioration of the Condition of the Slave Population in the West Indies," House of Commons, Debates, 16 March 1824, Hansard, 10:col. 1091–198 (quotation at 1093), available online at https://api.parliament.uk/historic-hansard/commons/1824/mar/16/amelioration-of-the-condition-of-the.

36. Marshall and Wood, *Burke Correspondence*, 122–23.

37. Drescher, "History's Engines," 749.

38. *Westminster Review* 42 (1844): 301–2.

Index

Abolition Act (1807), 1, 5–12, 23, 227, 243–46, 248, 257

Abolitionism

and African humanity, 16, 157, 159–60, 179, 255

and African narratives, 176–79

and American Revolution, 11–12, 119, 135–36, 179–84

and class, 142–43, 202–12, 253, 277n

and English identity, 179, 182, 255–56

and French Revolution, 217, 228–29, 256

and Haitian Revolution, 228–29, 237–46, 249, 256, 258

and humanitarianism, 14–16, 134, 179, 210, 246–48, 260, 265, 353n

and Industrial Revolution, 12–14, 133, 146–47, 150, 200–202, 208–12, 218, 247, 249, 253, 257, 351–52n

intellectual roots of, 131–35, 179, 185–86, 257, 266

and international context, 12, 15, 17–18, 119–20, 179–84, 217, 234–46, 249, 257

and Irish representation, 233–34

and mass politics, 148, 191, 228

and national interest, 225, 256–59, 266

and parliamentary strategy, 232–46, 256

and planter opposition, 219–24. *See also* Slave power

and political barriers to, 132, 190, 214, 216–28

and public mobilization, 16, 135, 179, 185–86, 257, 266

and public opinion, 139–51, 166, 185–86, 195, 213, 232, 264, 266

and overproduction crisis, 234–37, 257, 359n

and the press, 148–54, 162, 166–82, 197–98, 211

and Quakers, 7, 100, 102, 110–12, 120–22, 151, 189–92, 197, 199, 246

as social movement, 16, 135, 139, 146–48, 191–92, 196–200, 247, 252, 257, 266

and theory of hegemony, 13, 134

and urbanisation, 153, 200–203, 247, 266

and women, 145, 203, 266, 332n, 350n

Addington, Henry (Lord Sidmouth), 230, 232, 237

African Association, 62

Agency dilemma, 19, 63, 66–85, 92, 301–2n. *See also* Principal-agent theory

Age of Enlightenment, 16

Allans and Campbell, 309n

Amanyanabo (military leader), 64

American Antislavery Society (Philadelphia), 183, 346n

Angola, 50, 60

Anomabu, 50–52, 56, 60

Anstey, Roger, 233

Antislavery

and British liberty, 103–5, 107, 161–62, 182, 277n, 335n

and human progress, 131

and imaginative literature, 137–64

and philosophical works. *See* Hume, David; Hutcheson, Francis; Locke, John; Millar, John; Montesquieu; Paley, William; Scottish Enlightenment; Smith, Adam

and religion, 119–25, 181–82, 196, 201–3, 207, 211, 246, 257, 260, 352n. *See also* Abolitionism: and Quakers; Baxter, Richard; Benezet, Anthony; Godwyn, Morgan; Woolman, John